DEADLY
DICTATORS

Masterminds of 20th Century Genocides

Terry Stafford

ISBN: 1450531970
ISBN-13: 9781450531979

CONTENTS

Turning and turning in the widening gyre
The falcon cannot hear the falconer;
Things fall apart; the centre cannot hold;
Mere anarchy is loosed upon the world,
The blood-dimmed tide is loosed, and everywhere
The ceremony of innocence is drowned;
The best lack all conviction, while the worst
Are full of passionate intensity.

William Butler Yeats

Deadly Dictators Timeline
Years of Tyranny

Joseph Stalin
1924 - 1953

Raphael Trujillo
1930 - 1961

Adolf Hitler
1933 - 1945

Kim IL-Sung / Kim Jong-IL
1945 - Present

Mao Zedong
1948 - 1976

François Duvalier / Jean-Claude Duvalier
1957 - 1986

Idi Amin
1971 - 1979

Pol Pot
1975 - 1997

Saddam Hussein
1979 - 2003

Théoneste Bagosora
1994 - 1995

1900 1910 1920 1930 1940 1950 1960 1970 1980 1990 2000

PROLOGUE

"No cause is left but the most ancient of all, the one, in fact, that from the beginning of our history has determined the very existence of politics, the cause of freedom versus tyranny."

Hannah Arendt

Tyranny is not new. History speaks of many rulers who inflicted cruel oppression upon their subjects. During the twentieth century, however, dictatorial rulers reached the apex of depravity through the subjugation and murder of more victims than during any other one hundred year period in all of human history.

Military and civilian deaths as a result of armed conflict between January 1900 and December 1999 are reliably estimated at between 85 and 100 million. And yet, the twentieth century's death toll was far higher when it includes the purposeful killing of innocent civilians by their own governments. Genocidal violence and the extermination policies of dictatorial regimes during the twentieth century caused the deaths of approximately 262 million people, far exceeding the number killed in all the wars and armed conflicts of the century.

It seems ironic that while we have benefited from the astounding advances of science and technology during the past century, we endured a simultaneous and tragic lapse of humanity. Enormously destructive and lethal wars occurred during the twentieth century, but even more appalling were the monstrous crimes committed by ruthless despots against innocent civilians in their own countries and in states under their occupation. Perhaps we can avoid another century of slaughter by understanding these crimes and facing the failures of the past. In that spirit, *Deadly Dictators* is an examination of the most brutal regimes of modern history – and it illustrates how they have shaped our present and future world.

The twentieth century began during an enchanted age that spanned several decades, from the 1870's until the eve of the Great War. This era was called the Belle Époque and was epitomized by a fin de siècle world's fair extravaganza held in Paris, known as the Exposition Universelle of 1900. Towering over the exposition was the phallic symbolism of the Eiffel Tower and prominently featured among the exhibits were many wonders of industrial progress, including electricity that gave Paris its reputation as the "City of Light." More than 50 million visitors experienced the cosmopolitan creativity of Paris during the six months of the Exposition. The golden age of the Belle Époque prevailed during an extended time without war in Europe – a period that brought enormous strides in technological advancement to the world.

In the afterglow of the Enlightenment many believed that human depravity and barbarism were in retreat. The wide acceptance of representative government and the belief in the moral imperative to "civilize" primitive societies spawned the creation of vast European colonies in Africa and Asia. The bright optimism of the new century convinced the political leaders of many nations that "New Imperialism" was the pathway to even greater progress and prosperity.

Despite the growing sophistication of the privileged class, the gains in technology and productivity hid their dark side. Capitalist industrialization had caused great social and economic upheaval and landed aristocracies were threatened by newly created urban wealth. The migration of workers from countryside to cities produced a seething social disorder, because the new industrial system was often unable or unwilling to adequately provide for the working class and the poor.

Russian writer Fodor Dostoevsky wished to prevent Western capitalism from invading Russia, fearing that it would "upset the old order and give rise to divisive class conflict." And the new order produced contrarian philosophers of anarchy, who shared a "vision of a stateless society." These men communicated their ideas through the press and the pamphlet to an ever-increasing mass of people who suffered from hopeless poverty. As anarchists, they aimed to wage war against privilege, to abolish the state and do away with authority.

Even before the turn of the century their revolutionary movement shocked the world when a group of anarchists assassinated Tsar Alexander II of Russia in 1881. In 1887, a plot against Tsar Alexander III failed, but one of the conspirators, Alexander Ulyanov, was hanged. His execution had a powerful impact on the conspirator's younger brother, Vladimir, who became a dedicated revolutionary and was later known as Lenin.

Six anarchists, who participated in a strike in the United States at Haymarket Square in Chicago during 1885, became martyrs to the cause when they were hanged the following year for the murders of seven policemen. The growing spectacle of anarchist violence was fed by men like Russian Prince Peter Kropotkin, who wrote that, "a single deed is better propaganda than a thousand pamphlets." Others like the fiery Enrico Malatesta of Italy and a Frenchman known as Ravachol became purveyors of violence and political murder. They encouraged many desperate disciples to bring anarchist ideals to life through a series of violent bombings and political assassinations. The Anarchists would cast a long shadow upon the twentieth century. Those who believed in the anarchists revolutionary tirades against the bourgeois and their political allies lived in the shadow of industrialization. Barbara Tuchman in *The Proud Tower* has vividly described their world:

> *They came from the warrens of the poor, where hunger and dirt were king, where consumptives coughed and the air was thick with the smell of latrines, boiling cabbage and stale beer, where babies wailed and couples screamed in sudden quarrels, where roofs leaked and unmended windows let in the cold blasts of winter, where privacy was unimaginable, where men, women, grandparents*

and children lived together, eating, sleeping, fornicating, defecating, sickening and dying in one room, where a teakettle served as a wash boiler between meals, old boxes served as chairs, heaps of foul straw as beds, and boards propped across two crates as tables, where sometimes not all the children in a family could go out at one time because there were not enough clothes to go round, where decent families lived among drunkards, wifebeaters, thieves and prostitutes, where life was a seesaw of unemployment and endless toil, where a cigar-maker and his wife earning 13 cents an hour worked seventeen hours a day seven days a week to support themselves and three children, where death was the only exit and the only extravagance and the scraped savings of a lifetime would be squandered on a funeral coach with flowers and a parade of mourners to ensure against the anonymity and last ignominy of Potter's Field. [1]

The actions of a few anarchists who possessed the passion to act would eventually hurl the world into a maelstrom of violence that was unimaginable during the waning days of the Belle Époque. They killed unsuspecting victims by bombing opera houses, crowded bistros and train stations. They even bombed parliamentary chambers. The violence spread throughout Europe and vengeful sentiments were whipped into a revolutionary frenzy through such publications as *The Torch, Antichrist, New Dawn* and *Black Flag*. Anarchists were tried for their crimes and punished by firing squad and guillotine but they continued killing until many in the upper classes were afraid to venture out on the streets. Public fears grew into hysteria and French newspapers began publish a daily tally of the attacks under the heading, "La Dynamite."

At a Lyons Exposition, a young Italian zealot stabbed French President Sadi Carnot to death on June 24, 1894, as he publicly appeared in an open carriage. The assassin had become an Anarchist in Milan, while working as a baker's apprentice. He was sent to the guillotine and the French government staged a mass trial of Anarchists. In August 1897, Premier Canovas del Castil-

lo of Spain was shot three times causing instant death as he sat
with his wife on the terrace of a spa in the Basque mountains at
Santa Agueda. The killer admitted that the crime was committed in response to the Premier "ordering the mass torture and
execution of Anarchists." The assassin was executed by garrote.
In 1898, Empress Elizabeth of Austria, wife of Franz Joseph,
was stabbed to death by a vagrant Italian workman who had a
background of anarchist activities. When asked why he killed
the Empress, he replied, "As part of the war on the rich and
the great...It will be Humbert's turn next." The killer was sent
to prison, where he later hanged himself. The prophecy would
come true on July 29, 1900, when an Anarchist and silk weaver
from Patterson, New Jersey assassinated King Humbert of Italy.
The King was shot four times at close range and died almost
instantly. The plot was hatched in the United States among
a group who were followers of the Italian Anarchist, Enrico
Malatesta. The assassin was sent to prison where he committed
suicide.

What began as a few desperate acts by a small number of
deluded men had seemingly become an international conspiracy against heads of state. Government action to prevent
attacks and punish the perpetrators was ineffective against the
onslaught. But the anarchist movement grew not by conspiracy,
but contagion. One man who read an account of the assassination of King Humbert was a moody Polish-American named
Leon Czolgosz. He had been laid off during a strike. Czolgosz
was influenced by a Chicago Anarchist newspaper known as *Free
Society* and had attended Anarchist meetings sporadically. He
apparently read the press clipping of King Humbert's murder
repeatedly and kept it as a treasured possession, even sleeping
with it at night.

On September 6, 1901, in a receiving line at the Buffalo
Pan American Exposition, Czolgosz shot President William
McKinley twice in the chest. The President died eight days later
and Vice President Theodore Roosevelt succeeded him. The
assassin was hurriedly tried and electrocuted on October 29.
Congress amended the Immigration Act to exclude anyone
who preached or accepted "disbelief in or opposition to all

organized government." The new President told Congress that, "Anarchism is a crime against the whole human race and all mankind should band against the Anarchist."

Soon after the turn of the century anarchist believers began to affiliate with other revolutionary movements, primarily those of communist workers parties. These groups did not advocate anarchy, but they did promote violent revolution and the killing continued. During the next few years, revolutionaries assassinated several Russian ministers. In January 1905, a massacre occurred in front of the Winter Palace, which came to be known as "Bloody Sunday." Nearly one thousand workers were killed as they sought to peacefully petition the Tsar for improved working conditions and political reform. The leading advocate of Tsarist repression, Grand Duke Sergei, was blown to bits by a bomb thrown by a young man named Kaliaev in February, 1905. During his trial, Kaliaev told the judges, "We are two warring camps...two worlds in furious collision." The assassin was hanged and buried beneath the prison wall.

Anarchists were gradually incorporated into the movements against "industrialized tyranny," but not before they assassinated Russian Premier Stolypin in 1911 and Spanish Premier Canalejas in 1912. The spirit of anarchist revolutionary fervor continued to illuminate the stark divide in society between those with privilege and those in poverty. What the anarchists had unleashed upon the world was a commitment to violent revolution and political murder. As could be expected from their philosophy, it was characterized by lone acts without an organizing principle, but it set the stage for a reaction by repressive tyrannies of the twentieth century.

One assassination became the catalyst for global chaos. June 28, 1914, was the fourteenth wedding anniversary of Archduke Franz Ferdinand of Austria and his wife. On that day, they visited Sarajevo to inspect the troops. A secret plot against the Archduke had been developed by a group of schoolboys and was carried out by a revolutionary nationalist, who later professed to be motivated by "revenge and love." The Young Serbian who committed the crime was insulted that the "tyrant," as he called the Archduke, would visit Serbia on the anniversary of the Serbian defeat by Turkey in 1389. His muddled view of history was influenced by his admiration for Friedrich Nietzsche, and he was fond of quoting passages from the philosopher's autobiography, *Ecce Homo.*

Following the political assassination of the Archduke, European nationalism, imperial competition, entangled military alliances and a series of diplomatic miscalculations led Europe to literally stumble into the Great War that resulted in the deaths of nearly nine million soldiers. The fuse that was lit by the Anarchists reactively spawned a repressive age of dictatorship, war and genocide. Riding astride history's bloodiest century came the most lethal and murderous despots of all time – men who wrote an entirely new definition of cruelty for the world. *Deadly Dictators* tells ten of their stories as the twentieth century unfolded, from the Great Terror in Russia to the Rwandan genocide.

In the wake of the First World War, the tyrants of the twentieth century claimed power based upon their own naked ambition and desire for domination. They preyed on popular feelings of alienation, nationalism and upon grim social conditions to swell the ranks of their followers. Some of these tyrants were motivated by mankind's oldest and most primitive urges, including craven self-interest, tribalism and sadism. But most of the despotic regimes of the twentieth century were based on an overarching ideology. Hannah Arendt has suggested that ideologies of modern totalitarianism elevated evil to near religious veneration. She describes such fanatic faith as rendering human values inconsequential, when compared to the higher ideals of the totalitarian system.

The philosophical foundations of most totalitarian ideologies of the twentieth century were based on the ideas of Karl Marx and Friedrich Nietzsche. Marx believed that revolution was unavoidable, because "the imminent laws of capitalistic production," would lead to "mass misery, oppression, slavery, degradation and exploitation" of the working class. Marx did not allow for dissenting opinions or freedom of choice. Consequently, his system required a dictatorship to implement its early stages and the liquidation of the exploiting classes. Marx created an economic system, but more importantly, he created faith in its ultimate potential. When the utopian dream of the "higher stage of communism" failed to appear, the faithful protected their dream by forbidding any criticism of the system that promised it. The result was a nightmare of coercion and brutality that led to the very oppression that Marx had railed against.

Nietzsche rejected all external moral law and detested the Judeo-Christian tradition. In his view, a select few were entitled with a "will to power." He called for ruthless domination by the strong over the masses. "Accordingly," he wrote, "we must agree to the cruel sounding truth that slavery belongs to the essence of culture…the wretchedness of struggling men must grow still greater in order to make possible the production of a world of art for a small number of Olympian men." Nietzsche disdained all pity or compassion. But he went beyond that in his belief that domination – even cruel domination was a virtue:

> *To see others suffer does one good, to make others suffer even more: this is a hard saying but an ancient, mighty, human, all-too-human principle to which even the apes might subscribe; for it has been said that in devising bizarre cruelties they anticipate man and are, as it were, his "prelude." Without cruelty there is no festival…*[2]

With the essential philosophies of Communism and Fascism defined, mankind awaited the larger-than-life personalities of the twentieth century to begin the "festival of cruelty." The imposition of totalitarian values would elevate the most notorious tyrants of the modern era to positions of absolute power. Their drive for domination and conquest brought about the greatest armed conflicts the world has ever known and a "cold war" that lasted for more than a half century.

Movements aimed at social or political revolution led to perhaps the greatest evil in all of human history. These movements resulted in almost unimaginable destruction of human life, not just in war, but also as the conscious policy of governments directed against non-combatants. Samantha Power,

Executive Director of the Carr Center for Human Rights Policy at Harvard University tells us:

> *Though genocide has been practiced by colonizers, crusaders and ideologues from time immemorial, the word "genocide," which means the "killing" (Latin, cide) of a "people" (Greek, genos), had only been added to the English language in 1944 so as to capture this special kind of evil... Genocide differed from ordinary conflict because, while surrender in war normally stopped the killing, surrender in the face of genocide only expedited it. It was – and remains – agreed that the systematic, large-scale massacre of innocents, stands atop any hierarchy of horribles.[3]*

Several dictators of the twentieth century turned their governmental apparatus towards the annihilation of their own people. The massive exterminations in China, Soviet Russia and Nazi-occupied Europe are among the greatest atrocities in all of human history. But numbers alone do not tell the full story. On a per capita basis, the regimes of some small nation-states have proven highly lethal to their people. Extermination rates of 20-25% in Cambodia and North Korea represent an astonishingly large percentage of the populations of these tiny nations.[4]

In all, the governments of the twentieth century murdered more than a quarter of a billion of their own citizens – more than double the military and civilian deaths caused by all the wars that occurred during the same one hundred years. Millions of people escaped death, but have endured false imprisonment, torture and rape that condemned them to live out their lives as physical or emotional cripples.

The murderous dictatorships of the twentieth century shared many commonalities and some influenced subsequent tyrannical regimes. Four of the dictatorships profiled in this book were Communist – Stalin, Mao, the Kims and Pol Pot, although their interpretation of Marxist theory varied. Saloth Sar, a Cambodian student studying in Paris, who would later

become Pol Pot, was inspired by the writings of Peter Kropotkin, one of the anarchist movement's best-known theoreticians.
Saddam Hussein was a great admirer of Stalin and although
he believed in his own Ba'thist ideology, he designed the Iraqi
terror apparatus with Stalinism as a model. Hitler, Amin and
Trujillo generally adopted fascist policies. Trujillo expressed
admiration for the Nazi leader and Idi Amin praised Hitler's
extermination of the Jews. Amin's regime, in an anti-Semitic
rampage, culminated with the holding of Israeli hostages in
Uganda, in cooperation with Palestinian terrorists.

There is considerable evidence that most of these regimes
employed operational techniques refined by previous dictatorships, especially in the use of state terror, torture and political
murder. An example is the training provided to Trujillo's intelligence services by the "Spanish Police," some of Franco's most
feared operatives, who were themselves trained by the Nazis.

Most cases of mass killing examined within these pages
meet the technical criteria of genocide. The exceptions are
the North Korean starvation under the Kims and the massive
number of unnatural Chinese deaths that occurred during
Mao Zedong's "Great Leap Forward." Although North Korean
and Chinese policy did not exclusively exterminate people on
the basis of race, religion or ethnicity, the massive number of
deaths inflicted by the governments of those countries could
hardly be omitted. The Rwandan killing machine and the
gangsterism of the Duvalier's seem to have been without links
to earlier twentieth century political philosophies. And yet,
the wanton slaughter of innocent civilians in Rwanda and Haiti
was consistent with many aspects of the criminal regimes that
preceded them.

The despots who committed these crimes spoke different
languages and worshiped at many altars, but shared a "malignant energy" for the propagation of death and annihilation of the human spirit. The following ten concise histories
explore the dark forces behind the nightmare each dictator
unleashed. The authoritarian rulers profiled were not selected
arbitrarily. Inclusion required a dictator to have exhibited a
character of unambiguous evil. Each was a sole and absolute

tyrant who denied citizens their most basic human rights. They all established or fostered widespread corruption and employed grotesque forms of abuse. And, their despotism crushed the spirits of even those not directly targeted for repression.

Many strong men assumed positions of power during the twentieth century through the use of cunning and ruthless tactics, but did not commit truly heinous acts. Kemal Attaturk of Turkey is an example of a dictator who did not become a tyrant. Pinochet of Chile was a dictator who became a tyrant, but he established a path for his nation's return to civil life. The Armenian genocide of World War I and the atrocities of Argentina's "Dirty War," of the 1970's have not been included, because of the collective nature of the military and political leadership involved, which in no way diminishes the shame or significance of these crimes against humanity.

While a historical context is established in the case of each dictatorship, the emphasis is on the individual characteristics and idiosyncrasies that defined each despotic ruler. The backgrounds of these men are examined to expose the roots of the bloodlust that was directed against both their enemies and their subjects. Each dictator's cult of personality, private life, delusions and degenerate behavior is documented.

The tumult of the twentieth century may well be repeating itself in the social and economic dislocations of the new century. And there is the distinct possibility that terrorism in our time could become a prelude to a new wave of repressive dictatorships, just as anarchist violence was in the past. The world community cannot afford such an outcome. Mankind must confront and conquer its darker impulses before seeking the dawn of a more humane future.

Los Angeles, Winter 2010

CHAPTER 1
Stalin: Swordbearer of Terror

"A single death is a tragedy. A million deaths are a statistic."

Joseph Stalin

Russia's ancient homeland was established amid a vast expanse, stretching from the Arctic north to the southern steppes and from Scandinavia to the deserts of Asia. For several centuries, a struggle for dominance among tribes raged – a process that resulted in seemingly endless strife and subordination. Fierce Mongol warriors from the Far East, known as Tartars, overwhelmed Russia in the 13th century. This "Golden Horde," did not completely settle their conquered territory, but remained nomadic, while imposing heavy taxes on Russian lands. Upon rejection of the Tartars in 1480 by Grand Prince Ivan III, the principality of Muscovy rose to become "the nucleus of a new centralized Russian state." However, the final "gathering of Russian lands," and repulsion of the remnants of Tartar rule remained a task for his grandson, Ivan IV.

Ivan IV, who became known as Grozny, or "The Terrible," finally liberated his homeland from the Mongols, creating the modern Eurasian state of Russia and becoming its first Tsar. But Ivan bequeathed a more sinister legacy to Russia – his apparatus of state security. It became an instrument of terror for the vengeful destruction of Ivan's enemies, as determined by his own paranoia. Ivan created an autonomous jurisdiction, known as the Oprichnina, through which he ruled certain

Russian lands, solely and absolutely. Ivan's dominion was po-
liced by a military-religious order that showed no mercy for its
victims, who were drowned, strangled or flogged to death. In
the city of Novgorod, sixty thousand people were slaughtered
during a one-week orgy of violence. Ivan's Oprichniks, dressed
in black clothing, were mounted on black horses or traveled in
black carriages torturing and killing as they saw fit. The mission of the Oprichniks was to bite the enemies of the Tsar and
to sweep them away. Some symbolically carried the severed
heads of dogs or brooms on their saddles.[1]

In the same way that Ivan's Oprichniks targeted enemies of
the state, Stalin's secret police allowed him to gradually exert a
frightening degree of control over the Russian people. It was
not necessary to commit a proven anti-Soviet act to become
the victim of the secret police under Stalin's regime. Suspicion
alone was sufficient, as the apparatus was increasingly guided
by paranoia and caprice. By Stalin's word alone one could be
tortured or killed – or rescued and even rewarded. It all became a shadowy game that eventually led to the creation of a
dark netherworld, first named by Alexander Solzhenitsyn in
The Gulag Archipelago. Prisons of the Gulag existed like islands
from the Black Sea to Siberia incorporating literally hundreds
of forced labor camps. During Stalin's time, nearly 15% of the
Russian population became prisoners. Perhaps the best known
of the Gulag camp complexes was Kolyma, an area in the Far
East arctic about six times the size of France. The Gulag required a huge logistical support system, including its own railroads, ports and ships. At its peak, the Soviet detention system
was the largest employer in Europe.

Stalin became modern Russia's most powerful leader. He
venerated Ivan IV and in many ways emulated his methods.
While Stalin has been denigrated by much of the world for his
horrifying cruelty to the Russian people, today many Russians
still express nostalgia for Stalin, the "man of steel." A recent
Russian book, *Stalin: The Second Murder*, charges that his denunciation by Khrushchev greatly diminished the Russian people.
The writer, Elena Prudnikova, states her thesis very frankly, "the
murder of Stalin was also the murder of his people.

The country, deprived of high ideals in just a few decades, has rotted to the ground." This statement reveals an almost pathological denial of one of the darkest periods in Russian history. According to Nina Khrushcheva, the great granddaughter of Nikita Khrushchev, the Russian people's desire for a strong leader is a "cycle that will keep on repeating itself until Russia finally and fully confronts its past." [2]

Like Ivan Grozny, Stalin endured a traumatic early life. Joseph Vissarionovich Djugashvili was born in a shack in the Georgian village of Gori near the Kura River on December 6, 1878. Gori is a thousand miles from the center of Russia – nearer to Baghdad than to St. Petersburg. His father, Beso, was a drunken cobbler who violently beat young Joseph (nicknamed Soso). According to some reports, when Soso was seven he endured an especially savage beating that resulted in an infected elbow, nearly causing his death. The damaged arm remained disfigured for life. His mother, Keke, also beat the boy upon occasion, although she alternately offered him a possessive form of affection in an otherwise loveless childhood. Stalin was born with a foot deformity and he suffered facial disfigurement from smallpox. But his intelligence and early education, allowed him to attend a seminary. Stalin's paternity is in some doubt and Stalin himself once stated that his father was a priest. His mother, who eventually left Beso, had previously worked for priests.

Soso grew into a deeply insecure and vengeful youth. He became an atheist and was expelled from the seminary in 1899. He wrote poetry, had a mesmerizing singing voice and an appeal to women, despite his facial scars. But he was drawn to street gangs and soon proved to be a master of violent coercion and cruelty. He took the name Koba, from the outlaw hero of a novel. Young Stalin's first power base was the grimy oil town of Batumi on the Black Sea, where he practiced – in his words, "surveillance, spying, and invasion of inner life, violation of feelings."

He demonstrated a natural talent in the conspiratorial world of political revolution and was arrested for the first time in 1902. During the next few years he was sentenced to numerous prison terms in Siberia, although he escaped on more than one occasion. He became a follower of Vladimir Lenin and his banditry soon was an important source of funds for Lenin's revolution. As a young revolutionary, Stalin was a dashing and lawless figure. His first marriage was to Ekaterina "Kato" Svanidze, a young Georgian girl from a Bolshevik family. Although they had a child together, Koba, a dedicated political organizer, was rarely home. He was living the life of his namesake, robbing banks to support party activities. In 1907, Kato died of a respiratory illness and Stalin abandoned his young son, named Yakov, who was raised by Kato's family.

He formed a friendship with an older Bolshevik, Dergei Alliluyev whose Gypsy wife, Olga, was rumored to have been his lover. Young Koba had a powerful impact on the Alliluyev family, rescuing their young daughter, Nadya, from drowning in the Caspian Sea. This incident was the beginning of a relationship between Stalin and the woman who would become his second wife.

In 1913, he used the name Stalin for the first time, perhaps borrowing it from a buxom Bolshevik, Ludmilla Stal, with whom he had an affair. The new name was similar to Lenin, and because it meant "man of steel," it was a powerful metaphor. It became permanent and was the beginning of the self-created "hero" that Joseph Djugashvili was destined to become. Stalin had a natural aptitude for political intrigue. His highly regarded article, *"Marxism and the National Question,"* won praise from Lenin, who called him "this wonderful Georgian." After Lenin launched the October revolution in 1917, Stalin was assigned to the Commissariat of Nationalities. He remained close to the Alliluyev family and engaged Fyodor Alliluyev to be his secretary and Fyodor's little sister, Nadya, as his typist.

During 1918, the revolution faced a struggle for survival. Lenin was wounded in August, but survived. During his recuperation he relied heavily on Trotsky and Stalin, who were the only members of his entourage allowed access to Lenin without an appointment. When both were named to Lenin's Politburo, Stalin recognized Trotsky as an obstacle to his ambitions. Trotsky was a sophisticated party intellectual, while Stalin was a borderland bandit, operating as Lenin's enforcer. Dismissing Trotsky as an "operetta commander," Stalin began to oppose him at every turn. Lenin dispatched Stalin to Tsaritsyn by armored train, where he dealt with counter-revolutionaries swiftly and ruthlessly. Those suspected of disloyalty were simply shot. Stalin was comfortable with the Bolshevik cult of violence, and when urged by Lenin to be "merciless", he responded: "Be assured our hand will not tremble."

Stalin and Nadya became lovers while traveling in a blue silk lounge car that once belonged to a Gypsy torch singer. She was only seventeen and must have been both thrilled and terrified as she watched Stalin order executions on an almost daily basis. When he returned to Moscow he married Nadya and moved in with her family. In 1921, Nadya gave birth to a son, Vasily and five years later to a daughter, Svetlana.

By 1922 Lenin was Premier and the Head of State. He appointed Stalin to the position of General Secretary of the Central Committee, where he enjoyed extensive new powers. In May of the same year, Lenin suffered a stroke, which severely limited his ability to run the government. On January 21, 1924 he suffered a second and fatal stroke. Violating the wishes of Lenin's family, Stalin had the Party leader's body embalmed and put on display in Red Square, as a demonstration of his own power.

When a drop in grain production threatened the revolution, Stalin personally went into the agricultural countryside to investigate. To solve the food crisis, Kulaks (rural peasant-farmers) were ordered to deliver vast quantities of additional grain and then, to join collective farms. When they resisted, the stage was set for a colossal war between Stalin and the Kulaks, which would dominate Russia for decades to come.[3]

Stalin in Power

Stalin, always ruthless in his political life, was never reluctant to use extreme methods against his enemies. In the early days of his rule, he was not a tyrant. In fact, there was almost a family atmosphere in the Kremlin among high communist officials. They all lived together with their families in a village of apartments within the Kremlin walls.

The new leaders' appearance was rather ordinary – he was short in stature, with reddish hair, slightly Asiatic eyes and a full mustache. His right arm was disabled, causing his right hand to be thinner than his left. His demeanor was calm – almost eerily so. He spoke in a hushed voice, with a soft Georgian accent. Stalin had a savage gaze that could cause those around him to recoil in apprehension. In his eyes, a blaze of light in an otherwise dead stare, reminded many of the look of a ravenous wolf – like those he drew incessantly during Kremlin meetings.

At Stalin's right hand was Molotov – a forbidding political operative, with round spectacles and a cruel streak. His name was adopted for effect. Molotov means "hammer" in Russian and the name was chosen to signify the tough image he wanted to project to the party and the public. Molotov's volatile temper and legendary ability to out-drink his colleagues allowed him a certain swagger among the leadership, but he always remained in Stalin's shadow. Molotov and his highly intelligent and dynamic Jewish wife, Polina, were intensely dedicated Bolsheviks. Molotov idolized Polina and together they were an imposing couple within Stalin's inner circle.

Stalin was admired for his prodigious work ethic and his strong but anxious personality. According to Beria, future head of the secret police, "he dominated his entourage with his intelligence." Stalin embraced his loyal underlings with an intimacy that led each to believe that he was trusted above all others. He could use humor to ingratiate himself, but frequently it was tinged with discrete manipulation.

A suspicious loner, Stalin found the ideal organ for political coercion in the secret police organization headed by a "hollow cheeked ascetic," Feliks Dzierzynski, the son of a Polish nobleman. The organization was known as the Cheka, which had proven effective when it was unleashed following an attempt on Lenin's life in 1918. This event was known as the "Red Terror," and the Cheka was successful in liquidating much of the opposition. In the same way that Ivan's Oprichniks pursued enemies of the state, the Cheka allowed Stalin to terrorize the Russian people.

Stalin linked the Leninist goals of collectivization and industrialization to the building of a strong state. This was the essence of Stalinism – he was determined to accomplish both goals simultaneously and he would use whatever methods were required. But the revolution Stalin created did not begin with the people – it was truly a "revolution from above." During the early 1920's, Stalin's approach was gradual. Politburo theoretician Bukharin called him a "genius at dosage." He encouraged a rigorous effort to speed industrialization and collectivization, but he did not initially advocate extreme measures. The countryside remained backwards and yet conditions improved for many peasant farmers, who were not completely unfriendly to the new Soviet system. By 1927, only about 40% of peasant farms were members of collectives and industrialization lagged far behind original plans. Stalin needed a greater sense of urgency to speed up the revolution. The threat of war was the means he chose to justify more severe methods.

To dramatize the danger of war, in 1928 he arrested 53 engineers working in the coal industry, three of whom were German citizens. Known as the Shakhty case, it charged that the conspirators had deliberately mismanaged the mines causing explosions and arson in cooperation with Polish, German and French intelligence services. Physical and mental coercion was used to extract confessions from those arrested. Their trials received massive inflammatory publicity. Five men were executed and others were sentenced to prison. The Germans defendants were acquitted, which directly undermined the claims of foreign subversion. Nevertheless, the ploy worked, and became a vivid example of the war danger facing the Soviet Union. Stalin had demonstrated that the menace lurked not just from surrounding countries, but also from within. For Stalin, the Shakhty case validated the use of persecution, torture, false evidence and the conviction of innocents as tools for swaying public opinion. The cunning use of the coercive tools of state power would become Stalin's trademark.[4]

By the time Stalin celebrated his 50th birthday in 1929, nearly all of the leadership elite had accepted him as the Vozhd (strong leader) of the Russian state and the rightful successor to Lenin. He had achieved this stature as much through charm as through cold calculation within the Kremlin. Outside of this insulated world, a war of epic proportions raged as Stalin and Molotov supervised the complete destruction of the Kulaks as a class within Russian society. Kulaks, peasant farmers who owned about 90% of Russia's arable land, were divided into three groups: those to be "immediately eliminated," those to be imprisoned and those who were to be deported. The Bolsheviks were single minded in their pursuit of the war on the Kulaks, rampaging through the countryside in search of hidden grain and meting out vicious punishment. The Kulaks fought back by killing their own livestock, brazenly slaughtering over 26 million head of cattle and more than 15 million horses. The peasants believed that through these destructive acts they could pressure the government to rescind its orders. But Stalin's response was outright confiscation, a punitive policy that began in early 1930.

The murder of more than a million Kulaks, including women and children and the deportation of 1.6 million others was beginning to cause a rupture in Stalin's Kremlin family. Stalin began to suspect disloyalty and he confided to Molotov in a note, "The summit of state is afflicted with a terrible sickness." Food shortages became more serious by the summer of 1931 and the Politburo increased the pressure in the countryside. Prison camps were expanded and by 1935 nearly one million people had been sent to the Gulag. The camps were the successors of the Tsarist Siberian penal system, to which Stalin had once himself been exiled. The Gulag was usually punishment for "political crimes," but the system of forced labor soon became an essential component of state economics.

As the pressure on the Kulaks increased, Stalin's high-ranking Bolsheviks began to enjoy lovely dachas or country houses. Many were in Zubalovo, just outside Moscow. Life here was idyllic, especially for the wives and children, who loved escaping from the confines of the Kremlin. Stalin's daughter, Svetlana, recalled a "happy sheltered life," with gardens and pet animals. The comrades played tennis and rode horses. Stalin was partial to billiards, and was remembered as a charming host and a doting father. While the Party leadership enjoyed these times with family, they never forgot that, as Stalin's friend, Sergei Kirov put it, "A Bolshevik should love his work more than his wife."

By late 1931, the food shortages turned to hunger and soon thereafter to outright famine. In contrast, many of Stalin's leadership were traveling by private trains to what had become known as the "Soviet Riviera," or the dachas in the south. Despite the nightmare of starvation that was sweeping the nation, these state-owned country homes were liberally stocked with food, plenty of provisions and fresh fruit of every kind. Stalin took great pride in his gardens and the natural beauty of the region, going boating or hunting for partridges.

While the leaders enjoyed their seaside vacations, the peasants were living on rotten potatoes, and eating dogs, horses and even tree bark. An American radical, Fred Beal, visited a village in the Ukraine in 1932 and found all the inhabitants dead, with the exception of one insane woman. Rats were feasting on the partially frozen remains of villagers. Beal also found heart-rending messages attached to many of the bodies telling of the peasant's final agony and starvation. When Beal reported these grisly findings to the President of Ukraine, the reply was, "We know millions are dying. That is unfortunate, but the glorious future of the Soviet Union will justify it." Stalin and Molotov decreed that no deviation from quotas of grain would be permitted, regardless of the food emergency. Stalin blamed the famine on his enemies. While starvation increased, he was exporting grain to finance his industrialization schemes.[5]

Like Ivan "The Terrible" before him, Stalin had cultivated the Party into a religious-like order that had Messianic faith in its cause. Many members came from pious backgrounds, and although they rejected religion, they accepted a new creed that vested a God-like authority in their leader. They regarded Marxism as scientific truth and Party-mindedness as, "an almost mystical concept." Malcom Muggeridge, a British correspondent in Moscow during this period, wrote that the party

had "idealized and spiritualized evil." It was reminiscent of
the military-monastic order founded by Tsar Ivan, to serve as
Oprichniks. They too blended the sacred with the profane as
they sacked cities in the name of sweeping the nation "clean" of
the Tsar's enemies. Stalin actually referred to the Party members as "Swordbearers" within the Soviet state. His reference
was to the ancient military-religious Livonian Order, which was
reincarnated as Ivan's guardian-monks. Only Stalin, with his
sense of history and his unique identification with Ivan Grozny,
could have used such a metaphor for the Party faithful.[6]

The stress created by the massive number of deaths in the
country exacted a toll on Stalin's immediate family. Stalin's
wife Nadya became emotionally disturbed and physically ill.
Later her daughter reported that much of her suffering was
caused by a "most terrible, devastating disillusionment." She
suffered from excruciating headaches and abdominal pain and
her ailments were affecting the marriage. Stalin later confided
that he had not given enough attention to his suffering wife
during that time. "There was so much pressure on me... so
many enemies. We had to work day and night..." [7]

All of the officials of the Kremlin returned from their liquidation missions in the countryside to attend the anniversary
celebration of the Revolution on November 7, 1932. They
marched as a group to Lenin's tomb, in bitter cold, to view a
four-hour parade. Among them was Nadya Alliluyeva Stalin,
the thirty-one year old wife of the General Secretary. While perhaps ten million people were starving in snowdrifts, the poten-
tates of the Soviet State followed the parade with a sumptuous
feast, including Georgian wine and plenty of vodka.

During the banquet, Nadya received scant notice from
her husband and so she danced with her Georgian godfather.
Many witnesses said this enraged Stalin. She was seen flirting with other men, perhaps to get his attention. He was busy
focusing on the attractive wife of a Red Army commander.
Galina Yegorova was a smoldering brunette with a reputation
for extramarital affairs and provocative clothes. Stalin was seen
throwing bread balls at Galina in a shameless display of seduction that caused his wife to become extremely angry. Stalin was,

of course, used to female admirers and was the master of many
sexual conquests. But his wife was increasingly unhappy about
such dalliances and was nearing the breaking point.

Before this fateful night there had been some warning signs
of how profoundly fragile Nadya's emotional condition had
become. She might have easily been diagnosed as suffering
from clinical depression. Her withdrawal of affection for her
children was a sign of her illness, as was the manic nature of
her relationship with Stalin. Her condition was exacerbated
by the disillusionment she suffered by observing the monster
he had become. Nadya left the party, and Polina Molotova followed her outside. They walked around the Kremlin, where
Nadya expressed extreme pain at seeing her husband flirting so
publicly. Although Nadya "quieted down," she was not content
when she went to her room. No sounds were heard during the
night, but when dawn appeared, a Russian tragedy was revealed
that would change the nation.[8]

The Great Terror Begins

In the morning the housekeeper found Nadya on the floor
by her bed, in a pool of blood, her body already quite cold.
She had been shot with her own small pistol. Stalin's bodyguards and Nadya's Godfather were called. Meanwhile, no one
dared to awaken Stalin, who slept on seemingly unaware of the
tragedy that had occurred in his household. Nadya's family
and personal physicians were summoned and her angry letter
of denunciation, addressed to her husband, was read. It was
a blistering series of accusations aimed at Stalin and his political policies. The people in the room were stunned. The letter
subsequently disappeared.

Something inside Stalin died with Nadya, and darkness
descended on him. It was an emotional blow from which he
never recovered – not unlike the emotional darkness that dominated Ivan, after his beloved wife Anastasia died tragically at a
young age. It was in response to her loss that Ivan's paranoia
grew into something monstrous, leading to the organization of

his Oprichniks and the death and destruction they would bring down upon medieval Russia. In the aftermath of lost love, Ivan IV truly became Ivan "The Terrible" and Stalin became the father of the Great Terror.

Stalin, who had basked in the warm glow of Nadya's love, would awake on this morning to learn of both her death and her political and personal repudiation. His own sense of the betrayal by his wife was so severe that Stalin, despite his obvious grief, did not attend Nadya's funeral and he never visited her gravesite. According to his daughter, Svetlana, he said of his young and beautiful dead wife, "She went away as an enemy." For Stalin a sacred trust had been violated. He was completely alone, never again trusting another human being.

Stalin had imagined the presence of enemies before, but now he began to feel like the victim of a vast web of conspiracy. The nation was in shambles created by his coercive collectiviza-tion, but the idealized hero-figure of his own creation could not be blamed for such catastrophic failure. Nadya's death became a watershed event in Stalin's life, and in the life of Rus-sia. "She's crippled me," he said to his close comrades and he became so emotionally damaged that he was capable only of destruction.

No mention of suicide as the cause of Nadya's death was permitted. Such an admission would legitimize her desperate act as a personal and political protest. The public was told that Nadya died of appendicitis. Her State funeral was a macabre Bolshevik charade. Close associates in the Kremlin saw behav-ioral changes in Stalin as despair turned to depression and then to rage. A few days following the funeral, he was found in his apartment, spitting on the wall. After Nadya's death Stalin never slept in a bed, but his nights were spent on a divan wher-ever he happened to be reading.[9] In the past, Stalin had rarely been suspicious of his inner circle, but following Nadya's death all stood equally exposed to Stalin's delusions of treason. In his mind, he was a glorious revolutionary leader surrounded by traitors and potential assassins.

To deal with perceived threats, Stalin created one of the most sinister totalitarian regimes in history. Malcolm Muggeridge, once an enthusiastic Communist, saw enough in just eight months as a correspondent in Moscow to be horrified by the evil of Stalin's secret police and what it meant for Soviet citizens. In his third report to *The Morning Post*, in June 1933, he described the workings of the newly designated GPU, the primary organ of the Soviet police state:

> *No one who has not seen it for himself can understand the terror that this organization inspires, not merely in avowed enemies of the Soviet regime ex-bourgeoisie, priests, people who were for any reason privileged under the old social order – but the whole population.*

> *It is not so much that they dread what the GPU may do to them, though it can do anything without anyone, even their nearest relatives, knowing; they dread the thing itself, because of its nature, because it is utterly evil, because it is morbid, because it belongs to those fearful distortions and perversions that exist in all human beings, but that, in a civilized society, emerge only occasionally in some criminal or madman.*[10]

The food crisis eased due to better yields, reduction in exports and the fact that there were many less peasants to feed because of the Kulak extermination. But concern about the impact of Stalin's extreme policy had brought about a movement favoring "reconciliation with the people." A leader in this movement was the dynamic forty-seven year old Sergei Kirov, a Party chief from Leningrad. He was a rising star and a close ally of Stalin's. Collectivization had been accomplished in his region with greater efficiency and far less human damage than in other areas of the country. Kirov was reported to have called Stalin a "hysteric." A chill then fell over relations between Kirov and Stalin according to Politburo member, Nikita Khrushchev, who witnessed at least one sharp exchange between the two men. Kirov was the leader of the Politburo members who favored reconciliation and Comrade Sergo Ordzhonikidze was co-leader. The two men were extremely close both personally and professionally.

In 1934, delegates assembled for the sixteenth Party congress, scheduled to be "The Congress of Victors," a celebration
of the victory of socialism under the leadership of the Russia's
greatest hero – Stalin. But there was an undercurrent of dissent. Many of the regional leaders were concerned with the direction of the Revolution and alarmed by the cult of personality
now building around Comrade Stalin. The "Old Bolshevik's,"
who had come into leadership positions before the Revolution,
proposed that Kirov become the new leader. Kirov reportedly rejected the offer and expressed his loyalty to Stalin. The
movement for a leadership change died quietly and the congress concluded in extravagant praise for Stalin. The last speak-
er was Kirov himself, who was generous in his comments about
Stalin's leadership. But the delegates' adulation was clearly for
the dynamic Kirov. For Kirov it was a personal triumph. Stalin
abstained from final remarks and appeared to moderate his
policies. However, Kirov had become Stalin's rival and was now
a marked man.[11]

Stalin was not seriously threatened by public enthusiasm for
Kirov, but he was silently enraged by its potential. He became
convinced of the need to do away with the "Old Bolsheviks,"
who had favored Kirov as his replacement. On December 1,
as Kirov arrived at a meeting at Leningrad's Smolny Institute,
his personal bodyguard lagged behind, perhaps detained by
security men from Moscow who had suddenly appeared. A
young man, who had been stalking Kirov, overtook him while
he was unprotected in the stairwell and killed him with a gunshot to the head. Stalin arrived on December 2 to take personal charge of the investigation. Kirov's errant bodyguard was
summoned, but he fell from a truck and died en route. The
two NKVD (the newest name for the GPU secret police) men
who were guarding him were then shot. Kirov's assassination
became the triggering event in a massive purge of the Party.
It was announced that the murder was a small part of a much
larger conspiracy against the Soviet State. Stalin was depicted
by the press as the closest of Kirov's comrades.

Kirov's funeral was a theatrical extravaganza, complete with
velvet curtains, burning torches and arc lights illuminating the

coffin. The Bolshoi orchestra performed the funeral marches. On the following day, his dear friend, Comrade Sergo, placed Kirov's ashes in the wall of the Kremlin. They rest there today. By December 15, fifteen former Trotskyites were arrested in Moscow. A week later seven others were referred to an NKVD Special Board for prompt administrative action. Kirov's assassin was tried behind closed doors, found guilty and executed on December 29. There was no published transcript of the proceedings. Lists of members of the conspiracy were prepared. A "Leningrad Center" and a "Moscow Center" for investigation were created. It was so neat, and yet so clumsy, that it was clear even to the public what was happening.[12]

Many years later, Vera Panova, a journalist from Rostov, described her reaction to these events in a posthumously published memoir. When her husband Boris Vakhtin, a newspaper editor, called her to tell her of the Kirov killing, she wrote:

> Who killed him?" I ask, no answer comes, but I know what will happen now: after all, I've written about the burning of the Reichstag. And that night I have a dream but I don't dare tell it even to Boris: they themselves killed Kirov so as to start a new terror. Against whom? Against the "lefts," against the "rights," against anyone they want. But I can't keep the dream from Boris for long. After vacillating, I tell it to him. He gives me a strange look and is silent.[13]

The Executioner's Circle Expands

In the biography, *Stalin: The Court of the Red Tsar,* historian Simon Sebag Montefiore refers to Kirov's murder as the "crime of the century" and with good reason. It was the seminal event in launching the greatest planned mass extermination in history. Stalin conducted an extensive purge of the party by execution, deportation, and imprisonment in the Gulag. The purge spanned several decades. The process started slowly, and at first seemed to be a direct response to the killing of Kirov. But

soon, the great locomotive of terror began to gain speed and
momentum. Initially those purged were low-level party func-
tionaries with whom Stalin had little or no contact. Leading
figures in the Soviet government were almost untouched. During 1935 and early 1936, it was called "the quiet terror." Prime
targets were Leningraders, sometimes referred to in the camps,
in which they were imprisoned, as "Kirov's assassins."

The executioner's circle of victims gradually expanded
to include Old Bolsheviks, presumably for their disloyalty to
Stalin. Like many others, they were victimized through the
technique of guilt by association. Many were charged with the
especially damaging allegation of harboring "Trotskyite" views.
While Trotsky himself had been exiled in 1929, Stalin had con-
veniently placed him on an island in Turkey, the visible symbol
of a potential counterrevolution.

As Pravda railed against "Trotskyites and White Guard
scum," and warned of "capitalist encirclement," a second level
of propaganda was enhancing the cult of personality around
Stalin. In reality, the leader projected the kind of duplicity on
his victims that he himself was guilty of, while the propaganda
machine extolled his virtues as a great populist leader, who was
protecting all Russians from conspiracies and treason.[14]

To capture public attention and to highlight the potential
for treason, Stalin launched the first of a series of "show trials," in August of 1936. Two previously imprisoned Bolshevik's
pled guilty to false charges to save their families and were put
on trial with other alleged conspirators in the Kirov case. The
script for this trial was written by Stalin himself and coordinated by his Procurator-General, Andrei Vyshinsky. Public
outrage was whipped into frenzy by his hysterical rants: "These
mad dogs of capitalism tried to tear limb from limb the best of
our Soviet land – Kirov. I demand that these mad dogs should
be shot – every one of them!" And they were. Some of Lenin's
oldest and closest comrades were sacrificed and panic began to
spread, even among the Party elite.[15]

Replacing Kirov as Central Committee secretary was a man
who became known as "the bloody dwarf," Nikolai Yezhov, a
Lithuanian who was small in stature, but who became a giant at

his craft of political terror and murder. His personal life had been unsavory from his youth, when his father ran a brothel. He enjoyed orgies with prostitutes and was avidly bisexual. His high-strung personality made him vulnerable to nervous conditions including psoriasis, neurasthenia, and depression. He became a Stalin favorite, and the dictator gave him the nickname, "blackberry," because the name Yezhov sounded like the Russian word for the fruit. Following the first show trial, Yezhov turned on Nadya's godfather. Stalin had never forgiven what he perceived to be undue influence over Nadya. He was accused of being central to a terrorist cell in the Kremlin. More than one hundred of godfather Yenukidze's employees were arrested including such low-level staff as maids. Stalin eventually promoted Yezhov to lead internal affairs, replacing the slavish Yagoda, who had so loved his job that the bullets used to kill the two Trotskyites, were dug out of their skulls and preserved as macabre trophies in his office. Yagoda's blood lust was no longer enough for Stalin.[16]

Comrade Sergo, who ran heavy industries, questioned how Stalin could have innocent people arrested and shot for mere allegations of treason or sabotage. Sergo actually had the courage (or stupidity) to confront Stalin. Acting on Stalin's orders, Yezhov had Sergo's apartment searched by the NKVD. This was a clear sign that his days were numbered and Comrade Sergo went into a deep depression. Within days he shot himself to death. When his widow found the body, she called Stalin franticly saying, "Sergo's done the same as Nadya!" Stalin was insulted, and promptly hung up on her. Sergo was considered "the perfect Bolshevik," so his death could not be revealed as a suicide. The public was told that he died of a heart attack and he was given another cult burial as a hero of the Revolution. Stalin himself placed the urn of Sergo's ashes in the Kremlin wall, near Kirov's remains.[17]

The new head of the secret police, Yezhov, turned on his former mentor. He presented evidence that his predecessor, Yagoda, had been a German spy since 1907, the year he first joined the Communist Party. Yezhov, the sinister dwarf, explained the source of his strength, "I may be small in stature but my hands are strong – Stalin's hands." Yagoda was arrested and now only five leaders – Stalin, Molotov, Voroshilov, Kaganovich and Yezhov, shared power in the Politburo. Stalin had the machinery of repression completely under his control and his subordinates were now so fearful of Stalin that they would allow virtually anyone to be sacrificed. Molotov, for example, remained loyal to Stalin over the years despite the fact that his beloved wife, Polina, was eventually arrested and tortured in the anti-Semitic purges of 1949.

As the Terror moved up the organization chart, Stalin found that it was less necessary to develop fictional crimes to force confessions from his victims. The targets for terror were increasingly men whose crimes were well known because they had been committed on Stalin's orders. The circle of death and destruction widened, as friends, protégés, lovers and relatives frequently were punished along with the accused. Yagoda's brother-in-law and father-in-law were shot, along with group of writers with whom Yagoda associated. His wife and sister were exiled. Yagoda himself, a victim of the last great show trial, died in the Gulag, along with his parents. Nadya's godfather "Uncle Abel" Yenukidze was shot on December 20, 1937.

Stalin knew that the only one institution could threaten his power – the military, so the purge included those in uniform. By 1938, 40,000 military officers had been arrested and three of five marshals, fifteen of sixteen commanders, sixty of sixty-seven corps commanders and seventeen commissars were shot. The methods used to extract confessions were crude but effective. One General's confession actually had rust colored spatters on the paper, later found to be his blood. The General was eventually executed.

The Terror moved into high gear beginning in July, 1937. Orders were issued to local Secretaries to execute "the most hostile anti-Soviet elements." Three-man tribunals were empowered to facilitate these killings. Quotas were issued and each region was told that 72,950 people were to be shot and 259,450 were to be arrested. These arbitrary figures were later increased and other extermination orders were issued based on ethnicity. Yezhov issued order Number 00485 for the liquidation of "Polish diversionists and espionage groups," under which 350,000 people were arrested (including 144,000 Poles) and 247,157 were shot (including 110,000 Poles). The most recent estimates of the number of victims of this ethnic purge are 1.5 million arrested and 700,000 shot.[18]

Death or imprisonment in the Gulag was frequently random, while other times a personal grudge or an informers envy of someone's job could lead to arrest, torture and perhaps even death. In many purge cases, eager underlings actually exceeded their quotas, in an effort to please superiors. The families of those charged were in greater danger after July 5, 1937 when the Politburo ordered the NKVD to "confine all wives of condemned traitors... in camps for 5-8 years." Later, children between the ages of one and three years of age and "socially dangerous children between three and fifteen," were put into state-run orphanages. Many years after the Terror, Nikita Khrushchev explained his absolute power over an underling who had angered him: "Well of course, I could have done anything I wanted with him, I could have destroyed him, I could have arranged it so that, you know, he would disappear from the face of the earth."

Stalin's working style was nocturnal, partly because he had difficulty sleeping and partly because he enjoyed late night dinners, with a great deal of serious drinking and superficial merriment. He especially enjoyed humiliating his ministers and terrorizing them with ominous comments. Stalin cleverly played one against the other, a cruel game of cat and mouse that he relished. Invited guests always attended these all-night sessions because failure to appear could result in a fate none wanted to contemplate. They laughed at Stalin's jokes and listened intently to his stories, but beneath the veneer of pleasure and devotion, there was pure fear, for no one was safe in Stalin's world.

The purpose of Stalin's Great Terror was not merely indiscriminate killing. Like Ivan's purge of the nobility known as boyars, it was a means of crushing the treason that was suspected within the prevailing system, but it was also a means of bringing a new power structure into being. Like Ivan, Stalin wanted to

strengthen and centralize power while developing a new generation of leaders to fill the vacancies created by the purges.[19]

To the entire world, Stalin presented the Soviet system as
the precise opposite of the Nazi barbarism that was growing
in Germany under Hitler. In 1936, Stalin stated that the new
Soviet constitution would be "the most democratic of all the
constitutions in the world." While this contrast was being promoted in state-sponsored propaganda, Stalin quietly pursued
better diplomatic relations with Germany, primarily as a means
of forestalling a war that he knew Russia was not prepared to
fight.

Between 1937 and 1939 the full fury of the Great Terror fell
upon the Russian people. By this time, Stalin had completely
overshadowed the ideology that was the inspiration for so many
who originally joined the Revolution. He had replaced Lenin-
ism with Stalinism and a system of repression and fear that
gripped everyone, from the lowest worker to the loftiest leaders of the Party. According to biographer, Robert C. Tucker, in
Stalin in Power: The Revolution from Above:

> *Suffice it to say here that no major nation has ever suf-*
> *fered state terrorism of such ferocity as Russia did then,*
> *that those arrested and put to death or consigned to*
> *slave-labor camps numbered in the millions, and that*
> *the grief and hardship borne by their loved ones defy*
> *computation. The moral, spiritual, economic, military,*
> *and cultural damage to the Soviet state was likewise in-*
> *calculably great.*[20]

Stalinism was not Communism, but a mutation of it. However, a system of terror and political murder had long been
the official policy of the Communists. Lenin had made it clear
that extermination of enemies of the Revolution was necessary. Officially, the policy of arrest and extermination was first
documented openly in *Red Terror*, published on November
1, 1918. What changed during the time of Stalin is that one
did not need to be an enemy any longer to be subject to state-
sponsored terror. One only needed to help meet a quota, or

be from a specific ethnic group, be accused by a colleague or denounced by a prisoner under torture. Essentially, Stalin had people murdered "not because of what they had done, but because of what they might do." This process of terrorism, practiced upon Soviet citizens, continued for decades. Alexander Solzhenitsyn makes it clear in the powerful expose, *The Gulag Archipelago* that Russia's "sewage disposal system" began in 1918 and remained active until 1956.

A Nation Enslaved

Fear gripped the entire population of 165 million people under the Stalinist system. Nearly everyone lived in constant terror of making a fatal mistake. Regardless of their station in Soviet society, everyone knew that their life could change in an instant, based on a word, a glance, a false accusation or a rumor. Overnight, and for no discernable reason, anyone could vanish into the bowels of a vast penal empire, described by the Nobel Prize winner, Solzhenitsyn:

> *The Kolyma was the greatest and most famous island, the pole of ferocity of that amazing country of Gulag, which, though scattered in an archipelago geographically, was, in the psychological sense, fused into a continent – an almost invisible, almost imperceptible, country inhabited by the zek people [prisoners]*[21]

Average citizens were subjected to arrest and interrogation, and possibly some grotesque form of torture to secure a false confession of guilt. Prisoners were then sent through transit prisons and across a continent in overcrowded, pestilent trains, known as Red Cows. Some prisoners faced transport on ships to a final nightmarish destination. It was a journey into debasement, filth, disease, torture, rape, and finally, in many cases, death by execution, freezing or prolonged starvation. According to Solzhenitsyn, the Gulag "metastasized," into four hundred and seventy-six camp complexes under Stalin. Within each, often dozens, sometimes hundreds, of smaller camps were embedded.

The Gulag system became essential to the Soviet economy, and inmates worked in every form of labor – railroad construction, road building, canal digging, mining, agriculture and forestry, under the most primitive and inhumane conditions imaginable. The Gulag complexes were not technically death camps, but on the subsistence rations provided, most prisoners were capable of productive work for only the first few months of captivity. Killing exhausted prisoners and replacing them with fresh inmates helped to maintain high productivity. It was general practice to shoot the last man in line for work detail each morning as a laggard ("dokhodyaga"), too weak for useful work.

Yevgenia Ginzburg, in her memoir, *Journey Into the Whirlwind*, recalls her fear as murderers and thieves joined "politicals" on the transport ship to the Gulag in Magadan: "When I saw this half-naked, tattooed apelike horde invade the hold, I thought that it had been decided that we were to be killed off by mad women. The fetid air reverberated to their shrieks, their ferocious obscenities, their wild laughter and their caterwaulings . . . Within five minutes we had a thorough introduction to the law of the jungle." Ginzburg tells us that frequently ships transporting prisoners to Magadan would become frozen in the ice, where they sometimes remained trapped for weeks. Hundreds, sometimes thousands perished. Guards occasionally fed corpses to the living, but usually they tossed them overboard onto the ice, where they lay frozen solid until the summer thaw caused them to slowly decompose.

Other accounts tell us that while the secret police administered the operation of the camps, inside the barracks criminal leaders ruled, abusing the weak. Women in the Gulag were almost always considered prey. They were often raped on transport ships or in railroad cars, even before they reached the camps. Upon arrival at their destination they would be paraded naked in front of camp officials, who would select their favorites to provide sexual favors to their new masters. Women not selected became "prizes" for male (and sometimes female) inmates. The pitiful creatures inhabiting the world of the

Gulag suffered from starvation, exhaustion, exposure, and physical abuse on a routine basis. Uncooperative prisoners, of either sex, might be subjected to isolation, impalement, genital mutilation, or perhaps more mercifully, a bullet to the brain.

It is estimated that more than thirty million prisoners entered the Gulag during the four decades in which the system flourished. Historian Robert Conquest, who has done extensive research on the Gulag, estimates that one out of every three new inmates died during the first year of imprisonment and only half survived through the third year in the camps. He estimates that about twelve million people perished in the Gulag. Soviet dissident, Andrei Sakharov and others have suggested a much higher death count, ranging from 15 to 20 million. Professor R. J. Rummel, who has done careful research, estimates that 25.6 million persons were killed as a result of deportation, transit and imprisonment in the Gulag labor camps. He believes that the Soviet government killed a total of more than 61 million victims in the Gulag and through Stalin's extermination policies.

One question raised by such barbaric cruelty is why there was no organized resistance to the great crimes committed by the state. Solzhenitsyn and other eyewitnesses tell us that there were many efforts to resist, but sadly, word of those heroics never reached the outside world. He writes, "The secret of this struggle is kept by the Soviet regime even more zealously than that of the torments and annihilation it inflicted upon millions of its victims." He tells of one revolt during 1952, when prisoners gained control of their camp for 40 days, during which they restored many aspects of civilized life. The human beings who stood up to the power of the totalitarian state knew that they were doomed and the survivors eventually were subjected to mass shootings or even more ghastly punishments.

Stalin, Hitler and the Jews

Bolshevik ranks during and after the revolution included a large number of Jews in relatively high positions, both in the

Party and the government. Perhaps this was because Jews along with other ethnic peoples (including Stalin's native Georgians), had been persecuted by the Tsarists. While anti-Semitism did exist in the early years of the Soviet Union, there does not seem to be any official policy that was openly hostile to Jewish citizens, until later, when Stalin began his own pogrom in the 1940's.

Several of Stalin's top leaders were Jews, including Commissar of Railroads Kaganovich ("Iron Lazar"); Editor of Pravda Mekhlis; NKVD Leader Yagoda and Foreign Commissar Litvinov. For many years Stalin's bodyguard and head of personal security was Karl Pauker, a Jew from Budapest. Several of his key lieutenants, including Kirov, Molotov and Yezhov had Jewish wives. Major figures in the Revolution including Trotsky had been Jewish leaders in the Party, before they became Stalin's political enemies. A number of women in Stalin's social circle were Jewish too, including Yevgenia Yezhova, Kaganovich's sister, Rosa, Georgian opera singer and Stalin in-law Maria Svanidze and Molotov's wife Polina.[22]

The assault on the Jews began when Stalin ordered an attack on his own diplomats. His orders were "Purge the ministry of Jews. Clean out the synagogue." Stalin had become distrustful of Jews, whom he feared had insufficient dedication to the Soviet state. The Foreign Ministry was an early target, partly to please Hitler, with whom Stalin wanted a non-aggression treaty. Later, his suspicions of Jewish citizens would become full-fledged Jew hatred.

Stalin and Molotov arranged a non-aggression pact with Hitler, which was signed on August 23, 1939, just before Hitler invaded Poland. Stalin knew that eventually one of the two parties would breach this protocol, but he desperately needed to buy time to prepare his country to defend itself. He knew that Russia simply was not ready to face German Panzers. Secret provisions in the Soviet-German agreement, revealed only upon Germany's defeat in 1945, specified plans to carve up Northern and Eastern Europe into German and Soviet spheres of influence.

Stalin received advance warning of the German invasion of Poland, which was launched on September 1, 1939. Within days, the Russians also invaded Poland and began to assert dominance over their share of the spoils. The Poles, at first cheered the Russian advance, believing that the Russians were preparing to oppose the Germans, but they soon learned the truth. By November 1940, more than one million Poles had been deported by the Russians and soon thereafter a third of that number was dead.

During the German negotiations, Foreign Commissar Molotov's wife Polina was indicted for espionage. This was not the first time that Stalin had tested the loyalty of his leadership by investigating their wives, but it marked an ominous turn of events. Polina Molotova was spared for the time being, but she eventually became a target for terror. As the political killings increased, they moved closer to Stalin's inner circle. In early 1940, the noted Russian author, Isaac Babel was executed. Stalin's brother-in-law, Stanislas Redens, who had been accused of crimes by Yezhov, was shot the next month. His widow and children continued to be friendly with Stalin and his daughter, Svetlana, as if nothing had happened. Stalin demanded loyalty based on a fear so complete that it transcended even the murder of a loved one.

The rise of Laverenti Beria marked the beginning of the end for his boss, NKVD chief Yezhov. Just as Yezhov had done away with his predecessor, Yagoda, he too would fall victim to his own secret police. Yezhov and his promiscuous wife, Yevgenia were easy targets. Yezhov later told associates that he had been "compelled to sacrifice her" to save himself. She took Luminal and died two days later, never regaining consciousness. But Yezhov was not saved by even this desperate act and before his demise he descended into a prolonged series of drunken orgies with both women and his homosexual lovers. Beria became head of the NKVD and Yezhov was left to await a grim fate. He told his few remaining friends, "I never realized the depth of the meanness of all these people." The bloody dwarf finally felt the wrath of Stalin. He was targeted for death and Beria would become the new executioner.

Stalin proved that he could reach out to find and liquidate enemies anywhere. In 1939, he ordered that Trotsky be "eliminated within a year." Although Trotsky had fled Turkey for the security of a Mexico City villa, which had become an armed

compound, one of Beria's agents was able to get close enough
to plunge a pickaxe into Trotsky's skull. He died of his wounds
the next day, August 21, 1940.

While Hitler and the Soviet dictator were still technically
allies, Stalin decided to eliminate a large number of Polish officers who were being held in three camps near the Katyn Forest, outside Smolensk. These men were considered "spies and
saboteurs...hardened enemies of Soviet power." Beria moved
in with a precision operation, and personally supervised the systematic killing of these inmates by gunshot to the head. 7,000
were shot to death in 28 nights, during the spring of 1940.
The bodies were buried in scattered locations, but 4,500 officers from the Kozelsk camp were buried in a mass grave in the
Katyn Forest. At the Nuremberg trials this crime was originally
attributed to the Germans, but later evidence proved that Stalin
had issued direct orders to have these men murdered.[23]

In early 1941, Stalin clung to the hope of avoiding a war with
Germany and he deferred a mobilization order. Somehow in his
mind, if he did not prepare for war, it could not happen. Finally,
during the week of June 20, when the German Embassy was discovered burning documents, Stalin ordered 75% combat readiness.
The alert order was finally given just after midnight on Sunday
June 22, 1941. Shortly after that time, a German communist
deserter swam across the Pruth River with news that the invasion
order had been given to his unit. Stalin, enraged by the confirma-
tion of his worst fear, ordered the informant shot, "for his disinformation." At 3:30 a.m., on the very day that Napoleon had invaded
129 years earlier, the German Blitzkrieg rolled towards the Russian
steppes, following a wave of Luftwaffe bombers. The force was
more than three million men, 600,000 motorized vehicles, 7,000
pieces of artillery, 2,500 aircraft and 3,600 tanks. Whether Stalin
was ready or not, he had now been engaged in World War II.

War With Germany

When Molotov finally told Stalin in no uncertain terms
"Germany has declared war on us," Stalin collapsed into his

chair, "lost in thought." According to General Zhukov, it "was
the only time I saw Stalin depressed." He still did not want to
believe that war with Germany was real, but the size of the invasion left no doubt. He issued orders to Kanganovich to move
20 million people and to disassemble and relocate several factories away from the front, to deprive the advancing Germans
of the prize these could become. Then he went into seclusion
and left Molotov to address the nation and announce the onset
of war.

The situation quickly grew desperate – as the Nazi Panzers
drew closer to Minsk, more than 30 Russian divisions had already been destroyed. By June 28, Minsk, capital of Belorussia,
was encircled and some 400,000 people were trapped in that
city. The Western Front was in a state of complete collapse and
Stalin was on the hunt for scapegoats. Stalin's generals were in
hiding from his wrath and it took some time to locate those he
could hold responsible. Eventually, several commanders were
arrested and under torture others were implicated. On July 22,
the four officers commanding the front were shot. Local commanders were ordered to shoot the traitors in their midst.

The fall of Minsk was a terrible blow and perhaps Stalin's
greatest wartime crisis. He told his officials that he could no
longer be their leader and he dropped out of Kremlin life,
remaining at his dacha, wandering like a zombie, without
sleeping. Partly this was theatrics, following the example of his
"teacher," Ivan Grosny, who withdrew from political power to
test the loyalty of his boyars, but Stalin was clearly depressed. A
paralysis gripped the Kremlin and the Soviet government was
leaderless for more than two days as the German advance drew
closer to Moscow. Stalin's subordinates were careful not to sign
any documents in his absence, but something clearly needed to
be done – and quickly.

Beria proposed a State Defense Committee consisting of Molotov, Voroshilov, Malenkov and Beria with Stalin as the leader.
When the leadership group reached Stalin's dacha, they found
him, "thinner... haggard and gloomy." He looked at them
fearfully and asked, "Why have you come." Beria restated their
proposal, "You, Comrade Stalin, will be the head." In no other

system, could the architect of such a catastrophe have been renominated to lead. But Stalinism was a police state, without any preparations for succession. There was simply no one but Stalin. Later Beria would shrewdly comment, "We were witnesses to Stalin's moments of weakness. Joseph Vissarionovich will never forgive that move of ours." [24]

A recommitted Stalin finally hurled himself into the war. Armed with new confidence and new powers, he addressed the nation in an emotional speech that called for a sense of patriotism, but it also contained the threat of terror. "Cowards, deserters, panic-mongers", he told the Russians, would be destroyed in a "merciless struggle." Despite the horrific losses, including more than 2 million men, 6,500 tanks and more than 6,000 aircraft, by the end of the first month of the war the Russian military had not been completely destroyed.

Next Leningrad fell under attack and Stalin sent Zhukov to take control, as the situation was "almost hopeless." But Zhukov lived up to his name as a "fighting general," holding the city and forcing Hitler to lay siege to Leningrad. It was a nightmare of starvation that lasted for 900 days. With more than 2 million people trapped, the death toll was almost without precedent in modern warfare. The dead were everywhere throughout the city. Those still living were too weak to bury the corpses. Cannibalism was common and bodies were frequently seen with meat carved off of the thighs and breasts. Eventually, half of Leningrad's residents died of starvation.

Hitler continued to drive to the south, seeking oil and wheat from the Ukraine. His effort resulted in the surrender of the city of Kiev on September 19. Then on October 2, the Panzers renewed their drive on Moscow, but precious time had been lost and the Russian winter was drawing near.

Stalin had used a "scorched earth" policy to leave nothing for the advancing Germans. The arrest and execution of Soviet soldiers accused of treason continued at a brisk pace. During 1941 and 1942 more than 990,000 Russian soldiers were condemned and more than 150,000 were shot. With the retreat, NKVD officers transferred prisoners or killed those in their cells with grenades, also destroying the facilities. By October

14, 1941, order in Moscow had collapsed and looters were running loose in the streets. Air raids on the city were now almost constant.

Many of Stalin's senior leaders urged a prompt departure from Moscow. But, Stalin found himself unable to depart the capital. His movements during this time are not precisely known, but he slept in the Metro beneath the city, because the Kremlin did not have air raid bunkers. Eventually he began to both work and sleep in the subterranean Metro station under Kirov Street. On the evening of October 18, Stalin's staff reported him continually repeating, "What shall we do?" There was no clear answer. When they returned to Stalin's apartment to eat dinner, the ever-cheerful Valechka, Stalin's maid and mistress met them. As she served their meal, suddenly he turned to her, and asked, "Valentina Vasilevna, are you prepared to leave Moscow?" Her answer was emphatic, representing a Russian peasant sensibility, "Comrade Stalin, Moscow is our mother, our home! It should be defended." Her words seemed to strengthen the leader's resolve. Russian troops from the Far Eastern Army were rushed to Moscow and massed behind the capital as reserves for the final battle. The destiny of Moscow was still in doubt, but Stalin now had the troops to make a stand at the walls of the city.

In early November, the Russian winter took charge of the war and the fate of the German Blitzkrieg was sealed. Winter became a greater enemy to the Germans than the Russian army, as its deadly grip brought bone-cracking cold, icy gales and massive snowdrifts. In subzero temperatures human flesh fuses to metal and frostbite leaves soldiers and pack animals white and numb. Like Napoleon before him, Hitler would feel the frigid embrace of mother Russia.

On December 6, Russia launched an enormous counterattack on four fronts. The Russian assault was a success and the freezing, exhausted Germans were forced to retreat more than 200 miles. The Russian generals, clearly aware of the need to appeal to Stalin's vanity, declared the battle for Moscow a victory on that very day, Stalin's birthday. Moscow was saved, but the war raged on. By the end of 1941, the Russians had suffered grievous losses, including 3 million soldiers (its entire strength at the start of the war). Fully half of its economic base was in German hands. But Russia still had 9 million men of military age, (enough for 400 divisions) and the nation produced 4,500 tanks during that winter. Over time, in what was becoming a war of attrition, the Russians had the numbers to prevail.

Now in command of everything, including the war, Stalin was at the peak of his dictatorial power. He encouraged absolute subservience, but was irritated by "boot licking." He respected those who had the courage to speak their mind in his presence. However, once he had made a decision, there could be no questioning. Zhukov, in his memoirs, spoke glowingly of Stalin's "technique of organizing front operations," and of his "natural intelligence" and "professional intuition." Stalin was a natural leader, but fear was his primary management tool. Typically, he paced during meetings. When his pipe was unlit, it was a sign of trouble to underlings. Putting his pipe down was a prelude to one of his rages. When he displayed his legendary temper, his ministers and generals were terrified. Zhukov stated, "He virtually changed before one's eyes, turning pale, a bitter expression in his eyes, his gaze heavy and spiteful." [25] Stroking his moustache with the pipe was a sign of pleasure. It was incumbent upon his subordinates to carefully read Stalin's mood. Their very life might depend on it.

The war was turning in Russia's favor but the cost to the Soviets was overwhelming. More than 26 million people had died and a similar number were homeless. Famine was raging throughout Russia and there was a civil war in the Ukraine and reportedly treason in the Caucasus. Stalin still relied on Beria's use of terror to rid the country of seditious elements. In early 1944, Beria proposed the mass deportation of Moslems, Chechens and other ethnic peoples. More than 1.5 million people were exiled. About one third of these people died during their transfer or soon after arrival at the camps. It was an immense human tragedy, which today would be called "ethnic cleansing."

As the Russians advanced in their struggle against Hitler, they engaged in an orgy of revenge against the Germans. Two million German women were raped and some Russian troops even raped Russian women liberated from Nazi prison camps. When told of these atrocities, Stalin replied, "Well, then imagine a man who has fought from Stalingrad to Belgrade – over thousands of kilometers of his own devastated land, across the dead bodies of his comrades and dearest ones? How can such a man react normally? And what is so awful about his having fun with a woman after such horrors?"

As the war lurched towards a conclusion, the Russians had fought the largest contingents and the finest units of the German army and had crushed them. They occupied Eastern Europe with a huge military force and would soon be the first troops to enter Berlin, forcing Hitler to die by self-inflicted gunshot wound in his bunker.

On August 6, 1945, the U. S. dropped the first atomic bomb on Hiroshima, Japan. Stalin was convinced that the bomb was directed at him, to forcefully demonstrate that the balance of power had indeed shifted. Beria, who was in charge of the Soviet bomb project met with Soviet scientists on the next day when Stalin stated: "Hiroshima has shaken the whole world. The balance has been destroyed. That cannot be." Designated "Task Number One," the Soviet bomb project moved into high gear and was on a "Soviet scale," utilizing 400,000 people, including 10,000 technicians. Beria used persuasion as only he could, once telling a manager, "You're a good worker but if you'd served six years in the camps, you'd work even better." Beria was not kidding, for he soon started organizing the "Sharashki" – special prisons for scholars and scientists. Scientists whose skills were essential were identified, then fabricated charges were brought against them and they were sent to a "carefully chosen place of destination."

By the end of the war Beria had become "ugly, flabby and unhealthy-looking with a grayish-yellow complexion." His condition not only reflected his extreme work schedule for Stalin, but also his depraved personal life. Beria was a brilliant manager, but one of the most despicable figures in a Stalinist system that was filled with criminals. There were only three things of importance in Beria's life – power, terror and sex. He would seduce women where possible, but generally he would simply kidnap and rape them. Many times this occurred when women came to plead for a loved one who was held in the Gulag. Women in such a vulnerable state could not resist, with the life of a relative at stake. Beria's armored Packard was seen on many evenings prowling the streets of Moscow looking for female victims. His bodyguards would snatch women and bring them to Beria, where he usually gorged himself in a feast that included the kidnapped woman as the final course. These sessions must have been terrifying for the women involved, knowing that resistance to Beria's advances could result in the camps or death.

Beria was a maniacal serial rapist. As a secret policeman, he was also a compulsive list maker and his colonels kept detailed lists of his sexual victims. One list includes as many as seventy-nine women who he violated through intimidation, or outright rape, during his time in power. Most Soviet leader's wives understood that he was a dangerous sexual degenerate and avoided him at all costs. Many refused to be in his presence alone. Usually young women, who became pregnant after Beria's rape sessions, were provided abortions arranged by NKVD officers. He is thought to have fathered several children by rape. In 2003, excavations beneath the Tunisian Embassy in Moscow – the former home of Beria – led to the discovery of human bones.[26]

Stalin basked in the glory of victory, but had been visibly aged by the war. According to one of his lieutenants he now, "always looked tired." As Stalin became physically weaker, extreme paranoia emerged in his personality. In the late fall of 1945 after suffering an illness, Stalin became distrustful of several of his top leaders, including Beria, who he was now referring to as, "snake eyes." When Stalin made inquires about the secret police chief, he learned the full dimensions of Beria's corruption. Soon afterwards, Beria was retired from the secret police (by then called the MVD). His office was moved from Lubianka prison to the Kremlin where he continued as Deputy Premier in charge of the bomb project and missile production. Beria was terrified of his successor, Abakumov, the new and extremely ruthless secret police boss. One of Beria's trusted aides, Colonel Sarkisov, denounced Beria's sexual depravity and labeled him a "Bolshevik Bluebeard." Despite the pressure, Beria delivered on his assignment regarding the bomb. Four years after Hiroshima, Russia had atomic weapons.

During the war, the drunken midnight bacchanals orchestrated by Stalin became less frequent, but after the collapse of Germany, he began to enjoy these session more than ever. Stalin was now venerated and could rule by stealth rather than by sheer force of will. One of his lieutenants said, "He never gave direct orders." And Stalin himself recognized that he was able to dominate his subordinates in more subtle ways. He suffered from arteriosclerosis and Svetlana said that he had experienced a "minor stroke." But his poor health only made him more unpredictable and even more deadly. According to Khrushchev, "after the war, he wasn't quite right in the head." And Stalin's dark moods were driven by a strange fear that made him even more frightening. He once told Zhukov, "I'm afraid of my own shadow."

The leaders of the Soviet regime knew to always look Stalin in the eye, but not too often, or he could become anxious, which made him extremely dangerous. They had learned that it was important to remain calm, since Stalin could become agitated at the first sign of panic. They knew Stalin liked them to take notes, but not so much as to look like a "boot-licker." The ministers never met in private because Stalin knew their schedules and was deeply suspicious. "Danger lurked in friends and friendship," wrote Sergi Khrushchev, Nikita's son. Stalin enjoyed playing one leader against another to provoke them into angry exchanges. Although Beria was the greatest sycophant, he could also come back at Stalin. His wife frequently warned him of the danger of "playing with the tiger." All of these men's homes were bugged and Stalin kept them in complete terror of losing their career or even their life.

Potentates, Plunder and Pogroms

Life with Stalin had become an Orwellian pageant of suspicion, terror and betrayal and yet, for each of the ministers, escape from Stalin's grasp was impossible. The dictator increased the stress when he began to speak of retirement, triggering a multi-year struggle for succession. In October, 1945 he made it clear that he needed rest and signaled that his favored successor was Molotov. Stalin decided that he needed six weeks off and he departed by train for the Black Sea. The government was left in the hands of Molotov.

Only a few days into the trip, Stalin suffered a heart attack, causing rumors to sweep the capital that he was dying. Stalin learned of these rumors and simultaneously became aware that Zhukov and the generals were taking public credit for winning the war. Just as the international media began to proclaim Molotov as the successor to Stalin, the old dictator began to stir from his seaside retreat to confirm that he was still in control. He fired Molotov from his post as First Deputy Premier, and then reinstated him after a chastened Molotov begged forgiveness.

Stalin's distrust of his subordinates increased. Beria, Malenkov and General Zhukov were targeted for persecution. Stalin's newly favored secret policeman was Victor Abakumov, a swaggering, bon vivant, womanizer and expert torturer. This man was efficient and orderly in his work, spreading out a blood-stained carpet to protect his Persian rugs before beginning torture sessions in his office. He was a jazz lover who enjoyed the good life, keeping mistresses and war booty stashed in safe houses throughout Moscow. The spoils of war were corrupting almost everyone from the generals to the bureaucrats. At every level, junior officers and government officials paid off their superiors with loot as a form of tribute. The leader's women now dressed in Dior and Chanel, and were always wrapped in expensive furs. These were the years of the Bolshevik high life.

Stalin had created an extensive criminal culture that reached into every aspect of Soviet society. The dictator and his leadership ruled a cowed and terrified population. Soviet life was built upon a vast slave empire of millions of suffering souls, confined within the labor camps of the Gulag. Cruel barbarity became a virtue that allowed ascendancy to power. But it was also a system that suffered from a self-created malignant

necrosis, for no one – not the police, the military, political leaders or especially Stalin and the jackals surrounding his court,
could be trusted. Predictably, the system that Stalin created
gradually began to devour itself.

Stalin's natural distrust for Jews and his fierce nationalism
fed his suspicions that Soviet Jews were working with the "imperialists" for the overthrow of the Soviet Union. A well-known
Yiddish actor, Solomon Mikhoels, attempted to establish contact with Svetlana to ask her help to protect the Jewish community and to plead for a Jewish enclave in the Crimea. Stalin
raged about Jews, "worming their way into the family," a clear
reference to his daughter's relationships with two Jewish men.
Svetlana divorced her husband Morozov, reflecting a trend, as
many people began to divorce their Jewish spouses. Abakumov arrested Jews in the circle around the Alliluyev family and
many were tortured. Stalin had Mikhoels murdered in January
of 1948. The actor was injected with poison, then beaten and
shot.

On September 3, 1948 a representative of the new State of
Israel, Golda Meir, arrived in Moscow, causing a great stirring
of pride among Soviet Jews. Polina Molotova was highly visible
at the diplomatic reception hosted by her husband. Speaking
in Yiddish, Polina told Golda, "I'm a daughter of the Jewish
people." Stalin's reaction to this event was swift. On November
20 the Politburo abolished the Jewish Committee. Colleagues
of Mikhoels were arrested, along with a number of prominent
Jews, including writers and scientists. Those placed under
arrest were tortured to gain evidence against Polina. Stalin
told Molotov it was time to divorce his wife, as she had conspired against the state. Molotov slavishly accepted the order
although some historians have suggested that Molotov thought
the divorce might save Polina.[27]

A comprehensive case was assembled against the Jews. Its
central charge was the plan for a Jewish Crimea. The Politburo
was given the case against Polina including charges of "group
sex." Molotov later said when he heard these charges, "My
knees trembled." Molotov abstained from voting, but changed
his vote to guilty in a letter to Stalin, dated January 20, 1949.

On the next day, Polina was arrested along with her sister, her doctor and her secretaries. She was sentenced to five years in exile, which she spent in Kustanai, Central Asia. Her name was expunged from the records. Her identity became Object Number 12 and many people believed she was dead. Beria used his inside information to torment Molotov during Politburo meetings, by whispering in Molotov's ear, "Polina's alive!"

Anti-Semitism "grew like a tumor in Stalin's mind" said Khrushchev. An early victim was Professor Dr. Yakov Etinger, who had treated many Soviet leaders. He was arrested and under torture died of "heart paralysis." His torturer, Lt. Col. Mikhail Riumin, was supervised by Abakumov. The madness of Stalinism was growing in parallel with the sickness in Stalin's mind.

More than 2.6 million inmates were now held in the Gulag – the highest number during Stalin's rule. One case built upon another and entire groups of victims were swept into the maw of the meat grinder. Some were executed and the rest were sent to the camps. A large number of the victim's families were also taken prisoner. Most of these spent years at hard labor in freezing camps for crimes that were wholly invented. The Soviet Union under Stalin was one of the truly monstrous regimes of all time and by 1950, it seemed almost invincible.

The Final Anti-Semitic Frenzy

One of the characteristics of such a system is that it eventually consumes its own. Members of the secret police were not exempt from charges. Many of its members had committed crimes that were fully documented in their own files. When the short, fat and rather stupid torturer, Riumin sent a letter to Stalin detailing charges against Abakumov, the dictator was only too happy to turn the system on its own chief policeman. Riumin accused Abakumov of killing the prominent Jewish Dr. Etinger to conceal a huge conspiracy by the Jewish doctors against the leadership. This played on Stalin's worst fears. Perhaps the accusation was to cover Riumin's own tracks, since his excess zeal during torture sessions had actually resulted in Et-inger's death. Within two weeks, Abakumov was dismissed and arrested. His corruption was easily documented by searches of his homes. Abakumov lost his identity, becoming Object Num-ber 15 in the Gulag system.

In a process that might be called a systematic, preventative amputation, Stalin believed that he was cutting off diseased por-tions of the state to preserve its strength and vitality. But the disease that had metastasized in the Soviet body politic was due to the perversity in Stalin's mind. It started with the liquidation of the Kulaks during the 1920's and it continued to rage some thirty years later. Greater numbers of killings did not restore the state to health. It merely made the Soviet state an ever-expanding enterprise of terror and crime. Stalin finally began to pursue the medical professionals whom he called "killers in white coats," as the Terror turned on those who were looking after the physical health of the nation. Because of its increas-ing anti-Semitic character, what began as a purge became a pogrom.

Stalin wanted a number of doctors, mostly Jews, arrested and punished severely. He was infuriated that Professor Vi-nogradov, his personal physician, had suggested Stalin's re-tirement for health reasons. This prescription now became a threat to the health of the Professor. Stalin shrieked his orders: "Leg irons! Put him in leg irons!" When the persecution of the doctors did not proceed quickly enough, Stalin lashed out: "Re-move the Midget!" He wanted Riumin replaced with someone who would proceed more quickly and more harshly. Stalin was now almost in hysterics over the doctors. "Beat them until they confess! Beat, beat and beat again." he wrote in his orders, per-haps revealing a childhood fear and a lifelong obsession with beating as a punishment. Because the top doctors were mostly Jewish, the Doctors Plot and the anti-Jewish campaign became commingled in Stalin's mind. "Every Jew's a nationalist and an agent of American intelligence," he screamed.

The Doctors Plot broke into the open on January 13, 1953, when Pravda announced the arrest of the first group of doctors. "Ignoble Spies and Killers under the Mask of Professor-Doctors,"

read the headline. Stalin supervised the draft of a letter for
signature by prominent Soviet Jews requesting deportation from
cities for their own protection. Stalin's intent was to force them
to sign as an example to others. Two new camps were under
construction, presumably for the large number of Jews soon to
be caught up in the net. Polina Molotova was returned to Moscow to be the star witness in the Jewish case.

On February 28, Stalin hosted a fearful Beria, Khrushchev,
Malenkov and Bulganin for movies at the Kremlin, and then
they drove to his dacha for dinner. They talked of the doctor's
interrogations, with Stalin asking, "Have the doctors confessed?
Tell Ignatiev (Riumin's replacement) if he doesn't get full confessions out of them, we'll shorten him by a head." It was 4 a.m.
in the early morning of Sunday, March 1, 1953, when Stalin saw
his guests out. They reported that he was "pretty drunk...in
high spirits." He stretched out on a divan in the dining room,
telling his security men, "I'm going to sleep. You can take a
nap too. I won't be calling you."

At 10 p.m., when the mail from Moscow arrived, the senior
man in the security detail, Peter Lozgachev, entered the dacha,
making noise, to avoid startling Stalin. He found the dictator
on the carpet in pajama bottoms and an undershirt. Lozgachev
asked, "What's wrong, Comrade Stalin?" The only response was
a mumble. Stalin was conscious but unable to speak and was
leaning on one hand "in a very awkward way." Stalin was inca-
pacitated and lying in his own urine. His security men lifted
him onto the sofa and called the secret police boss, Ignatiev,
who was too afraid to take any action. Lozgachev called Stalin's
most important ministers, but they too were afraid to respond.

At 3 a.m. on Monday, March 2, Beria and Malenkov arrived
at the dacha. It had been more than four hours since the first
call went out. They berated Lozgachev for causing such concern. The instructions they issued were somewhat mysterious,
"Don't bother us, don't cause a panic and don't disturb Comrade Stalin." They were clearly aware that something extraordinary had happened. Some believe that Stalin was murdered
with warfarin, a blood thinner, and they have suggested Beria
as the most likely poisoner. Beria fueled these suspicions later

with the statement "I did him in! I saved you all!" Certainly Beria had good reason to want Stalin dead, since he was very close to arrest himself. Most historians agree that the ruling committee stalled on seeking treatment, allowing Stalin to reach a state of near death. Calling a doctor may have put them all in danger, since Stalin himself had ordered the nation's top doctors arrested.

The guards at the dacha were now frantic, fearing that Stalin might die on their watch. The decision-making circle was expanded and Molotov, Mikoyan and Voroshilov were contacted. The entire group, plus Kaganovich arrived early the next morning to see Stalin. Molotov has noted, "Beria was in charge." It was a chilling moment when Stalin opened his eyes and looked at each of his lieutenant's one at a time – then he closed his eyes again. The doctors led by Professor Lukomsky arrived. They had not previously treated Stalin and all were terrified. The diagnosis was a cerebral hemorrhage and they pronounced his condition as "extremely serious." Stalin's children, Svetlana and Vasily were summoned.

This macabre scene became more twisted as Beria began to spew a vitriolic hatred for Stalin, who seemed to be dying. Then, when the patient would open his eyes or his eyelids would flicker, Beria would drop to his knees and begin kissing Stalin's hand, like a groveling dog. This went on for hours as Stalin's life hung in the balance. Stalin's ministers, however, began to act in a coordinated way, with a twenty-four hour vigil established, each shift to be manned by a pair of leaders. The torture of the doctors was interrupted so they could be asked for medical advice. This single act revealed the complete insanity that Stalinism had become. It was absurdly deranged that these men would be given a break from their own torture sessions to help save the life of the very man who had ordered them arrested and tortured.

Late the next afternoon, Stalin took a turn for the worse and Beria rushed to the Kremlin to search Stalin's safe for any incriminating documents. Soon afterwards he was joined by Khrushchev and Malenkov, who removed and destroyed evidence that Stalin was keeping on each of them. Back at the death vigil, the ministers lined up and each shook hands with the dying Stalin. He was limp and unresponsive. By 9:30 p.m. Stalin had almost no pulse and he began to drown in his own fluids. According to Svetlana, "He literally choked to death as we watched. The death agony was terrible...At the last minute, he opened his eyes. It was a terrible look, either mad or angry and full of the fear of death." In a last gesture, he raised his left hand "like a greeting," according to a nurse who was present. Svetlana said he "seemed to be pointing upwards somewhere or threatening us all." When one of the doctors began artificial respiration, Khrushchev said, "Stop it please! Can't you see the man's dead?" Svetlana has written of the moment that his features became, "pale...serene, beautiful, imperturbable. We all stood frozen and silent." Beria was the first to kiss the body after death, then the others lined up to follow. Stalin's "secret wife" Valechka, led the staff in mourning as she lay across the corpse wailing and sobbing.[28]

Stalinism after Stalin

Stalin died on March 5, 1953. His body was embalmed and placed in the mausoleum beside Lenin. Beria emerged as the power behind Malenkov, who became Premier, but Beria was soon targeted by his own colleagues. On June 25, he was arrested, as was his wife Nina and their son Sergo and daughter-in-law. Beria was dispatched with a single shot to the head. Khrushchev out maneuvered Malenkov and then Bulganin and upon becoming General Secretary of the Party, he began to dismantle the Gulag. In 1956 he addressed a closed session of the Twentieth Party Congress, exposing the great crimes of Stalin. He told shocking truths to a stunned and silent Congress:

> Stalin...practiced brutal violence, not only towards everything which opposed him, but also towards that, which seemed – to his capricious and despotic charac-ter–contrary to his concepts. Stalin... instead of proving his political correctness and mobilizing the masses often

chose the path of repression and physical annihilation, not only against actual enemies, but also against individuals who had not committed any crimes against the Party and the Soviet Government.[29]

Stalin's remains were removed from the mausoleum and placed into the Kremlin wall. Over time, the Soviet state began to wither. But this was Russia, and despite a new age of perestroika and glasnost, people were confused by the emergence of crime, poverty and oligarchy that came in the wake of new freedoms. Because the Russian people had little self-esteem outside of their identification with the state, they began to long for the days of stability, even though it came at a terrible price. The yearning in the Slavic soul for a strong leader brought nostalgia for the former Soviet Union and its sense of empire.

There are distinct signs that some of the old ways are returning. Today, in the twenty-first century, the press has described Vladimir Putin's Russia as a system of "soft authoritarianism." The secret police (now called FSB) are back in control and "vertical power" has returned. Putin, a former secret policeman, cancelled gubernatorial elections and appointed regional leaders himself. Aggressive, nationalistic and revisionist, Russia under Putin is attempting to manipulate elections in adjacent countries and recently used the power of the pipeline to cut off its neighbors from supplies of oil and gas. Russia apparently intends to reclaim some former Soviet satellite nations through military force, as demonstrated by the war against Georgia of August 2008. Putin is not shy about the similarities between his ruling style and that of Stalin – he keeps Stalin's personal papers in his office and frequently enjoys reading them along with the Soviet dictator's handwritten notations in the margins. Putin has essentially selected his own successor and has extended his rule as Prime Minister with seemingly unlimited power.

According to Russia's Glasnost Defense Foundation, freedom of the press is being reduced and censorship is on the rise. NGO Freedom House downgraded Russia in their 2004 rating from "partially free" to "unfree." There are increasing reports of intimidation and even murder of reporters who have been

critical of the regime. The most prominent of these killings is
the murder of the courageous journalist, Anna Politkovskaya,
who was shot in October of 2006. This killing served notice
that the publication of truth that criticized the state will not be
tolerated. A former FSB agent, Alexander Litvinenko, living in
London, publicly accused Putin of authorizing the Politkovskaya murder. He too was killed, the victim of poisoning from
a little known radioactive element, polonium 210. His killing
had all the earmarks of a secret police assassination, demonstrating a similar global reach to Stalin's, who in 1940 successfully ordered the murder of his enemy, Leon Trotsky in Mexico.

Perhaps most ominous of all, is the fate that awaits those
who are perceived as a political threat to the power of the
Kremlin. Political dissenters now face long sentences in prison,
for even minor infractions. The former head of Yukos Oil
Company has been sent to a forbidding prison camp 6,000
kilometers from Moscow in Russia's frozen Far East, near the
Chinese border. Mikhail Khodorkovsky's crimes had nothing
to do with taxes or anti-trust – they were simply crimes of political dissent from the current regime. Khodorkovsky's mother
believes that she may never see her son alive again.[30]

With a menacing tone from the leadership, increasing
political persecution, and rampant corruption centered upon
newly acquired oil wealth, Russia is retreating from the hope-
ful promise of an open society into a state that is reminiscent
of its dark and repressive past. Languishing in frozen camps
are a growing number of dissidents and each day, more join the
ranks of those behind the barbed wire of the new Gulag. They
are no longer citizens with the right of free expression. They
have been silenced. The luminous image of greater Russian
freedom and human rights is fading into mere shadows in the
snow. Stalin has been dead for more than a half century, but in
Russia today, a modern form of Stalinism is alive and growing.

CHAPTER 2
Raphael Trujillo: Sexualized Tyranny

"He who does not know how to deceive does not know how to rule."
Raphael Trujillo

In the autumn of 1492, a Genoese merchant captain and about ninety men crossed the Atlantic Ocean and changed the world. Sailing under the flag of Spain, they had expected to find the orient, but instead they discovered the Caribbean archipelago between North and South America. The men who accompanied Columbus and those who followed were adventurers with a thirst for gold and a religious intolerance bred by the Spanish Inquisition, which "came to border on paranoia." [1]

Columbus did not establish a colony until he reached a place he called "La Isla Espanola." Today the island of Hispaniola or "Little Spain" is shared by the Dominican Republic and Haiti. When Columbus arrived, a large population of friendly and attractive Taino Indians inhabited the island. Columbus' intentions towards these people were revealed when he wrote, "They…brought us parrots and balls of cotton and spears and many other fine things…They would make fine servants… With fifty men we could subjugate them all and make them do whatever we want." [2] Columbus established the first colony in the new world, on the island's northern coast. He named the colony Navidad.

Leaving 39 men at the newly established colony, Columbus sailed for Spain on January 16, 1493. When he returned he found that every Spaniard had been killed by the Tainos in retribution for stealing native women. The second voyage of Columbus was not a journey of discovery, but a full-scale invasion with 17 ships, and 1,300 men and 20 mounted cavalry to subdue the natives. During this excursion, the sexual subjugation of Indian women became commonplace. Cuneo (probably a close friend of Columbus) received a "gift" of a captured native woman from his captain. His journal entry tells of this conquest:

> *While I was in the boat I captured a very beautiful Carib woman the Lord Admiral gave to me, and with whom, having taken her into my cabin, she being naked according to their custom, I conceived desire to take pleasure. I wanted to put my desire into execution but she did not want it and treated me with her fingernails in such a manner that I wished I had never begun. But seeing that (to tell you the end of it all), I took a rope and thrashed her well, for which she raised such unheard of screams that you would not have believed your ears. Finally we came to an agreement in such manner that I can tell you that she seemed to have been brought up in a school of harlots. [3]*

The Spanish conquistadors exploited the new land using military force, followed by seizure of the native's women and gold. Indians who resisted were cut down by swords, muskets and ravenous dogs that were frequently set upon the Indians for entertainment by the conquering Spaniards. A system known as the encomienda was established that granted concessions to Spaniards, who utilized Indian slave labor for mining and agricultural production. The indigenous population was decimated at the hands of the conquistadors through murder, a cruel system of slavery and deadly diseases introduced by the Europeans, for which the Indians had no immunity. By about 1512, only 15,000 natives survived on the island of Hispaniola, out of a population of more than 2 million in 1492. A similar pattern followed in South America and in Mexico. [4]

The island of Hispaniola and its capital, Santo Domingo, became the seat of government for the Spanish Indies. In 1664, the French West India Company began to colonize western Hispaniola. The French developed a highly profitable slave-based economy in what became the colony of Saint Dominique (See chapter six). Following a slave rebellion, the French colony became the independent nation of Haiti, in January 1804. The following year Haiti invaded the Dominican Republic, bringing about a 22-year occupation that would forever poison the relationship between Dominicans and Haitians. The Haitian occupiers immediately abolished slavery in the Dominican Republic. [5]

The Dominican Nation

The history of the Dominican Republic is inexorably linked with Haiti since both nations share the island of Hispaniola. Like two cocks that fight in a single arena, they have suffered and struggled repeatedly for more than five centuries. They are divided by culture and race – Haiti is African, influenced by French culture and language, while the Dominican Republic reflects its early role as the center of the Spanish Indies. Dominicans are a mixture of Spanish and Indian blood with only a smattering of African heritage.

Dominican rebels won a great victory over the Haitian occupation on February 27, 1844. The initial joy of liberation gave way to an extended period of turmoil and political chaos. After three decades of disorder, the Dominican Republic was ripe for someone to reclaim the powers of the conquistadors, who despite their brutality had provided the only orderly governance the country had ever known.[6]

Ulises Heureaux, a black man and an unlikely leader of the Dominicans, became interior minister and then commanding general of the national army. Heureaux was elected President in 1886. His real power base remained the army and an extensive secret police network. He ruled as a caudillo or strong man and assumed dictatorial control of the nation. During subsequent elections, soldiers and police terrorized his detractors and drove opponents into exile. Dissent was met with repression, as he filled the prisons. In 1891, the Dominican government signed a controversial trade treaty with the United States prompting nationalistic Dominicans to wage protests throughout the country. The protests spawned extreme violence, which resulted in Heureaux's assassination in 1899.

Convulsive political turmoil followed the death of the dictator and disagreements with the United States led to U. S. intervention in Dominican affairs. The assassination of another president, Ramon Caceres, brought direct intervention by the United States. A proclamation was issued on November 29, 1916, which began an eight-year occupation of the Dominican Republic by U. S. Marines.[7]

The Dominican culture's Iberian roots shaped the temperament of its people, which emphasized family and spiritual values. Even today, paternalism dominates the culture. A sense of personal honor is a strong characteristic of the Dominican temperament. Another pervasive characteristic throughout Hispanic America is machismo. This refers to manly courage and forceful action, but it also embodies the Latin male's skill in the conquest of women. Machismo is an expression of the early conquistador's personal traits of valor and sexual masculinity.

As family life has evolved in Hispanic America, there has been a tendency towards a formal family unit that is often supplemented by the head of household taking a mistress or engaging in multiple extramarital relationships. In the formal family, the mother is generally motivated by honor and reputation, but she is usually subservient to her husband. The Latin father figure is frequently aloof and is generally authoritarian. In Hispanic America, the patriarch has become legendary.

The Roots of Tyranny

José Trujillo Monagas was a Cuban police captain in the seething Cuatro Caminos section of Havana. He was known as a "tough hombre," who took advantage of opportunities for graft that were available. As a result of corruption, in 1862 he was forced to flee his homeland for Santo Domingo. Later he moved to the small village of San Cristobal, on the west bank of the Haina River, some eighteen miles inland from the capital. There, he took a room in a boarding house owned by a mulatto woman, Silveria Valdéz. An intimate relationship developed that lasted for less than a year. José Trujillo Monagas returned to Cuba, but he left Silveria pregnant and in 1864 she gave birth to José Trujillo Valdéz, known as Pepito.[8]

Silveria was a strong woman with a renegade streak. She was intensely political and she lent her "considerable and unscrupulous talents to intrigues and violence," as the local organizer for the dictator Ulises Heureaux. She lived to be 105 years old. When Pepito was in his early twenties, he married Altagracia Julia Molina, the illegitimate daughter of a Haitian army officer. The couple was married in San Cristobal on September 29, 1887.

Pepito was amiable and modestly successful, dealing in lumber tobacco, coffee and cattle. As he traveled the countryside on horseback, he was described as "licentious to an extreme degree," but he was well liked and was a solid supporter and friend of the dictator, Ulises Heureaux, as his mother had been. His wife Altagracia, considered a saint by her neighbors, was described as "generous and kindhearted, a simple and honorable woman." Together they raised nine children. Theirs was a traditional Dominican family with a Haitian influence from the mother and a youngest son, born so black he was nicknamed "Negro." Their third child, Rafael Leonidas Trujillo Molina, was born on October 24, 1891. He grew up in San Cristobal.

While Rafael was still in school he stood out from other children in only one way – he was extraordinarily neat, clean and obsessed with personal grooming. Considered the best-behaved child in his family, he was nicknamed Chapita (bottle top), for his love of wearing bottle caps on his shirts like military metals. His leisure time in San Cristobal was spent playing with toy horses and swimming in the Nigua River with his friends and siblings. As a teenager Rafael developed an "extreme interest in women." His other passions were horsemanship and dancing. He was frequently seen riding around town on his father horse, smartly dressed, and looking fastidious.

Rafael was not a model citizen. He and his brother Petán were headstrong and prone to trouble. They stole mules, horses and cattle. In 1911, Rafael was hired as a clerk in a telegraph office, but was fired when he was caught stealing three English saddles. In 1913, at the age of 22, he impregnated and then married Aminta Ledesma, a country girl with little education. They soon had two children, both of whom died as infants. Rafael developed an interest in politics and became a supporter of the National Party of Horacio Vásquez, known as Horacistas. Rafael and his street friends were involved in a political riot in 1915. After their arrest, a local minister of Justice, Jacinto Peynado, sent Trujillo home without reprisal. For this gift of mercy, nearly three decades later, the minister would reap a grand reward.

In 1916, Rafael Trujillo descended more deeply into criminality when he joined a group known as "The 44." This gang robbed bodegas (small stores serving sugar field workers), and provided muscle for hire when violence was necessary to settle scores. They also engaged in low-level graft and blackmail. Rafael worked in the sugar cane industry, at first weighing cane at a field station, and later as a guarda campestre, which has been described as a "combination of watchman, troubleshooter and private policeman." Rafael's marriage dissolved in 1925 and its only lasting product was a third daughter, who survived. Her name was Flor de Oro or Flower of Gold.[9]

The U. S. Marine occupation presented many opportunities for an enterprising young Dominican to make money. Rafael proved eager for his share. His uncle Teódulo introduced him to a hard-drinking Marine Major named McLean, who enjoyed the company of Dominican whores and the powerful island rum. Teódulo suggested that his nephew, "the pimp, Chapita" could be valuable to the Marine intelligence service. The Major immediately saw the advantages of Chapita's contacts. Rafael knew the local women and he knew the bandits who were considered rebels by the Marines. The Marines introduced him to one of his future favorite tortures, which was a rope twisted ever tighter around the head until the victim goes mad. It was especially appealing because it is bloodless. John Gunther wrote in *Inside Latin America*, "The Untied States Marines liked Trujillo...They said, 'He thinks just like a Marine!'"[10]

Rafael Trujillo joined the National Guard on January 11, 1919 and he was granted a commission as Second Lieutenant. He now had a career that perfectly suited him. Lt. Trujillo could wear the medals that little Chapita had coveted as a child and he could also flaunt his machismo with glamorous women and men of power and importance. To the meticulously groomed Trujillo, the "splendid uniforms, the parades, the music, the martial pomp all nourished his feeling for drama and display." Although he was only 5 foot 7 inches tall and weighed 126 pounds, he was always crisp in his uniforms and he achieved increasingly high military ratings. Marine Major Thomas E. Watson wrote, "I consider this Officer one of the best in the service." But Trujillo's military exploits did not add to his social status and he suffered snubs that left deep scars in his psyche. He romanced the daughter of a powerful landowner and applied for membership in a social club in Seibo, but was spurned in both endeavors. Trujillo never recovered from these rejections. He began to wear makeup and powder to hide the "blackness," which might reveal his Haitian blood.

Trujillo was promoted directly to Captain, skipping the rank of First Lieutenant – the only officer given such an honor. The National Guard became the Dominican National Police and Captain Trujillo was assigned to Santiago, a town in the north. In 1924, Trujillo was promoted to Major and given the post of Commandant of the Northern Department. Trujillo enhanced his prospects for promotion when the officer he replaced died under unusual circumstances. The former Commandant, Major J. César Lora, had seduced a married woman, whom he met regularly for romantic trysts under a bridge. It is reported that Trujillo informed the cuckolded husband regarding the lovers' next rendezvous. The husband "took the ancient form of vengeance," when he caught them in flagrente delicto. They were gunned down together, opening the path for Trujillo's promotion.

In December of 1924, President Horacio Vásquez appointed him to the position of Chief of Staff and Trujillo was again promoted, this time to the rank of Lieutenant Colonel. Trujillo's rise fortuitously coincided with the end of the U. S. occupation. Vásquez was reelected in March, 1924 and in June 1925 Trujillo was named Colonel Commandant of the National Police. He reached this high rank only six years after receiving his commission as a Second Lieutenant.

Another officer had originally been selected as Commandant, but in a premature drunken celebration he had boasted of his pending promotion. When the Minister of Interior learned of this indiscretion, Trujillo was given the position instead. It was later learned that an informant had been sent to the Minister's office by Trujillo. His climb through the ranks had been nothing short of meteoric and, to be sure, much of this achievement was due to his aptitude for military life, his tireless energy and his gift for administration. But as the informant matter and the previous Lora affair suggest, he was not averse to advancing his career through treachery.

Trujillo married Bienvenida Ricart, a young Dominican woman from an excellent family in Monti Cristi. The wedding was held in the hometown of the bride shortly after Trujillo's promotion to Brigadier General, in August of 1927. Bienvenida soon discovered the General's affairs with many women. Even worse, Trujillo had become the regular lover of a "high-spirited young woman" who was openly his paramour. On June 5, 1929, the mistress, Maria Martínez gave birth to Trujillo's first son. Rafael Leonidas Trujillo Martínez, who would be known as Ramfis, nicknamed for the High Priest of Egypt in the Giuseppe Verdi opera, *Aïda.*

The Quest for Power

Trujillo seethed with a barely suppressed ambition for power and social position. He had secured the complete loyalty of the National Police, but elite Dominicans still considered him uncultured and socially unacceptable. When rumors swept the capital that Trujillo was in league with anti-government conspirators most advisors to President Vásquez urged him to fire Trujillo. General Trujillo denied any political ambitions and professed complete loyalty to President Vásquez.

As evening fell in the northern city of Santiago on February 23, 1930, a long line of trucks assembled at a local garage. The armed men in the vehicles proceeded towards the nearby Fortress San Luis. They carried old weapons, some rusted so badly that they were inoperable. Others carried only machetes. Rafael Estrella Ureña, who had designs on the presidency and the implied assurance from the armed forces that he would be allowed to prevail, led this "popular revolt." When they reached the Fort a few shots were fired and the army capitulated. Now numbering about 1,500 men, the convoy turned south towards Santo Domingo in the early hours of February 24.

Learning that the column was approaching the capital, President Vásquez began to panic and he went to Ozama Fortress to confront General Trujillo personally. Only the president and two military aides were admitted inside, but when the General appeared, he saluted President Vásquez, and requested presidential commands. The president ordered Trujillo to send an armed detachment to intercept the conspirators while they were still outside the city. Trujillo appeared to comply. But an interception did not occur and by February 26, when the convoy entered the capital, it became clear that Trujillo was enabling the revolution. A settlement brokered by the American Embassy called for President Vásquez to resign and Estrella was established as the Acting President. American diplomats were pleased that they had arranged a bloodless, constitutional succession and had blocked the path of the ambitious Trujillo.

But the final act of this little pageant had not yet occurred. Estrella Ureña was merely a pawn in a web of intrigue that Trujillo had been weaving for more than a year. Acting in his position as commander of the armed forces, Trujillo seized all weapons in the possession of the rebels and made a nationwide collection of arms, to "preserve order." Slowly, the new president began to realize the precarious nature of his position. He had the presidential title but no guns, while Trujillo lacked the title, but possessed all of the guns.

The spring political season began with the slogan, "No puede ser" ("It cannot be"), referring to the ascension of General Trujillo to the presidency. But the Dominican Republic soon was subjected to a campaign of terrorism. Opposition rallies were raked with gunfire and dozens were killed. Thugs, who appeared brandishing weapons, disbursed political meetings. Those planning to speak against Trujillo lost their audience, as terrified voters hurriedly fled public campaign appearances. There were literally hundreds of episodes of violence throughout the Dominican Republic during the election of 1930. Trujillo's brothers were recognized among the gunmen on several occasions.

On May 16, an election was held, but only a few citizens were brave enough to go to the polls. Just 25% of those eligible actually voted and a fraudulent tally elected Trujillo. His opponents appealed to the Appellate Court in Santo Domingo to declare the election invalid. At the hour the Court's decision was to be read, a group of men with machine guns entered the building and stood facing the clerk of the court. The clerk was struck dumb with fear and the decision was never rendered. On May 30, a completely intimidated Congress certified the election and Trujillo's inauguration was scheduled for August 16.[11]

During the interim, Trujillo worked skillfully to secure U. S. support. Meanwhile, the terror continued as a gang of gunmen ran wild throughout the country cutting down Trujillo's enemies in fusillades of automatic weapons fire. A leading poet and an outspoken opponent of Trujillo's, Virgilio Martinez Reyna, was gunned down at his mountain home on June 1. The victim's pregnant wife rushed into the room and was also shot dead. The next day Moncito Matos, the leader of the opposition to Trujillo in Barahona province, was murdered. The opposition leader in Moca, Elisio Esteves, was similarly dispatched, as was Juan Paredes, the most prominent political opponent of Trujillo in San Francisco de Macoris province.

Other members of the opposition did not wait for their turn under the gun. Several opposition leaders fled to Puerto Rico.

A three-day inauguration began on August 16, 1930, with parades, fireworks and great ceremony. Trujillo wore a newly designed uniform for the festivities, which included the plumed hat of former President Heureaux that had been preserved as a national treasure. The symbolism was not lost on the public. Pledging stability, the General warned that he would, "punish with all the severity provided by the law, those who disturb public order." He had succeeded in gaining the presidency through intimidation and violence and now he made it clear that "public order" would be defined by Trujillo alone, as the nation's caudillo.

The new dictator of the Dominican Republic was 39 years old. He was a short but powerfully built mulatto, with bronze skin and black hair. An American female journalist had written that he had "bedroom eyes," and there is no question that he strongly appealed to women. He also had a magnetic presence in the company of men, who were drawn to his imperial bearing and his obvious abilities in the use of power. He was a man of great energy, rising at 4 a.m. each day for exercise, breakfast and morning newspapers. He was always in his office by 9 a. m., where he worked until noon. He then took one hour for lunch, usually with government officials. After lunch he took a long walk, followed by office work until 7 p.m. Usually, he would visit his mother after dinner and take an evening walk with assistants, discussing affairs of state. He ate modestly and partook of only one kind of alcohol, Carlos Primero cognac. He could be a good listener and was frequently gracious to visitors. But Trujillo trusted no one and had no personal friendships outside of the political sphere.

The Hurricane

On September 3, the eastern sky darkened and a storm broke over Santo Domingo that was more terrifying than anything ever seen before. A powerful hurricane, with pounding rain and shrieking wind speeds up to 180 miles per hour, struck the island. Trees were ripped from the earth and blown great distances. Roofs were torn away and structural walls crumbled under the force of the wind. In poor neighborhoods, many homes disappeared entirely. The largest bridge in the country fell into the surging Ozama River. Flying glass and deadly shards of metal roofing slashed like giant spinning razors, killing many residents in the capital. Some were found decapitated; others were literally cut to pieces.

Flooding and fallen trees isolated the city, leaving it without power or water. It was estimated that in Santo Domingo 2,000 people died and 6,000 were injured. More than 9,000 structures were destroyed in the capital and no one knew the extent of the damage or loss of life in the countryside. The Dominican Congress quickly gave full emergency power to Trujillo and a massive airlift of supplies from other Caribbean nations and the United States poured into the country. Trujillo's administrative talent and prodigious energy became a national asset as he worked effectively to get the nation back on its feet. Eventually the nation's governmental structure became so centralized under Trujillo that only three Special Commissioners ruled all localities, and they were under the personal direction of General Trujillo. Once Trujillo had seized absolute power he would never relinquish it as long as he was alive.

Trujillo's prisons were filled with political detainees, many of whom were sick with malarial fever. Some had become insane due to the miserable conditions of their imprisonment or by virtue of rope torture to the head. Still others had been tortured on an ancient rack that Trujillo had pressed into service. Many of these prisoners were shot to death in remote places but official records listed them as victims of the hurricane.

Trujillo's subordinates deeply feared their leader and were never able to feel secure in their ministerial positions. He shifted his position frequently, causing great uncertainty among governmental leaders. Occasionally, a siren sounded in the capital – a signal that Trujillo had changed ministers. All of official Santo Domingo would quake with fear when the siren wailed, until the identity of the disgraced official was revealed.

Trujillo was Napoleonic in his ambitions, fueled by deep feelings of inferiority, perhaps due to his Haitian bloodline and his limited physical stature. It may have also been partly due to his roots in a criminal culture. At the core of his being was a voracious, almost primitive need for total domination, in politics, in business and in the bedroom – where "his sensuality and his sexual drive were extraordinary." His nation was destined to become an estancia, operated for the benefit of one man that would eventually make him one of the ten richest men in the world.[12]

Despite his masculine characteristics, Trujillo had an almost feminine love of finery. He was obsessed with neckties and he owned more than ten thousand of them. More than two thousand suits and uniforms were in the closets of his many homes along with 500 pairs of shoes. Trujillo had a high-pitched voice that became nearly falsetto in tone when he became agitated. He enjoyed gossip and innuendo.

According to a biographer, "He delighted in the company and the bodies of women, although he was indifferent to their minds. His taste was Caribbean in these matters. He preferred mulatto females and he preferred them plump." To maintain a continuing supply of women for his "conquests," he used the casual services of associates, but later the role was formalized. He did not use physical force on his victims but his methods of coercion were not subtle. Some terrible fate might befall a member of the woman's family if she did not enthusiastically submit to his lust.

As soon as he took power, his libido was unleashed upon the young women of the nation. As he got older, the ages of his sexual victims became younger, eventually reaching the age of puberty. His preference was for virgins, because he enjoyed the power to dominate and to deflower young and helpless girls. He believed himself to be a Dominican Don Juan, but his subjects came to call him "The Goat" behind his back. They did not view the conquests of the dictator as seduction, but as sexual violence. The selection process was ritualized into a bizarre festival, acted out regularly at the National Palace:

*In his office in the Palace, perhaps twice a week, there
was assembled a group of eligible's, perhaps thirty on
each occasion. From these, Trujillo indicated his choice
or choices for the week. Those who had been selected were
given appropriate instructions as to time and place. Trujillo generally went to bed with each woman once or twice.
A few favorites were kept on a more consistent basis.[13]*

Trujillo provided financially for any children he fathered. His
affection, however, was reserved for children from his wives and
those legitimized by his acknowledgement of paternity. No one
knows how many children he left to the Dominican people in
this national ritual of "Eros de la Patria." He penetrated the soul
of the nation when he penetrated the bodies of its young women
as a demonstration of his personal and political machismo.

In 1932, the Dominican Party was established and the nation became essentially a one-party state. The Party became the
implementing agency for welfare payments, medical assistance
to the poor, financial aid for church construction and highway
programs. It also became the dictator's instrument of benevo-
lence to his subjects, essentially binding the nation to his political machine. Unexplained violence and killings continued.
Some of Trujillo's former gang members provided the gunmen
who operated on his behalf. Sometimes elements of the Army
would be used, but the gangsters were used for the dirtiest jobs.

During 1933 large meetings were held to demand that
General Trujillo continue to serve, despite his stated intention
to withdraw to private life. It was all a theatre, scripted by the
General himself. The fawning acclaim grew to grotesque proportions when the nation's largest paper declared, "May God
preserve our Emperor." The political ticket of General Trujillo
and his old protector, Jacinto Peynado won an overwhelming
victory in 1934. In recognition of the victory and of the fifth
birthday of the General's illegitimate son, his sycophants sent
the following telegram:

*One hundred friends and fellow partisans of yours are
at this moment raising their glasses in your honor and*

*we ask you to place upon the pure forehead of the little
eagle, who is proud of your name, your blood, and your
race, the beloved Ramfis, the kiss of love, of our loyalty
and our adherence to you, which have no limit except
death. God and Trujillo!* [14]

The Triumph of Gangsterism

Political repression in the land of Trujillo was ramped up
during the second administration. Mail was not safe from
inspection, telephones were frequently bugged and Trujillo's
spies were everywhere. In upper class homes, many domestic servants became informers. While there were a few plots
against the regime, there was not much difference between a
seditious plot and a minor slight to Trujillo in the eyes of the
government – all were deemed to be violations of state security.

Political terror had a strong impact on the people. They
were terrified to speak ill of Trujillo and felt compelled to
engage in the sycophantic hyperbole that he demanded. Anything less was considered a crime. Evidence of such involuntary
adulation is the act of Congress that renamed Santo Domingo
as Ciudad Trujillo in 1936.

Those who were unfortunate enough to be arrested faced
absolute horror in Trujillo's prisons. A glimmer of the truth
reached the outside world after Oscar Michelena was arrested
in 1935. Because he was both a Dominican and American citizen, U. S. Embassy officials were allowed to interview him at the
Ozama prison. He had been held incommunicado for seventy-
two days and no charges had been filed. He was confined in
a cell that was 15 feet square, and home to 20 prisoners. Michelena was repeatedly beaten with an iron whip, known as the
cantaclar, until his flesh was torn and bloody. One of his arms
became paralyzed from the beatings. For several days, he was
too weak to eat and he was not allowed to bathe for the entire
time of his incarceration. He contracted grippe and malaria.
His family business and property were attached and he was denied legal counsel. Michelena was released from prison thanks

to his American citizenship and the efforts of the U. S. Ambassador. He became an exile in his birthplace, Puerto Rico.

Rafael Trujillo and his siblings were a family of gangsters. Virgilio, the oldest, was untrustworthy and disagreeable, but he expected to be treated with great deference as the eldest in the Trujillo clan. The dictator gave him government positions, but eventually had to remove him because of his embarrassing criminal behavior. Anibal was reckless and essentially immoral, spending his life engaged in a good deal of whoring and low level criminal activity. Pedro was on the family dole, rising to the position of Major in the army through sheer nepotism. He was enterprising enough, however, to run a substantial prostitution business in Santo Domingo. Pipi was a prostitution kingpin and dealt in human trafficking throughout the Caribbean. He referred to the girls and women in his business as "skins." Hector, known as "Negro" due to his dark complexion, was not bright and his criminality was limited by his lack of imagination. The sisters of the family were less ruthless but no less addicted to wealth and excess. Marina and Japonesa were housewives but both were married to men in high positions with the Trujillo government. Julieta was married to a man who ran the government lottery that produced a small fortune. Nieves Luisa operated a thriving prostitution ring in Cuba, in which she acted as both a whore and the madam.

Trujillo had no ideological philosophy other than his lust for power and domination. He was devoted to money for the opulence and luxury it provided. Bribery and intimidation advanced his business and political schemes. Trujillo acquired a huge amount of land for his herds of cattle and had a near-monopoly on the meat and dairy business. He used his political muscle to order the health ministry to close twenty-nine outlets that did not carry milk products from Trujillo properties. They soon fell into line. He gradually gained control of the rice business, a staple in the Dominican diet and he dominated rice exports through the Trujillo-owned Exportadora Dominicana.

Trujillo expanded his holdings of staple food products through a wildly profitable salt production company, Salinera Nacional, and he muscled his way into a commanding position in the highly respected Dominican tobacco business. By 1937, he had a monopoly in edible peanut oils and army boots, as well as control of the lumber industry. He received a percentage on all sugar exported from the Dominican Republic and a huge share of the national lottery. By 1938, the Trujillo family controlled more than 40% of all economic activity in the Dominican Republic. A special organization known as "The Personal Office of the Generalissimo" was developed to administer Trujillo's growing economic empire.[15]

Trujillo had a number of strange health practices and beliefs. He dabbled in African superstitions, believed that heart disease was related to mental illness and had a great fear of cancer and tuberculosis. As a result, he was serious about fitness, although he suffered from recurring bouts of malaria. Tortoise eggs, eaten to promote sexual virility, were part of his regular diet.

Trujillo adored his illegitimate son. As a child, Ramfis had been declared a Colonel in the Dominican Army, with full military honors and privileges, including a tiny uniform. Trujillo tired of his wife Bienvenida, who was unable to bear children. In December of 1934, at Trujillo's suggestion, Bienvenida sought medical treatment abroad to deal with her propensity toward miscarriage. Two months after her departure, a new law was enacted by Congress that made five years of childless marriage grounds for divorce. A divorce decree was issued on April 30, 1935 and Trujillo married Maria, the mother of Ramfis, on September 28, at the home of his former protector and now Vice President, Jacinto Peynado, in a small, intimate ceremony. When Bienvenida returned to the Dominican Republic, the dictator established a residence for her in the city of Santiago and in early 1936 he began seeing her again. He could not completely renounce anything he once possessed and so there was a strange reversal –"just as the former mistress had become the wife, so the former wife now became the mistress." Bienvenida, became pregnant, and gave birth to a daughter, Odette, who was granted recognition as Trujillo's child.

In the late summer of 1935, Trujillo had surgery for urethritis, usually a sexually transmitted condition. The surgery

was a success, but Trujillo's health was compromised. Those
expecting his demise included his brother, Petán, who lusted
for power and conspired to replace the dictator. He already
ruled like a feudal despot in the small town of Bonao. Petán
operated a crooked construction business and numerous illegal activities. He gave full license to his raging sexual appetites
and revived the practice of droit du seigneur, sexually initiating
young women prior to their wedding nights, as the price of his
permission for them to marry.

Petán's political treachery was discovered by the dictator's
secret police and he was ordered arrested and brought to the
National palace "dead or alive." But the arresting officer knew
that if he killed the dictator's brother, he would probably face
his own death sentence. So he sought the counsel of their
mother, Julia Molina, who persuaded Petán to surrender voluntarily. Petán was temporarily banished to Puerto Rico, while all
who had conspired with him were killed.[16]

The Carnival of Death

Carnival in Santo Domingo, as in other Hispanic settings,
has traditionally been a celebration of life and culture. At
night, the festival's many colored lights are outlined against the
darkened tropical sky and music blends with shrieks of revelry.
The combination of sights and sounds overpower the senses.
The enticing smell of food from the vendor carts suggests the
influences of many regional flavors. The soft, humid darkness
enhances the pulsating meringue rhythm that conveys a strong
erotic energy. This spectacle of "incoherence and delirium,"
is an apt metaphor for the time of Trujillo in the Dominican
Republic. The events of the 1937 Carnival define the Trujillo
era, which has been vividly described in the novel, *The Feast of
the Goat.*

During one of his daily strolls in 1937, Trujillo spotted a
woman who took his breath away. She was tall, lithe and beautiful. Lina Lovatón was the only daughter of Ramon Lovatón, a
prominent attorney from a prestigious Dominican family. She

was also a debutante and a contestant for the title of Carnival Queen. In addition to being from the old aristocracy, and of privileged social position, she was described as "young, beautiful, cultivated, virtuous, distinguished, aristocratic, while being simple and generous." The dictator desired her as the "ultimate accoutrement and sign of Trujillo's unfulfilled bourgeois ambitions." But his erotic dream became complicated when Trujillo fell passionately and hopelessly in love with Lina. With Trujillo as her benefactor, of course, she became Carnival Queen.

The Carnival that year was unlike any other. It has been described as "a two-month-long feudal masquerade ball." The government sent representatives to the court of Queen Lina and she presided over ceremonies with great pomp. She even received the dictator himself as if he was a visiting dignitary and she was given a twenty-one-gun salute. The culmination of the celebrations came on February 23, to commemorate Trujillo's assumption of power, with the unveiling of a massive 40-meter obelisk, a "phallic token of Trujillo's fecund and promiscuous dominion."[17]

Following Carnival, Trujillo pursued Queen Lina with fierce determination. At first she resisted his seduction, but ultimately she succumbed to his advances, as had so many Dominican women before. Later that year, enraptured by his sexual liaison with the beautiful Carnival Queen, the benefactor wrote and had published these words in her honor:

> *She was born a queen, not by dynastic right but by the right of beauty, and so when the chords that filled the air during her splendid reign—laughter, music, fantasy – fell silent, she still reigned with the power of that right— her beauty.*

> *There is nothing under the sun comparable to the bewitchment of her eyes—stars for the sky where the nightingale wanders giving voice to the mystery of the night. Her hands—silk, amber, perfume—have been made for the ermine of the glove and for the passion of the kiss.*

On her lips, whose fire evokes the pomegranate flower,
lingers always her smile—irresistible seal of charm and
conquest! — that is as sweet and soft as those pink and
blue tints announcing the aurora.

The seductive power of Anacaona, the poetess Queen of
Jaragua, abides in her eyes as an immortal bewitchment,
as a remote enchantment.

Such is Lina: one of those beautiful women whom di-
vinity sends to the world only rarely, so heaven's voice
may come to earth and poetry sings its glory with silver
trumpets.[18]

Trujillo sent Lina to live in Miami and he provided her with
a magnificent mansion once owned by former General Mo-
tors chairman, Alfred P. Sloan. Trujillo visited her secretly and
often. On occasion, she was flown into the Dominican Republic by private seaplane. The Generalissimo acknowledged the
children she bore by him, named Yolanda and Rafael Jr.

Life for Trujillo during 1937 was not solely consumed
by sexual conquest or love poetry. During that year, long-
simmering difficulties with Haiti evolved into one of the darkest chapters in the Trujillo legacy. Border disputes with Haiti
had occurred with some regularity for 150 years. Early in his
regime hundreds of Dominicans fled the Trujillo dictatorship
by slipping across the border. Haiti gave them sanctuary and
resisted the dictator's demands for extradition. There was a
steady encroachment into the border regions of the Dominican
Republic by Haitians, a problem that was exacerbated by the
continuing conflict over the precise border between the two
countries. Trujillo regularly issued bellicose statements about
Haitian breaches of the border.

Trujillo commanded a brutal sweep of nearly the entire
Dominican Republic to end the "Haitian problem" for good.
During thirty-six hours beginning on the night of October 2,
1937, the massive slaughter of Haitians was swift and skillful,
made possible by considerable advance planning.

The Dominican army rounded up Haitians, mostly in border areas, but as far away as Santiago and usually decapitated them by machete. The border offered no sanctuary from Trujillo's killers. In an area near the border, aptly named the Massacre River, many Haitians tried to gain safety on the Haitian side, only to be chased down and cut to pieces under the blade. Sometimes the only way to determine who was Haitian was by accent. All who spoke in French patois were killed. The night was filled with the screams of the dying and trucks soaked in blood transported the mutilated bodies of the victims to secret dumping grounds. In some border villages the Haitians did not resist or cry out, but lined up like cattle, with grim but patient resignation, awaiting their own slaughter. In a few Dominican homes, even devoted family servants were sacrificed to the will of the dictator.[19]

In only a few cases the Dominican army resorted to the use of rifle fire to dispatch their victims, for Trujillo had specifically ordered the use of the one weapon that was in the hands of peasants. In this way, he planned to dismiss the slaughter as the spontaneous outrage by Dominicans, who had grown tired of the crimes of their Haitian neighbors. One account tells us about the Dominicans use of the machete during the slaughter:

> In every town and every village in the provinces of Monte Cristi and Santiago, Negroes were dragged from their homes, lined up in streets and hacked at with machetes. Seldom were guns used. The machete looks like a butcher's instrument. Its blade is two to three feet long. Used primarily to fell brush and cut the sugar cane, it is rarely finely sharpened. It tears rather than cuts. [20]

Trujillo revealed his own chilling inhumanity regarding the massacre when he described what had taken place. "He smiled and said, 'While I was negotiating, out there they were going sha-sha-sha.'" The Generalissimo simulated the sound of a machete severing the neck as he made a cutting gesture with his manicured hand. Estimates of the number of Haitians murdered range from 15,000 to 25,000. In 1937 Haiti was a small, impoverished nation of about 3 million people. The murder of 15,000 of its citizens is a death rate that can be compared proportionately to killing more than 1.5 million persons in a country the size of the U. S. today.

The Dominican media buried all reports of these events and the Haitian government was complicit in the cover-up. The Haitian President even visited with Trujillo at Estancia Fundacion, one of the Generalissimo's homes, and participated in a joint communiqué that whitewashed the entire affair. An indemnity of $275,000 in cash was paid by Trujillo to the Haitian government as a result of U. S. pressure. The money was eagerly divvied up between greedy Haitian politicians. Following the final settlement, Trujillo and Haitian President Vincent were photographed at the border together smiling and embracing in mutual affection.

God and Trujillo

An adverse international reaction to the Haitian massacre caused Trujillo to withdraw from public life, surprising the citizens of the Dominican Republic. In a radio address on January 8, 1938, he announced that he would support the campaign for the Presidency of his Vice President and longtime friend, Jacinto Peynado and for the Vice Presidency, he endorsed Manuel de Jesus Troncoso de la Concha. He added in his speech, "Until my heart shall have lost its final beat, the Dominican fatherland shall never lack either my vigilance or my services. I can withdraw from public life only conditionally."

Trujillo's withdrawal from political office was not the act of a man who was giving up the exercise of power. Quite the opposite, his statement was the pronouncement of a leader who enjoyed total power and commanded complete subservience, regardless of his position or title. When he invited the new U. S. representative, R. Henry Norweb, to meet the next President, Norweb noted that Trujillo called Peynado into the room "with the air of whistling for a well trained dog." Peynado was indeed dog-like in his devotion to Trujillo. It was Peynado who had popularized the saying "God and Trujillo," and he and his wife had placed a huge neon sign on the roof of their home with that message for all to see how subservient the ministers of state had become to the tyrant.

The Inauguration invitation did not even include Peynado's name. Trujillo spoke at the event and then allowed the new President a final word. Peynado gave a groveling salutation to the benefactor, calling him "a Knight of the Divine Order of Genius." But Trujillo may not even have heard this adulation, because as he left he motioned to the band to begin playing, effectively drowning out the new puppet President as he fumbled with his speech.

When President Peynado's diabetic condition caused his death, he was succeeded by Vice President Troncoso, who became Trujillo's second puppet President. Shortly after this succession, Trujillo suffered a serious case of anthrax and surgery was performed quietly at Estancia Ramfis to prevent speculation about the dictator's health. Upon his recovery he took a leisurely cruise to Europe aboard his private yacht. His daughter Angelina was born in Paris during that trip. Trujillo also visited the United States, demonstrating full confidence in his grip on power. In Washington, on September 24, 1940, he and Secretary of State Hull signed a treaty that returned all of its own financial controls to the Dominican Republic. In Ciudad Trujillo a bronze tablet bears the inscription, "Eternal glory to Trujillo, Benefactor of the Fatherland, to whose effort and sacrifice the Dominican people owe the recovery of their financial sovereignty." A more colorful tribute was given by Secretary of State Cordell Hull, who said of Trujillo, "He is a son of a bitch, but he is our son of a bitch."[21]

On November 15, 1940, a new political party was established, known as Partido Trujillista or the Trujillo Party. The new Party was, in essence, an inner circle of Trujillo political loyalists. Partido Trujillista nominated Trujillo for the Presidency in the 1942 elections. Trujillo accepted the new party nomination astride an Arabian stallion at Estancia Fundacion, where he provided his supporters a new rallying cry: "And I will go ahead on horseback." The newspapers ran photos of the leader on horseback and repeated his slogan, comparing him with the great medieval Spanish hero, El Cid. On Calle Conde in Ciudad Trujillo a poster of the leader was hung. It quoted his words: "I will go ahead on horseback." The people depicted in the poster responded "And we will follow on foot." President Troncoso resigned making Trujillo's immediate ascension to the Presidency possible.

World War II presented an incredible economic opportunity for Trujillo. Worldwide shortages of many of the Dominican Republic's leading products brought about soaring export volumes. Dominican exports were $29 billion in 1945, and by 1947 they had skyrocketed to a total of $73.7 billion. In 1943, Trujillo's wife Maria gave birth to a second son, who also was named for a character in the Verdi opera *Aïda*. The name of the second son was Rhadamés.

In 1945 Trujillo's corrupt brother, Petán, began to operate a government radio station, La Voz Dominicana, which he used it to arrange sexual liaisons with "stage struck young women." Some of these relationships involved outright coercion and brute force. He maintained residences for a flock of "adopted" girls who were twelve or under for his most prurient acts of criminal sexuality. Trujillo never intervened, perhaps because he considered it a family privilege and because he enjoyed similar pursuits.

Trujillo understood the weaknesses of his underlings, and pandered to their character flaws, to secure their loyalty. Then he would turn on them with a vicious attack creating panic. To regain the favor of their boss, whom they often called El Jefé, they were frequently willing to do almost anything. Recognizing that El Jefé increasingly found younger virgins attractive, Trujillo's morally bankrupt subordinates would give him even their most precious possessions, for his personal pleasure. Bernard Diederich in his biography of Trujillo, has described this sacrifice to the dictator:

> *And this man, who had once pimped for his Marine superior, had reached a height where he could expect from a "loyal" subject, tribute in the form of a daughter's virginity, to satisfy his extraordinary sexual appetite.* [22]

Despite his wanton rape of the bodies and minds of his subjects, Trujillo was the recipient of deification by the people as they cowered in fear of his police state. Literally every shop, business and home in the nation had a portrait of the dictator on prominent display. Cars and trucks frequently exhibited crude hand painted declarations, such as "Trujillo is my protector." Simple roadside stands often displayed signs of worship, such as "God and Trujillo are my faith." Theodore Draper, an American reporter said, "it is as if the dictator were everywhere, watching everything, knowing everyone." The professions of faith in the dictator were a plea for political protection – a verbal talisman against terror. Biographer German E. Ornes has described this relationship:

> *The Government hospitals are decorated with signs reading "Only Trujillo Cures Us." At village pumps, "Only Trujillo Gives Us to Drink." Beside each irrigation ditch the posters read: "Trujillo Is the Only One Who Gives Us Water," "Seeds Grow Because of the Water Trujillo Gives Us" or "Crops Are Plentiful Because Trujillo Has Given Us All the Water We Need." These placards are set up, of course, by the "grateful" farmers themselves. They do it, however, on their own free will – or else! Those who do not show the required enthusiasm are denied access to the irrigation facilities by the Departamento de Recursos Hidráuticos – always on account of some minor technicality; nothing to do with politics indeed!* [23]

In late 1948, Trujillo learned from his secret police that his brother Aníbal had made threats against the life of the Benefactor himself. On December 2, 1948, Aníbal was visited by a group of army officers in his home on Isabel la Católica, a picturesque and historic street in Ciudad Trujillo. There is no official record of the events of that day, but those who heard a shot in the street rushed into the house found Aníbal dead in the bathroom of a gunshot wound. They were told that he had committed suicide. The newspapers reported a "tragic accident." There was no investigation and Trujillo did not attend the funeral. After nearly two decades of repression, every detail of life in the Dominican Republic was under the control of Trujillo and even his own family members were not safe from his retribution. Biographer Germán E. Ornes suggests the psychological effect of Trujillo's use of unseen political terror:

> *A man arrested for actual or imaginary offenses may be shot or hanged (the rope is Trujillo's favorite method of execution) in a prison backyard. Kidnappings, murders and mysterious disappearances are as much part of the system of repression as they were in the early days of the regime. Cases of quiet disappearance are still common, so common in fact that people have coined a graphic phrase to apply to a man who leaves his home never to return. They simply say: "Se perdió" (he got lost), and everybody understands.*[24]

Long suffering Dominicans developed a resistance movement in exile following World War II. They assembled a force and began to call themselves The Caribbean Legion. The Legion launched an assault on the Dominican Republic from their Guatemalan sanctuary on June 18 and 19 of 1949. The ill-fated invasion was doomed to failure from the very beginning. Of the fifteen men who reached Dominican shores ten were killed and five were captured when their Catalina seaplane was attacked and sunk by Dominican coastal patrols, near Puerto Plata. While the invasion failed, the attempt awakened the Dominican people to the possibilities of revolution.

Trujillo was suspicious of nearly every regime in the Caribbean, especially Haiti. When Haitian authorities' uncovered details of a Trujillo plot to kill Haitian officials, The Organization of American States (OAS) launched an investigation. On April 8, 1950 the government of the Dominican Republic was rebuked for its efforts to subvert Caribbean neighbors. Trujillo put forward another puppet, as he had in the past, when his reputation was tarnished by his own illicit actions. This time it was his simpleton brother, Hector, known as "Negro."

By 1955, the dictator had enjoyed a quarter century of rule. He lived at the expansive Estancia Rhadames, which combined the styles of Miami, the Middle East and Spain in a confusing jumble of tasteless extravagance. No expense had been spared – the Estancia had a swimming pool, a theater, a barbershop and a skating rink. His other residences included a luxurious home in Santiago, another in Constanza, a country home in La Cumbre situated on a high ridge with a magnificent view of the Atlantic Ocean, a huge beach home at Playa de Najayo and a massive cattle ranch, Estancia Fundacion near San Cristobal. The mahogany villa known as Casa Caoba, part of Estancia Fundacion, was where Trujillo enjoyed most of his "virgin sacrifices." He also owned a summer home at San Juan de las Matas and he maintained a personal headquarters in every major Dominican city. He controlled approximately 1.5 million acres of developed land, and "vast tracts" of undeveloped property. His businesses and factories employed 60,000 people and his holdings in the Dominican Republic and abroad were estimated to be worth $500,000,000 – the equivalent of several billion in 2008 dollars, making Trujillo one of the richest men on earth.

In celebration of 25 years under Trujillo, the nation held a Free World's Fair of Peace and Confraternity. Fully one third of the national budget for 1955 was spent on this extravaganza. It lasted for a year and included trade fairs, exhibits, dances and various cultural performances that culminated in a "Floral Promenade," which featured the dictator's sixteen-year-old daughter Maria de los Angeles del Corazon de Jesus Trujillo Martinez, known as Angelita, who was crowned during the Carnival parade as Queen of the Fair. Angelita had an entourage of 150 princesses. Her regal ensemble was in stark contrast to the poverty of the campesenos in this poor little Caribbean nation:

> *Queen Angelita's white silk and satin gown was beyond fantasy proportions: it had a 75 foot train and was decorated with 150 feet of snow-white Russian ermine— the skins of 600 animals–as well as with real pearls, rubies, and diamonds. The total cost of the gown was*

> *$80,000, a significant fortune at the time. In full re-galia, her costume replicated that of Queen Elizabeth I, replete with erect collar and adorned with a brooch and scepter that cost another $75,000. For $1,000 two imperial hairdressers were flown in from New York to set the royal coiffure…Her royal entry was made on a mile of red carpet and in the company of hundreds of courtiers."* [25]

1955 was proclaimed the "Year of the Benefactor," and the dictator was lauded by a Dominican Senator as "Trujillo…our course and our helm, our star and our sail, our compass and our motive power." The dictator had seduced a nation through "a combination of wits, will, sartorial style and cojones [balls]." At the pinnacle of his power, he paraded his daughter Angelita, just as he had his mistress many years earlier, reveling in his male dominance over women, as both the sexual conquistador and the father or "Benefactor," of all Dominicans. Thousands of busts and plaques were dedicated in his honor and he held literally hundreds of titles, awards and decorations, many of which were developed in his own overheated imagination. According to biographer Robert Crassweller:

> *Vanity and the need for adulation had ascended from obsession into a monomania and now hovered on the fine edge of imbalance, an abnormality that was passing into an illness.* [26]

Perhaps no other dictatorship in history has employed the use of sexual power as a means to dominate a nation. While the adulation of Trujillo was seemingly unending, the people were repeatedly degraded through his well-known abuse of the nation's virgin daughters. He enthusiastically flaunted this degradation of women and girls. From his exploitation of the womanhood of the nation to the torture chambers and dungeons of his secret police, the Dominican Republic suffered from a menacing state apparatus, designed and built by "The Benefactor." Trujillo was, however, beginning to display signs of emotional decay and paranoia that became increasingly evident even as he reached the apex of his power.

The War Against All Enemies

The Trujillo regime had long maintained a level of repression of its citizens that rivaled almost any military dictatorship in the world. Every person living in the Dominican Republic, including those who were foreign-born had a serial number and was required to carry Cedula Personal de Indentidad (personal identification card) once they reached the age of sixteen. Beyond the careful monitoring of individuals, the security services of the Dominican Armed Forces wiretapped, opened mail and broke into homes whenever they suspected subversion. Those who worked within this labyrinth of security were not exempt from suspicion by El Jefé. Even his most intimate associates and security officers were subjected to surveillance, coercion and blackmail.

By 1956, Trujillo began to consolidate his network of informers and spy's into one agency that would be in charge of all security, from surveillance and torture to espionage and assassination. He established the position of Secretary of Security and appointed Major General Arturo Espillat to the post. The new agency had more than 5,000 security officers and spies in its ranks, and included the dreaded "Spanish Police," an elite corps of about one hundred former Spanish secret service agents who had been trained by the Nazi's and Spanish dictator Franco.

In early 1956, a Spanish Basque exile named Jesus de Galíndez was completing a dissertation to earn a doctorate degree at Columbia University in New York. A Republican loyalist in the Spanish Civil War, Galíndez had fled Franco's Spain in 1939, and settled in the Dominican Republic. After a few years, Dominican authorities became suspicious of his political views, prompting him to flee to America. His strong criticism of the Trujillo regime was the subject of his dissertation – a paper that was never presented. On the night of March 12, 1956, he entered a subway station at 57th Street and Eighth Avenue in New York City and was never seen again.

The Galíndez disappearance became such a political sensation that President Eisenhower was forced to comment about the case on two occasions. Galíndez had been drugged, kidnapped and flown on a charter aircraft, piloted by an American named Gerald Murphy, to a location near Monti Cristi on the northern coast of the Dominican Republic. He was taken to the grounds of Estancia Fundación, and to Casa Caoba, the mahogany lair of Trujillo. The dictator, wearing riding clothes and holding a copy of the dissertation, confronted the glassy-eyed captive. He threw the manuscript at the drugged man, screaming "Pendejo, pendejo!" (A Hispanic pejorative that literally means pubic hair, and is widely used to indicate complete disrespect). He then struck Galíndez across the face with his riding crop, and stalked out of the room.

Although the body was never recovered, it has been reported that Galíndez was lowered into a vat of boiling water, inch by inch, to inflict extreme suffering. After death, his remains were fed to sharks, a favorite means of disposal that left no incriminating evidence. Trujillo's agents had confiscated Galíndez's dissertation, but two copies survived. One copy remained with Columbia University, and a Spanish language version was published in Santiago, Chile in June 1956 and became a best seller in Latin America. Surprisingly, while it was critical of Trujillo, it did not contain documentation of his worst abuses.

A witness to the Galíndez kidnapping, the American pilot, Gerald Murphy, was overheard indiscreetly telling a companion in a bar in Miami that he had flown a "cancer patient" to the Dominican Republic in March. During the last days of his final visit to Ciudad Trujillo, Murphy was summoned to the National Palace. He disappeared and his car was found on a coastal promontory near the area known as "the swimming pool," where the bodies of Trujillo's enemies were often fed to sharks. Gerald Murphy's death became a cause that rivaled the Galíndez case. Murphy's fiancée, a Pan American Airlines stewardess named Sally Clare, was certain that he was the victim of foul play. She beseeched members of Congress to investigate.

A Dominican pilot was arrested, based on the story that he had killed Murphy during a violent fight on the bluff where the car was found. The fight was supposed to have been prompted by the homosexual advances of Murphy. Octavio de la Maza (known as Tavito), a Dominican Air Force Captain, refused to confess to this contrived saga. Trujillo's henchmen then arranged for Tavito's death in prison, and clumsily tried to make it look like a suicide, complete with a note from the dead man. U. S. authorities had become active in the investigation because it involved a missing American and the FBI later proved the suicide note to be a crude forgery. The Galíndez disappearance and the two subsequent murders by the Trujillo regime to cover-up this killing would start a chain of events that would eventually bring down the Trujillo government. [27]

With the reelection of Trujillo's brother, "Negro," things in Ciudad Trujillo went on as before, but the dictator felt compelled to insure that events would never again spin out of his control. To accomplish this, he established the Servicio de Inteligencia Militar (SIM) – the ultimate incarnation of his secret police. The head of this new agency was Johnny Abbes Garcia. He had become involved in the "dark side" of police work while in Mexico observing Dominican exiles considered subversive by the Trujillo regime. His personal life was also controversial and he was said to be the lover of Nene Trujillo, the dictator's half brother. When Abbes returned from his clandestine assignments in Mexico and Central America, he rose to a position of top confidant of El Jefé and was installed as the head of SIM in late 1957.

Trujillo's well-known support of the Batista regime placed him squarely in the sights of the new Cuban dictator, Fidel Castro. On June 14, 1959, an unmarked C-46 aircraft off loaded fifty-six fighting men of Cuban origin in the Cordillera Central. The small invasion force was easily crushed by Trujillo's security forces. This attempted overthrow of the regime became a symbol to the quietly growing Dominican resistance, who longed for freedom from the tyranny of Trujillo.

The massive costs of the Free World's Fair of Peace still burdened the nation and the economy began to suffer as a

result of Trujillo's military adventures and his personal corruption. Inflation was rampant and new taxes on staples were
not enough to curb the country's huge deficits. The economic
circumstances and a simmering hatred of the Trujillo regime
for the first time spawned a serious, organized underground in
the Dominican Republic. The clandestine group was named
Catorce de Junio ("known generally as IJ4"), in commemoration of the invasion attempt of June 14, 1959. The regime
responded to the developing underground by stepping up
the repression. Thousands of dissidents from all walks of life
were arrested, including professionals, students, businessmen,
society women and priests, many of whom were formerly Trujillistas. Some were tried and sentenced to hard labor for periods
of up to 30 years.

The SIM employed barbaric instruments such as an electric chair that was used for shock torture during the slow and
painful executions of their victims. Screams of the suffering
were broadcast throughout the cellblocks of the prisons by
loudspeakers, to create extreme fear in other inmates. Another
instrument was the Pulpo (Octopus), a horrifying multi-armed
electrical device that was attached by small screws into the skull.
A rubber "collar" was also used and tightened gradually to sever
a prisoner's neck. An electrical rod ("the Cane") was employed
to shock the genitals of prisoners. Trujillo's torturers also used
nail extractors, leather-thonged whips and scissors that were
especially designed for castration.

The Beginning of the End

The crackdown by Trujillo's police attempted to suffocate
the resistance but it only fueled more hatred for the regime.
The streets were alive with secret policemen, informers and
spies. A fleet of black Volkswagens driven by SIM agents constantly menaced the public with street surveillance and preventative arrests. Large speed bumps were installed near foreign
embassies to slow traffic and Trujillo's agents were posted
nearby with orders to shoot anyone suspected of seeking

sanctuary or political asylum. On January 31, Catholic churches in the Dominican Republic read a pastoral letter to all attending mass. The letter professed solidarity with the "many families affected by the wave of mass arrests" and called on Trujillo to "dry the tears and heal the wounds." All six Catholic bishops of the nation signed this letter.

Trujillo had long hated the leftist tendencies of Venezuela, which had always opposed his government in the Organization of American States. Through SIM leader Abbes, Trujillo had sought to undermine Venezuelan President Rómulo Betancourt, to no avail. Abbes and the aging and increasingly paranoid Trujillo finally decided to resort to murder. On June 24, as President Betancourt departed for an Armed Forces Day Parade in Caracas, his limousine was blown across the street by a powerful bomb that had been detonated from a parked Oldsmobile.

An aide, a chauffeur and one bystander were killed, but the Venezuelan President was only injured. Betancourt suffered severe burns and from his hospital bed he accused Trujillo of having a "bloody hand" in the attack. The Venezuelan accomplices in the plot were soon apprehended, and they confirmed the Dominican role in the assassination conspiracy. The OAS took action on August 26, when all member nations, including the United States, severed diplomatic relations with the Trujillo government. A complete economic boycott began within a few months against Trujillo's regime, plunging the Dominican Republic into an economic death spiral.

The United States began planning to remove Trujillo. CIA operatives within the Dominican Republic began active talks with dissidents to identify a group that could be trusted to bring down the regime. Betancourt gave the Americans an increased incentive to proceed with their plans when he told Secretary of State Christian Herter, "If you don't eliminate him, we will invade." [28]

In August, Negro resigned from the Dominican Presidency in a familiar ploy that Trujillo used when he was under siege. The new President, Dr. Joaquin Balaguer, an intellectual described as an "honest and poor man," was quite out of place in

the world of Dominican tyranny. But reshuffling titles at the
top accomplished nothing.

The anger of the Dominican people was finally captured by
one crime above all of the thousands of political killings committed by Trujillo. Three beautiful young sisters, Dr. Minerva
Mirabal de Tavarez, María Teresa Mirabal de Guzman and Patria Mirabal de Gonzalez were active in the political opposition,
and all had been previously arrested by the regime as subver-
sives. The oldest was thirty-eight and the youngest was twenty-
five. They had become inspirational leaders of the freedom
movement and were beloved and revered by the Dominican
people. They were released from prison, but their husbands
were still in custody.

The three women were granted permission to visit their husbands, but instead, SIM agents intercepted the sisters. Trujillo
biographer Crassweller states, "Fresh abominations were practiced upon them." They were then beaten to death in a cane
field and their bodies were placed in their own jeep, which
was hurled over a cliff. One agent reported to Abbes that they
"floated through the air like dummies." Their death caused a
wave of outrage and the story of the young women became a
legend. They became known as "las Mariposas" ("the Butterflies"). A grieving nation responded as if their own children or
sisters had been sacrificed. The sisters came to symbolize all of
the cruelty and abuse that had been so savagely inflicted upon
the Dominican people, and especially upon its women, by Trujillo. Despite the viciousness of the murder and the reaction of
the people, the increasingly macabre dictator could not resist
the temptation to visit the scene of the crime:

> During a trip to the Cibao, Trujillo chose a mountain
> road to Puerto Plata where the jeep had been pushed over
> the cliff with its load of dead passengers. With him was
> an intimate associate who knew the details of the Mira-
> bal assassinations. Trujillo paused, gazing silently over
> the precipice and down the deep slope. Then to the ee-
> rie surprise of his companion, he said, "This is where
> the Mirabal women died – a horrible crime that foolish

people blame the government for.   Such good women,
and so defenseless! [29]

Antonio de la Maza, the brother of "Tavito," who was murdered in prison to cover up the killings of the American pilot
and Jesus Galíndez, was especially outraged at the Mirabal murders. He told his friend Salvador Estrella, "Look what they are
doing to women now…we must do something to finish with this
madman." Antonio and Salvador were active members of the
underground who were working to end the regime.

Within two months of the death of the Mirabal sisters,
guided by the CIA, the resistance developed a plot to kill Trujillo under the leadership of retired general Juan Tomás Díaz,
a childhood friend of Trujillo from San Cristobal. The group
included men thought to be loyal to Trujillo, including former
general Antonio Imbert Barreras, Salvador Estrella, the son of a
general and General José René ("Pupo") Román, who was married to Trujillo's niece. The CIA had provided the conspirators
with three .30 caliber M-1 carbines, extra magazine clips and
500 rounds of ammunition.

Then, the U. S. shifted its policy, in the wake of the Bay of
Pigs debacle. The Americans believed that a failed attempt
on the life of Trujillo might "further destabilize" the Caribbean. President Kennedy and his advisors were also questioning whether a successful assassination might open the way for
a leftist government that could be politically more dangerous
than the current regime. The Dominican resisters felt deeply
betrayed when informed that additional weapons would not be
available.

Despite the setback, members of the resistance agreed that
the best operational approach would be a simple plan, "to
intercept El Jefé and his chauffeur en route to San Cristobal."
They named it the "Avenida" plan, because it involved chasing
down the dictator in fast cars on the Avenida George Washington, a broad avenue, which passed the Fair Grounds and then
became a straight stretch of road running along the Caribbean
Sea. Only two hundred feet beyond the highway was a sheer
cliff descending to the crashing surf. At night there would be

little traffic to divert the conspirators from their prey. Along this quiet highway, the only nighttime sounds were the rustle of the wind in the palms and the thunder of the waves against the coral below the cliff. The conspirators began to concentrate on the operational aspects of the plan. The weapons and the cars were ready. All they needed was the target to become available. On the evening of Tuesday, May 30, 1961 the plotters were on station – the third consecutive night of a vigil they had vowed to maintain until the man they awaited made his appearance. At seven in the evening they got the news, "Trujillo is going tonight."

The Death of the Goat

The action group that night was a team of seven men in three cars. Antonio Imbert would drive the chase car, de la Maza's black Chevrolet Biscayne. He would primarily be responsible for overtaking the dictator's car. In the right hand seats, positioned to do most of the shooting, would be de la Maza and Lieutenant Garcia, an Aide to Trujillo. Both were expert marksmen. Garcia had a .45 pistol and one of the M-1 carbines, while de la Maza had a 12 gauge sawed off Remington semi-automatic shotgun and a .45 caliber pistol. The other man in the chase car was Salvador Estrella, who was carrying a .38 caliber pistol. The vehicle was parked where the Avenida begins at the Fair Grounds. They planned to await Trujillo's car and follow it to the dark stretch of road, then pull out to pass, allowing the shooters to do their work, blasting the dictator and his driver with gunfire.

A black 4-door Oldsmobile was posted at kilometer 7. This car was supposed to wait for the chase car to make its passing move, at which time the chase car would provide a flashing headlight signal. On the signal, the Olds would move up to block the highway and prevent Trujillo's escape, in case the dictator's driver had evaded the chase car. In this vehicle was Pedro Livio a former army officer, with the other M-1 carbine and Huascar Tejeda, an engineering professor, armed with a

9mm Smith & Wesson pistol. At kilometer 9, in Salvador Estrella's Mercury was Roberto Pastoriza, who was to act as a final
interceptor of the Trujillo car, if everything else failed. The
members of the action team were in place and ready before
8:30 p.m.

Dressed in an olive uniform that he usually wore to the
country, the seventy-nine year-old Trujillo visited his daughter
Angelita. He waved good-bye at 9:40 p.m. and departed for
Casa Caoba, where his staff was preparing for his arrival. Only
when he was comfortably settled would he "send out an order
for his current young mistress to be brought to the house." He
was traveling in a blue Chevrolet Belair. Army Captain Zacarías
de la Cruz, who had been the Generalissimo's driver for eighteen years, was at the wheel. The dictator's car carried three
submachine guns and several revolvers. The car motored down
the Avenida and passed the black Chevrolet chase car, which
swung out into the highway and began to accelerate behind the
blue Belair.

As the cars raced onto the dark portion of the highway,
Imbert drew alongside Trujillo's car to pass. When de la Maza
fired the first time, he was no more than fifteen feet from
his quarry. The back window was quickly blown out and the
"shredded curtain fluttered in the wind." The next shotgun
shell jammed and by the time de la Maza could fire again,
the chase car was pulling away, passing the Belair. The Belair
slowed after El Jefé had shouted "Cono, I've been hit." The
chase car, unable to brake quickly enough, overshot the Belair
as de la Maza screamed, "Stop! Stop! Carajo, stop!" By the time
the chase car had halted it was well ahead of Trujillo's car, but
Imbert quickly did a u-turn and brought the assassin's vehicle
along side of the target car, facing the opposite direction. By
now Trujillo was ready for a fight and despite a serious wound
he said, "Pendejos, pendejos, get the guns, we fight, get the
maldito guns!"

His driver realized that their only escape was to quickly
return to the city, and he protested, "But Jefe, there are a lot
of them ...better we get out of here, Jefe." He began to turn
the car around to flee for safety. Then, inexplicably, Trujillo

shouted "No, no, no," as he struggled to open the back door. Perhaps Trujillo felt invulnerable to danger or his response was a visceral reply to the audacity of these young men that compelled the General to stand and fight. The attackers pumped a fusillade of bullets that ripped into Trujillo's Belair as the dictator's car siren wailed in the darkness. Zacarías was hit several times in the legs. As Trujillo held onto the fender of his car, he managed to get several shots off from his .38 and then he slowly moved directly towards his attackers.

De la Maza crossed the road, moving in for the kill. As he reached the rear of the Belair, he looked up to see Trujillo, the man who had ordered his brother's murder, the tyrant himself, standing unsteadily, illuminated by the headlights. Taking careful aim he gave the old man a full blast of the ball bearing shot. Trujillo collapsed on the side of the road, in tall grass. Approaching the lifeless body of Trujillo, de la Maza "kicked the corpse over on its back." Then with the words, "This hawk won't kill any more chickens," he gave a final coup de grace with a handgun through Trujillo's jaw. The entire assassination took less than four minutes. The Oldsmobile arrived making a violent stop and Pedro Livio fell out of the vehicle, struck by a .38 slug. He had been shot by fire from the chase car, whose occupants thought his fast-approaching vehicle was the SIM, arriving to help Trujillo. They stood over the dictator's body, stunned, not really believing what they saw with their own eyes.

In a state of shock and confusion, the action team pushed the Belair to the side of the road. They placed the body of the tyrant in the trunk of the black Chevrolet and departed, their car almost rendered inoperable by bullet damage. All four men in the chase car had been shot and Pedro Livio was bleeding heavily. The team had left the unconscious but still alive Zacarías by the side of the road. The action team attempted to notify "Pupo" Román, so he could take charge of the government, but the general could not be found.

General Román, without firm knowledge that Trujillo was dead, hesitated in his mission to take over the government. This failure would cost him dearly because, as the investigation would later determine, he had been in league with the assassins for months. The action team hid the car holding Trujillo's corpse, but SIM investigators found it at the home of former General Diaz within a few hours. When they opened the trunk, "everyone froze." It was several minutes before anyone could speak or take action – the sight of the Generalissimo's mangled, bloody remains was overwhelming. When the SIM finally called Hector Trujillo's office, General "Pupo" Román answered. He went completely pale upon learning of the death of the dictator. His panic was palpable, because he had waited too long to seize the government. He was a conspirator trapped among the Trujillistas.

The capital filled with SIM Volkswagens and Trujillo's killers were pursued in every neighborhood. By 2:00 a.m. the airport was closed. The public was not told of Trujillo's death but official radio stations began to play "mournful chamber music" and government buildings flew flags at half-staff on May 31. President Kennedy was in Paris when Secretary of State Dean Rusk called him to say, "Trujillo has been killed."

The first of the seven assassins arrested was the badly wounded Pedro Livio. Huáscar Tejeda was seized after his entry into a church attracted attention. He was brought to face Ramfis Trujillo, who had taken charge of the investigation. Huáscar talked, naming the entire band of conspirators, including General Román and the roundup accelerated. A few of the conspirators fought before they died. Lt. Amado Garcia shot and killed a SIM agent before he was himself shot dead by other secret service members. A gang of SIM agents cornered Juan Tomás Díaz and Antonio de la Maza on the street. Both were killed in a hail of gunfire.

Ramfis Trujillo and a team of torturers were at the center of the SIM manhunt. They subjected a growing number of mostly innocent people to diabolical cruelties. Ernesto de la Maza was electrocuted and beaten so badly that he died from his injuries. The Diaz family houseboy was tortured to death and the family barber, who knew nothing, was electrocuted when he was unable to provide information to his tormentors. The torture continued, despite a visit by an inspection team from the OAS, which was shown a sanitized version of the roundup. Those tortured were moved several times to avoid detection by inspectors.

In the torture chambers themselves, there were macabre incidents that had no intelligence gathering value, but apparently satisfied the rage and bloodlust of the torturers. A Diaz family member was given a hearty meal, for which he thanked his jailers and then he was told, "You're eating your son's flesh." He reacted with incredulity, as if it could not be true. Then the SIM torturers brought him the head of his son, "on a tray." Báez Diaz died moments later of a coronary occlusion.

On the occasion of the state funeral for the fallen dictator, Trujillo's widow, Maria, became hysterical screaming, "One of the killers is in this room." But it was not until June 5, that Ramfis took action against the "traitor in the family." General "Pupo" Román's head was shaved and his eyelids were stitched to his eyebrows, so sleep would be almost impossible. He was tortured for months. Acid was poured over his body, electric rods were inserted into his urinary tract and his colon and electrical charges were fired into his orifices. To end his suffering, he attempted suicide by eating a light bulb and bashing his head on a toilet. General Román was found guilty of treason. He did not die however, until an October session with Ramfis and another officer, who brandished a loaded revolver in his face, which went off. Ramfis then blasted Pupo's body with his own revolver, which he reloaded twice during the frenzied fusillade. The General Román's body was fed to sharks.

The military was unable to maintain order, as the Dominican people were determined to gain their freedom during the months that followed the death of the dictator. Unwilling to return to a life under repressive rule, rioters fearlessly faced machine guns and tanks. On November 19, Ramfis ordered all surviving conspirators removed from the jails and brought to the family compound at Hacienda Maria, a seven thousand acre seaside estate. There, he and his drunken friends enjoyed cocktails on the veranda and took turns shooting the six remaining prisoners who were handcuffed to trees. Their bodies were never found. Following the Hacienda massacre, Ramfis and his entourage left the Dominican Republic, never to return.

The prospect of a bloody wave of executions by the two remaining Trujillo brothers was averted. "Instead of facing the wrath of the SIM, the populace awoke next morning to find the big gray ships of the United States riding offshore." U. S. Consul John Calvin Hill came to the national palace to assure the "wicked uncles" that if they stayed in the country, U. S. Marines would invade. At 11:45 p.m. that evening, November 19, Hector and Petán Trujillo boarded a chartered Pan American DC-6 and flew into exile in Florida. On November 20, the Dominican Congress changed the name of the capital back to Santo Domingo.[30]

Rafael Leónidas Trujillo Molina was, in many ways, a typical Latin American dictator. The tools he utilized to control his people were terror, torture and political murder. But Trujillo was perhaps the most insidious of all of all Latin American caudillos, because of his domination of the mind, body and soul of all Dominicans. Jesús de Galíndez, wrote in the doctoral dissertation for which he was killed, "The most serious things are not the illegal arrests, or even the murders; more serious is the total destruction of the spirit of a people."

Trujillo's crimes were amplified by his grotesque political pornography. His despotism was unparalleled in its preoccupation with the violations of the woman of the Dominican nation. Trujillo's sexual crimes were degrading not just to the women and their families, but to all Dominicans.

While the memory of Trujillo and his three-decade reign of terror in his small country has faded, the recollections of his crimes against women have not. The Mirabal family home in Saucedo has been turned into a national shrine and museum. The only surviving sister, Dedé, has dedicated her life to the memory of the three "Mariposas" who were murdered. Their story was the subject of a widely read novel and an American film. A 137-foot Obelisk that was planned as a tribute to Trujillo became a monument that "eulogizes the struggle of many women and men for Dominican liberty." It is a memorial to the victims of Trujillo's tyranny.

In 1999, the United Nations General Assembly designated November 25, the date of the murder of the Mirabal sisters, as the International Day for the Elimination of Violence Against Women.[31] It is appropriate that the most enduring legacy of the criminality of Rafael Trujillo is a remembrance of his crimes against the women of his nation.

CHAPTER 3
Hitler: Mythology and Madness

"...I am acting in accordance with the will of the Almighty Creator: by defending myself against the Jew, I am fighting for the work of the Lord."

Adolf Hitler

It began with a kiss – the most infamous betrayal in all of recorded history. When Judas Iscariot delivered Jesus to the Romans, he established the rationale for centuries of anti-Semitism. St. Paul proclaimed that the Jews "killed the Lord Jesus and the Prophets and drove us out, the Jews who are heedless of God's will and enemies of their fellow men..."(I Thessalonians 2:15-16). By the time Christianity became the official religion of the Roman Empire in 380 A. D., anti-Jewish sentiment had become a serious threat to the very existence of the Jewish people.

In 1096, crusader armies attacked Jewish communities on the way to the Middle East, forcing Jews to choose between baptism and death. The leader of the first crusade, Godfrey Bouillon, pledged "to leave no single member of the Jewish race alive." During the thirteenth century church leaders in Germany forced Jews to wear cone shaped hats and yellow badges on their clothing so they could be easily identified. Thus marked, Jews were easy prey for Christians who wanted them banished or killed.

Jews were expelled from England in 1290, from France in 1394 and from Spain by the Spanish Inquisition in 1492. By the

fifteenth century most surviving Jews in Europe were isolated
into the forced segregation of ghettos. Martin Luther, a priest
who led the Protestant Reformation in Germany, wrote that
their synagogues and homes should be burned, "so that you
and we may be free of this insufferable devilish burden – the
Jews." Luther's well-read pamphlet, printed in 1545, was entitled *The Jews and their Lies.*

A few voices of moderation and for civil rights resulted from
the French Revolution (1789-1799) and the Enlightenment
brought a general easing of discrimination. German nationalism, however, continued its long tradition of "Jew-hatred."
Johann Gottlieb Fichte, widely recognized as the father of modern German anti-Semitism and German nationalism, argued
against Jewish emancipation as early as 1793.

The nationalistic concept of "Volk" came to mean German
heritage and cultural identity as well as inner creativity. *German
Volkdom*, published in 1810 by Friedrich Ludwig Jahn, explained
the concept: "A state without Volk is nothing, a soulless artifice;
a Volk without a state is nothing, a bodiless airy phantom, like
the Gypsies and the Jews. Only state and Volk together can
form a Reich, and such a Reich cannot be preserved without
Volkdom."

Although anti-Semitism was present in other European
countries, there was a special virulence that accompanied the
Jew-hatred that was intrinsic to German nationalism. The Jew
was looked upon as a homeless wanderer who belonged no-
where and who had no roots – no "Volk." The philosophies of
Hegel and Treitschke, both prominent academics during the
mid-nineteenth century at the University of Berlin, appealed
to a growing national spirit that incorporated German Volkdom, Prussian militarism and Teutonic mythology. The advent
of "race science" introduced the concept of racial superiority
that went well beyond religious issues. Christian Lassen, at the
University of Bonn, argued that Aryans and Semites were direct
opposites in terms of anthropological development. A French
diplomat, Arthur de Gobineau, wrote *Essay on the Inequality of
Races*, which placed the pure "Aryan German" at the apex of
civilization.[1]

Expressions of Teutonic racial superiority became fused with Jew-hatred in the artistic philosophy of Richard Wagner, the brilliant but profoundly controversial composer, who was an important contributor to German Romanticism during the period between 1850 and his death in 1883. Wagner used myths, metaphors and highly emotional music to convey his vision. The Wagnerian portrait of Jews as physically malformed creatures, with a foul stench, made its way into the collective unconscious of the German soul.

Wagner's anti-Semitism was first documented in an article, which linked the "spirit of Judaism" with the artistic decline of society. Wagner's statement, "I felt a long-repressed hatred for this Jewry, and this hatred is as necessary to my nature as gall is to blood," expresses his fundamental racial views. Wagner was the first to use the expression, "the Jewish problem" and it was Wagner, who coined the phrase, "the final solution," by which he meant the disappearance of Jews and Judaism.[2]

Germany and Adolph Hitler

The German people first appeared in a historical context through the writings of Roman historian Tacitus, who described Germania as a collection of tribes living near the Rhine River. Their dominant tribe, the Franks, became the founders of a German State. Charlemagne, ruler of the Franks, a powerful warrior and an enlightened ruler, expanded his authority over a number of kingdoms, establishing the First Reich (empire) in about 778. It is said that "by the sword and the cross," Charlemagne became the master of Western Europe. On Christmas day in 800 A. D., he was crowned by the pope as ruler of nearly all of the territory that today includes Italy, France and Germany, becoming the first Holy Roman Emperor.

Charlemagne's empire lasted less than a century, after which it was divided into the West Frankish Kingdom, which became France, the Eastern Frankish Kingdom, which became Germany and Austria, and the land in between, then known as the Middle Kingdom. These realms were further fragmented by a series of duchies that enjoyed political autonomy. Germany remained disunited while power was centralized in France and England. Martin Luther's Protestant Reformation had a transforming effect on the German people. But while it would have seemingly unified the culture, it actually vested greater power in local rulers, whether Protestant or Catholic. And because there was no longer one single religion, Germans continued to be a fragmented people.

Fredrick I, was crowned as ruler of the German State of Prussia in 1701. Fredrick's successor, Fredrick the Great, transformed Prussia into a true European power, seizing Silesia and participating in the partition of Poland. In 1792 French troops invaded and occupied the Rhineland for more than twenty years. The failure of Prussia in its war against France prompted social and military reform. A revitalized Prussia participated, along with Austria and Russia, in the defeat of Napoleon at the Battle of Leipzig, in 1813.

Germany continued to suffer from political disunity until King Wilhelm I of Prussia named Otto von Bismarck, an aggressive Prussian nationalist, as his minister. Bismarck's policies led to a Prussian victory in the Franco-Prussian war and the German states agreed to accept Wilhelm as the Kaiser (emperor) of a united Germany.

The unification established the second German Reich. Bismarck was dismissed in 1890, following a power struggle with Wilhelm II. Germany then suffered a series of foreign policy blunders and the formation of a web of interlocking alliances. Due to a lack of diplomatic statesmanship, Europe's great powers allowed the unthinkable to happen – the disaster of a World War, sparked by the assassination of the Archduke Franz Ferdinand in Sarajevo on June 28, 1914. [3]

While the German people were seeking political unity, anti-Semitism grew into a lethal virus that would provide the basis for one of history's most vicious racial policies. But a formal government program that would order the extermination of the Jews awaited the emergence of one man: Adolf Hitler.

He was born into obscurity and, like many despotic rulers he was from the cultural and geographic periphery. It has been said that Adolf Hitler's family tree was twisted by a "malignant incestuousness." Its roots were in Waldviertel, a district in Lower Austria near the Danube and close to the borders of Bohemia and Moravia. Adolf's paternal grandmother, Maria Schicklgruber gave birth to an illegitimate son on June 7, 1837, whom she named Alois. Five years later she married a wandering miller, Johann George Heidler. Heidler may have been the child's father, but he did not legitimize the son, who grew up as Alois Schicklgruber. Maria died in 1847, when the child was only 10 years old. Afterwards, Heidler vanished for 30 years. When he reappeared at the age of 84, the spelling of his name had been changed to Hitler. He testified that he was the father of Alois and the parish records in the nearby village of Döllersheim were revised accordingly.

Alois' parents never lived together, even after they married, which fueled speculation about their family relationship. There was also a rumor of "other blood" – that a member of a prominent Jewish family from Graz, in whose household Maria was previously employed, may have impregnated the woman. According to historian Alan Bullock, "In all probability, we shall never know for certain who Adolf Hitler's grandfather, the father of Alois, really was. It has been suggested that he may have been a Jew, without definite proof one way or the other." The memoir of Nazi leader Hans Frank, before his execution at Nuremberg, provides yet another strange twist to this tale of the bloodline of the future Füehrer:

> *Not two months after Hitler invaded Austria, in May 1938, an order was issued to the Land Registries concerned to carry out a survey of Döllersheim (Alois Hitler's birthplace) and neighbourhood with a view to their suitability as a battle training area for the Wehrmacht. In the following year the inhabitants of Döllersheim were forcibly evacuated and the village together with the surrounding countryside was blasted and withered by German artillery and infantry weapons. The birthplace of Hitler's father and the site of his grandmother's grave were alike rendered unrecognizable, and today this whole*

tract of what was once fertile and flourishing country is
an arid desert sown with unexploded shells.[4]

Such destruction could never have occurred without Hitler's personal approval. It appears that Hitler wanted to destroy
evidence of something in that village.

Alois Hitler became a customs service policeman and
married a woman fourteen years his senior, who was in poor
health. They had no children. Hitler biographer John Toland describes a young woman, a second cousin, Klara Po-
elzl, to whom Alois was drawn. She was as an attractive teenager "with abundant dark hair...installed with the Hitler's
at an inn where Alois was already carrying on an affair with
a kitchen maid, Franziska." Alois married Franziska upon
the death of the first Mrs. Hitler. Franziska promptly sent
away her rival, Klara. Franziska's marriage to Alois resulted
in two children before she was stricken with tuberculosis.
When she left home to seek treatment, Alois again sought
out Klara. She remained in the household, even after the
death of Franziska, "and this time", writes Toland, "she became housemaid, nursemaid and mistress." Alois wanted to
marry Klara, but because they were related he had to petition the Catholic Church for permission. Rome granted the
petition for dispensation, allowing the blood relations to
marry, but despite their marriage, Klara continued to call
Alois "uncle."

A first child was born to Klara and Alois four months after
their marriage, but the child died in infancy, as did a second
child in 1886. Adolf, the third child, was born on the evening
of April 20, 1889 in Braunau am Inn, Austria, just across the
border from Bavaria. A fourth child, Edmund was born in
1894, but lived only six years. The fifth and last child, Paula,
was born in 1896. Only Adolf and Paula lived to adulthood and
Paula survived her infamous sibling.

The family moved several times and Adolf attended five
different schools by the time he was fifteen. He spent two of
those years at a Benedictine monastery at Lamback, where he

considered joining a holy order. He went to high school in
Linz. His father may have abused him, although he did not
specifically write about this in Mein Kampf (My Struggle).
However, the book described a drunken father who raped his
wife in front of a confused and helpless three-year-old son.
U.S. psychologists later came to believe that this was an episode
from Hitler's own life, which helped to explain the rage that
boiled within him – even as an adult. Hitler's recollection in
Mein Kampf was that he fought with his father over becoming
a civil servant. Adolf was said to be a "bad tempered," "self-
opinionated" young man, who displayed a "lack of self-con-
trol." He was a poor student and dropped out of high school
without graduating.

Alois died in 1903 of a lung hemorrhage, when Adolf was
thirteen. Klara moved with Adolf and Paula to a suburb of
Linz, where she continued to struggle with her son over his
career. He dearly loved his mother, but he refused to consider
the civil service. The next few years were, in the words of Hitler
himself, "the happiest days of my life." He enjoyed freedom
from attending school and the pleasure of being "mothers dar-
ling." Adolf did not work. He whiled away the days dreaming,
roaming the countryside, exploring the city or listening to the
music of Richard Wagner. He is remembered as a shy, sickly
boy who was, "capable of sudden bursts of hysterical anger."
Adolf enjoyed drawing and became an avid reader of German
history and mythology.

In 1907, Hitler attempted to gain admission to the Vienna
Academy of Fine Arts, but his drawings were judged unsatis-
factory. He was nineteen when his mother died and he remembered that, "it was a dreadful blow...I had honored my
father, but my mother I had loved." Without an education
or a trade, he set out for Vienna where he endured what he
called, "the saddest period of my life." The city of Vienna was
known for its charm and its music, its fine architecture and its
pleasure-loving citizenry. Hitler made a living as a common
laborer and attempted to sell some of his very mediocre paint-
ings. He frequently went hungry.

Hitler became a keen observer of the Viennese political scene and the use of both fear and propaganda in the exercise of political power. He concluded in Mein Kampf :

> *I understood the infamous spiritual terror which this movement exerts, particularly on the bourgeoisie, which is neither morally nor mentally equal to such attacks; at a given sign it unleashes a veritable barrage of lies and slanders against whatever adversary seems most dangerous, until the nerves of the attacked persons break down, just to have peace again...*
>
> *I achieved an equal understanding of the importance of physical terror toward the individual and the masses...For while in the ranks of their supporters the victory achieved seems a triumph of the justice of their own cause, the defeated adversary in most cases despairs of the success of any further resistance.[5]*

The basis of future Nazi tactics for seizing and maintaining power is here in these observations by a homeless young man, who was wandering through Vienna. He believed that the Pan-German movement suffered from an inability to arouse the masses. His movement of National Socialism would one day suffer from no such disability. It was during the years as a vagabond in Vienna, when he first noticed a Jew and this discovery formed a lasting impression:

> *Once, as I was strolling through the Inner City, I suddenly encountered an apparition in a black caftan and black hair locks. Is this a Jew? was my first thought. For, to be sure, they had not looked like that in Linz. I observed the man furtively and cautiously, but the longer I stared at this foreign face, scrutinizing feature for feature, the more my first question assumed a new form: Is this a German?[6]*

He found the answer to this question in trashy anti-Semitic literature that was readily available in Vienna. And Hitler asked another question that, in its own warped prose, provided an answer: "Was there any form of filth or profligacy, particularly in cultural life, without at least one Jew involved in it? If you cut even cautiously into such an abscess, you found, like a maggot in a rotting body, often dazzled by the sudden light – a kike!" Hitler continues, "When for the first time, I recognized the Jew as the cold-hearted shameless and calculating director of this revolting vice traffic in the scum of the big city, a cold shudder ran down my back."

According to William L. Shirer in *The Rise and Fall of the Third Reich,* "There is a great deal of morbid sexuality in Hitler's ravings about the Jews." Hitler wrote in Mein Kampf of the "nightmare vision of the seduction of hundreds of thousands of girls by repulsive, crooked-legged Jew bastards." "Gradually," Hitler wrote, "I began to hate them...I had ceased to be a weak-kneed cosmopolitan and became an anti-Semite." This hatred would become a burning passion for Hitler and the driving obsession of his Third Reich. He left Vienna in 1913 for Munich, but still he did not find work. When war broke out the next year, he joined the Bavarian regiment and his political ambitions began to grow.

The Rise of the Nazi Party

On the darkest day in German history, November 10, 1918, Adolf Hitler received the news of the German defeat and the abdication of the Kaiser from a pastor who was serving in a military hospital. Corporal Hitler was recovering from a case of temporary blindness, inflicted by a British gas attack. He has related his shock and horror at the news: "...So it has all been in vain. In vain all the sacrifices and privations; In vain all the hours in which, with mortal fear clutching at our hearts, we nevertheless did our duty; in vain the death of two millions who died...Had they died for this?...Did all this happen only so that a gang of wretched criminals could lay hands on the Fatherland?" Hitler broke down and wept for the first time since the death of his beloved mother.

He would cling to the belief that Germany was not defeated in the war, but was instead "stabbed in the back," by, "miserable degenerate criminals." He held the Jews responsible and he wrote in Mein Kampf, "There is no making pacts with Jews; there can only be the hard: either-or." Hitler returned to Munich in 1918 and took a job with the army's district Political Command Press Office. In September of 1919, the Political Command sent him to speak to a group called the German Workers Party. He appeared in a dreary beer cellar to speak to about 25 men. A man named Anton Drexler thrust a Party pamphlet into his hands. He read the booklet and found that it reflected many of his own political ideas. He was soon enrolled as the seventh member of the German Workers Party. The organization included men like Ernst Roehm, a bull-necked, scar-faced professional soldier and brawler who, like Hitler, despised the "November criminals" and the democratic Republic that prevailed after the war. They shared a vision of a strong nationalistic Germany built upon the support of the masses. Like many others in the early Nazi movement Roehm had a seedy past, but he brought many ex-soldiers into the movement.

Hitler assumed responsibility for Party propaganda in 1920 and delivered a speech that articulated the twenty-five-point program of the German Workers Party. He spoke of plans to abrogate treaties, impose harsh policies upon Jews and to unite all Germans into a "Greater Germany." The little group began to grow. By summer the organization's name was changed to the National Socialist German Workers Party, known as the Nazi Party. Strong-arm squads in brown uniforms, commanded by ex-convict Emil Maurice became the storm troopers (Sturmabteilung), or the S. A. Hitler consolidated power to become absolute leader of the Nazi Party. They adopted the swastika and began to use banners of red, black and white, emblazoned with the new symbol and the words "Deutchland Erwache! (Germany, Awake!)"

As the Party grew it attracted men like Rudolph Hess, a student and anti-Semitic pamphleteer; Alfred Rosenberg, a graduate architect with a burning hatred for Jews and Bolsheviks and Hermann Goering, a famed pilot and hero of World War I.

The Party also attracted many unsavory characters including blackmailers, Jew-baiters, pimps and sexual perverts. Fund raising increased, with contributions from the wives of rich industrialists, affluent anti-Semites and wealthy families who believed in a militarized Germany.

The backdrop of the Nazi Party's growth was Weimar Germany, an experiment in parliamentary democracy that was tumultuous in the extreme. The capital, Berlin, was paralyzed by general strikes. The competing forces swirling about Germany made effective governance nearly impossible. The communists were plotting revolution in the style of the Bolsheviks, while the upper classes and the industrial magnates favored a right-wing political solution. The military pledged loyalty to the new democratic government, but they were unenthusiastic. The civil service and the Army were generally in favor of some kind of authoritarian regime. Nearly everyone was afraid of the anarchy that threatened to consume the nation. Liberals and socialists were aggressively prosecuted for their protests, but right wing attacks on the government were treated with leniency. Communists were beaten in the streets and their leaders murdered. Beset on every side by hostility, the Weimar government struggled to survive under the shadow of the treaty of Versailles. [7]

The treaty that ended the war virtually disarmed Germany and assessed reparations that crushed the nation with an impossible financial burden. This caused the Mark's value to slip from 4 to the dollar to 75. It continued to fall and by early 1923 it was 7,000 to the dollar. The German government requested relief from the reparations payments, but the victorious nations refused. By July 1, 1923 the Mark was 160,000 to the dollar and by August 1 it reached 1,000,000 to the dollar. It would eventually extend into the trillions, making the German mark completely worthless. The people and the nation were impoverished.

In times of extreme stress human behavior often becomes bizarre and in the early 1920's the Germans began to behave in unpredictable ways. A bohemian culture was spawned, especially in Berlin. New artistic movements sprung up with a spirit

of free thought among the artistic and creative elite. A kind of
madness took over and people were drawn to the strange, the
unusual and the repulsive. Otto Freidrich tells us in *Before the
Deluge*:

> *When the money became worthless, it destroyed the whole
> system for getting married, and so it destroyed the whole
> idea of remaining chaste until marriage...Not every girl
> was a virgin when she was married, but it was generally
> accepted that one should be. But what happened from
> the inflation was that the girls learned that virginity
> didn't matter any more.*[8]

According to Stefan Zweig, "all values were changed, and
...Berlin was transformed to the Babylon of the world." More
than 100,000 financially desperate women and girls sold their
bodies for a pittance and a popular novelty was mother-daugh-
ter prostitution teams. It was a world in which morals had lost
all value, along with the currency.

Hitler cultivated a relationship with war hero General Erich
Ludendorff. In November 1923, Hitler and his "brown shirt"
thugs took control of a beer hall meeting in Munich and declared a revolution. The following day, Hitler and Ludendorff
led some three thousand armed storm troopers behind Nazi
banners to carry out the revolt. Police crushed the march and
put Hitler, Ludendorff and eight others on trial. Ludendorff
was acquitted, while Hitler and the others were found guilty,
but the trial made Hitler a hero among ultra rightists. Hitler
served less than nine months of a five-year term in Landsberg
prison, where he was treated as an "honored guest." It was during this confinement that he began to write Mein Kampf.

Hitler's threats against the government led to an official ban
on his speeches and he responded by channeling his energy
into organizing and expanding the Nazi party. He signed up
thousands of dues-paying members and launched Nazi organizations for young people and women. He created the Schutz-
staffel or SS, which had originated as a bodyguard detail. The
Nazi Party's formal organization included a number of odd

characters among their leadership. Paul Joseph Goebbels, a frustrated playwright, fell under Hitler's spell. In late October 1926, Goebbels was appointed Gauleiter or political leader of Berlin. Meanwhile, Hitler waited out his public speaking ban and used the time to complete Mein Kampf.

In the summer of 1928, Hitler leased a villa and persuaded his widowed half-sister Angela Raubal to become his house-keeper. Angela brought along her two daughters, Geli and Friedl. Hitler fell in love with the young and beautiful Geli. He and Geli later rented a luxurious apartment in a fashionable suburb of Munich.

The Party leader's open relationship with his twenty-year-old half-niece began to cause a scandal. The rising politician's past was also coming under scrutiny, especially his "family history." In late 1930, according to Hitler confidant and lawyer Hans Frank, Hitler learned of the attempt by relatives living in England to sell a story about the origins of the family. Hitler told his half-nephew, William that "These people must not know who I am. Nobody must know where I come from."

Hitler met with Frank at the Munich apartment he shared with Geli Raubal to address what Hitler called a "disgusting blackmail plot." According to Frank's written account: "The press reports in question suggested that Hitler had Jewish blood in his veins and hence was hardly qualified to be an anti-Semite." After making "confidential inquiries," Frank found explosive documents, which he said, were "in the possession of a woman living in Wetzlsdorf near Graz [Austria] who was related to Hitler through the Raubals." What Frank learned is the following:

> *Hitler's father was the illegitimate son of a woman by the name of Schicklgruber from Leonding near Linz who worked as a cook in a Graz household...But the most extraordinary part of the story is this: when the cook Schicklgruber (Adolf Hitler's grandmother) gave birth to her child, she was in service with a Jewish family called Frankenberger. And on behalf of his son, then about nineteen years old, Frankenberger paid a maintenance*

allowance to Schicklgruber from the time of the child's birth until his fourteenth year. For a number of years too, the Frankenbergers and Hitler's grandmother wrote to each other, the general tenor of the correspondence betraying on both sides the tacit acknowledgement that Shicklgruber's illegitimate child had been engendered under circumstances which made the Frankenbergers responsible for its maintenance...Hence the possibility cannot be dismissed that Hitler's father was half Jewish as a result of the extramarital relationship between the Schicklgruber woman and the Jew from Graz. This would mean that Hitler was one quarter Jewish. [9]

And, according to Frank, Hitler "did not dispute the authenticity of the paternity correspondence." What is more interesting is Hitler's response to this information when Frank presented it to him in Munich in the winter of 1930. According to Frank:

Adolf Hitler said he knew...that his father [was not the child of]the Schicklgruber woman and the Jew from Graz. He knew it from what his father and his grandmother told him. He knew that his father sprang from a premarital relation between his grandmother and the man she later married [Georg Heidler]. But they were both poor, and the maintenance money that the Jew paid over a number of years was an extremely desirable supplement to the poverty-stricken household. He was well able to pay, and for that reason it had been stated that he was the father. The Jew paid without going to court probably because he could not face the publicity that a legal settlement might have entailed. [10]

Despite the cover story, Hitler himself was uncertain if he was "infected by Jewish blood," and perhaps this explains his obsession about even the slightest amount of tainted blood creating a "racially divided being." The point is not whether Hitler was part Jewish, but that he believed it was a possibility, which could have contributed to his obsessive efforts to exterminate the entire race.

Perhaps the greatest scandal to threaten Adolf Hitler's rise to power was a violent incident that occurred in his household in the late summer of 1931, as Hitler was considering a bid for the presidency. Hitler left his residence on a Friday afternoon to attend a political meeting and following his departure his lover and niece, Geli Raubal, was seen leaving his bedroom. She appeared agitated. No one heard any unusual sounds, but the next day her body was found in her bedroom, shot through the chest with Hitler's handgun. A police investigation concluded that it was a suicide, but no one could establish a motive. Rumors in Munich were rampant with suggestions of a possible homicide.

Other rumors suggested perversion in the private life of Hitler and his young half-niece. A Berlin newspaper, *Neue Montags Zeitung*, attributed the suicide to Geli's "bitter disappointment at the nature of Hitler's private life" and a Bavarian weekly was more to the point: "Hitler's private life with Geli took on forms that obviously the young woman was unable to bear." Press reports at the time even included a story with the headline, "The Legend of Hitler's Suicide Maidens."

Walter Langer, a psychologist who prepared a 1943 report for the American OSS on Hitler's mental condition included this passage: "The idea that Hitler had a sexual perversion particularly abhorrent to women is further supported by a statistic: of the seven women who, we can be reasonably sure, had intimate relations with Hitler, six committed suicide or seriously attempted to do so." In addition to Geli Raubal, "Mimi Reiter tried to hang herself in 1928…Eva Braun attempted suicide in 1932 and again in 1935; Frau Inge Ley was a successful suicide, as were Renate Mueller and Suzi Liptauer."

Hitler biographer, Konrad Heiden, suggested that Hitler entertained perverse fantasies about Geli that came to light through a letter that Hitler wrote to her in 1929, disclosing "masochistic coprophilic inclinations bordering upon what Havelock Ellis calls 'undinism' (the desire to be urinated upon for sexual gratification)… The letter probably would have

been repulsive to Geli if she had received it. But she never did."
The letter was intercepted by the landlady's son, forcing Hitler
and Geli to change lodgings.

Perhaps Otto Strassner, brother of Nazi leader Gregor
Strassner, provided the most direct information on this matter.
One evening in 1931, according to Otto, through bitter tears,
Geli disclosed that Hitler demanded things of her that were,
"simply repulsive...." In a debriefing for the OSS he became
specific, stating what he was told by Hitler's niece:

> *Hitler made her undress [while] he would lie down on
> the floor. Then she would have to squat down over
> his face where he could examine her at close range,
> and this made him very excited. When the excitement
> reached its peak, he demanded that she urinate on him,
> and that gave him his sexual pleasure. Geli said that
> the whole performance was extremely disgusting, and
> although it was sexually stimulating [to him], it gave
> her no gratification.[11]*

Despite scandal and the tragedy of the Geli Raubal affair, Hitler took advantage of the economic misery created
by the depression to increase his political power in Germany.
With factories closed and more than six million people un-
employed (a rate of more than 30%), Germany was ready
for radical change. In 1932, Hitler ran for President and
received nearly one third of the vote, forcing a runoff and the
reelection of war veteran Paul von Hindenburg. In July 1932,
Hitler's Party won 230 seats in the Reichstag, and became the
largest party in the 608-member body. The German Republic
continued to be unstable and the leading politicians were unable to form a lasting governing coalition. As Hitler's 400,000
brownshirts mobilized menacingly, a series of frantic political
maneuvers concluded with the in 84 year-old Hindenburg
forming a government that included Hitler. In a vain attempt
to neutralize the Nazi's through assimilation, the elected
president appointed Hitler to the principal operating position of the government. At noon on January 30, 1933, Adolf

Hitler formally became Chancellor of Germany and the long, dark slide into tyranny began.

Hitler in Power

Brownshirt thugs promptly unleashed a campaign of violence and terror directed at the communists as well as the Social Democrats and even the Catholic Center Party. By early February, the Hitler government had banned the Communist Party and closed all communist newspapers. The next Reichstag election was scheduled for March 5 and Hitler's political operatives urgently needed a sensational event that would stampede the public into their corner before Election Day. The event occurred on the evening of February 27, 1933 when the Reichstag building burst into flames. Arriving at the scene, Hitler declared it a "communist crime."

There is considerable evidence that the Nazi's planned the arson and utilized a third party as a cover for their activities. Members of the S. A. used underground passages to gain entry to the building, where they torched the structure with gasoline and other propellants. A "half-witted Dutch Communist with a passion for arson," named Marinus van der Lubbe did attempt to set the Reichstag on fire, but the proper job was done by storm troopers under the command of Karl Ernst. Hermann Goering admitted as much at a luncheon in 1942, and testimony at the Nuremberg trials established these facts beyond question. Hitler seized this opportunity to urge upon President Hindenburg a decree suspending seven sections of the constitution that guaranteed civil liberties. With this decree, Hitler gained the power to crush his opponents and to persecute ordinary citizens who might not support the Nazi Party.

On March 23, 1933, the Reichstag passed the Enabling Act, which provided dictatorial power to Hitler and his cabinet for the next four years. This was the last legislation passed under the Constitution of the Republic. The German parliament had essentially committed suicide by granting Hitler the power to outlaw democracy. And it had all been accomplished within the system, for as we are told by *The Rise and Fall of the Third Reich*, "It was this Enabling Act alone which formed the legal basis for Hitler's dictatorship." Hitler biographer, Allan Bullock has written, "The street gangs had seized control of the resources of a great modern state, the gutter had come to power."

In the Spring of 1934, Hitler gave an arrogant speech on the anniversary of his elevation to the position of Chancellor. The speech included a litany of Hitler's personal achievements:

> *Within twelve months he had overthrown the Weimar Republic, substituted his personal dictatorship for its democracy, destroyed all the political parties but his own, smashed the state governments and their parliaments and unified and defederalized the Reich, wiped out the labor unions, stamped out democratic associations of any kind, driven the Jews out of public and professional life, abolished freedom of speech and the press, stifled the independence of the courts and "co-ordinated" under Nazi rule the political, economic, cultural and social life of an ancient and cultivated people.* [12]

In a secret meeting with Anthony Eden of Great Britain, Hitler proposed to partially disarm the S. A. as a means of showing good faith on the disarmament issue. Word leaked to brownshirt leader Roehm, who was outraged. Relations between the military and the S. A. leadership soon became bitter. The S. A. had grown to some 2 ½ million armed storm troopers who posed an eminent threat to the military. By agreeing to suppress Roehm's ambitions, Hitler gained the support of the military high command as the successor to Hindenburg, whose health was failing.

On June 30, Hitler claimed to have received urgent messages during the middle of the night that S. A. units were ordered to assemble. He referred to these reports as evidence of a "mutiny." Himmler then ordered a special detachment of the S. S. and Goering's special police on alert and Hitler flew to Munich to confront Roehm. Upon his arrival, he was informed that an S.A. leader had been discovered in bed with a young man.

Hitler ordered the immediate execution of key S. A. leaders. Roehm and a number of others were shot by the S.S. According to Hitler, "for their corrupt morals alone, these men deserved to die." The final death toll from the purge was nearly 1,000 men, half of whom were leaders of the brownshirts.

On July 13, Hitler told the Reichstag that, "In this hour I was responsible for the fate of the German people, and thereby I became the supreme judge of the German people. It was no secret that this time the revolution would have to be bloody; when we spoke of it we called it "the 'Night of the Long Knives.' Everyone must know for all future time that if he raises his hand to strike the State, then certain death is his lot." The S.S. organization under Himmler and Heydrich would expand to become Hitler's instrument of extermination during the remaining existence of the Third Reich. When the German military leadership accepted Nazi lawlessness, they essentially relinquished all power to Hitler.

On August 2, 1934 the last potential impediment to Hitler's absolute control of Germany was removed with the death of President Hindenburg. Three hours after his death the cabinet enacted a law combining the offices of Chancellor and President. Adolf Hitler assumed power as the head of state. A new sacred oath of allegiance was required for all members of the armed forces that recognized Adolf Hitler as the "Füehrer of the German Reich" and swore fealty to him personally.

The racial laws that were enacted in 1935 aroused little scrutiny, because they were cloaked in Nazi "master race" theories that were generally popular with nationalistic Germans. The Nuremberg Laws of September 15, 1935 relegated Jews to the status of "subjects." Laws enacted during the next few years would further deprive them of the right of citizenship and even the opportunity to earn a living in Nazi Germany. German Protestants were influenced by the views of Martin Luther, who had been a ferocious anti-Semite and a believer in strict obedience to political authority.

As early as 1933, German culture began to undergo a transformation, evidenced by torchlight parades that included the burning of books by respected writers. Joseph Goebbels was responsible for both propaganda and culture, which was strictly regulated and essentially "Nazified." Music was less restricted, but works by Jewish composers like Mendelssohn were banned, as were modern compositions. Dr. Goebbels regulated every aspect of the arts as well as the media, including the press, radio and films. All publications and newspapers that would not submit to Nazi control were forced out of business.[13]

Under Hitler, Germany became a ruthless police state, in which the rule of law ceased to exist. Dr. Hans Frank, Commissioner of Justice and Reich Law Leader, told judges "The National Socialist ideology is the foundation of all basic laws, especially as explained in the party program and in the speeches of the Füehrer." He suggested as a guideline for judges to ask this question: "How would the Füehrer decide in my place?" If legal proceedings were not to the liking of the state, Nazi officials had the right to drop prosecutions or to take the accused into custody.

The Gestapo had originally been established in Prussia by Goering in 1933 and became essentially the "Secret State Police." The Gestapo was provided with a special legal status that put it beyond all judicial review. During Hitler's first year in power, fifty concentration camps were established. Their purpose was not just incarceration, but they were used as a tool to terrorize the public and to deter any resistance. By 1936, the entire police structure was nationalized and complete control resided with the Nazi state under a sadistic former chicken farmer, Heinrich Himmler.

Germany Prepares for War

While the economic growth of the Reich seemed a relief from the chaos of the Weimar government and the deprivation of the depression, the underlying cause of the economic recovery was rearmament. From 1934 on, economic activity was referred to as the Wehrwirtschaft or war economy. Gradually the controlled economy began to take away the freedoms that private enterprise cherished most. Without trade unions or collective bargaining workers became serfs.

By the end of 1934 the size of the army had reached 300,000, triple its original size. The Navy was ordered to build new fleets in complete secrecy. A universal conscription law was enacted in to support an army of 500,000. Hitler continued his "peace" offensive with speeches that included assurances designed to mislead the world. At first he moved cautiously. He had a strong case for returning the Saar district to Germany, since the people there had never consented to French rule. They voted overwhelmingly for return to Germany in January 1935. On March 7, 1936, a German force invaded and occupied the demilitarized zone of the Rhineland.

On November 5, 1937 Hitler met with his generals to review military planning. He told them, "The aim of German policy was to make secure and preserve the racial community and to enlarge it." He expressed the desire for greater living space, or "Lebensraum." To the shock of the military leadership, Hitler made it clear that he was ready to use force to annex Austria and Czechoslovakia. Hitler was able to bring pressure on the government of Dr. Kurt von Schuschnigg, the Austrian Chancellor. He forced the Chancellor's resignation. As Hitler arranged to make his triumphant entry into Austria, the place of his birth, he was described as "being in a state of ecstasy." Austria lost its independence and was absorbed into the Reich. Not a shot had been fired.

Soon thereafter a wave of terror swept through Austria. Jewish men and women were forced wash the gutters on their hands and knees. Hundreds of other Jews were forced to clean the latrines of storm troopers. Thousands were arrested. Many had all their personal possessions seized. It became an "orgy of sadism." Germans bought businesses at bargain prices, especially from Jews, who wanted to escape Austria. Himmler established an "Office for Jewish Emigration," and built a concentration camp known as Mauthausen. The former Chancellor was arrested, forced to endure sleep deprivation and completely degrading treatment. He was later sent to Dachau and Sachsenhausen, with his wife and child. The former Austrian first family was scheduled to be executed by the S.S., but before the sentence could be carried out, almost miraculously, the Americans freed them near the end of the war. [14]

"Peace In Our Time"

As 1939 dawned, *Time* magazine named Adolf Hitler as its
"Man of the Year," describing him astride a "cringing Europe
with all the swagger of a conqueror." The magazine portrayed
a "moody, brooding unprepossessing 49-year-old Austrian
ascetic with a Charlie Chaplin mustache," but this description
failed to capture the essence of Adolph Hitler. He was barely
5 feet 9 inches tall, hardly the swaggering figure described by
Time. With an almost ghostly pallor and a forelock of black hair
swooping across his forehead above the left eye, he appeared to
be a comic caricature of a man. His hands were "finely struc-
tured" with long, rather graceful fingers. He used his hands
to punctuate a symphony of hate in fiery speeches delivered at
torchlight rallies throughout Germany.

But even his oratory, as charismatically emotional as it
was, did not convey the core of Hitler's personality. Without
question, Hitler's most distinguishing features were his pale,
phosphorescent gray eyes that have been called "startling and
unforgettable." His eyes penetrated everyone who met him,
casting an almost hypnotic spell upon men and women alike.
Frequently the fire in his eyes would erupt into a volcanic temper, expressed through withering sugar-fueled rages. Hitler's
smoldering hatreds formed the molten core of the man.

His well-known hyper-cleanliness was an outward manifestation of an inner fear of impurities that he believed endangered the Aryan race. He would often speak of "the Jewish
poison …penetrating the bloodstream of our people." Contrary to the comic depictions of cartoonists, his passion for
conquest and murder was constantly seething just below the
surface.

Hitler could be charming, especially with women, who he
treated with polite respect in public. Hitler loved pornography
and enjoyed watching pornographic films in a private viewing
room that were provided by his official photographer. But Hitler's fascination with women's bodies was excessive and perhaps
even pathological. Former Nazi leader Hermann Rauschning
hinted at Hitler's deviant personality when he wrote, "most

loathsome of all is the reeking miasma of furtive, unnatural sexuality that fills and fouls the whole atmosphere around him, like an evil emanation."

By January of 1939, Hitler was nearly ready to unleash the retribution of his Third Reich upon the nations that had subdued Germany only two decades before. He planned to mislead Europe into a false sense of security by duping their hapless leaders with his hypnotic charm. Hitler had perfected the technique of fomenting unrest in a country he coveted, while using his excellent propaganda machine to highlight the difficulties of German citizens in that country. This assured Hitler that the military action or annexation would seem justified to the Western Democracies. He began that process in Czechoslovakia in early 1938. France and Great Britain's eagerness to avoid war allowed Hitler to simply take what he wanted without much of a trumped-up pretext. British Prime Minister Neville Chamberlain met with Hitler and accepted his assurances that the Czechoslovakian Sudetenland would be his "last territorial demand" in Europe. Chamberlain returned home, declaring that there would be "peace in our time," as Nazi Germany prepared to swallow the remainder of Czechoslovakia.

Hitler's final political gambit was to threaten that Czech failure to accept annexation would result in Germany bombing the beautiful city of Prague into rubble. On Wednesday, March 15, 1939, the Czech president signed a document stating he had "confidently placed the fate of the Czech people and country in the hands of the Füehrer of the German Reich." This was the first of Hitler's non-German conquests. Again, not a shot was fired.

The Western Democracies merely watched in stunned silence as Hitler flagrantly breeched the Munich agreement before their eyes. Belatedly the British Prime Minister realized how his appeasement policy had played into Hitler's hands. But by now, Hitler was ready to turn on Poland.

Within a month of signing the Munich agreement, Hitler began to pressure Poland for the "return" of the Danzig corridor, a small strip of territory west of the Vistula River that separated East Prussia from Germany proper. The Poles stood firm, refusing to be intimidated. They sought a guarantee of independence from Great Britain, which was granted on March 31. It was a startling turnabout for Chamberlain, who earlier might have prevented aggression in the Rhineland or the Sudetenland. The British also had an opportunity to block Hitler before he moved on Austria and Czechoslovakia. Hitler's next bite of Europe meant war and everyone knew it.

On April 13, war alliances were conjoined when France and Britain issued a military guarantee to Greece and Rumania. U. S. President Roosevelt sent a telegram to Hitler requesting assurances that he would not attack a list of 31 nations. The list included Poland. On April 28, 1939, Hitler made a broadcast speech to the Reichstag that answered Roosevelt. He had the attention of the entire world and he denounced the British, offered an extension of the German-Polish non-aggression pact (with terms set by Hitler) and answered the President's questions with sarcasm. He named each country on Roosevelt's list, that he would not attack, but he cunningly left out Poland, which went unnoticed to many in his audience. While his words said peace, his rhetorical sarcasm said war.

Gestapo action to create a fake attack on a German radio station near the Polish border was prepared, using concentration camp inmates dressed in Polish uniforms. The code name for these sacrificial victims was "canned goods." Hitler now needed only to secure his eastern front before launching a war in Europe. Agreement on the provisions of a non-aggression treaty with Russia was reached on August 21. Final negotiations went on until August 31,1939, the very day that Hitler gave the attack order for September 1 against Poland. Through a combination of strategic blindness, timid appeasement and flawed diplomacy, the European Democracies had assured that the Blitzkrieg (Lightning War) would fall upon them with its full fury.

As the clock struck midnight on September 1, 1939, Europe and the world were about to be plunged into the greatest armed conflict in history. The terrible fate that awaited the world on that morning was under the control of one man – and at the mercy of his highly unstable personality. Perhaps the most revealing assessment of Hitler's personality disorder was prepared

for The United States Office of Strategic Services (OSS).
Dr. Walter C. Langer and his team wanted to provide understanding and insight into Hitler's thought processes and potential future actions. This report tells us:

> The world has come to know Adolph Hitler for his in-
> satiable greed for power, his ruthlessness, cruelty and
> utter lack of feeling, his contempt for established institu-
> tions and his lack of moral restraints. In the course of
> relatively few years he has contrived to usurp such tre-
> mendous power that a few veiled threats, accusations or
> insinuations were sufficient to make the world tremble.
> In open defiance of treaties he occupied huge territories
> and conquered millions of people without even firing a
> shot. When the world became tired of being frightened
> and concluded that it was all a bluff, he initiated the
> most brutal and devastating war in history - a war
> which, for a time, threatened the complete destruction
> of our civilization. Human life and human suffering
> seem to leave this individual completely untouched as
> he plunges along the course he believes he was predes-
> tined to take.[15]

A sense of the personality of Adolf Hitler can be derived
from these conclusions of the report:
- *A survey of all the evidence forces us to conclude that Hitler
  believes himself destined to become an Immortal Hitler, chosen
  by God to be the New Deliverer of Germany and the Founder of a
  new social order for the world.*
- *These attitudes are probably the outcome of his early experiences
  with his mother who first seduced him into a love relationship
  and then betrayed him by giving herself to his father. Nevertheless, he still continued to believe in an idealistic form of love
  and marriage, which would be possible if a loyal woman could
  be found. As we know, Hitler never gave himself into the hands
  of a woman again with the possible exception of his niece, Geli
  Raubal, which also ended in disaster.*

- *To him it [the defeat of Germany] was as if his mother was again the victim of a sexual assault. This time it was the November Criminals and the Jews who were guilty of the foul deed and he promptly transferred his repressed hate to these new perpetrators.*
- *In Hitler's case this earlier experience was almost certainly the discovery of his parents in intercourse and that he interpreted this as a brutal assault in which he was powerless. He refused to be- lieve what his eyes told him and the experience left him speechless.*
- *That this interpretation is correct is evidenced by his imagery in dealing with the event later on. Over and over again we find figures of speech such as these: ...by what wiles the soul of the German has been raped ...our German pacifists will pass over in silence the most bloody rape of the nation.*
- *It may be that his nightmares will yield a clue. These, it may be remembered, center on the theme of his being attacked or sub- jected to indignities by another man. It is not his mother who is being attacked, but himself... Under ordinary circumstances, we would be inclined to interpret this as the result of an un- conscious wish for homosexual relations together with an ego revulsion against the latent tendency. This interpretation might apply to Hitler, too, for to some extent it seems as though he reacted to the defeat of Germany as a rape of himself as well as of his symbolic mother.*
- *Just as Hitler had to exterminate his former self in order to get the feeling of being great and strong, so must Germany extermi- nate the Jews if it is to attain its new glory. Both are poisons, which slowly destroy the respective bodies and bring about death.*
- *Hitler might commit suicide... This is the most plausible out- come. Not only has he frequently threatened to commit suicide, but from what we know of his psychology it is the most likely possibility... In any case, his mental condition will continue to deteriorate. He will fight as long as he can with any weapon or technique that can be conjured up to meet the emergency. The course he will follow will almost certainly be the one which seems to him to be the surest road to immortality and at the same time drag the world down in flames.*[16]

The World at War

Like a scene from a Wagnerian Opera that would indeed "drag the world down in flames," the war began. At first light on September 1, 1939, the German war machine descended upon a completely unprepared Poland. The Nazi Blitzkrieg, destroyed Polish defenses in a matter of a few days. On September 3, Britain and France declared war on Germany and began a general mobilization. Although Russia had been given an early warning of the invasion, their leaders were caught by surprise when German armor reached the outskirts of Warsaw by September 8. Germany had committed naked aggression against Poland and Russia belatedly moved in like a hyena, for a share of the spoils. The Russians advanced into Poland on September 17.

Following the invasion, Nazi terror assaulted the citizens of that vanquished country. The fate of Poland would serve as a foreshadowing of what would soon befall all of Europe. Long time Hitler crony Hans Frank was appointed Governor-General. Frank would create a slave labor force, while he liquidated the intelligentsia and prepared Polish Jews for the "Final Solution." His intent was clearly stated, when he said, "We must annihilate the Jews." Within one year of the invasion, 1.2 million Poles and 300,000 Jews had been relocated to the east. On February 21, 1940 a new "quarantine camp" was established at Auschwitz. This was to become the first of many extermination camps operated by the S. S.

Denmark was attacked by Germany and capitulated the same day. Norway tried to make a fight for freedom, but superior German forces sealed their fate. Surrounded by Russian and German occupied nations, Sweden maintained an uneasy neutrality. Dutch resistance lasted only five days. Churchill flew to Paris on May 16 and looking down from his aircraft as it crossed the French coast, he was absolutely horrified to see more than seven million people – soldiers, civilians and refugees fleeing from the German onslaught. Every road and highway south of Paris was filled with exhausted and terrified French citizens in horse carts, automobiles and on foot.

There was only a glimmer of hope for the Allied forces. By the morning of June 4, more than 330,000 British and French soldiers had been successfully evacuated across the English Channel. The "miracle of Dunkirk," was a great achievement, but as Churchill himself pointed out, "wars are not won by evacuations." The French, who had fought the Germans for more than four years during the Great War, now capitulated to Hitler in less than six weeks. The Germans controlled most of Europe and had the mightiest war machine on earth. They predicted that they would be masters of a "thousand year Reich."

Hitler was so sure that the British would accept a peace treaty that he made no further plans against Britain. But the British remained defiant and the battle for Britain would be fought in the air. The island nation was bombed unmercifully by the Nazis. Despite overwhelming numerical superiority, the Luftwaffe was unable to establish a promising rate of attrition of British aircraft. This was due to the skills of the British Fighter Command and the unique capability of radar that was available to British forces. Courageous British airmen made a valiant defense of the homeland and RAF fighter pilots became national heroes. A German invasion of the British Isles never occurred, which was fortunate for the allies. The rollback of the Nazi conquests was only possible because Britain was available as a staging area for the invasion of Europe.

The Nazi dictator believed that Britain was finished and would eventually beg for peace to stop the bombing. During the summer of 1940 he began to make comments to his military leaders that indicated he was seriously considering an invasion of the Soviet Union. In fact, he believed that removing Russia as a potential ally for Britain, he would be speed the conclusion of the war in the west.

Hitler instructed his generals to prepare for an assault on Russia, telling them, "The mass of the Russian Army in western Russia is to be destroyed by daring operations." Hitler's goal was to crush the Russians before they were fully prepared for war and before the end of the war against England. According to General Halder's notes Hitler said, "The war against Russia will be such that it cannot be conducted in a knightly fashion. This struggle is one of ideologies and racial differences and will have to be conducted with unprecedented, unmerciful and unrelenting harshness."

The attacking German force numbered more than three million men and 3,400 tanks, divided into three groups. One aimed north for Leningrad, one for Moscow and a southern force targeted the Ukraine. The German Blitzkrieg exhibited the same precision and fury that had been evidenced in the invasion of Poland. Minsk was captured within six days. The Germans massacred large numbers of Russians in that city, as Hitler's bloody policy had decreed. A few weeks later, Leningrad was surrounded and the Germans had advanced deep into the Ukraine. The panzers rolled onwards towards Moscow with Russian resistance faltering before them.

On October 3, Hitler addressed the German people, stating "I declare today, and I declare it without any reservation, that the enemy in the East has been struck down and will never rise again...Behind our troops there already lies a territory twice the size of the German Reich when I came to power in 1933." Hitler was exhibiting the megalomania that would ultimately be his undoing. His declaration was clearly premature. The Russians, after reeling from the initial shock of the German advance, were beginning to stabilize their defenses. It was also dawning on the German generals that they had badly underestimated the size and strength of Russian fighting forces.

Hitler believed that his commanders, who disagreed with his strategy, did not realize his genius. The Füehrer insulted all of his principal generals by denouncing their "minds fossilized in out-of-date theories." Hitler's directed his troops to follow the same fateful road that Napoleon had taken to Moscow as the Russian winter drew near.

In Russia, winter does not arrive suddenly. It is preceded by cold autumn rains, which turn the roads into quagmires. During October, the greatest enemy of the Germans was mud. Each gun required a team of horses and every wheeled vehicle sank up to the axels in slime. As bitter cold arrived, the Germans had no winter clothing or provisions. The German supply lines were broken by Russian flank assaults, resulting in food shortages. The Wehrmacht generals began to despair. They now faced fresh Siberian troops who were fully equipped for winter fighting. Nazi generals could not understand the ferocity of the Russian fighting men because they failed to recognize that Soviet soldiers were not fighting for communism, but for Mother Russia.

After failing to seize Moscow, as the Grand Army of Napoleon had done 130 years earlier, the Germans began to retreat. By January 1942, the Germans had been forced back more than 200 miles. Hitler himself assumed the position of Commander in Chief of the Army, now convinced that he was surrounded by fools. The German army found itself under the command of a mad corporal. On the Eastern front the war turned into a disaster and then into a catastrophe for the Third Reich. [17]

Hitler's "Final Solution"

While a master plan for Nazi society was never developed under Hitler, the Füehrer did have a vision for the future:

> *A Nazi-ruled Europe whose resources would be exploited for the profit of Germany, whose people would be made slaves of the German master race and whose "undesirable elements" – above all, the Jews, but also many Slavs in the East, especially the intelligentsia among them – would be exterminated. The Jews and the Slavic peoples were the Untermenschen—subhumans.* [18]

Hitler's goal was to make Europe "Jew-free." At first, it appeared to many that deportation was his intent and that Jews would be resettled in the East. But a darker plan had been developed in Hitler's mind and was detailed in Mein Kampf, some two decades before. Scholar and teacher Lucy Dawidowicz, author of the book, *Hitler's War Against the Jews*, deals with the origins of Hitler's policy of ritual race murder. She tells us that extermination was his plan from the earliest days, but his sinister objectives were frequently obfuscated for purposes of deniability. Dawidowicz was a young American woman, who made a "reverse migration" from New York to Berlin in 1939, to discover the truth about Hitler's intentions regarding the Jews. Her thesis about concealment of the true plan through the use of words that had several meanings is borne out through an analysis of Hitler's speeches that use such words as "Entfernung," "Aufräumung," and, "Beseitigung," which mean "removal," "cleaning up," and "elimination." But there are several instances where Hitler used other words of far less ambiguity. Consider this passage from a speech in 1922:

> *Once I really am in power, my first and foremost task will be the annihilation of the Jews. As soon as I have the power to do so, I will have gallows built in rows - at the Marienplatz in Munich, for example - as many as traffic allows.*
>
> *Then the Jews will be hanged indiscriminately, and they will remain hanging until they stink; they will hang there as long as the principles of hygiene permit. As soon as they have been untied, the next batch will be strung up, and so on down the line, until the last Jew in Munich has been exterminated. Other cities will follow suit, precisely in this fashion, until all Germany has been completely cleansed of Jews* [19]

In public Hitler was rarely this specific about his plans for the actual killing of Jews on a wholesale basis, but in private he was far more candid. Consider for example, his choice of words when having a private conversation with Foreign Minister Chvalkovsky of the Nazi-backed Czech regime. Hitler told his guest, "We are going to destroy the Jews." There is no ambiguity here. Destroy does not mean to relocate or even to eliminate. It means just what it says – destroy, as in exterminate, annihilate, liquidate, murder.

Lucy Dawidowicz and others have cited a very particular speech that Hitler made to the Reichstag on January 30,1939 as evidence of what she calls his "declaration of war against the Jews":

> *Today I will be a prophet again: If international finance Jewry within Europe and abroad should succeed once more in plunging the peoples into a world war, then the consequences will be not on the Bolshevization of the world and there with a victory of Jewry, but on the contrary, the destruction of the Jewish race in Europe.*[20]

Here again, Hitler is specific, using the "destruction of the Jewish race in Europe," which does not allow any misinterpretation. These words could not be construed to mean anything like resettlement or deportation, for no part of Europe would be a haven since he meant to destroy Jews in every part of the continent. And consider the words of Albert Speer, one of Hitler's most intimate colleagues and the Minister of Wartime Production for the Reich, describing that very speech, where he interpreted the word destruction as meaning "extermination":

> *The hatred of the Jews was Hitler's driving force and central point, perhaps even the only element that moved him. The German people, German greatness, the Reich, all that meant nothing to him in the final analysis. Thus, the closing sentence of his Testament sought to commit us Germans to a merciless hatred of the Jews after the apocalyptic downfall. I was present in the Reichstag session of January 30, 1939 when Hitler guaranteed that, in the event of another war, the Jews, not the Germans, would be exterminated. This sentence was said with such certainty that I would never have doubted his intent of carrying through with it.*[21]

Hitler cannot be dismissed as merely a madman although his unsound mind is well recognized. Hitler exhibited a conscious and "obscene delight" at the prospect of exterminating an entire people, revealing "a Hitler fully conscious of his malignancy."

History tells us that Hitler wanted to engage in ritual extermination based on race and his own definition of "sub-human" beings, who he believed did not deserve the right to bear children, who might carry on their name and their traditions. This darkest of all deeds is perhaps the most famous genocide in history – the crime for which the very word "genocide" was developed.

The policies of human extermination actually began in Germany during the early 1930's when German "eugenics" laws were passed that required genetic "inferiors" to submit to forced sterilization. About 350,000 people were subjected to surgical or radiation procedures. Later institutionalized or handicapped patients were transferred to special gas chambers where they were killed, simply because they were "incurable." "Babies, small children, and other victims were thereafter killed by lethal injection, pills and forced starvation."

The extermination of the Jews began on November 9, 1938 on Kristallnacht, or "Night of Broken Glass." Nazi thugs roamed streets throughout Germany, breaking windows, vandalizing Jewish businesses and burning synagogues. These attacks resulted in the destruction of more than 100 synagogues and 7,500 Jewish businesses. More than 25,000 Jews were arrested and sent to camps. Hundreds were attacked and beaten and more than 90 Jews were murdered. Orchestrated by Himmler and the S.S., the Kristallnacht rampage was less formalized than the later mass killings, but for the victims, it was no less lethal.

As the Third Reich expanded by conquest, the number of laborers pressed into slavery greatly increased, resulting in millions of deaths through malnutrition, disease, neglect of hygiene, lack of medical care and overwork in extreme conditions. Many of the victims of these labor schemes were Jews, Gypsies, homosexuals, Slavic peoples and Russian prisoners of war, whose treatment was a "flagrant violation" of the Geneva conventions. Gestapo killers complained that exhausted Russian captives often fell dead before their executioners could savor a last measure of cruelty. In the conquered lands the Nazi's followed a policy of deliberate terror under the Nacht und Nebel Erlass ("Night and Fog Decree"). Hitler personally devised this grotesque policy, which authorized seizure of those thought to be security risks. Hundreds of thousands of victims then vanished into the night and fog, without a trace.

The systematic machinery of death was the most chilling aspect of the Nazi slaughter of innocents. Within the Third Reich, this program became known as the "Final Solution." It began with mass shootings in the occupied territories, by Nazi's known as "Einsatzgruppen," mobile killing squads who followed the invading German military assaults to carry out Hitler's orders. Near Kiev, at a location known as Babi Yar, an estimated 33,000 persons, mostly Jews, were shot to death during two days. Hitler's desire to increase the kill rates was the subject of a formal conference that was held on January 20, 1942 at a lakeside villa in Wannsee. While the final protocol issued from this conference was deliberately vague, in the meeting there was little attempt at obfuscation. The group agreed that their ultimate objective was the extermination of millions of European Jews, who lived in some 20 countries. The Wannsee conference was the catalyst for the organization of the state machinery of death and it greatly enhanced the Nazi capability for mass murder, through the application of technology.

Six weeks before this conference, the S.S. had achieved a significant improvement in efficiency over the procedure of shooting by instead using sealed vans and carbon monoxide gas to suffocate their victims at Chelmno, in Poland. Most of the victims were Polish Jews. For the remainder of 1942, thousands of train cars transported men, women and children from all over Europe to designated killing centers, Belzec, Sobibor, Treblinka, Chelmno, Majdanek and Auschwitz-Birkenau, all located in Germany and Poland. By the end of the year, the Germans had achieved a new level of automated death and had exterminated more than 4 million people. According to Holocaust survivor Elie Wiesel:

> *While not all victims were Jews, all Jews were victims. Jews were destined for annihilation solely because they were born Jewish. They were doomed not because of something*

they had done or proclaimed or acquired, but because of who they were, sons and daughters of Jewish people. [22]

What went on in these centers of organized slaughter can never be fully comprehended by anyone who did not experience it firsthand. The only way to even get a glimpse of the macabre process of systematic killing is to learn from someone who survived it. What follows are excerpts from a powerful book entitled, *Five Chimneys*, by Olga Lengyel, a survivor of the death complex at Auschwitz-Birkenau. She describes the mass murder of innocent people from the time they arrived on daily transport trains:

While the deportees were being disembarked, the camp orchestra, inmates in striped pajamas, played swing tunes to welcome the new arrivals. The gas chamber waited, but the victims must be soothed first. Indeed, the selections at the station were usually made to the tune of languorous tangos, jazz numbers and popular ballads. To one side the ambulance trucks waited for the sick and aged... The old, the sick and children under 12 were sent to the left, the rest to the right. To the left meant the gas chambers and the crematory of Birkenau, to the right meant temporary reprieve in Auschwitz...

Distressing episodes resulted from the separations, but the Nazis showed that they were not petty. When a young woman insisted that she would not be separated from her old mother, they often gave in and let the deportee rejoin the person she did not want to leave. Together they went when they left to quick death.

Then, always to the sound of music - I could not help but think of the Pied Piper of the legend - the two corteges began their procession. In the meantime, the service internees had assembled the baggage. The deportees still believed they would get their possessions back when they arrived at their destinations.

*Other internees placed the sick into the Red Cross am-
bulances. They handled them tenderly until the march-
ing columns were out of sight, then the behavior of the
SS slaves changed completely. Brutally, they threw the
sick into the dumping trucks, as if they were sacks of
potatoes, for the ambulances were now filled. As soon
as everybody was pushed in, with the prisoners groan-
ing and shouting out of sheer terror, the cargo was sent
off to the crematory ovens... To the captivating tunes
played by the internee musicians, whose own eyes misted
with tears, the cortege of the condemned wound toward
Birkenau.*

*Fortunately, they were unconscious of the fate that
awaited them. They saw a group of red-bricked buildings
agreeably laid out and assumed it was a hospital. The
SS troops escorting them were irreproachably "correct".
They were hardly that polite dealing with selectionees
from the camp, whom it was not necessary to treat with
kid gloves; but the newly arrived had to be handled properly to the very end. The condemned were led into a long
underground viaduct called "Local B", which resembled
the hall of a bath-house. Up to 2,000 persons could be
accommodated.. The "Bath Director", in a white blouse,
distributed towels and soap - one more detail in the immense show. The prisoners then removed their clothing
and disposed of their valuables on a huge table. Under
the clothes hangers were plaques declaring in every language, "If you want your effects when you get out, please
make note of the number on your hanger".*

*The "bath" for which the condemned were being prepared
was nothing but the gas chamber, which was right off the
hall. This room was equipped with many showers, the
sight of which had a reassuring effect upon the deportees. But the apparatus did not function and no water
came to the faucets.*

Once the condemned had filled the long, low, narrow gas chamber, the Germans stopped the play. The mask was off. Precautions were no longer necessary. The victims could not escape nor offer the least resistance. Sometimes, the condemned, as though warned by some 6th sense, recoiled at the threshold. The Germans pushed them in brutally, not hesitating to fire pistols into the mass. As many as possible were crowded into the room. When one or two children were left out, they were thrown on top of the heads of the adults. Then the heavy door shut like the slab of a crypt.

Horrible scenes took place within the gas chamber, although it is doubtful that the poor souls even suspected then. The Germans did not turn on the gas immediately. They waited. For the gas experts had found it was necessary to let the temperature of the room mount by a few degrees. The animal heat given off by the human herd would facilitate the action of the gas.

As the heat increased, the air fouled. Many of the condemned were said to have died before the gas was turned on. On the ceiling of the chamber was a square opening, latticed and covered with glass. When the time came, an SS guard, in a gas mask, opened the peephole and released a cylinder of "Cyclone B", a gas with a base of hydrate of cyanide which was made at Dessau.

Cyclone-B was said to have a devastating effect. Yet this did not always happen, probably because there were so many men and women to kill that the Germans economized. Besides, some of the condemned may have had high resistance. In any case, there were frequently survivors; but the Germans had no mercy. Still breathing, the dying victims were taken to the crematory and shoved into the ovens.

*According to the evidence of former internees at Birke-
nau, many eminent Nazi personalities, political men
and others, were present when the crematory and the gas
chambers were inaugurated. They were reported to have
expressed their admiration for the functional capacity of
the enormous extermination plant. On the inauguration day, 12,000 Polish-Jews were put to death, a minor
sacrifice to the Nazi Moloch.*

*The Germans did let a few thousand deportees at a time
live, but only to facilitate the extermination of millions
of others. They made these victims perform their dirty
work. They were part of the "Sonderkommando." Three
or four hundred serviced each crematory oven. Their
duties consisted of pushing the condemned into the gas
chambers, and after the mass murder was accomplished,
of opening the doors and hauling out the corpses. Doctors and dentists were preferred for certain tasks, the latter to salvage the precious metal in the false teeth of the
cadavers. The members of the Sonderkommando also
had to cut the hair of the victims, a reclamation that
provided additional revenue for the National Socialist
economy...*

*For, paradoxical as it may seem - and this was not the
only paradox in the camps - the Germans furnished a
special doctor to care for the slaves in the extermination
plant...From the eyewitness reports, one can gather what
the spectacle in the gas chamber was after the doors were
opened. In their hideous suffering, the condemned had
tried to crawl on top of one another. During their agonies some had dug their fingernails into the flesh of their
neighbors. As a rule, the corpses were so compressed and
entangled that it was impossible to separate them. The
German technicians invented special hook-tipped poles,
which were thrust deep into the flesh of the corpses to pull
them out.*

Once extracted from the gas chamber, the cadavers were transported to the crematory. I have already mentioned that is was not unusual that a few victims should be still alive. But they were treated as dead and were burned with the dead.

A hoist lifted the bodies into the ovens. The corpses were sorted methodically. The babies went in first, as kindling, then came the bodies of the emaciated, and finally the larger bodies. Meanwhile, the reclamation service functioned relentlessly. The dentists pulled gold and silver teeth, bridges, crowns and plates. Other officials of the Sonderkommando gathered rings, for despite every control, some internees had kept theirs. Naturally, the Germans did not want to lose anything valuable. The Nordic Supermen knew how to profit from everything. Immense casks were used to gather the human grease which had melted down at high temperatures. It was not surprising that the camp soap had such a peculiar odor. Nor was it astonishing that the internees became suspicious at the sight of certain pieces of fat sausage. Even the ashes of the corpses were utilized - as fertilizer on the farms and gardens in the surrounding areas. The "surplus" was carted to the Vistula. The waters of this river carried off the remains of thousands of unfortunate deportees. [23]

The Nazi's were meticulous in their planning and implementation of the "production schedule" for these facilities. Each camp had a Totenbuch (death book) and until very late in the war, they were carefully kept. At Auschwitz-Birkenau the S. S. processed 360 corpses every half hour or 17,280 corpses during each 24-hour shift. According to Olga Lengyel it was, "An admirable production record – one that speaks well for German industry."

There had been intense competition for contracts to provide the machinery of death to the camps. Correspondence between the S. S. and their contractors was first revealed at the Nuremberg trials in which mass death was discussed very matter-of-factly, with references to "electric elevators for raising the corpses," and "for putting the bodies into the furnace, we suggest simply a metal fork moving on cylinders." As the war collapsed around Germany, an effort was made to kill as many Jews as time would permit, despite the obvious outcome of the war. This tends to support the sworn statement of Albert Speer, that only the extermination of the Jews had true and lasting importance to Hitler. Frequently, Allied troops would arrive at death camps to find the ovens were still warm.

There were also ghastly medical experiments at the camps that spoke of a personal level of sadism and inhumanity that went beyond a "lust for mass murder." The experiments were carried out on Jews, Polish inmates, Russian POW's and even a few German prisoners. They were subjected to "high altitude" tests, "lethal doses of typhus and jaundice" and freezing experiments where they were left naked in icy water in the snow to slowly freeze to death. At Dachau and Buchenwald experiments were performed on gypsies to see how long they could live on salt water. At Ravensbrueck camp for women, the so called "rabbit girls" were given gas gangrene wounds and others were subjected to horrible bone grafting. These were slow, sadistic murders, with no scientific purpose, conducted by doctors with no regard for medical ethics.

A mad scientist named Professor August Hirt insisted on maintaining a "large collection of skulls" for racial comparisons. Hirt suggested severing the heads from the body while alive and hermetically sealing them in cans for his collection. Human skins were collected by the Nazi's for use as lampshades, a favorite décor item of Frau Ilse Koch, wife of a camp commandant, known to inmates as the "Bitch of Buchenwald." Especially prized by Frau Koch was skin that was tattooed. But the "Bitch" was not the only customer. A Czech physician prisoner, Dr. Frank Blaha testified at Nuremberg that at Dachau, demand for such skins far outran supply.

Jews died in many other ways under the Third Reich. During the summer of 1942, reports of mass murder at the killing centers reached the Warsaw ghetto. A surviving group of mostly young people formed an organization called the Z.O.B. (a Polish acronym for Jewish Fighting Organization). In January 1943, Warsaw ghetto fighters fired upon German troops who were sending a group for deportation to the camps. On April 19, 1943, German troops and police entered the ghetto to deport those who still survived. Seven hundred and fifty courageous fighters fought the heavily armed Germans and held out for nearly a month. On May 16, 1943, the Germans crushed the resistance. Of the more than 56,000 Jews captured, about 7,000 were shot and most of the others were sent to death camps.

The Collapse of the Third Reich

As the extermination of Jews continued the war raged on, but news from the front was not good for the Nazi warlord. After the fall of Stalingrad, Hitler still had visions of regaining the initiative on the Eastern Front, but his hopes were dashed with the complete defeat of Hitler's Operation Citadel in March of 1943, near Kursk, Russia. In only five days, the Wehrmacht lost more than 30 divisions and more than a half million men. German forces would never again be on the offensive in the East. Even worse for Hitler, the Russians were advancing on the Fatherland at an alarming rate. Allied bombing was beginning to hurt Germany badly, with the British bombing by night and the Americans bombing in daylight. Morale was declining along with war production.

In June of 1944, the Allied forces successfully landed a huge invasion force on the beaches of Normandy, France. By July 4, the Russians were converging on East Prussia and all available reserves were rushed to protect the German Fatherland. Without reinforcements in the west, the Germans were doomed to face an ever-growing invasion force that continued to land men and equipment in France. Germany now faced its greatest fear – a two front war.

There was a serious plot to kill Hitler by his own military on July 20, 1944 by use of a bomb at a conference center in East Prussia. Although traumatized and singed, Hitler escaped with his life. Retribution against the perpetrators was swift and violent. The final death toll of conspirators was 4,980 although Gestapo records show more than 7,000 arrests. By the time of these killings there was little time left for Germany and for Hitler.[24]

The Allied armies in the west retook Belgium and the Netherlands within weeks, and by August 23, Paris was largely under the control of French resistance fighters. With astonishing speed American, British and Canadian forces swept towards Germany, not allowing the Germans to set up a defense. By the end of August, the Germans had lost 500,000 men on the Western Front. Hitler denounced his generals for a defeatist attitude:

> *If necessary we'll fight on the Rhine. It doesn't make any difference. Under all circumstances we will continue this battle until, as Frederick the Great said, one of our damned enemies gets too tired to fight any more.*[25]

Hitler was losing touch with reality. He ordered a "total mobilization," sending thousands of young boys and old men to their deaths. Speer had been right – Hitler did not care about the German people, only about his own glory and the extermination of the Jews, which proceeded at a frenzied pace despite the collapse of Germany. Hitler had only one gamble left and he called his generals together to plan a last stand. Those who were present on the evening of December 12, 1944 described Hitler's appearance:

> *A stooped figure with a pale and puffy face, hunched in his chair, his hands trembling, his left arm subject to a violent twitching, which he did his best to conceal. A sick man… When he walked he dragged one leg behind him.* [26]

In December of 1944, the Germans attempted a final Western offensive, known as the "Battle of the Bulge," a major military effort that ultimately failed. American losses were severe, but the Americans had reserves and the Germans were depleted. In the East, General Zhukov's Soviet armies crossed the Vistula and took Warsaw on January 17,1945. With 180 divisions, the Russian onslaught was unstoppable. By January 27, Russian forces were at the Oder River, one hundred miles from Berlin. As the German armies withdrew on both fronts, war production plummeted. The great German war machine went into a death spiral.

Hitler's rage now turned from his enemies to the German people, who he said, "must have been too weak." But Hitler himself was now in a tragically weakened state taking weird, poisonous drugs given to him by his "quack physician, Dr. Morrell." He had suffered a complete breakdown in late 1944, and although his health had improved slightly, "he never recovered control of his terrible temper." As more dreadful news came from the fronts, he frequently flew into bouts of "hysterical rage." When he became overwhelmed by events, he began to shake uncontrollably.

In this completely unstable state, Hitler made a fateful decision to destroy all military, industrial and communications facilities in Germany to prevent them from falling to his enemies. He ordered Germany to be made a wasteland. According to Albert Speer, "Hitler, his mission as world conqueror having failed, was determined to go down, like Wotan at Valhalla, in a holocaust of blood – not only the enemy's but that of his own people."

Götterdämmerung: Hitler's Final Days

On April 20, Hitler celebrated his final birthday in the Füehrerbunker, an underground series of chambers under the Chancellery Garden in Berlin. Life inside the bunker had degenerated into a claustrophobic nightmare of meetings regarding the military situation, chaired by an increasingly deranged Hitler who continued to issue orders, while subordinates maintained the pretense of his sanity.

The Füehrerbunker became a nest of vipers during the next few days, as both Göering and Himmler attempted to seize power from Hitler. One officer noted that by now Hitler was in, "terrible shape, dragging himself along slowly and laboriously from his living quarters to the bunker conference room,

throwing his upper body forward and pulling his legs along...
Saliva often trickled from the corners of his mouth." Hitler
prepared a final document on April 28, which was signed the
next day. This document included a personal will and a political testament.[27] In the text, he noted the treachery in their
midst:

> *Apart altogether from their disloyalty to me, Göering and
> Himmler have brought irreparable shame on the whole
> nation by secretly negotiating with the enemy without
> my knowledge and against my will, and also by illegally
> attempting to seize control of the State.*[28]

After denouncing the treachery that surrounded him, he
appointed Navy Admiral Doenitz as his successor. Hitler then
prepared for his final act by marrying Eva Braun, his mistress of
twelve years, in a simple ceremony that was followed by a wedding breakfast.

On April 30, with Russian soldiers now just blocks from the
Chancellery, Hitler and Eva said their final farewells. Hitler's
last words were, "It is finished, goodbye." The Nazi dictator and
Eva Braun then retired to their quarters while their loyal subjects waited in the corridor. Within a few minutes they heard
a single gunshot and although they waited for a second shot, it
never came. They entered Hitler's quarters to find the death
scene. Adolf Hitler lay dead in a pool of his own blood, shot
fatally in the mouth. Eva was at his side, but had not used her
own weapon. She had taken poison. The time was 3:30 p.m.
on April 30, 1945. Nothing was said as the sound of artillery
shells continued to thud in the garden above.

The corpses were taken to the garden during the next lull
in the shelling and a small party, which included Bormann and
Goebbels gave the Nazi salute as the bodies were soaked with
gasoline and torched. After the fall of Berlin the remains were
shipped to East Germany. Hitler's remains were kept until
1970, and then "secretly cremated by the KGB and dumped into
the river Elbe." As we are told by the files of Britain's MI 5, "Part

of Hitler's jaw and the top of his skull, containing the bullet wound from which he died, were removed and preserved. They are today stored in the Russian Federal Archives in Moscow." [29]

The death toll directly attributable to Hitler's regime is simply staggering – more than 75 million victims. The Nazi genocide of Jews, Gypsies, homosexuals and Slavs totaled approximately 16.3 million people. What has been categorized as "institutional killing," added another 11.3 million victims, including deaths caused by euthanasia, forced labor, prisoners of war and concentration camps. The mass murders of people in occupied Europe added another 19.3 million. Finally, there are the 28.7 million war dead, including more than five million Germans who died during the war. [30]

Germany was left in ruins and the German people were sacrificed by the millions for their support of Hitler's fantasy of a "thousand year Reich." How could someone who was once a drifter and a vagabond, without background or education use his malevolent, hypnotic charisma to seize control of greater Germany and plunge the world into total chaos? How is such a mystery explained?

Within Adolf Hitler, an "empty vessel," there occurred an evil alchemy of mythic Teutonic superiority and the most advanced race-hatred in history. What he created was a social poison that infected everything touched by his Nazi regime. Perhaps most chilling of all, the mystique that surrounded both the mythology and madness of Hitler seems to have grown beyond the life of the man.

Hitler's most extreme hatred, anti-Semitism, lives on. This was his most fervent hope, according to the final words in his political testament, which was discovered in the bunker. Even when facing his own destruction, Hitler had one final hate-filled order to issue, when he wrote: "Above all I charge the leaders of the nation and those under them to scrupulous observance of the laws of race and to merciless opposition to the universal poisoner of all peoples, International Jewry."

CHAPTER 4
Kim Il-Sung and Kim Jong-Il: Despotic Dynasty

"One is pleased to see the bugs die even though one's house is burned down."

Kim Il Sung

The oldest myth of the Korean people tells of their creation by an act of heaven. A heavenly son was transformed into an earthly creature named Hwanung, who descended to earth upon a sacred mountain. Hwanung married a bear-woman. The child of the divine son and the she-bear was Tan gun, King of Sandalwood. He became the first citizen of Old Choson, or the "Land of Morning Calm."

During the third Millennium B. C., Tan gun built his royal palace near Pyongyang, in Old Choson. According to the she-bear myth, the Korean people are the descendants of spirits that joined heaven and earth and they trace their origins to the sacred crater-lake mountain, Paektu. Koreans strongly identify with the location of their creation mythology, in the towering mountain ranges of northeastern Korea near Manchuria. A volcanic lake, known as the "Pond of Heaven," is located close to Mt. Paektu, near the Sino-Korean border. It has been described as a place of "monumental grandeur... where the broad surface of the lake, appears to be motionless, even when storms are raging overhead... one of the most enthralling sights on earth." The Korean people revere this place of legend and beauty because it provides a link to their founder, the spirit world and the kingdom of heaven.[1]

In 108 B. C., Old Choson was invaded by the Han Chinese. Later, Korea's Three Kingdoms emerged, but China continued to dominate the political and economic life of the Korean peninsula. In 635 A.D., the Han Chinese were driven north and power was assumed by the Silla Kingdom. During the Silla period, which began in 668 A.D., the people of Korea became unified. This period marked the beginning of Korean cultural development. During successive Dynasties the Koreans adopted Confucianism as the country's official religion. With the arrival of Western traders in the 19th century the nation closed its borders and became known as the "Hermit Kingdom."

The first leader of modern North Korea is said to have battled for Korean independence on the slopes of the sacred Mountain of the creation myth. He was born in the Korean village of Mangyongdae on the banks of the Taedong River, on April 15, 1912. His name was Kim Song-ju. He was born nearly two years after "National Humiliation Day," August 29, 1910, when the Japanese occupied Korea. A violent anti-Japanese uprising in 1919 was widely supported by the Christian community. Kim's parents were devout Christians and he attended a mission school run by American Presbyterians. When Kim was seven, the family made an exodus across the Chinese border into Manchuria to escape from the hated Japanese. Kim felt as if his family was set adrift, "like fallen leaves to the desolate wilderness of Manchuria."

Kim's father became a traditional medical practitioner and a Korean independence activist. Before his eleventh birthday Kim's father sent the boy back to Japanese occupied Korea to gain a "good knowledge" of his native country. His teacher in Korea was a Methodist minister and a strong nationalist, who taught patriotic songs along with Christian doctrine.

In 1923 a great earthquake in Japan provoked the Japanese to attack and kill hundreds of Korean émigrés, accusing them of taking advantage of Japanese misfortune. Kim has said that following this event he realized that the Japanese "despised

Korean people, treating them worse than beasts." He returned
to Manchuria and went to the city of Jilin, the provincial capital and a hotbed of political ferment. In 1928 he enrolled in
a Chinese school, where he met a communist teacher named
Shang Yue, who became his mentor. Opposition to Japanese
imperialism blended easily with his newly found communist
philosophy. Despite his communist views, Kim attended Christian services regularly and he retained a reverence for the beliefs of his ancestors. Kim was arrested for distributing political
handbills and he spent the frigid Manchurian winter of 1929 in
the Jilin prison. Upon his release, Kim became a revolutionary.

The Korean Patriot

During the 1920's, the Japanese exploitation of Korea
became increasingly brutal. Rice harvests were plentiful, but
Korea served as the "Rice Bowl" of Japan while the Korean
people went hungry. The Japanese occupiers ruled Korea with
extreme cruelty, using torture and disfigurement routinely as
punishment. Local women were used as sex slaves for the occupation army and Korean men were conscripted to fight for the
Japanese, as Japan's imperialist aims expanded to Manchuria
and China.

In the spring of 1930, Kim Song-ju changed his name to
Kim Il-sung. It was the name of a legendary Korean freedom
fighter, who was killed just as Kim was released from prison.
Kim joined the Chinese Communist Party in 1931 and in the
spring of that year he joined the guerrilla movement in the
Manchurian mountains. Manchuria was under the heavy hand
of a puppet government, which ruled the colony of "Manchu-
kuo" on behalf of the Japanese. Kim's revolutionary activities
consumed his entire life. He attempted to return home to see
his mother before she died, but he arrived too late. This event
seems to have evoked a strong sense of filial piety in Kim, perhaps due to shame or guilt.

In 1932, Japanese military pressure forced Chinese and
Korean nationalist forces to retreat into the Manchurian-Soviet

border area and many of Kim's comrades became common
bandits. It was a difficult time for Kim and his group of seventeen teenaged Korean guerrillas, "isolated in a bleak, wild
territory called Luozigou." With their provisions exhausted and
their clothes in rags, they hid in the mountains under the care
of an old man who took pity on them. When they emerged
from their revolutionary hibernation, they stepped into a world
of destruction. According to Kim, the Japanese were "killing
everyone, burning everything and plundering everything."
His band served in the Chinese Communist "guerrilla zones"
in Manchuria, where several small revolutionary communities
were established.

Kim later claimed that during 1933 people began to urge
him to become Korea's "Ho Chi Minh." The fact that he was
very young and had no true military experience makes this
claim seem highly doubtful. All he possessed was a name that
was stolen from a dead revolutionary. However, during the
next few years, he achieved limited success as a guerrilla leader.
In 1935, a Comintern (Communist International) report described Kim as "trusted and respected within the anti-Japanese
movement." The Japanese referred to Kim and his men as
bandits.

When the Japanese targeted Kim by name, he abandoned
the revolution and fled across the Soviet border. His first child,
Kim Jong-il, was born to a common law wife during 1942, in a
Soviet army camp located in Siberia. Under the protection of
the Soviets, Kim survived the war, rising to the rank of captain
in a combined unit of Chinese and Korean soldiers. Following the bombing of Hiroshima in August of 1945, the Soviets
entered the war against the Japanese. Upon the unconditional
surrender of Japanese forces, the Soviet military moved quickly
into Northern Korea while the Americans occupied South Korea. Kim's return to Korea, on September 19, 1945, was inaus-
picious. He was 33 years old, his arrival was on a Russian ship
and Kim was still wearing the uniform of the Soviet Army. [2]

Kim was a young and attractive figure, who wore his uniform smartly. He had handsome dark eyes, a square jaw and a
burning desire for political power. When the Soviets decided

to establish a puppet government in Pyongyang, the notorious leader of the Soviet Secret Police, Laverenti Beria, selected Kim to be their front man, with Stalin's approval. Kim was poorly educated and almost unknown in Korea but Beria and Stalin had no use for a well-known nationalistic leader with a loyal following of supporters. Kim favored Stalin's preference of Korean trusteeship under the Soviets and opposed immediate unification with the South, which put him at odds with most nationalists. He was Stalin's man and his public persona was the creation of Soviet military propagandists. According to NKVD Officer Leonid Vassin:

> *We created him from zero...we had to destroy real heroes of the national liberation movement...this is how the hero became the enemy and how the puppet we pushed forward became a hero....[3]*

The Soviets discredited the South Korean assertion that their choice was not the real Kim Il-sung and promptly smashed the reputations of other Korean leaders who were true nationalists. The Soviets arranged for Kim Il-sung to become chairman of the Korean Communist Party in December of 1945. He was named Chairman of the Interim People's Committee, making Kim the highest-ranking Korean official in the North.

Many charges of cruelty and rape were leveled at the new Russian occupiers of North Korea and in some cities students marched against the Soviets. But Kim was devoted to the ideas of Stalin and imposed a Soviet-style collective system on the country. These heavy-handed policies resulted in the migration of more than a million North Koreans to the capitalist south. Moscow provided specialists to fill the vacuum created by the exodus of these mostly upper class citizens and by the end of 1946, 90% of North Korean industry was in the hands of the state.

In the south, Dr. Syngman Rhee was elected to head the government of the Republic of Korea, which was formed on August 15, 1948, with the active support of the United States. The Cold War then settled over the Korean Peninsula. As the new ruler of the North, Kim mercilessly purged the Party of anyone opposed to his policies. On September 10, 1948, Kim announced the creation of the Democratic People's Republic of Korea (DPRK), with himself as its first Premier. He soon became the object of a self-created cult of personality. Stories were disseminated claiming that the new Korean leader had personally provided land reform and food to his impoverished people. One typical story was about Kim and a village elder:

> *Old Pak Jang-ban, given the first potato, held it in his hands, sobbing, and bowed his white-haired head deeply. Suddenly he buried his head on the Leaders chest and began to cry loudly. All his life the old man had been treated like a slave and used like a horse or bullock. Now he was treated for the first time like a human being – by no other person than General Kim Il-sung, the great Respected and Beloved Leader!* [4]

Kim modified his views on reunification and began to build a massive army. He appealed to Stalin to provide the heavy weapons and aircraft necessary to invade South Korea, telling him that he wanted to "touch the South with the point of a bayonet."

The Korean Conflict

Most of the speeches that Kim delivered had been written for him by Soviet propaganda officers and the uneducated Kim was plagued by deep feelings of inferiority. He was only able to sooth his ego by demanding "absolute obedience and lavish praise." Kim established a society that valued order above all else. His enforcement mechanisms utilized all of the coercive elements of state power. As we learn from *Rogue Regime:*

> *By 1949, his DPRK was a fully-fledged Stalinist dictatorship with labor camps, purges, arbitrary arrests, public executions and a personality cult. Kim erected*

the first statue to himself in 1949, before he was even 40 and began calling himself "The Great Leader," or Suryong. [5]

In early 1950, Kim again requested support from Stalin for his goal of reunification by military means. Stalin invited him to Moscow. Khrushchev's diary reveals that Kim presented a case based on the complementary economics of the North and South. The North had minerals and resources, but little agricultural land. The South had a better climate, vast rice paddies and excellent fisheries. After some consideration, Stalin accepted Kim's proposal. Both the Soviets and the U. S. had withdrawn their troops from Korea and America's unwillingness to fight for Taiwan was interpreted by Stalin as an abandonment of Korea as well. The Americans favored a policy of "containment" of Communism, but downplayed military guarantees to the South Korean government, fearing that such a commitment might encourage the South to launch the very war the Americans were determined to avoid.

During May of 1950, Kim visited China's Chairman Mao, at Stalin's urging, to seek support for the invasion plan. When Mao approved, Stalin gave Kim the green light to begin the war. Stalin had cleverly maneuvered China into the role of front line supporter of the forthcoming conflict, allowing the Soviets to maintain a position of influence without much risk. With the elements of military superiority and surprise on their side, the communist leaders assumed that the invasion of South Korea would be an accomplished fact before a reluctant Washington could react.

Although American diplomats believed that an invasion "had been coming since 1946," they were still shocked when a massive artillery barrage began in the early morning of Sunday, June 25, 1950. The barrage was followed by an assault of 150 Soviet T-34 tanks belonging to the Korean People's Army (KPA). Seven North Korean divisions swarmed behind the armored attack and the South Korean defenses collapsed. The North Koreans took Seoul in only three days and bewildered South Korean soldiers fled southward in a state of complete disorder. The North Koreans expected the southern people to rise up against their capitalist "oppressors." Perhaps the Communists believed too much in their own propaganda because the uprising did not occur. Although a few citizens welcomed reunification, when the North Koreans began to arrest and execute Southern "reactionaries" the mood in Seoul quickly darkened.

Kim's propaganda machine informed the North Korean people that the advance into South Korea was in response to an invasion by the Republic of Korea (ROK) and their U. S. allies. Popular anger was whipped into a frenzy of nationalistic hatred. The "Song of General Kim Il-sung," which glorified the leader, was taught to every Northern schoolchild. As North Korea prepared to declare victory, the United States requested an urgent meeting of the U. N. Security Council. The Council adopted a resolution demanding an immediate cessation of hostilities and a withdrawal of all North Korean forces to the established border near the 38th parallel.

American General Douglas MacArthur flew to Korea. Upon witnessing the inept defense by ROK troops at the Han River, south of Seoul, he recommended the commitment of U. S. forces. Thanks to a Soviet boycott of the Security Council, a UN resolution was passed that authorized the formation of a multinational force to combat North Korean aggression.

The initial American effort to delay the North Korean advance was remarkably unsuccessful. The power of the Soviet T-34 tanks and the North Korean's "disregard for human life" stunned U. S. forces. U. S. air power eventually slowed the KPA assault at the Nakdong River, north of Pusan, a port on the southeast tip of the Korean peninsula. The Americans were forced into a small and precarious enclave, but were able to avoid total defeat by protecting the "Pusan perimeter." Under the banner of the United Nations, twenty-seven other countries contributed assistance and a buildup within the perimeter began.

The KPA had taken nearly all of South Korea but their long supply lines were increasingly vulnerable to UN Command (UNC) attacks from the air. The UN Aircraft were conducting carpet bombing missions so the KPA, "could neither fight nor move during daylight." UNC reinforcements poured into the perimeter. By mid-September, the U. S. Eighth Army command-ed more than 500 medium tanks and were bolstered by a flow of fresh troops.

Chairman Mao sent word to Kim to beware of a landing at Inchon that could cut Korea in two, but Kim was focused almost solely on Pusan. Mao proved prescient. As the U. S. prepared for a breakout from the Pusan perimeter, General MacArthur was developing a plan to make an amphibious landing at Inchon on the Yellow Sea, midway up the western coast of the Korean peninsula, just twenty-five miles from Seoul. A two-division force successfully made the Inchon landing on September 15, despite dangerous tides and high sea walls. UNC forces took the capital and returned Seoul to President Rhee on September 29.

The advance of the U. S. Army out of the Pusan perimeter broke the stranglehold of North Korean forces, forcing many KPA soldiers to flee into the mountains to escape. The U. S. agreed to accept General MacArthur's proposal to press on to Pyongyang, unaware that Mao had already established the 38th parallel as a "trip wire" for his direct intervention.

A shocked Kim Il-sung vowed to "fight until the end" and ordered his troops to defend Pyongyang at all costs. However, KPA forces had been decimated in the south and were unavail-able for the defense of his capital. On October 19, American forces and their South Korean allies stormed the Northern capital and seized Kim's command bunker. It was found to contain portraits of Stalin in every room and plaster busts of both Stalin and Kim in his private office. Kim was driven into a mountain hideout and was forced to send his family to China for safety. Watching the unfolding calamity from Beijing, Mao had always suspected that Chinese troops would be needed and he had positioned several elite units near the Chinese-North Korean border as early as July.

On October 8, just after the American First Cavalry Divi-sion crossed the 38th parallel into North Korea, Mao ordered the "Chinese People's Volunteers," as his forces were known, to "march speedily to Korea and join the Korean comrades in

fighting the aggressors and winning a glorious victory." The
U. S. 24th Division reported taking Chinese prisoners near the
Yalu River in the far north, but no one believed them. Soon
headquarters was forced to face the fact that a 300,000 man
Chinese force had joined the war. While the Americans were
bogged down on North Korea's rutted roads, Chinese troops
traveled lightly, carrying only "a bag of rice, an army coat,
ammo and a rifle." The Chinese attacked at night in massive
numbers and UNC units began to take heavy casualties. The
United Nation's front lines crumbled just as the bitter North
Korean winter set in. On November 28, General MacArthur
notified Washington that "we face an entirely new war."

UNC forces abandoned Pyongyang on December 5 and
their retreat was swift. During the next two years the Korean
War became a savage struggle, during which Seoul again fell to
the Communists. They were repulsed for a second time and
prolonged talks about an armistice began while casualties on
both sides mounted. General MacArthur was relieved of his
command for contravening U. S. policy and he became a somewhat tarnished national hero. By late 1952 the conflict seemed
destined to become a bloody stalemate.

Former U. S. General Dwight D. Eisenhower campaigned
for President on a promise to "go to Korea," which voters assumed would mean an end to the war, even if it required extreme measures. The unexpected death of Stalin in March of
1953 and a threat by the Americans to use nuclear weapons finally brought an end to the fighting. A ceasefire agreement was
signed on July 27, 1953 at the neutral village of Panmunjom. It
established a 155-mile long, two-and-a-half-mile-wide "demilitarized zone" between the two Koreas. The South Koreans angrily
refused to sign the agreement. The line was established roughly
where it had been when hostilities broke out in 1950.[6] The war
had gained nothing but the human toll was dreadful:

> *Altogether, three million civilians lost their lives and*
> *another five million became refugees. During the brief*
> *occupation of the south, 84,000 were kidnapped and*
> *200,000 pressed into the North's military...Seoul alone*

changed hands three times. The war created 100,000
orphans and a million people fled from the North to be-
come refugees in the South. [7]

As many as one million Chinese died in the Korean war,
including one of Chairman Mao's sons. The U.N. Command suffered more than 550,000 casualties, including
nearly 95,000 dead. U. S. casualties totaled 33,629 Americans killed, 103,284 wounded and 5,178 missing in action
or captured. North Korea lost 2.5 million people, or about
one quarter of its pre-war population. At the conclusion of
the conflict the northern nation was in ruins. The devastation was far worse than had been suffered under Japanese
occupation. In almost any political system in the world, Kim
Il-sung would have been deposed and perhaps killed by his
own people. But Kim's propaganda machine convinced the
people that his brilliant leadership had saved them from the
"imperialists." The population was completely oblivious to
the fact that his reckless adventurism had caused the slaughter one fourth of the nation for no gain whatsoever.

Kim's strategy for dealing with abject failure was to continue to proclaim that North Korea had won a great victory.
"At the time when we had been able to live a worthy life,
built up on our own after the liberation, the U. S. imperialists ignited the war," he told his people. The official biography of Kim Il-sung is blatant propaganda but it has been
accepted as truth by North Koreans:

> *The People's Army and the whole Korean people stood*
> *like a mountain towering in the sky, brandishing their*
> *sharpened arms. On top of the mountain stood Com-*
> *rade Kim Il-sung, the iron-willed brilliant commander,*
> *who held in his hands the general outcome of the war,*
> *looking down upon the panic-stricken U.S. imperialist*
> *aggressors with calm and shining eyes.* [8]

The Chinese "volunteer" army remained in North Korea until 1958 but Pyongyang's propaganda made no official mention

of their role in the war. On July 28, 1953, the title of Hero of the
Democratic People's Republic of Korea, the National Flag First
Class and the Medal of the Golden Star was conferred on Marshal Kim Il-sung, who had "organized and led the Korean people and the People's Army to a shining victory in the Fatherland
Liberation War." The people were fed slogans and lies about
their leader while Kim's perceived enemies, including about
90% of his Generals were purged, to prevent any criticism of his
leadership. The victims of these purges were exiled, imprisoned
at hard labor or killed. Kim held show trials for many who were
framed on charges of collusion with the United States.

A tactic favored by Kim was to award promotions to gain
favor with his subordinates, "then, at the moment they became
careless or inattentive, he would either purge or remove them
like a lightning bolt out of the blue." He drew North Korea
behind a wall of secrecy making it the most isolated nation on
earth. When the people had been completely subjugated, Kim
Il-sung proceeded to construct one of the most frightening
slave states the world has ever seen.

The God King

Following the war, a quasi-religious cult that worshiped Kim
was developed. Knowing nothing of the outside world, the
North Koreans believed that the small improvement in their
standard of living was a great achievement. "Meetings of revenge," were held in almost every village, in which the people
were taught about the "bloody atrocities" of North Korea's
enemies. They were told that American pilots dropped disease-
bearing insects, plague, anthrax, and other hideous afflictions
on them during the war and that only the protection of the
"Fatherly Leader" had saved them from the horrors of these attacks. The people were expected to be forever grateful to Kim.
Every community swarmed with spies and informants of the
regime to assure Kim of the undying loyalty of every citizen.

What the North Korean people believed to be an "egalitar-
ian paradise" was achieved with massive foreign aid from both

the Soviet Union and China. By 1954, Kim had developed collective farms modeled after the Soviet system and the Chinese "Great Leap Forward." These were programs that eventually brought economic disaster to both nations. Complete control of North Korea by the Communist Party was achieved through isolation, coercion and a form of mind control that pervaded the entire country. Kim's philosophy of "Juche" or self-reliance became the mandated belief of every citizen. There was no opposing view. As the Soviet Union and China began to show "revisionist" tendencies, North Korea held fast to its "Juche" ideology, which more closely resembled "Neo-Confucianist" thinking than Communism. Kim imposed a belief system that was remarkably similar to a religious orthodoxy prevalent from the 16th to 20th centuries in Korea, which suppressed all other thought systems, especially Buddhism.

Kim's synthesized belief system manifested Confucian principles of feudalism, which allowed the concept of dynastic succession, but was completely at odds with all recognized forms of Communism. Some experts have compared "Juche" to State Shinto, which was practiced by the Japanese imperialists. Under this peculiar form of state religion Kim Il-sung was elevated to the status of a living God who commanded a fanatic following. "Juche" became a form of "xenophobic nationalism," with distinctly racist overtones. Kim demanded absolute mental subordination to the "Fatherly Leader" through a system that relentlessly reinforced devotion to dogma.

Deviation from the state-mandated philosophy was punished severely. At the conclusion of the Korean War, Kim established 17 labor camps to house the regime's political enemies. In 1958, a massive purge was conducted that resulted in the murder of about 9,000 party members and permanent exile for thousands more. Any indication of deviant thought among the people would result in harsh retribution. Security agents abducted suspect individuals from their homes or places of work and most were never seen again.

Kim Il-sung was housed in "almost unimaginable luxury," and he sired many children by his two official wives, many mistresses and innumerable concubines. Kim remained handsome into middle age, except for a protruding goiter on the left side of his neck that grew to the size of a grapefruit. The unattractive growth was retouched out of all official photographs and portraits, since a God-King could not reveal such an earthly imperfection.

The number of Kim's biological children is unknown. More than one observer has noted the resemblance to the "Fatherly Leader" in many young members of the official class. Defectors from high North Korean circles have reported that his many children were raised at several of his mansions. According to biographer Bradley K. Martin, "One need only look into Korean history, though, to find the Confucian patterns that repeated themselves in the heredity North Korean ruling class that Kim Il-sung built." [9]

The God-King consumed food grown in special greenhouses, farms and orchards. Each grain of rice he ate was polished individually, "so he would get not a single bad grain." All party workers were required to wear lapel badges with a picture of the Leader as proof of their love and affection for him. As he aged, Kim Il-sung received medical and dietary aid to extend his life and to improve his sexual potency. The medical experts of the Kim Il-sung Institute of Health and Longevity prescribed regular consumption of dog penises, of "at least seven centimeters (2.8 inches) long," for this purpose. His sexual appetite increased to a degree that required extensive organization to secure women to satisfy his lust. Kim subscribed to the belief that frequent sex with young women would prolong life and virility. This was a belief that he shared with China's last emperor, Mao Zedong.

Kim Il-sung imposed the "droit de seigneur" (rite of the lord) upon the women of Pyongyang and he took those he wanted, even kidnapping some when necessary. He was routinely serviced by a group of young women from a "volunteer" corps, which grew into a large sexual procurement bureaucracy. The "kippeunjo" or Happy Corps was made up of actresses and singers who entertained at parties and had sex with the Leader. However, the "manjokjo," or Satisfaction Corps, "was more explicitly focused on sexual services." Sexual favors were also provided by the "haengbokjo," or Felicity Corps. These were women recruited from the Workers' Party and from Kim's female bodyguards. They performed menial services in Kim's mansions and they were also expected to offer sex whenever the Leader requested it.

The women who made up these cadres were selected from among the most attractive young women in the country. Specialized sexual training was taught at a location known as Tongi-ri, a large mansion complex. The training was conducted in strict secrecy and the girls were taught the "special characteristics and preferences of Kim Il-sung." One of the more bizarre practices was called "the human bed." The Leader would sleep on a mattress made of naked female bodies, which was "arranged so that both top and bottom people are comfortable."

As Kim aged, he craved increasingly younger girls for his sexual satisfaction and he sought their "ki," or life force, which he believed would increase his longevity. A few of the "most beautiful thirteen-year old Happy Corps recruits" were assigned to each mansion for "training" so they would be available by age fifteen to the Leader. He enjoyed them sexually as they matured, because he believed this was "good for his health." When the women of the various sexual organizations reached retirement age in their mid-twenties, they were "given husbands chosen from among party members, including bodyguards."

A retired concubine who became a widow might be recycled. Many of them became members of the "Kwabu-jo," a new division of the female companion corps that satisfied the sexual needs of other high government officials in North Korea. But the Leader was mostly focused on the young and he articulated his affection towards children in many public statements. The following statement from Kim can be construed to have a double meaning:

> *Mix with children, share their feelings, and you will feel a strong urge to live, and you will understand that they bring beauty and variety to people's lives. You will also feel inspired with a sense of the noble duty of bringing them to full bloom and safeguarding the ideals glowing in their eyes.*[10]

The people of North Korea did not question the sexual proclivities of their "Fatherly Leader." We have learned from defectors that citizens of the nation were "happy to give their daughters to Kim Il-sung." It was an honor and an opportunity to demonstrate absolute loyalty and it assured the girls family of preferential treatment in Kim's collectivized state.

A long tradition of Shamanism (spiritual healers) and the historical assimilation of Buddhism and Confucianism are indications of a deep religious impulse that underlies the Korean character. In recent times Korean religious fervor in both the North and the South has been exceptionally strong. The North has been subjected to Kim Il-sung's bizarre form of state religion, strengthened by an extremely powerful and intrusive government propaganda campaign. The North Korean Government officially describes Kim Il-sung as a God:

> *The Sun of Love – superior to Christ in love, superior to Buddha in benevolence, superior to Confucius in virtue and superior to Mohammed in justice. The sun of the nation…not only protected the political life of the people but also saved their physical life, his love cured the sick and gave them a new life, like the spring rain falling on the sacred territory of Korea.[11]*

Divine Succession

Kim Il-sung's first-born child, Kim Jong-il, was born in Soviet territory during 1942. As a child, he was known by the Russian nickname of Yura. A younger brother, known by the Russian name Shura died in North Korea, when the six-year-old Yura repeatedly pushed him into a pond until he drowned. Kim Jong-il grew up as a "guilty and lonely child." He was raised by his father's paramour, whom he despised. She had been the rival of his mother, who died in 1949, a year after the fratricide. Jong-il developed a deep hatred for his younger stepbrothers, Pyong-il and Yong-il, who became rivals in the court of Kim Il-sung for the right of divine succession. Kim Jong-Il was devoted to only one person in his life, his younger sister, Kim Kyong-hui. They spent their childhood together in China, during the Korean War. After the war, Kim Jong-Il attended school in Pyong-yang with the children of top officials, exhibiting what has been called "self-centered and impolite behavior." By the time he reached college it was clear that his ambition was to succeed his father and to assume absolute power.

Kim Jong-Il was always short – about five feet, two inches and extremely self-conscious about his height. Indulged on a diet of delicacies, he grew into a fat, pie-faced young man, with a penchant for "wild partying, fast driving and sexual escapades." But the young Kim also had a taste for politics and he was given responsibility for North Korea's counterpart to the Chinese Cultural Revolution soon after he graduated from the University in 1964. He worked for the Central Committee and was directly involved in party propaganda. The young Kim briefly worked in his father's bodyguard detail, the closest Jong-Il ever came to military service.

Jong-Il instinctively understood that involvement in political struggle could enhance his position in his father's eyes. He assumed a role within the Central Committee to root out "bourgeois ideas and criminal acts of anti-party elements." In May of 1967, at the age of 25, Kim Jong-Il called a plenary meeting of the Central Committee and "unveiled the nature of anti-party, counter-revolutionary elements." His example led others to join in the denunciation of suspect party members. The young Kim's accusations resulted in the murder of every official targeted by his witch-hunt. The success of this purge allowed him to take his struggle for revolutionary purity on the road, where he "emerged as a leading theoretician," according to a North Korean spokesman in Tokyo. The young Kim used ideological struggle and political persecution to destroy his rivals while he shamelessly fawned over his father's deification. His goal was to assure his own ascendancy to the pinnacle of power.

He also was interested in cinema and opera. Kim Il-Jong indulged his fascination for propaganda in his nationalistic film "Sea of Blood." When "Sea of Blood" premiered in July of 1971, the production was hailed with a standing ovation and it helped to "solidify his status as the most likely successor to his father."

As the aging Kim Il-sung became more addicted to adulation, his obsequious son fed this obsession with tributes and endless sycophancy. In 1972, on the occasion of the father's sixtieth birthday, the young Kim enshrined his father as a permanent God figure by introducing a new constitution that legally established unlimited personal rule by the Fatherly Leader. This decree would also serve the ends of the eventual successor. During the birthday celebration, Kim Jong-Il unveiled a 70 foot-high statue of his father, which had been placed in the center of Pyongyang. It was covered in gold leaf and had cost more than $800 million. A new political theory, presumably inspired by Kim Jong-Il, called the "Theory of the Immortal Socio-Political Body" was announced. It stated that:

> *The Suryong (Leader) is the supreme brain of a living body, the Party is the nerve of that living body, and the masses are only endowed with life when they offer their absolute loyalty...without the Suryong, which is the brain, and the Party which is the nerve, the masses will remain dead bodies because they are no more than arms and legs...* [12]

Soon after this celebration, Kim Jong-Il's foremost rivals, his uncle and his younger half-brother "disappeared from view." The young Kim was formally anointed at a secret Workers Party politburo meeting in April, 1974 as the successor to his father, with title of "Dear Leader." Initially he kept a low public profile. Official publications began to refer to "The Party Center," as the collective leadership of father and son. Behind the scenes, Kim Jong-Il worked to win the military leadership's acceptance of his succession.

The younger Kim's portrait began to appear beside that of his father in public displays and on official buildings. But in early 1977, just when it appeared that Kim Jong-Il had successfully assured his ascent to power, his portrait was removed from public places. This episode in North Korean politics has never been fully explained. But it occurred just a few weeks after North Korean troops killed two American soldiers at Panmunjom with axes, as the Americans trimmed a tree that was obstructing their view of the truce zone. One story regarding this event asserted that Kim Jong-Il's extreme form of revolutionary leadership had inspired the embarrassing incident. Kim Jong-Il was forced to retreat into the shadows.

For more than three years the younger Kim became almost invisible to the outside world. During this time it is likely that a power struggle was taking place within the inner sanctum of the Hermit Kingdom. The details of how this impasse was resolved have never been revealed but gradually the clouds began to part. The secret struggle for succession concluded in 1980, when the Public Security Minister told western journalists that "antagonistic elements" had been "completely isolated" and would soon be "shattered." After years of working tirelessly to assure his ascendance to power, Kim Jong-Il achieved his lifetime ambition. He was rewarded with official acknowledgment of his future role as unquestioned leader of North Korea. In the fall of 1980, a Party Congress declared that the succession plan was complete, with this statement:

> *The cheers shaking heaven and earth…were an explosion of our people's joy, looking up at the star of guidance [Kim Jong-Il] shining together with the benevolent sun [Kim Il-sung].*[13]

The police and security services had grown to more than 300,000 members and a system of spying was expanded until "one out of every five students was a secret agent of the State Security branch." People learned "not to voice their innermost thoughts, even at home." Phones were tapped, letters and packages were inspected. Kim Jong-Il's thought police were everywhere, seeking out anyone who was insufficiently loyal to the regime. The punishment for any deviation from orthodoxy was more terrible than most people could ever imagine.

The entire population of North Korea was divided into three classes of people – the Core Class, The Wavering Class and the

Hostile Class. The Core Class, which included some twelve sub-groups were given priority in social and political opportunities. They were considered loyal citizens of the DPRK. The Wavering Class, the largest category, consisted of some 18 sub-groups who were considered potentially loyal. These people were allowed advancement in North Korean society, but were forced to constantly prove their loyalty to the regime. Members of the Hostile Class and all of their relatives, comprised about 27% of the population, or more than six million people. These unfortunates fell under constant police surveillance. This permanent classification meant exclusion from military service, government jobs and even educational opportunities. Those who were condemned in this way, were forced to live in a condition described as "arbitrary terror." Every member of the Hostile Class was exposed to the potential of execution or long-term imprisonment for the purpose of reeducation.

The North Korean Gulag

When Kim Jong-Il took over the Party security apparatus in 1973 the number of inmates in the camps "swelled phenomenally," according to a South Korean human rights report. The expansion and reorganization of these camps, "terrified the Party elite into submission." More than 15,000 new inmates were accused of opposing Kim Jong-Il's succession. The construction of an additional four camps was authorized following the announcement in 1980 that he would succeed his father. The new facilities would soon house thousands of prisoners, who were subjected to suffering, starvation and death.

From the early days of the dictatorship in North Korea, successive rounds of purges did not increase Kim Il-sung's feelings of security. The "Fatherly Leader" told Soviet leader Andropov that he could not let up on ideological education even for one day "without fearing that subversive thoughts might creep into the minds of his subjects."[14] Every North Korean citizen was expected to attend weekly "instruction inspiration and self criticism" sessions at one of the nation's 450,000 Kim Il-sung Revolutionary

Research Centers. An offense as minor as listening to a foreign radio broadcast, writing a "reactionary" letter, or even sitting on a newspaper photo of one of the leaders could doom a citizen to the Gulag. One woman was arrested for singing a South Korean pop song. Once incarcerated in the North Korean penal system, victims were subjected to an unimaginable level of savagery. For thought crimes, such as belief in a religion, Kim Il-sung had made it clear that his security officials would show no mercy: "those of religion can do away with their old habits only after they have been killed," he stated.

Two distinct prison systems have long existed in North Korea, both of which have committed egregious violations of internationally recognized human rights. The political penal-labor colonies, known as Kwan-li-so, were reserved for persons suspected of political and thought crimes. Prison labor facilities, called Kyo-hwa-so, were meant to house prisoners charged with criminal offenses. Punishment by interrogation, torture and forced labor was practiced on North Koreans forcibly re-patriated from China. Reports from Human Rights Watch and The U. S. Committee for Human Rights in North Korea have provided gruesome details of a system of incarceration in which people are literally worked to death. Brutality is officially en-couraged and guards are actually rewarded for killing inmates who break the rules or attempt to escape. [15]

Prisoners condemned to the Gulag, live in a nightmarish world of torture, savage beatings, gnawing hunger, starvation and summary executions. The fetuses of pregnant women are aborted by injections. If that fails, their infant could be mur-dered by strangulation upon delivery. When entering camp Number 11, one former guard described seeing creatures so short and crippled he "wondered if they were human." He described a truly horrifying scene:

> On average they were about 4 feet 11, walking skeletons of skin and bone…Their faces were covered by cuts and scars where they had been struck. Most had no ears; they had been torn off in beatings . Many had crooked noses, only one eye, or one eye turned in its socket. [16]

Most inmates suffered from a 90-degree curvature of the
spine because they had repeatedly been forced to carry heavy
loads on a bodily frame that was emaciated from a starvation
diet. Up to three generations of extended families have been
held in these camps, since all relatives of the condemned have
traditionally been considered suspects. Many have been incarcerated for a lifetime of brutal labor in mining, timber-cutting
or farming. Prisoners were often seized by security people,
then tortured into confessions before being sent to the political
labor camp.

A former prisoner, identified as Lee M. by Human Rights
Watch, described rations for loggers in the Number 15 camp at
Yoduk as "450 grams of corn and wheat boiled into "a gruel."
This is less than 16 ounces of food per day. Work usually began at 5:30 in the morning and continued until 11:00 at night.
There were typically only two toilet breaks a day and "there
is only one toilet for every 300 prisoners." Chul-Hwan Kang,
became a prisoner at Yodok camp at the age of nine, when his
entire family was incarcerated. He survived there for ten years:

> *Few people at Yodok survived more than ten years. I had
> a strong will to survive. There was nothing I did not
> eat: snakes, rats, frogs, whatever I could lay my hands
> on . Some of us would find worms in the ground or from
> the river. Some could not do this. Those who could not
> eat anything just perished.* [17]

Inmates were routinely beaten with iron chains, rubber
belts, wooden sticks, hung upside down, electrocuted and
force-fed water. Punishments included isolation cages so small
that there was no room to stand or sit. Some have been punished by being forced into positions that cut off blood circula-
tion, eventually causing paralysis or death. Prisoners have been
killed for small infractions. One was beaten to death for trying
to eat the leather handle on a whip. Another, who attempted
to escape, was killed by being dragged behind a car. Fellow
prisoners were forced to place their hands on his bloodied
corpse. One prisoner, who cried out at this grisly scene, was immediately shot to death.

Eyewitnesses have testified that some prisoners were subjected to tests for chemical or nerve agents. Written directives have been smuggled out of North Korea verifying this human experimentation. The documents provide biographical details of each person used for such purposes. The victims of these experiments nearly always died an agonizing and hideous death.[18]

There are numerous accounts of human experiments, such as the following from Camp Number 22, by a former North Korean official, who changed his name to Kwon Hyuk:

> *I witnessed a whole family being tested on suffocating gas and dying in the gas chamber. The parents, son and a daughter. The parents were vomiting and dying, but till the very last moment they tried to save the kids by doing mouth-to-mouth breathing. (Hyuk has drawn detailed diagrams of the gas chamber he saw) ....The glass chamber is sealed airtight. It is 3.5 meters wide, 3m long and 2.2m high. [There] is the injection tube going through the unit ...Scientists observe the entire process from above, through the glass.* [19]

Lee Soon-ok, best known for the book, *Eyes of the Tailless Animals*, which chronicles her years in a woman's re-education camp, gave similar testimony:

> *An officer ordered me to select 50 healthy female prisoners. One of the guards handed me a basket full of soaked cabbage, told me not to eat it but to give it to the 50 women. I gave them out and heard a scream from those who had eaten them. They were all screaming and vomiting blood. All who ate the cabbage leaves started violently vomiting blood and screaming with pain. It was hell. In less than 20 minutes they were quite dead.* [20]

Unnatural death is treated as an ordinary event in the North Korean Gulag. Ahn Myong Chul, a former prison driver at Camp 22 described an occurrence in 1991, in which the guards engaged in a competition to win a college education.

One was creative enough to lure five prisoners into climbing the camp's barbed wire fence. Then he shot them dead and qualified to be rewarded with free college tuition. Prisoners learned to expect death around them every day. One former border guard who escaped to China and then was repatriated, had been an inmate in Number 606 detention camp. He was charged with economic and political crimes and he described his experience:

> *During my stay there, 1,200 people were sent to the facility and I saw only seven people who left without physical injury or harm. Many people died because of an epidemic, and many others were shot to death. The facility generally released people when they believed that the person would no longer survive...There were about three hundred people in the camp, with a group of thirty in each room. About one hundred people were sent each month, and about ten people were dead every day. If someone didn't receive one meal per day, he would be so weak from starvation that he could not move properly. Since there were no coffins, they put the bodies on a plank and carried them to a hill and buried them.*

> *I cannot describe the situation properly. Can you imagine expecting the person next to you to die, and when the person dies, taking the corpse's clothing off and wearing it? Since the roof leaks on rainy days, the mattress is always wet. Lice are crawling all over the corpses, but the inmates use the blankets of dead people as soon as they die...When newcomers arrive at the camp, they are first taught how to bury corpses. When they enter, they are surprised to see that the detainees were only skin and bones, with faces that look black and a bad smell. The guards would shout at them, "Put your head down on the ground!" If they raise their heads, they are beaten. After having them bury corpses, the guards force them to wear the clothing off the dead bodies. [21]*

It is difficult to estimate the death rate in the camps. The constant population has been between 200,000 and 300,000 prisoners. The rate of death is thought to be in the range of 10% annually, so it is possible that up to one million people have perished within the system during the past five decades. Almost everyone living in North Korea knows someone or has a relative who has disappeared into the Gulag. The awareness of the camps has created so much terror among the people of North Korea that the entire population is in a state of perpetual fear. Any deviation from prescribed behavior could result in abduction and imprisonment. Fear of the camps has caused many to attempt escape from the country. Thousands flee into China each year, only to be returned to a mandatory minimum sentence of seven years of labor reeducation. The Gulag system has succeeded in imposing complete mind-control upon the people of North Korea but it has a second purpose – slave labor:

> *Beyond its political purpose of terror and control, North Korea's gulag has an economic dimension of which the world has been previously unaware. This side of the atrocity has only come into focus as former North Korean political prisoners and prison camp guards have risked their lives to defect to South Korea in recent years...For the cash-starved regime, political prisons and concentration camps have become a vital cog in the production machine... To fill their institutional quotas, prisons must obtain – by any means necessary – fresh supplies of prisoners to replace the considerable number who die under the draconian conditions.*[22]

The regime depends on prison production to meet both domestic and export goals. While the system serves a security function, until recently its economic role has been obscured. Perhaps the worst thing about the North Korean Gulag is that it still exists today after more than a half century. Kim Jong-Il has expanded the brutal penal system built by his father and today he continues to command an absolute slave state.

The Deification of the Prodigal Son

A new mythology was developed around Kim Jong-Il that was more audacious in its disregard for truth than the distorted glorification that had surrounded his father. The tale of his birth was given mystic overtones, "When he was born at the foot of Mount Paektu on February 16, 1942, a double rainbow appeared and a comet traversed the sky," according to the official account of his birth. The official biography did not disclose his true Soviet birthplace, but relocated it to the sacred mountain of the Korean creation myth. By the 1980's, state propaganda had embellished the legend to include religious relics in the form of "slogan bearing trees," with such revelations as "We inform you of the birth of the bright star on Mt. Paektu." Scientists were said to have discovered auto-carved slogans, as if nature itself had confirmed the arrival of the man the state called "The God of the Contemporary World" and "The Saint of All Saints."

This "saintly figure" expanded North Korea's police state, augmented its penal system to accommodate more victims, widened the definition of "thought crimes," and ramped up the brutality in the black hole of the North Korean Gulag. As he tightened his grip on power, the young Kim began to marginalize his father. Kim Il-sung had allowed his personal vanity to become dependent on the adulation his sycophantic son had created. This fawning tribute eventually included 70 bronze statues of Kim Il-sung, 40,000 plaster figures, 250 monuments to his achievements, 350 memorial halls and 3,500 "towers of eternal life." Every citizen was required to wear a Kim Il-sung badge on their clothing and to keep a photo of both father and son in their home and workplace. The adulation of both Kims cultivated a "grotesque climate of mutual flattery," that obscured the worsening economic conditions that had begun to grip the nation.

Kim Jong-Il enjoyed life in a style befitting a dictatorial god-figure. The young Kim kept at least eight pleasure palaces that were equipped with golf courses, stables, garages full of luxury cars, motor bikes, shooting ranges, swimming pools, movie theatres and hunting grounds stocked with wild deer and duck.

Two thousand servants, including doctors, nurses, cooks, maids, valets, gardeners, masseurs, dancing troops and bodyguards staffed his palaces. The palaces were occupied at all times, to obscure his whereabouts to potential enemies. For security reasons, his constant companions, a trio of very young and attractive women, were replaced every six months. He drove about in a collection of 100 imported limousines. "In [a] real sense, he is the richest man in the world. There are no limits on what he can do," according to a former bodyguard Lee Young-guk.

Kim Jong-Il enjoys the company of foreign women, prostitutes and strippers as well as entertainment acts, such as Russian pop singers, Turkish belly dancers and American professional wrestlers. His leisure time is filled with the enjoyment of foreign foods, wines, books, clothing and jewelry. He is especially fond of films and considers himself an auteur and a filmmaking genius.

The "Dear Leader beat his first wife, Hong Il-chon, the daughter of a revolutionary," when she failed to produce children. He divorced her in 1973, when he became the presumptive heir to the regime. Later that year, his father insisted that he marry the daughter of a general. Although she bore him a daughter, he soon had a love affair with a beautiful film star, named Sung Hae-rim, who was already married to the brother of a former schoolmate. The unfortunate husband was forced to divorce her when Kim impregnated the actress. Because she was from a wealthy family and considered politically untrustworthy she was "an unsuitable consort," so their relationship was kept a secret. When their son was born, the pressures of secrecy became even greater. Eventually Sung Hae-rim was hospitalized in Moscow for depression, where she died in 2002.

The son from this marriage, named Kim Jong-nam, was raised in secret, much like a prisoner. He later attended schools in Switzerland. His very existence was never revealed to his grandfather, Kim Il-sung. Kim Jong-Il had two daughters with Son Nui-rim, the sister of the North Korean ambassador to Russia. Kim discarded her when she became mentally ill in 1991. Another daughter of Kim Jong-Il's was born to a nineteen-year-old daughter of the Director of the North Korean

Judo Association. One of Kim's lovers, Wu In-hui, a Japanese born actress, was accused of being unfaithful and was shot on orders from Kim Jong-Il in 1979, in front of a crowd of 5,000, as the mob shouted, "Kill, kill." A mistress, who was once a singer with the Pyongyang Art Troupe, drowned herself in the Tae-dong River when Kim grew tired of her in the late 1970's.

Kim Jong-Il has had affairs with three actresses who gave birth to two sons and a daughter by the dictator. The eldest son, Kim Jong-chul might become Kim Jong-Il's successor, since the fall from grace of his first-born son, Kim Jong-nam, who was deported from Japan in 2001 at the age of 33, when he was found carrying a forged Dominican Republic passport. He and his companions said they were in Japan to see Disneyland.

The absolute power held by Kim Jong-Il allows him to order the kidnapping of anyone. He has done this repeatedly, snatching beautiful girls from Europe as well as prostitutes and entertainers from all over the world. In order to indulge his interest in cinema, he ordered the abduction of South Korean film director Shin Sang-ok and his actress ex-wife, Choi Un-hee. She was kidnapped in 1978, and used as bait to snare the Di-rector. Kim gave his hostages a large budget and a production staff to make films. Kim was directly involved in the creative process and they produced a total of seven films. The South Korean couple made a daring escape to Vienna in 1986. They have described their ordeal with the power-mad Kim in a mem-oir, *Kingdom of Kim.* In this book, Shin tells us that Kim watches film to help him understand the real world, with favorites being James Bond, Rambo, and Daffy Duck.

Kim's personal film collection includes more than 15,000 titles from all over the world. He has his women dress up in the national costumes of a country he selects once a week and serve him the cuisine of that nation. For many years he regularly became completely drunk at weekend parties that sometimes lasted for several days. His Japanese chef, named Kenji Fujimoto (a pseudonym), in his own book, has described these drunken events filled with "malicious levity." Once, after drinking all night, Kim asked Fujimoto if he had pubic hair. When he answered "yes" he was ordered to prove it by disrobing only to discover that he had been shaved while he was drunk and passed out.

Kim's drinking has increased over the years and insider reports indicate that he suffers from a serious drinking problem and sometimes goes on binges for days or weeks at a time. He maintains a massive 10,000-bottle wine cellar, perhaps the largest personal wine collection the world. He begins each day by sampling a few bottles.[23] Like his father, Kim has made his pursuit of private pleasure into an institutionalized obsession. His womanizing and the "systematic, even official exploitation of girls and young women," has affected the women as well as many North Korean men. On many occasions, his paramours have been married off to unsuspecting men after they became pregnant with Kim's children. Most of these men have raised Kim's children without ever learning the truth.

While Kim Jong-Il has used abductions to satisfy his whims and selfish desires, he has also engaged in clandestine activities for political reasons. The most serious was an unsuccessful assassination attempt on South Korean President Park Chung Hee in 1974, which resulted in the death of the South Korean first lady. The South Korean government claims that more than 450 of its citizens have been abducted by the North and remain in detention. Japan has charged that dozens of Japanese citizens have been abducted by Kim's agents and Kim has admitted to several abductions, claiming that most of these people have died while in his country. He has never explained the reasons for these kidnappings.

In October of 1983, North Korean agents attempted to assassinate South Korean President Chun Doo Hwan, while he was visiting the capital of Burma. Although the President was spared, a bomb used in the plot killed 17 senior South Korean officials and injured 14 others. Four Burmese nationals were also killed in the attack and more than 30 were wounded. In November of 1987, a South Korean Airline passenger plane and all 115 people on board disappeared over the Andaman Sea, off the coast of Burma. Two North Korean agents were blamed for the bombing that downed the aircraft.

At about the same time, North Korea began work to develop a nuclear weapons program at a facility in Yongbyon, located north of the capital. All of these activities were instituted and directed by Kim Jong-Il, who continues his plan to make North Korea a world power through military might. In support of this goal, the Korean People's Army has been built up to 1.2 million troops, making it the fourth-largest military in the world.

The Road to Starvation

While Kim Jong-Il was preoccupied with pleasure and fantasy, the collapse of the Soviet Union and the subsequent destruction of the world socialist market caused the economy of the DPRK to shrink. After Russia and China began demanding settlement of trade in hard currency, the North Korean economy plunged by nearly 30% in one year alone. In 1991, a new propaganda slogan urged the people, "Let's eat two meals a day instead of three," hinting at official recognition of a looming crisis. But this was not the beginning of food shortages in North Korea.

Lee Min-bok, a North Korean agricultural expert first noticed a man dying of hunger during a research trip to the northeast in 1987. Alarmed, he began to study the problem and became convinced that the nation's agricultural production was dangerously inadequate and that the food distribution system was no longer working. By his estimates the nation was short by perhaps as much as a million tons of food per year. This is enough to feed about three million people. "The problem was not outside factors, nor our farming skills, but the whole economic system," Lee said, "Everyone knew how to please the Great Leader – all you had to do was lie."

At first local officials falsified the records to show that their quotas had been met. When officials from Pyongyang arrived to confirm the harvests, borrowing from neighboring districts would cover the shortages. The grain would be returned after the inspection to the district of its origin. Real shortages existed but they were not reflected in the records. Lee reported this finding to the government on May 31, 1990 along with his observation that peasants working individual plots produced several times more food than those working in collective fields. He expected to be rewarded for identifying the food shortage problem and was shocked when he was told that he was engaging in "reactionary activities." He was advised to keep his mouth shut. The government has maintained an almost fanatic belief in the Soviet-style collective system, despite the fact that the Soviets themselves warned the North Koreans to "avoid the mistakes it had made in 1928."

Food production in North Korea had already begun falling when the Soviet Union broke up and the Chinese began to experiment with capitalism. But North Korea continued to rely on a collective agricultural system, while supporting the growing demands of a huge military build-up. In the spirit of Juche, or "self reliance," a series of massive, ill-conceived and wasteful agricultural projects costing billions of dollars were attempted during the 1980's. They all failed. Severe droughts in 1997 and 1998 exacerbated crop failures caused by a shortage of hydroelectric power. Without the normal power, the electrical grid began to collapse. *Rogue Regime* explains the domino effect:

> *The whole system wound down like a piece of clockwork. The trains could not shift the coal because there was not enough electricity and vice versa... Without basic necessities like food, nobody wanted to work. The most productive part of the economy were the slave labor camps because the prisoners were forced to work and they regularly produced five times as much coal and food as outside workers. It is a curious paradox of all such dictatorships like North Korea's – despite all the terror and the relentless exhortation, people still cannot be compelled to work effectively. They put up a passive resistance...*[24]

During the 1990's, outsiders became aware of the gathering famine. They reported seeing emaciated people in ragged and filthy clothing with blackened faces, probably from the effects of pellagra, a potentially deadly disease caused by nutritional deficiency. The food crisis caused tension between the "Fatherly Leader," and his son, but in reality there was little Kim

Il-sung could do to regain control by this point. In December 1991, the younger Kim became supreme commander of the People's Army and in April 1993, he became chairman of the Party's Military Commission. Although the DPRK had begun operation of a nuclear reactor, they signed the Nuclear non-Proliferation Treaty and the U. S. withdrew its nuclear weapons from South Korea. The future looked promising for reduced tensions, when the DPRK joined the United Nations, in May of 1991. The North and South signed a Joint Declaration on the Denuclearization of the Korean Peninsula followed in 1992 by an Agreement on Reconciliation, Non Aggression, Exchanges and Cooperation.

In October of 1992, the U. S. and South Korea announced resumption of Team Spirit joint military exercises, to which North Korea reacted with hostility. The DPRK then announced its intention to withdraw from the Nuclear non-Proliferation Treaty. On March 8, 1993, Kim Jong-Il put the nation on a "semi-war" footing and threatened to turn Seoul into a "sea of fire." By this time, the famine in North Korea had become extremely serious. The disaster was not a famine caused by natural events – in a very real sense it was manmade. According to a detailed report by Amnesty International:

> *The actions of the North Korean government exacerbated the effects of the famine and the subsequent food crisis, denying the existence of the problem for many years, and imposing ever-tighter controls on the population to hide the true extent of the disaster.* [25]

As the food crisis began to reach truly catastrophic proportions, the political structure of the DPRK was suddenly confronted by the greatest political shock in its history. On June 28, it was announced that the leaders of North and South Korea would meet at a summit in Pyongyang in late July, the first such meeting since 1945. The 'Fatherly Leader" was in the Myohyang mountains, at his favorite summer retreat, to personally inspect accommodations for the visit of South Korean President Kim Young Sam. On July 7, 1994, he suddenly suffered a massive heart attack. He died the following day without being revived or taken to a hospital.

A high level defector later reported that the leader's coronary occurred while father and son were engaged in a heated shouting match regarding the planned summit. According to Lee Young-guk, a former bodyguard for Kim Jong-Il, the son allowed no one, including his father's doctors, to attend the stricken leader. Suspiciously, every member of Kim Il-sung's personal entourage was killed in the crash of a pair of helicopters during their return trip to Pyongyang.[26] The summit was cancelled and a period of extreme uncertainty hovered over Korea. The old leader was mourned deeply by the people of North Korea, and became in death," The Eternal Leader."

Food production continued to fall. Reports from the countryside showed increasing death rates among the very young and the very old, with many grandparents quietly going into the fields to die, in an attempt to relieve the hunger of the younger members of their families. These deaths frequently went unreported, allowing the family to continue receiving the same allotment of rations to share among fewer family members. During the month following the death of Kim Il-sung there were no public executions. Then Kim Jong-Il announced that he wanted to "hear the sound of gunshots again." Public executions were resumed and soon the pace of the killing escalated. Large crowds attended these grim spectacles, including schoolchildren who were brought by their teachers. "While several thousand people watch silently, the official reads the charges against the prisoners over a loudspeaker and asks if they admit their guilt." Usually the prisoner, already "half dead from beatings," mumbles or nods his admission and then is shot to death.

Sometimes people were executed for killing a cow or pig to feed their family, an act forbidden by the state. Others were executed for stealing food. A family of five was shot to death in Heidong, near the Chinese border for "luring small children to their house, drugging them, chopping up their bodies and mingling the flesh with pork which was then sold in local markets." The youngest family member executed in this case was 12 years old. Kim Chul Soo, a factory worker

from near the port of Hamhung, was quoted by Don Kirk of
the *International Herald Tribune* as stating, "When Kim Il-sung
was alive, when people died, the government provided a coffin. Now people are just put in the ground. At night people
go to the burial of a recent corpse, dig it up, cut it apart, cook
it and eat it. It happens, It really happens." In many villages,
"special" meat was displayed on straw mats for sale. "People
know where it came from, but they don't talk about it," said
a refugee. Another witness, named only as Lee, 54, said he
feared that his missing grandsons, aged eight and eleven had
been killed for food. As he searched widely for them, the
boys' friends said they had vanished near a market. Mr. Lee
said police who raided a nearby restaurant found body parts.
The business's owners were shot. [27]

A report from the United States Institute of Peace written
by Andrew Natsios, an internationally respected expert on the
North Korean food crisis, confirms "beginning in 1995, North
Korea's central authorities reduced the grain ration for farm
families from 167 kilograms per person per year to 107 kilograms, which was insufficient to live on." This policy change
was an incentive for farmers to cultivate private plots for household use, further reducing food national production. North
Korea's annual grain production of 9.1 million tons in 1990 fell
to 7.0 million tons in 1994, to 3.4 million tons in 1995 and to an
all-time low of 2.5 million tons in 1997 – the peak of the food
crisis. International aid to North Korea began when the UN's
World Food Program (WFP) appealed for massive supplies of
food to be rushed to North Korea in 1995. Nine years later international aid organizations were feeding more than 8 million
people in that country, nearly half of the population.

Despite the largest and longest emergency food aid operation in history, the United Nations relief effort did not really
succeed. Food distribution was controlled by Kim's regime and
the food aid was allocated based on the political usefulness of
the people to the leadership. The military and the elite were
fed first. Those despised by the regime, generally people in
the Gulag, and those considered "hostile" to the government,
were left to die. Amnesty international has reported that some

detainees in North Korean detention facilities were given 80 kernels of corn per meal, three times a day, while some were only given three to four spoons of corn meal in a small bowl of hot water three times as day. These inadequate rations amounted to a virtual death sentence. At the height of the food crisis, in 1997, Kim Jong-Il issued orders to set up facilities, known as "927 camps" to forcibly confine citizens who were caught outside their village or city without a travel permit, including people found illegally foraging for food. The regime valued order so much that it expected people to sit obediently in their homes and starve to death for Kim Jong-Il.

Aid workers were prevented from visiting many parts of the country where the crisis was most acute. The aid organizations were faced with an enormous moral dilemma about continuing with a feeding program that was corrupted by government interference or pulling out altogether, leaving millions to starve. By September 1998, many groups of NGO's including Doctors Without Borders, Action Contre la Faim, Oxfam, Medecins du Mond and Help Age International withdrew from the food operation. Save the Children partially withdrew. In many respects, according to Jasper Becker, author of *Rogue Regime*, "the United Nations [became] a silent partner in the North Korean holocaust." However, he admits that, "the system was never designed to respond to a situation where a government is prepared to let its own people die in huge numbers rather than adjust its policies or agree to minor conditions."

Although mass deaths from the famine continued well into the middle of 2004, the death rates began to abate once the most vulnerable 15% had died and there was more food for the remaining population. No one knows how many people died in this man made famine, but high-level defector, Hwang Jong Yop, estimated that the death toll was approximately 2.5 million.

From the time the "Fatherly Leader," took power in 1945 until the present moment, through the Korean War, the horror of the Gulag, extermination of enemies, diabolical human experiments, nuclear weapons development and mass starvation – the despotic dynasty has deliberately killed more than 7 million of their fellow Koreans. While some of these victims have been

South Koreans killed through infiltration, kidnapping, murder and assassination, the overwhelming majority of deaths have been people from North Korea. This level of killing represents a death rate greater than 28% of North Korea's population, one of the highest mass murder rates ever recorded. All of this suffering was to satisfy the blood lust and quest for power of two men and to provide them with personal lives of decadence and debauchery.

A Criminal State gets the Bomb

Kim has used extortion to seek payments from governments who wish to influence his behavior. He demanded a billion dollars a year from the U. S. to discontinue selling missiles to rogue states and he demanded a payment of $10 billion in reparations for Japan's colonization of Korea. While these demands were not met, other extortion attempts have been successful.

In 1997, the new leader of South Korea, Kim Dae-jung, announced the "Sunshine Policy" designed to improve relations with North Korea through generous aid and business arrangements between Pyongyang and South Korean companies. The Hyundai Corporation moved quickly to become a leader in this effort. Samsung Electronics, LG Company and the Unification Church's Tong-il Heavy Industries followed suit, but the highly controlled nature of the North Korean regime made most business ventures unworkable. The "Sunshine Policy," did progress on a diplomatic level. Kim seemed mildly receptive to the idea of reunification talks, and proved a gracious host for the summit that was finally held in mid-2000. South Korea's president, Kim Dae Jung, came to Pyongyang for the first-ever meeting of the two countries' leaders. In late 2000, U. S. Secretary of State Madeleine Albright visited Kim in Pyongyang. She reported that he seemed "knowledgeable, good humored and relatively normal."

Soon thereafter North Korea made the stunning admission that it had kidnapped thirteen Japanese citizens for training to become North Korean agents. Kim also admitted that North Korea had violated a 1994 agreement freezing its nuclear weapons program. Charges surfaced that South Korean President Kim Dae-jung's aides, operating through Hyundai, had actually bought the summit in 2000 through a payment of $500 million, which was deposited directly into the North Korean leader's account. In August 2003, Chung Mong-hun, son of Hyundai founder Chung Ju-yung, leapt to his death from the twelfth floor of the Hyundai building in Seoul. He left a note reading: "This foolish person has committed a foolish thing." The scandal called into question the Nobel Prize that Kim Dae-jung won for arranging the summit meeting.

The summit was called "Kim's coming out party," by researcher Andrew Scobell of the Strategic Studies Institute. Since the Summit Kim has visited Russia and Japan once each and China three times. He hosted Japanese Prime Minister Koizumi and Chinese President Hu Jintao in Pyongyang. But a diplomatic accord negotiated by the Clinton administration known as the Agreed Framework failed to slow nuclear weapons development in North Korea. When George W. Bush became president, he pulled out of the talks and denounced Kim's regime for cheating on the previous accords. North Korea was named as a member of the "Axis of Evil," during the 2002 state of the union address. Following this threat against Kim Jong-Il, the pace of Pyongyang's nuclear development quickened and international weapons inspectors were expelled by the regime.

In July 2006, North Korea launched seven missiles over the Japanese archipelago, posing a direct threat to Japan. The DPRK announced its first nuclear test on October 9, 2006. The failure of U. S. policy was underscored by Carlos Pascual, director of foreign policy at the Brookings Institution, when he stated, "by opting for terminating our engagement, we opened the door to North Korea's becoming a nuclear power."

Kim Jong-Il rules a highly lucrative criminal state. Through a state-owned conglomerate, known as Daesong, he heads a shadowy directorate, called Bureau 39, which is undoubtedly one of the world's largest criminal empires. Operating out of a

gray concrete building in Pyongyang, this state-run crime syndi-
cate is engaged in the production and trafficking of opium and
heroin, the manufacture and sale of billions of counterfeit cigarettes and the printing of tens of millions of dollars in forged
U. S. currency. His distribution network includes many of the
world's top crime organizations.

According to Time Magazine, as of July 2007, the North
Korean leadership was earning about $1 billion a year from this
"business." When compared to the total annual exports of the
country of about $1.7 billion, it becomes clear that Bureau 39
is Kim's largest single source of hard currency. Although the
U. S. was successful in freezing $25 million of Kim's illicit funds
in Banco Delta Asia, located in Macau, these funds were later
released as a condition of the agreement struck through the
six party talks to essentially bribe Kim into cooperation on the
nuclear question. The six parties are the U. S., China, Russia,
Japan and South Korea along with the DPRK.

Kim has become a powerful player on the world stage who,
if not admired, is at least feared. He believes that he is invulnerable, by virtue of the weapons he possesses. In the words of
researcher Andrew Scobell:

> *Kim appears eccentric, egotistical, ruthless, and extremely
> ambitious. His peculiar tastes in Western fashion and
> fascination with show business and the arts make for an
> odd mix. Observers often comment on his penchant for
> platform shoes and bouffant hairstyles, almost certainly
> intended to make him appear taller than his five foot-two
> inch stature.*[28]

The international community cannot feel secure knowing
that world leaders have allowed a man of Kim's unpredictable
character to assume the level of power he now wields. But
Kim has some glaring weaknesses. He maintains control of
the regime through an apparatus of terror, but the armed men
he keeps around him might kill him at any time. His regime
devotes an enormous amount of its financial resources to maintain the loyalty of the military and spends about 30% of its GDP

on the military establishment. The police state required to maintain absolute discipline among a populace of about 22 million people is very costly. Andrew Scobell's *SSI report* clarifies:

> *While totalitarianism is a powerful and intimidating system, it places tremendous strain on a state and a society – demanding constant activity and mobilization of personnel and exploitation of resources. The costs of maintaining heightened ideological indoctrination, an ever-vigilant coercive apparatus, and a large national defense organization are high and ultimately debilitating.*[29]

While criminal enterprises and sale of missiles to rogue states like Iran and Syria produce substantial income, the nation still suffers shortages and deprivations. In some respects, Kim is locked into a trap of his own making. Opening up the system to reform will expose the corruption and cruelty of the leader himself, which he cannot allow. This negates the possibility of gradual easing of restrictions, at least until Kim Jong-Il passes from the scene.

Kim Jong-Il continues to starve his people, to terrorize and imprison them for even the most trivial offenses while he proceeds with development of the world's most dangerous weapons. According to former State department official David Asher, "the [North's] growing ties to organized crime groups and illicit shipping networks could be used to facilitate weapons of mass destruction shipments." It would seem unlikely that Kim would ever give up the nuclear weapons that have proved so successful in extorting other nations and maintaining a global threat. Meanwhile the UN is freeing up money that allows him to maintain his power, by continuing to feed about a third of the North Korean people.

In June of 2008, although North Korea failed to live up to disclosure commitments made to members of the Six Party Talks, the Bush Administration agreed to remove North Korea from the list of state sponsors of terrorism. This virtual capitulation to Kim Jong-Il allows North Korea to become eligible for American aid and loans from the World Bank.

Asian intelligence services have reported that Kim Jong-Il suffered a stroke in August of 2008 and he was not seen in public for several months. When he made his first state appearance since his health crisis, on April 12, 2009, he appeared grayer, considerably thinner and he walked with a slight limp. North Korea made a rocket launch on April 5 and conducted a nuclear test in May, both of which may represent saber-rattling as part of a campaign to build national unity around the successor who will eventually rule North Korea.

South Korea's National Intelligence service reports that Kim Jong-Il has "apparently chosen his third son, still in his 20's as his heir," according to the New York Times. The heir apparent is Kim Jong-un, who exhibits many characteristics of the father. There are unofficial reports that the young man is being referred to as "Commander Kim." The international community has so far failed to effectively deal the Kim Dynasty, which has starved its own people, engaged in criminal behavior, exacted diplomatic extortion and has attained nuclear weapons without significant consequences.

CHAPTER 5
Mao Zedong:
Revolutionary Emperor

"Political power grows out of the barrel of a gun"

Mao Zedong

The Forbidden City lies behind the Gate of Heavenly Peace at the center of Beijing. Today it is one of China's greatest attractions, luring millions of visitors to its great halls and magnificent towers. But nearby is another place that is truly forbidden and is hidden from tourists. The compound of Zhongnanhai, steeped in the ancient history of China, is where the true power of the empire has been centered for centuries.

The name Zhongnanhai means central and southern seas and it is often referred to as the "sea palaces." There are a number of heavily guarded access gates in the vermilion walls that surround the complex, but the main entrance is just to the west of Tiananmen Square. Behind the red lacquer door stand a group of palaces, some built by Kublai Khan. Here emperors and empresses, their ministers and concubines took their pleasure and ruled their empires. Its beginnings can be traced to the Liao Dynasty before 1125. It became the favorite summer resort of Ming emperors (1368-1644) and Qing Dynasty emperor Qian Long established it as a secret enclave in the 1750's. Within its walls imperial lakes are fed by crystal waters from the Jade Fountain, a spring that originates west of the city in the Fragrant Hills. The waters of the lakes are said to possess aphrodisiac qualities, incorporating the principles of female and male, yin and yang. It is difficult to get into Zhongnanhai, and once you are in, it is even more difficult to get out. Some who attained entrance did not escape alive.[1]

Chinese Philosophy says that "knowledge of the past is essential for an understanding of the present," and so it was in 1949 that one of the greatest students of Chinese history, Mao Zedong, decided to establish his regime in the sanctuary of Zhongnanhai. He was not called an emperor but the power he wielded rivaled that of any of his predecessors. When Mao's Red Army was on the verge of complete victory over Chaing Kaisheck's Nationalists, the communist leader virtually disappeared from public sight. He abandoned his Shaanxi Province stronghold in Yan'an but he did not rush to Beijing. Derk Bodde, a Fulbright Scholar in the capital city, noted in his diary, "So quietly and gently that one is hardly aware of it, yet inexorably, the 'red tide' draws near." [2]

Mao made his residence in the Fragrant Hills, at the Villa of the Two Wells where he could see the lights of Beijing from his terrace each evening. He had much to think about before he moved into the Study of Chrysanthemum Fragrance to become the leader of China, and he lingered in the Fragrant Hills from the early spring until October. Mao must have contemplated what a long and unusual journey he had taken. It began in the village of Shaoshan, deep in the countryside of Hunan province.

He was born in the Year of the Snake, on a day that corresponds to December 26, 1893. His father, Rensheng, was a mean-spirited, grasping peasant who had accumulated land and a small measure of prosperity. He was known to financially squeeze his neighbors after buying their mortgages. Mao's mother was named Wen Qimei, which means literally, "Seventh Sister." It is a common practice in China for girls to be simply called by their number in the family. She was a devout Buddhist and Mao was raised with Buddhist teaching and practice. At the age of six he began to help out in the fields and at age eight he attended a village school.

Mao was a rebellious boy and he detested his father, who frequently beat him for insolence. He defied authority, even defacing the village temple, then setting it on fire. His mother, however, remained devoted to the boy and sided with Mao against his father. But his life was not dreadful. He had his own bedroom, a luxury not common in Chinese village life at the time. When he was thirteen his father decreed that he should go to work to support the family. At fourteen he was betrothed to an older girl who moved into the family home. The marriage was never consummated and Mao soon left home to live with a friend.

Although Mao's father was not educated, he recognized that his willful and disobedient son was, in his words, "the family scholar." Throughout his entire life Mao maintained a love of books. In those times China was under the domination of the hated Japanese. But geopolitical events did not penetrate into Hunan province until food riots occurred in its capital city, Changsha, during the spring of 1910. This was an event that Mao said, "influenced my whole life." Mao and other young Chinese were humiliated by the weakness of China when faced with oppression, first by the Japanese and later by the Russians who were the real powers behind the Chinese throne. A famine was causing widespread hunger and starvation. The food rioters were crushed and the leaders of the revolt were dragged through the streets in cages, decapitated and then their heads were hung on lampposts.

In 1911 a revolutionary spirit began to sweep through China. The people sought the overthrow of the imperial system and the tyrannical Manchu dynasty. Calls for the Han Chinese to rise up against their Manchu rulers grew into a true revolution led by the Chinese patriot, Sun Yat-sen. The young Mao Zedong, now eighteen, became a soldier and served in the revolution. The emperor was forced to abdicate and on New Year's Day in 1912, Sun Yat-sen was sworn in as China's first President. Mao decided to return to his studies, but like many young Chinese, he was forever changed the events of that year.

The revolution may have changed the face of the government, but it had not changed China's weakness in dealing

with outside forces. The Japanese continued to exercise what
amounted to a protectorate over China. They also shared a role
with Russia in ruling Manchuria. Mao, who had become an accomplished poet, penned these lines:

> *Repeatedly the barbarians have engaged in trickery,*
> *From a thousand li they come again across Dragon*
> *Mountain.*
> *Why should we be concerned about life and death?*
> *This century will see a war*
> *The eastern sea holds island savages*
> *In the northern mountains hate-filled enemies abound.* [3]

His reference to the Japanese as "island savages," and the
Russians as "hate-filled enemies," demonstrate Mao's feelings
of patriotic distress at Chinese weakness in the face of foreign
domination.

When Mao received his teaching diploma in 1918, he departed his native province for Beijing to begin a new chapter in
his life. In Beijing he obtained a low level job at the University
library, located near the Forbidden City, where the deposed emperor still lived. Both of Mao's parents died, first his mother,
due to lymph inflammation, followed only a few months later
by his father from typhoid. He was filled with guilt because
he had failed to return home to seek care for his mother, who
died from a treatable condition. Mao, however, continued his
activism. He produced a weekly publication, the Xiang River
Review, which agitated for reform. Mao wrote: "Today we must
change our old attitudes…Question the unquestionable. Dare
to do the unthinkable." His writing in the Xiang River Review
drew wide praise and some notoriety.

By 1920 he realized that reform could only take place under
the auspices of some kind of political organization and he was
increasingly drawn to communist thinking. Mao was one of only
thirteen delegates who attended the Party's founding congress,
secretly convened in Shanghai in July 1921. The Republic of
China was by now recognized as an abject failure and warlords
ruled Mao's home province of Hunan. He returned home to

become principal of a primary school in Changsha. That winter he married Yang Kaihui, the daughter of his late former professor, and his life settled down for the first and only time. The couple moved into a small house and began to raise a family. The first son, Anying was born in October 1922, a second, Anqing arrived in November 1923 and then a third, Anlong in 1927.

The Rise of Chinese Communism

Mao became a labor organizer, working the streets and factories with little to show for his efforts. He began to suffer from neurasthenia, a form of depression, characterized by insomnia, dizziness, headaches and high blood pressure. Mao suffered from this condition for the rest of his life. The young revolutionary was a clever provincial, who shared with Hitler and Stalin an overbearing father and a doting mother. Mao's personality frequently revealed a smoldering lust for power that was almost physically visible. He was not especially muscular in appearance, but he had a lean, almost animal-like quality that made his political enemies wary. Mao exuded an extreme tenacity that, in his early years, was his greatest strength and eventually became his most terrible weakness.

Mao's work organizing in the countryside would become the hallmark of his eventual success. He believed that revolution could prevail only if the peasants were liberated and the power of their landlords crushed. He spoke of these beliefs in passionate, visionary terms:

> *In a very short time, several hundred million peasants in China's central, southern and northern provinces will rise like a fierce wind or tempest, a force so swift and violent that no power however great, will be able to suppress it. They will break through all the trammels that bind them and rush forward along the road to liberation. They will, in the end, send all the imperialists, warlords, corrupt officials, local bullies and bad gentry to their graves.[4]*

Mao foresaw a "brief reign of terror in every rural area," that would lead to an eradication of feudalism and he differentiated between revolutionary violence and the violence of war. Revolution was aimed at those who were enemies not because of what they did, but because of who they were. This was class warfare, just as the Soviet Bolsheviks had used it.

The fear of Chinese communism gave rise to organized repression by landlord militias, who meted out brutal reprisals upon peasants. It began on May 21, 1927, a day of violence and mayhem. Mao reported these events and their aftermath in June:

> In Hunan...they beheaded the chief of the Xiangtan General Labor Union and kicked his head about with their feet, then filled his belly with kerosene and burned his body. In Hubei... the brutal punishments inflicted on the revolutionary peasants by the despotic gentry include such things as gouging out eyes and ripping out tongues, disemboweling and decapitation, slashing with knives and grinding with sand, burning with kerosene and branding with red-hot irons. In the case of women, they pierce their breasts, and parade them around naked in public or simply hack them to pieces...[5]

There had been nothing like it since the gruesome repression of the Taiping rebellion during the 1850's. The death toll in Hunan province alone was more than 300,000. But following this bloodbath, which became known as the "Horse Day Incident," a telegram came from Stalin supporting the creation of a communist army, something long championed by Mao.

The Red Army

Although Mao had served for a brief time as a soldier in the 1911 revolution, he was primarily a political theorist. His work as a labor organizer in Changsha did not prepare him for the struggle that he now faced – that of helping to form an effective

fighting force from a gaggle of peasants, bandits, and mutineers from the Nationalist Guomindang army. But his vision
was clear, as this statement in August 1927 demonstrates:

> *We used to censure [Sun] Yatsen for engaging only in a
> military movement, and we did just the opposite, not un-
> dertaking a military movement, but exclusively a mass
> movement. Both Chaing and Tang rose by grasping the
> gun; we alone did not concern ourselves with this. At
> present though we have paid some attention to it, we
> still have no firm concept about it. The Autumn Har-
> vest Uprising, for example, is simply impossible without
> military force… From now on we should pay the greatest
> attention to military affairs* [6]

The newly militarized communists launched an armed rebellion in Changsha, in response to the "Horse Day Incident."
Mao took a central role in the Autumn Harvest Uprising, but it
was a disaster. In only eight days, through casualties or desertion, a 3,000-man force was reduced by half. Mao was dismissed
from the Politburo. Although this was a period of defeat and
pessimism, Mao formed an alliance with Zhu De (who had
defected from the Nationalists) and was soon brought back
into the party fold. Together they formed the Zhu-Mao army,
known officially as the Fourth Red Army.

Mao became a serious student of military strategy and tactics. He was especially impressed by the strategy of a mountain
bandit named Old Deaf Ju, who used the slogan: "All you need
to know about warfare is circling around." This approach,
especially useful for outnumbered forces, would provide distance from the enemy's main force, by leading them around
in circles, and then allowing an effective strike at the enemy's
weakest point. This would become the overriding strategy of
the Red Army in the future. Zhu and Mao even made it into a
rhyme:

> *Enemy advances, we withdraw. Enemy rests, we harass.
> Enemy tires, we attack. Enemy withdraws, we pursue.* [7]

Mao and Zhu's political philosophy embraced fair and proper treatment of peasants, for they saw the peasantry as a "sea" in which red army guerrillas could swim.

Mao had abandoned his family and his personal life was sacrificed to pursue his total commitment to the revolution. These acts were early examples of Mao's ruthless ambition and amoral behavior. In early writings he describes himself as *wu fa wu tian,* which literally means, "without law, without heaven." One passage in his journals reads, "People like me only have a duty to ourselves; we have no duty to other people." Mao met an eighteen-year-old girl named He Zizhen, who was also a devoted communist. She was a slender girl with a boyish body and a scholarly orientation. While working together they fell in love and soon she moved in with Mao and bore his child.

Nationalist leader Chaing Kaishek launched a series of military campaigns designed to use warlord forces to crush the fledgling Red Army. Using the tactics of the military rhyme, Mao denied Chaing the quick victory the Nationalists wanted by drawing in their forces, using circling, zig zag movements. Mao then struck Chaing's troops at a weak point. As a result of these engagements, seventeen Nationalist regiments were destroyed and more than 30,000 of Chaing's troops were killed, wounded or taken prisoner. These early successes were only skirmishes in a much wider war. In the fall of 1931, when Japanese troops invaded Manchuria, the situation in China changed profoundly.

Caught between the communists and the invading Japanese, Chaing was forced to fight a bloody two-front war. In the cities controlled by Nationalists forces, warlords and landowners hunted down and killed large numbers of suspected communists and communist sympathizers. Chaing's troops and his warlord allies simultaneously conducted a reign of terror throughout the countryside. They followed a policy called "draining the pond to catch the fish." Every man in a village was killed, then the village was burned and all grain and foodstuffs was seized or destroyed. During one of these raids, Mao's abandoned family was taken prisoner and his first wife, Yang

Kaihui, was beheaded. Their children were sent to Shanghai, where one died. Nationalists initially used severed heads to keep count of their victims, but when this proved cumbersome, they took ears instead.

Communist reprisals were similarly brutal and, according to reports from westerners in China, the battle took on "the intensity of religious wars." The communists conducted military sweeps that caused the deaths of thousands of landlords and rich peasants. Complicating things for the Red Army were blood purges against their own followers, as factional struggles for control raged among party leaders. Mao was, as always, in the midst of the fray, and his position in the party ebbed and flowed. The conflict between communist factions was sometimes based on ethnic rivalries or political differences, but behind these issues it was always about power.

Finding itself nearly encircled, the Red Army could not maneuver, but could only fight on Chaing's terms. The army was trapped in the southern province of Jiangxi, surrounded and threatened with annihilation. Mao vigorously supported a breakout. Their only hope was a desperate flight to safety.

For Mao personally, things were not much better. All he owned was bedding, a few personal items and some books. He Zizhen was pregnant again and his role in the leadership of the party was still uncertain. On Thursday evening, October 18, Mao crossed the Gan River by torchlight. Behind his group more than 40,000 troops followed. They were what remained of the Red Army. It took three days for the entire force, with an additional 40,000 bearers, to cross the river. The "Long March" had begun.

March to the West

There was nothing glorious about what was then called the "march to the west." The base area the communists had spent years developing was now lost. They were facing extermination at the hands of Chaing Kaisheck's Nationalist Army, which was larger and better equipped. Chaing attempted to stop the communists once and for all at the Xiang River. After a week-long battle the communist force was reduced to no more than 30,000 men. An experiment with static warfare had failed. There was talk of mutiny as the remnants of the Red Army entered Hunan province.

Soon, bitter defeat would force deep soul searching by the Red Army leadership. At the time of the terrible losses at the Xiang River, a three-man troika held power. Bo Gu was a 27-year-old ideologue and the Comintern's man in China. Zhou Enlai, despite his mandarin roots, was the political leader of the Red Army. Otto Braun, known as Li Teh, was a German military advisor. When they reached the town of Liping, the Politburo held a formal meeting to decide fighting tactics and the Army's destination. Mao's suggestion of establishing a new base near the border region of Guizhou and Sichuan was adopted, signaling a shift in power towards Mao. Zhou Enlai cast the key vote.

The Politburo met again on December 31, in the small trading town of Houchang. The politburo gave a preliminary endorsement for a return to Mao's mobile warfare principles. A final, decisive meeting was held on January 15, 1935 in Zunyi, west of the Wu River in Guizhou province. The Red Army had taken the city without bloodshed. The real battle of Zunyi would be fought with words between members of the Politburo. In an upstairs room at the home of a former warlord, twenty men conducted a long and acrimonious debate over the direction of their revolution. With braziers lit to warm them from the biting winter cold, the meeting became similarly heated. Bo Gu, as acting leader of the Party, reported that the losses they had suffered were not due to poor policy, but to the strength of their enemy. Zhou Enlai was next and he made the same case, although he admitted that errors had been made. Next, it was Mao's turn.

Mao said that it was a serious mistake to abandon the successful strategy of mobile guerrilla warfare and replace it with a defensive war dedicated to holding territory. Mao insisted that the Red Army was of paramount importance. An army that had been preserved could recapture territory. He attacked the

Politburo leaders for their "rude method of leadership" and accused them of allowing military mistakes to go uncorrected. Supporters of Mao spoke, as did those who supported the Politburo leaders. Otto Braun rancorously described Mao's actions:

> *It was obvious that [Mao] wanted revenge... In 1932... his military and political [power] had been broken... Now there emerged the possibility – years of partisan struggle had been directed at bringing it about – that by demagogic exploitation of isolated organizational and tactical mistakes, but especially through concocted claims and slanderous imputations, he could discredit the Party leadership and isolate...Bo Gu. He would re-habilitate himself completely [and] take the Army firmly into his grasp, thereby subordinating the Party itself to his will.* [8]

When the conference reconvened the next day, Mao attacked his opposition at their weakest point, targeting the discredited Bo Gu and the disliked foreigner, Otto Braun. Wisely, he left Zhou Enlai a face saving way out and Zhou took it. Zhou admitted that the military strategy had been "fundamentally incorrect." This would mark the beginning of one of the most enduring political partnerships in history between Zhou Enlai, the urbane mandarin administrator and Mao Zedong, the peasant visionary from Hunan.

Soon after this fateful meeting, the troika was dissolved and Mao was named Zhou's chief military advisor. By February, Bo Gu was replaced by one of Mao's supporters. Zhou escaped condemnation, but his power had been diluted. There would be political struggles in the future, but no one would ever again challenge Mao for leadership of the Party. In a humble rural village, a small group of men had, in effect, selected the next emperor of China.

Of course, no one could have foreseen such an outcome at the time. The bedraggled Red Army would flee into the wilderness and proceed on the legendary "Long March," through the Great Snowy Mountains, across perilous gorges, and over the Tibetan highlands, fighting the Nationalists, hunger and bitter cold. The epic journey would take a year and would cover more than 8,000 miles. The journey would involve suffering that was almost indescribable. The death toll was frightful, but under Mao's leadership, the Red Army persevered.

On September 21, 1935 the Red Army entered Hadapu in southern Gansu province and for the first time since beginning their journey, they were welcomed into a Han Chinese village. Finally, they reached Shaanxi province, where Mao would spend the next twelve years. The long march was over, but of more than 80,000 original members of the Red Army, less than 5,000 had survived.

The Philosopher of Yan'an

In the summer of 1937, considerable international attention was focused on the small walled village of Yan'an, a traditional trading center and caravan crossroads located in north-central China. Here, in the shadow of an ancient pagoda that towers over the city, Mao made his headquarters. Radical thinkers, expatriates and idealistic young Chinese made their way to the border region in Shaanxi province to be a part of what one English aristocrat called "the heroic age of Chinese communism." Survivors of the long march north had become folk heroes and attracted the adulation of those who looked to communism as the new wave for China.

Chaing Kaishek was gradually losing his hold on the population. He had been "arrested," in a mutiny of his own troops for failing to actively engage the Japanese invaders. He was later freed, but no longer enjoyed the trust of his officers. Chaing was the head of state, and he bore responsibility for the welfare of the people. This was a burden Mao did not have. Late in 1937, Chaing abandoned his headquarters in Nanjing (Nanking) leaving the city open to the Japanese, who committed some of the most gruesome atrocities of the war there, murdering as many as 300,000 men, women and children.

Tillman Durdin, a reporter for the New York Times was an eyewitness to the horror. He has called "The Rape on Nanjing" one of the "greatest atrocities of modern times. The Japanese conquerors engaged in wanton killing of Chinese and all over the city, women and girls as young as twelve were gang raped. By one estimate, 20,000 women in Nanjing were raped by Japanese troops. Many were killed and their bodies burned along with thousands of other victims of Japanese brutality. Still others were made "comfort women" and served out the war as sex-slaves for the Japanese.

In Yan'an, by contrast, the days were pleasant and leisurely. Mao spent much of his time developing a comprehensive Marxist theory. He wrote:

> *China's revolutionary war... is waged in the specific environment of China and so has its own specific circumstances and nature...[and] specific laws of its own... although we must value Soviet experience... we must value even more the experience of China's revolutionary war, because there are many factors specific to the Chinese revolution and the Chinese Red Army .[9]*

Mao was developing a communism that would be independent from Moscow and free from the treachery of Stalin, who had repeatedly undermined Mao, while continuing to prop up Chaing Kaishek. It was clear that Stalin harbored a fear of Mao as a rival for leadership in the communist world. With the publication of Edgar Snow's *Red Star over China*, the outside world was first exposed to an idealized view of the heroes of the communist revolution, and Mao's world began to change.

Mao became the philosopher king of a guerilla army. He was very appealing to the influx of attractive young women who had made their way to this backwater outpost from the cosmopolitan centers of China's coast. He Zizhen was one of those displaced by the new, livelier companions who came to Yan'an. One of them was a former Shanghai "actress" named Jiang Qing, a woman with a sordid background. Her father was a drunkard, who beat both his wife and child and her mother was

a concubine. As a young girl she was sold into prostitution, to
the sinister Kang Sheng, who would later become Mao's security chief. According to one observer who knew her in the early
years, all the men in Kang Sheng's family used her sexually.
Jiang Qing had many casual lovers and at least two marriages.
Following the Japanese invasion she made her way to Yan'an.
Kang Sheng may have been responsible for making her available to both her former husband and Mao, by acting as kind of
a proletarian pimp to advance both of their ambitions through
Jiang Qing's smoldering sexuality.

Some said Jiang Qing bore a resemblance to the woman she
replaced, He Zizhen, with a slight, boyish body a bright smile
and jet black hair. In rural Yan'an, she was regarded as a star.
She was skilled on horseback and played cards with the men.
She was twenty-three years old and her own clothes were cut to
fit tightly, to show off her young figure.

In 1940, Jiang Qing bore Mao a baby daughter – his ninth
child, including two that were given to peasants during the "Long
March." After she conceived again, she had an abortion and was
sterilized. Jiang Qing did not intend to go through the ordeals
that her predecessor had suffered. She wanted a political role,
although Mao had forbidden it. Most party members never really
accepted Jiang Qing, but she was considered Mao's wife and was
to remain so, at least for appearances, through the rest of his life.

Mao underscored his belief in violence with this statement,
"Every communist must grasp this truth: Political power grows
out of the barrel of a gun." Savagery and repression were effective tools in the hands of the new leader. Ever-present guards
enforced a philosophy that allowed no deviation or intellectual
dissent. Mao's intention was "rectifying mistaken ideas, not
the people who held them." This cunning tactic foreshadowed
later political purges when opponents were lured into exposing their views, and then destroyed by Mao's devastating counterattack. It allowed Mao to change his ideological position
on a whim, and then force devotion to his line through fear of
repression and repudiation.[10]

The first victim of the purges was writer Wang Shiwei, who
exposed what he called the "darkness of the proletariat." A sham

trial subjected him to collective denunciation, a technique that would be expanded and used against all dissidents in the future. He was sent to prison as a Nationalist spy.

The Rectification Campaign of 1942 began a long tradition of torture as a political tool in communist China. Kang Sheng was encouraged to impose secret police tactics to locate "spies and bad elements" or Nationalist sympathizers. The use of torture was expected to bring "redemption" in the form of a confession. According to Kang Sheng, seventy percent of the recruits were not politically reliable. By the conclusion of the rectification process, some 40,000 people had been expelled from the party. A later investigation of the purge showed that more than ninety percent of the accused were innocent.

A growing cult of personality resulted in adoring followers and devoted cadres of communists who venerated Mao as a man of destiny. The Red Army numbered only a few thousand men, and was by no means assured of eventual power, but Mao viewed himself as a historical figure on a par with the ancient emperors of China. Photos and illustrations of Mao with rays of the sun behind his face were repeatedly used – a graphic that had been associated with Chinese emperors throughout the ages. In 1943, Mao was elevated to Chairman of the Politburo and the term "Mao Zedong Thought" was first used. His portrait soon appeared on buildings and village walls throughout communist-controlled China. Mao's personality and ideology merged into one.

The Chinese Civil War

The collapse of the Imperial Japanese forces left Mao and Chaing to face each other in a final struggle for the leadership of China. Mao developed a plan to seize the great cities of the nation. As recruiting for his military gained increasing success, Mao eventually commanded a huge force, numbering in the millions.

As 1946 drew to a close, Chaing Kaishek was still confident. All indications were that the Red Army (now called the People's

Liberation Army or PLA), was in retreat and Chaing continued to believe that his encirclement plans would eventually wipe out the communist military force. The Nationalist Guomindang Army continued to spread themselves very thin, over-extending their line of communications and control. Mao's intelligence chief, Kang Sheng, ruthlessly purged anyone who might even consider helping the Nationalist enemy. Meanwhile, he had effectively placed spies in the highest echelons of Chaing's officer corps, which enabled Mao to be kept fully informed of Nationalist plans.

The Nationalist army maintained their troop strength by conscripting villagers who were literally dragged from the fields, leaving their families to face starvation. Instead of receiving basic training, they were guarded as prisoners. When the Nationalists took a village they left nothing in their wake. Wells were filled in, foodstuffs were contaminated, villagers were executed and the women were raped. In the cities, secret police repression and the corruption of the Guomindang was so systemic that legitimate business became almost impossible. Despite an estimated $300 billion in U. S. aid, the Nationalists were ready to collapse, and the time was right for Mao to go on the attack. The people no longer trusted or supported Chaing Kaishek and his troops had sealed their fate with the masses through their cruel treatment of Chinese citizens.

Shifting away from the strategy of mobile guerilla warfare, Mao ordered a three-pronged attack on the principle cities of China. These maneuvers were carried out with lightning speed, completely inverting the power equation of China. They were launched in mid-September of 1945 and by January of 1946 victory was within Mao's reach.

As the PLA tightened the noose around the northern cities, 200,000 Nationalist men were assimilated into the PLA. A defeated Chaing Kaishek resigned the presidency. In just over four months his army had lost more than 1.5 million men. Nanjing fell, then Hangzhou on May 3, Shanghai on May 27, forcing the Nationalists to escape to Taiwan. Taking his air force, navy, his elite combat units and more than $300 million in gold, silver and foreign currency reserves, Chaing retreated across the Formosa Straits.

All of Mainland China now belonged to the communists and to its new emperor, Mao Zedong. When the PLA detachments entered the capital of Beijing, British journalist Alan Winnington reported that the streets were lined with "shouting, laughing, cheering people." On October 1, 1949, from the Gate of Heavenly Peace, Mao announced the founding of the People's Republic of China. Ten days before this momentous event, Mao had been named head of state and his remarks included this statement:

> *The Chinese people, comprising one quarter of humanity, have now stood up. The Chinese have always been a great, courageous and industrious nation; it is only in modern times that they have fallen behind... [Today] we have closed ranks and defeated both domestic and foreign aggressors... Ours will no longer be a nation subject to insult and humiliation.*[11]

Mao had come a long way from the early days in Hunan, when he felt so despondent at the humiliating treatment of his people by their Manchu rulers and the despised foreign imperialists. After nearly 40 years of organization, struggle, and political infighting he had become the savior of modern China. He had overcome the warlords and the Nationalists and, with a small cadre of dedicated revolutionaries, had made the almost unimaginable "Long March." Mao was to rule a quarter of the world and would soon take his place as emperor, in the enclave of Zhongnanhai.

The Study of Chrysanthemum Fragrance

A month after founding of the Peoples Republic of China, Mao took up residence in specially prepared quarters in the secret world of Zhongnanhai. Mao's personal residence became the former library, which had been built for Emperor Qian Long in the middle of the 18th century. The structure, known as the Hall of Beneficent Abundance, had a shaded inner courtyard with lovely pines and cypress trees. His private quarters, known as the Study of Chrysanthemum Fragrance, included a large dining room, a vast bedchamber and a study / salon combination. It was connected to Jian Qing's bedroom and her living accommodations by a walkway. The study would become Mao's cocoon, where he was protected by three rings of guards, and served by a staff of secretaries.

His food was grown on a special farm and was tasted before it was served, as a security precaution. Mao had a personal physician and a security team that carefully advanced his every movement. He traveled by armored train. Not long after his arrival at Zhongnanhai, Mao brought back the Saturday night dances, one of his favorite pastimes from the days in Yan'an. This was his meeting place for an endless stream of increasingly younger women, sometimes in groups, whom he invited to his bed. He maintained a collection of Daoist texts containing the secrets of immortality. They suggested frequent intercourse with young girls combined with the conservation of one's "essence" as a means to prolong life.

A special group of lovely young women were recruited to serve Mao's sexual desires. These were not concubines, but were simple country girls who were awe struck by their good fortune to become Mao's bed partners. Mao was known to make love like he danced – rather clumsily but with versatility and vigor, according to one of his former partners. His behavior was clearly at odds with proletarian morality. But, Mao was not just the leader of the nation – he was China itself – and he served as both emperor and a living god of the communist regime.

His relationships with his wives were complex, and at times he arranged for them to "receive treatment" in Soviet hospitals – interludes that were perhaps a necessary emotional respite from life with Mao. He Zizhen was sent to Moscow for treatment in 1937. And during the great celebration of October 1, 1949, Jiang Qing was missing from the group of dignitaries who stood atop the Gate of Heavenly Peace. She was, at that very moment, en route to Moscow for treatment, just as He Zizhen was en route back to China. Some have speculated that their trains may have passed each other in Siberia.[12]

Mao was a brilliant poet, statesman and military strategist, but beneath it all he was still a peasant. He had what the Chinese call *tu*, or an earthy quality. Mao did not bathe, but instead had rubdowns with hot towels provided by his servants. He was never comfortable with flush toilets, but instead he preferred chamber pots, which were taken on his trips and state visits, so he could avoid the newer contraptions.

Inside the Study of Chrysanthemum Fragrance, Mao spent a great deal of his time in his enormous bed, which was well beyond king size. In addition to the young girls, Mao kept many volumes of Chinese history along with state reports on his bed, so he could spend hours reading and reflecting, bringing the ancient history of the Chinese empire to bear on his contemporary exercise of power. According to his personal physician, he was not concerned about morality and he identified with some of China's most ruthless emperors.

Mao's first great challenge as leader of the Peoples Republic came with the Korean War. As Chinese leaders celebrated the first anniversary of the Peoples Republic, the combined American and South Korean forces had pushed the North Koreans to the point of collapse when Mao agreed to send "Chinese Peoples Volunteers" into the war to prevent the presence of an American force on his border. But Stalin reneged on his offer of Soviet air support. To Mao this was the bitterest betrayal of many by Stalin and it caused a breach that never healed.

Mao used the strategy he knew best in Korea – luring his enemy into a deep penetration and then launching a counter-attack. It worked well but was costly. In the end, the Chinese lost more than 140,000 men in Korea, including Mao's eldest son, Anying. The stalemate in Korea convinced Mao that China needed to become a modern and fully armed nation to assume its rightful role in world affairs.

Fragrant Flowers and Poisonous Weeds

Partly as a result of the Korean conflict, a wave of paranoia and repression swept over China. Counter-revolutionaries by the tens of thousands were identified and executed. Some were driven to suicide. During 1950 and 1951 more than 700,000 suspects were murdered. At least 1.5 million people were sent to labor camps to have their political views reformed. Mao was personally involved in the "reform through labor" scheme, and he urged ruthless methods. "Persons …have to be executed to assuage the people's anger," Mao declared.

In 1932, before the revolution, a Western study of the Chinese economy had depicted the rural peasant standing up to his neck in water and leading a life so precarious that "even a single ripple is sufficient to drown him." Recent evidence suggests that peasants were not any better off under Mao. His policies of land reform could be summed up in one word: liquidation. Landlords were dragged before mass meetings and declared enemies of the people. They were then either beaten to death, or condemned to public execution. Mao wanted the ordinary people to do much of the killing, believing that this would firmly bond them with the revolution. By the end of 1952, more than one million landlords had been murdered merely because they were guilty of owning property.

A succession of campaigns against corruption, waste and bureaucracy were launched. The methods used during these campaigns were brutal. Workers turned in their bosses, children informed on their parents, wives turned against husbands. Mao would employ these procedures for his entire reign. Mass condemnation was used as a means of terrorizing the population. By the end of 1953, after more than two million people had been murdered, Mao fully controlled the political and social dialog in China.

Mao planned to radically change the Chinese countryside through the establishment of Agricultural Producers' Cooperatives. Although some opposition to Mao's rapid collectivization was voiced, he launched swiftly effective counterattacks on his critics and plunged more deeply into his goal of complete socialist transformation. His success was remarkable, and by 1956 the collectivization of agriculture was 97% complete. At almost the same time, he achieved complete state control of all private businesses in Beijing, through joint ownership.

Following the lead of Lenin, who said: "the unity of opposites is temporary; antagonistic struggle is absolute," Mao created and perpetuated a series of revolutions in China. The new emperor was a true revolutionary who believed that struggle was eternal. As a young man Mao had written, "it is not that we like chaos, but simply that... human nature is delighted by sudden change."

Mao told his followers that "crude methods" were things of the past. "Let a hundred flowers bloom, a hundred schools of thought contend...What is there to fear from the growth of fragrant flowers and poisonous weeds? There is nothing to fear... Among the bad flowers there might be some good flowers." With this declaration he urged people to bring forth their ideas. On May Day, 1957 *The People's Daily* featured the "Hundred Flowers" slogan on the front page. Every paper in China followed this lead.

Slowly, the idea caught on, and the people of China practiced active "blooming and contending." The people did not know that Mao had confided much the opposite to party leaders in private. He told the people that the bourgeoisie had shown great progress but he told party leaders that they were not trustworthy. He told the people that poisonous weeds should grow, but he told party leaders that the weeds would be cut down and turned into fertilizer.

The people began to voice their feelings. It was said that the communist system had become "an aristocracy divorced from the people," that China had become a "family domain all painted a single color," that the leaders received special treatment and treated the people as "obedient subjects," or "to use a harsh word, slaves." Mao had set his trap. He stated: "Some say they are afraid of being hooked like a fish... Now that large numbers of fish have come to the surface, there is no need to bait the hook." [13]

On June 8, 1957 Mao launched a savage counter offensive. More than a half million people who had spoken or written against the government were sent to labor camps, exile in the countryside, or to work in communes. Mao, isolated in his cocoon in Zhongnanhai, was removed from all restraint and reality. He exercised complete social and political control over 600 million people and beyond that he had added thought control. The stage was set for Mao's greatest and most ghastly social experiment.

A Leap into the Abyss

Without an understanding of or education in economics, Mao was ill equipped to develop a plan for China to join the top economies in the world. But he was flush with success in converting the nation to complete state control and there was no political opposition that could question his plans. At the Central Committee meeting in October of 1957, Mao announced radical and far-reaching goals for China. He pledged the greatest crop yields in the world and said that China would attain 20 million tons of annual steel production within fifteen years. This was a quantum leap over 1956 production levels. He also instigated a bizarre plan of the four no's – no rats, no sparrows, no flies and no mosquitoes. Mao believed that agricultural nuisances could be defeated with this policy. People were reported to be running about in the streets screaming and waving flag-like sheets on poles to prevent sparrows from landing. Millions of sparrows died from exhaustion. But Mao had failed to listen to the warnings of experts that extermination of the sparrows would allow caterpillars to infest agricultural crops.

In early 1958, Mao left the capital on a four-month armored train tour of the provinces, so that he could be informed through inspections at the grass roots level. But Mao was so isolated by his entourage that he learned nothing. In fact, the tour gave him the dangerous impression that he was well informed and encouraged him to believe that nothing was beyond his grasp. He announced that steel production would exceed forty million tons annually within fifteen years, double what he had predicted only two months before. He pledged to overtake Great Britain as an economic power. The annual steel production estimate was raised again and again. Eventually he was predicting that China would overtake the U. S. within a few years and produce more steel than all other countries in the world combined – some 700 million tons within a decade.

The steel forecasts along with fantastic projections for agricultural production were a clear indication that Mao had lost touch with the real world. Mao launched other infrastructure projects, but the heart of his scheme was the drive for more steel. A policy of "backyard furnaces" was established and the entire countryside began to glow from peasant-run smelters. Party committees went from house to house collecting pots and pans to be melted down for steel. By the fall of 1958, nearly a quarter of the population was participating in the steel effort. This was to be Mao's greatest legacy. It was called "The Great Leap Forward." In April 1958, Mao wrote:

China's 600 million people have two remarkable peculiarities: they are first of all, poor, and secondly blank. That may seem like a bad thing, but it is really a good thing. Poor people want change, want to do things, want revolution. A clean sheet of paper has no blotches, and so the newest and most beautiful words can be written on it, the newest and most beautiful pictures can be painted on it.[14]

Mao envisioned himself as the painter, who would use the blank sheet of paper – the Chinese people – upon which to paint his beautiful pictures. His arrogance and blind ambition was a formula for a catastrophe of epic proportions.

By the spring of 1959, it had become clear that the steel produced by the peasants was of literally no value whatever. Not only had the country been stripped of steel and metal objects, but wooden homes, fences and fruit trees had been sacrificed to provide fuel for the furnaces. Food production was de-emphasized for home steel production and urban industrialization. The consequences of Mao's policies soon became evident. Food shortages, at first confined to the cities, began to appear. The Army was pressed into service to move grain to the areas where the suffering was extreme. PLA recruits reported scenes of severe hunger in the provinces. Some said that their own families were hungry and entire communities were without food.

On July 2, at a mountaintop conference at Lushan, Mao encouraged "making criticisms and offering opinions." An air of expectation existed in the working groups because the situation was dire and becoming worse. Defense Minister Peng Dehuai decided that the Chairman needed to know the truth about the "Great Leap." He tried to see Mao personally, during the early morning, but was told the Chairman was asleep. Peng then sent Mao a "letter of opinion." While the letter contained praise for some achievements of the "Great Leap Forward," there was considerable criticism, some aimed at Mao personally. The letter was distributed to all delegates by Mao's staff, which signaled that Peng's criticisms would be on the table at the general session.

In an acrimonious rant, Mao denounced Peng and charged him with conspiracy. Mao suggested that Peng was somehow involved in a plot with the Russians. Peng defended himself, but was crushed by Mao's overwhelming attack:

> *You wanted to bring about the disintegration of the Party. You have a plan, you have an organization, you have made preparations, you have attacked the correct line from a Rightist standpoint. (Then referring to comments by Peng from the days in Yan'an, Mao continued) [You say that] at [Yan'an], I fucked your mother for forty days. So this time, there are still twenty days to go. For you to be satisfied you want to fuck my mother for forty days this time. I tell you, you've fucked enough.*[15]

Mao's intimidating words found their mark and the Central Committee passed a resolution that branded Peng as heading a "Rightist opportunist anti-Party clique," and of directing "vicious attacks" at the Chairman. Peng was stripped of his governmental position. Peng was evicted from his residence in Zhongnanhai and lived for years under virtual house arrest. Lin Biao, a Mao loyalist, was named the new Defense Minister.

An early draft of the document denouncing Peng had been flown to Jang Qing, who was at a beach resort in Beidaihe. She called Mao telling him that she would come to Lushan immediately. He told her "don't come, the struggle is too acute." She ordered a plane and hurried to Mao's side. This was a dramatic development, both politically and personally for Mao and Jang Qing. During the years of their marriage she had become marginalized and she was kept out of Mao's political life. His constant infidelities were an insult to her pride and her illnesses had become more pronounced over the years. She lived in constant fear of being abandoned by Mao. She exhibited a violent temper with servants, who were terrified of her. Mao's personal physician has written, "Jiang Qing was the most pathetically dependent, the most slavishly loyal, and the most unabashed flatterer of anyone in the inner circle." She now joined Mao in his hour of need and she would remain in high profile for the remainder of his life.[16]

The condemnation of Peng shattered the brotherhood of the Long March. For the first time, Mao was faced with a true national crisis and his leadership itself was in serious dispute. The party had to decide – they were either with Mao or with the dissidents, led by General Peng Dehuai. But Mao had an almost primal power, much like a force of nature that could sweep over everything, like a raging storm, changing the landscape into his own unique design. It was a force that he used repeatedly to maintain absolute power. Mao prevailed and what began as a purge of a few critics became a full-fledged political bloodletting.

A campaign against "Rightist opportunism" was unleashed, which eventually snared six million people, who were banished or forced into "Reeducation." Many communist cadres were eager to prove loyalty to Mao. Their actions caused a redoubling of the government's commitment to the "Great Leap," making a serious situation worse and even more lethal.

The gruesome results of the "Great Leap" increased and the death toll continued to rise. The continuing dispute with the Soviets added to the crisis. Russian technical advisors were withdrawn and all Russian aid was terminated. The breach between former communist allies was now an open wound. The Soviet action did extreme damage to the Chinese economy and conditions continued to worsen in China. More than one hundred million acres of land were rendered useless by the worst drought in a century. And then, in a strange twist of fate, nature brought a devastating flood that covered fifty million acres. China descended from hunger into famine.

The famine was hidden from Mao. When he visited a model commune, he saw piles of vegetables placed along the main road. "Officials told him that the peasants had dumped the vegetables because they had grown so much food they did not know what to do with it." His train passed fields with bumper crops as far as the eye could see. This was Potemkin agriculture, in which transplanted crops had been brought from other locations. They were usually placed close together to give the appearance of extravagant abundance. Mao's advance team left nothing to chance, even painting over the trees that had been stripped of their bark by starving peasants who had eaten it in desperation. Exports of grain were stepped up to bolster the Chairman's image abroad. Every ship that departed China's harbors condemned thousands more to death.

Agricultural production levels plummeted as the crisis became more severe. Party officials ordered troops into the villages. Peasants were tortured and murdered for refusing to hand over secret stores of grain that did not exist. The few meager foodstuffs that could be found were seized for the Army and the leadership. Large numbers of peasants were essentially starved to death by their own government. The suffering during this time was beyond anything ever imagined in the West.

Jasper Becker, a BBC journalist, who lived for several years in China, has documented the full story in his 1996 book, *Hungry Ghosts: Mao's Secret Famine.* It is a devastating account of a man-made disaster, and probably the greatest famine in all of human history. Becker expresses the belief that Mao's famine was "a deliberate act of inhumanity" and asserts that, as a mass murderer, Mao should be ranked with Hitler and Stalin. The death toll eventually reached between 60 and 80 million people and assures Mao's infamy.[17]

The disastrous famine was easily hidden from the world, because westerners were given little access to China. Those who were allowed visas were leftists, enamored with Mao and his social experiments. A leading example of such disinformation are the writings of Edgar Snow, who visited China at the height of the famine and wrote: "One of the few things I can say with certainty is that mass starvation such as China knew almost annually under former regimes no longer occurs . . ." What Snow did not know or would not tell was that in some provinces the conditions were simply so nightmarish that peasants were reduced to cannibalism to survive. In order to gain enough protein to live for a few more days, people regularly consumed the bodies of family members who had died of starvation or malnutrition.

In the most desperate of all human acts, some families reported killing and eating their own children. This was not an isolated event, but routinely became the final act of dying families. Children understood what was happening, and they were terrified of being "given" to another family. The horror of consuming the young was so painful that families exchanged children, so they would be spared the macabre ritual of killing and eating their own.

In the fairyland world of Zhongnanhai, preparations were underway for Mao's sixty-sixth birthday celebration, in December of 1959. The banquet was a sumptuous feast. According to Mao's personal physician, it was, "as extravagant as any I have ever had, consisting of the finest, most expensive delicacies Chinese cuisine can offer. We had real bird's-nest soup with baby doves, one of the rarest of Chinese dishes, and shark's fin soup cooked in a special clay pot, also rare and expensive."

Many have suggested that Mao did not know of the suffering throughout China, but those in attendance that night say otherwise. "Mao was still losing face because of the food crisis and did not want to indulge in extravagance when so many ordinary folk were suffering," according to an official. Nevertheless the leadership enjoyed opulent surroundings and sumptuous dining. One member of Mao's inner circle (called Group

One) told Mao's personal physician, Dr. Li Zhisui, "survival in Group One requires us to violate our consciences." Mao's physician confesses shame that while they were living a life of plenty, millions were starving. According to Dr. Li:

> *We in Group One had no rules. There was no law. It was a paradise, free from all restraint, subject only to the whim of Mao and the guilt that gnawed those of us whose consciences remained intact.* [18]

Mao continued to enjoy the decadence of an absolute emperor. Since he never bathed, his genitals were never washed. His doctor warned him about the potential for disease, and in fact, Mao was later found to be the carrier of a mild form of venereal disease. But Mao was unconcerned, and continued to enjoy greater numbers of ever-younger girls. "I wash myself inside the bodies of my women," he told Dr. Li. The doctor reported, "I was nauseated." Mao never brushed his teeth, only rinsing with green tea and his oral hygiene was deplorable. And yet, the young girls continued to parade into his giant bed, convinced they were making love with a god.[19]

Mao became a depraved caricature of the hero he believed himself to be. But his entourage protected him and catered to his every whim. Behind their obedient service was a bone-chilling fear of condemnation by the Party and perhaps banishment to a work camp or the countryside for "Reeducation." A still worse fate awaited anyone who might challenge Mao's authority. The more radical members of his entourage dominated Mao's inner circle. As deprivation and misery stalked the Chinese countryside, the most diabolical figures within this cadre of gangsters were increasingly using the apparatus of power for their own selfish purposes.

"He Who Does Not Work Shall Not Eat"

A bond between Mao and Jiang Qing was renewed and for the first time since the days in Yan'an, she shared his bed.

Others too, emerged with added powers, including the radical Chen Boda, the new Defense Minister Lin Biao and the ever-sinister Kang Sheng. As the famine deepened, corruption in the party grew progressively worse. During work hours Mao and his top command developed extreme economic schemes to cure what they had created and by night they enjoyed music, dance troupes, acrobats and stars of the Beijing Opera. Despite the horror that the "Great Leap" had become, Mao forged ahead with such massive construction projects as Tiananmen Square, which was constructed by a labor force of twelve thousand "volunteers."

Kang Sheng had been assembling an extensive collection of erotica for Mao, to enhance his personal collection of pornography. Included in this collection were such ancient volumes as *The Golden Lotus,* China's most famous erotic book. Others, such as hand colored "pillow books" provided foldout picture guides to sexual positions. Since Mao was now practicing sex for both pleasure and longevity, these books were essential for his enjoyment and practices in search of immortality. Mao's pornography collection soon equaled the greatest of such collections from the Qing and Ming dynasties.

Mao's sexual partners enjoyed the Chairman's attention in a "transcendent, almost mystical experience." The young women were expected to be loyal and most received permission to marry only when he was finished with them. At sixty-six, Mao was still a man of extreme sexual appetites, and he enjoyed engaging in group orgies with several of his young paramours. Dr. Li has reported that Mao's trysts were not exclusively with women. He sometimes engaged in sex with his bodyguards. Dr. Li has speculated: "...I concluded that it was simply an insatiable appetite for any form of sex."

In many provinces armed rebellions were launched by starving peasants. The PLA was called out to suppress these uprisings. Some 25 million residents of the cities were forcibly moved to the countryside to reduce the pressure on food supplies in urban areas. Slowly, the nation began to recover from the food shortages, but not until the amount of land authorized to be privately owned was increased. The concept of more pay for more work was emphasized and the old Leninist slogan, "He who does not work, shall not eat," was resurrected to serve as an acceptable communist cover for increased privatization.

By 1962, the nation was sufficiently stabilized for Mao to call a meeting to plan a fresh start after the dreadful results of the "Great Leap." He made a perfunctory statement assuming responsibility for "mistakes," but there was no apology or expression of remorse. In the countryside, relieved of quotas for home steel production, more people went back to farming the fields, boosting output enough to begin the process of recovery. The people needed to be fed regardless of the political ideology expressed by China's leadership. Deng Xiaoping used an old Sichuanese proverb to point out the obvious: "It doesn't matter if the cat is black or white; so long as it catches the mouse, it is a good cat." [20]

By any rational standard, a government that had forced the starvation of millions of its citizens would be expected to moderate its failed policies. But in Mao's China the government was no longer rational. The Chairman remained dedicated to the concept of perpetual revolution. Those who had begun a move toward privatization were unknowingly placing themselves in mortal danger.

Mao ordered Chen Boda, his leading radical, to draw up a Central Committee resolution declaring absolute support for a collective economy. Sensing danger, Deng tried to have all written texts of his "black cat, white cat" remark expunged. Mao was furious about the moderate tone that was being expressed throughout the government. He wanted steadfast opposition to imperialism abroad and capitalism at home and he believed that his disciples were backsliding on him. He warned of an attack by the forces of "feudalism and capitalism," and stated: "We must nip their counter revolution in the bud." Desperate to show loyalty to Mao's latest directives, in 1964 the leadership launched a sweeping purge of the Party in rural areas.

With the publication of the "Little Red Book," Mao's inner circle began to intensify their efforts to maintain and expand the cult of personality around him. Mao was destined to become the greatest revolutionary spokesman in the world – a virtual icon. He had considered the possibility that China could become affluent and he had rejected it, because a prosperous China would no longer be a revolutionary China.

Mao had learned nothing from the catastrophe of the "Great Leap." He would not let pragmatism come between him and his revolutionary obsession. He began to speak darkly of "leaders taking the capitalist road" and of a capitalist class "drinking the blood of the workers." He said he would deal with the "wolves" first then the "foxes." Soon China would understand what the emperor had in mind and the nation would be plunged into another devastating revolutionary struggle.

The Final Revolution

It began in a typically Maoist fashion – indirectly. The plan was to isolate and destroy many in the high command of the Party. Their response to the disaster of the "Great Leap" had been to slide back into what Mao considered "the capitalist road." The ultimate targets of the planned purge were Liu Shaoqi, his second in command and the General Secretary, Deng Xiaoping. Following the dictum that "war is politics and politics is war by other means," Mao plunged into political war against his own government.

University students put up wall posters condemning all conspirators who the Chairman imagined were a threat. Chen Boda became head of the *People's Daily*, which expressed support for Mao's "Cultural Revolution," editorializing: "Chairman Mao is the red sun in our hearts. Mao Zedong Thought is the source of our life..." The student population was whipped into a white-hot revolutionary frenzy as the witch-hunt gained momentum. Radicals at Beijing University staged struggle meetings, forcing those charged to wear dunce caps. The faces of the accused were blackened, they were forced to kneel in submission to students who kicked and punched them and bound them with ropes. They became objects of scorn and raw hatred.

Symbolizing his readiness to dive into the political fight, Mao plunged into the Yangtze River swimming and drifting downstream for over nine miles. Photos of the swimming 72-year old Chairman were published throughout the world. At the first Politburo Standing Committee meeting called in more than four years, Mao characterized those who opposed the Red Guards as acting like Guomindang warlords and he stated that Liu and Deng had carried out "an act of suppression and terror." He portrayed his enemies in the most menacing terms: "There are monsters and demons among the people present here." When these remarks were published, all who read them were electrified. The Central Committee approved a document, which outlined plans for the daluan or "great chaos" that would sweep over China for the next several years.

The Chinese people and especially the youth were motivated by an almost hysterical adoration of Mao and a cold fear of the consequences of opposing him. Targets of Mao's national witch-hunt were expanded to include "all those people in authority who are taking the capitalist road." Within a few weeks a million Red Guards from all over China gathered in Tiananmen Square in the first of ten huge rallies to formally launch the new revolution. Mao appeared with the first rays of the rising sun at 5 a.m., wearing his military uniform as a signal of revolutionary struggle.

The "Cultural Revolution" became a frenzy of political warfare with the young students ready to die and kill for Chairman Mao. Struggle meetings were held throughout the nation, and leaders, teachers and intellectuals were shamed, tortured, beaten and killed, usually by radical student groups. In one such struggle session more than 300 people were killed, including a six-week old baby and a man in his eighties.

The entire nation became terrified of the Red Guards as the children's revolution became more and more crazed with its own power. Teachers were shot or buried alive. Some people were pushed off the roofs of buildings. Others were forced to blow themselves up with explosives. As happens in many violent social upheavals, the rebels eventually turned on their own. They began to split along class lines, based on the social position of their parents. The violence targeted those believed to be insufficiently committed to the cause. Red Guards became both predators and prey.

People's heads were shaved on the street corners, temples and tombs were desecrated, priceless artifacts were plundered and monasteries were vandalized. Nearly a third of all homes were subjected to search and confiscation missions by Red Guard fanatics. In Shanghai alone, such missions resulted in the confiscation of 32 tons of gold, 150 tons of pearls and jade, 450 tons of jewelry and over six million dollars in cash. Books were special targets of the mob, with some of the most revered texts of China put to the torch.

Everything that had gone before was condemned and was to be replaced by "Mao Zedong Thought." Mao was more deified than ever before and he was thrilled by the zeal and militancy of the Red Guards. Their movement had become so powerful that no one dared to question or oppose them. During the celebration of his Seventy-third birthday, Mao proposed a toast to "the unfolding of an all-round nationwide civil war." Mao had now created another monstrous movement that led China into chaos, but his ego was completely delighted by the veneration.

By late 1966 the Cultural Revolution was closing in on the targets of Mao's wrath – Liu Shaoqui and Deng Xiaoping. Mao directed the pressure to be increased on them and others in the "Party Center." Red Guards began to terrorize these leaders and their families. A special group was set up with Mao's authorization to examine the past of high officials on Mao's hit list.

When Mao left the compound, Zhongnanhai itself fell under siege from raging Red Guards. Urged on by Jiang Qing, Chen Boda and Kang Sheng, the radicalized students even held Zhou Enlai captive for a time. Liu, Deng and their wives along with other officials were called before the struggle groups, which were conducted within the compound that was once a refuge from the outside world. These high officials were terrorized and beaten by the mob. An increasingly shrill Jiang Qing became the hands-on director of the purge. About Liu Shaoqi, she shouted: "He deserves a slow death by a thousand cuts, ten thousand cuts." Eventually, Liu died in Henan Province on November 12, 1969, while lying naked on the cement floor of an old prison. His medical care had been withdrawn and he died of pneumonia. His home had been reduced to rubble by the mob. His oldest son was beaten to death in Mongolia. Other children died in prison or killed themselves. Only his wife survived and was eventually released.

Deng Xiaoping and his family were treated less violently, but they were banished, shipped to Nanchang and placed under house arrest. Their life was Spartan, but they maintained their equilibrium. Deng was a strong individual and his family showed a similar inner strength. He was allowed the life of a simple peasant and his family was spared further brutality with the exception of two family members. One committed suicide or was murdered by Red Guards. Another, Pufang, a brilliant student at Beijing University, was seized by Red Guards and beaten badly during torture. Later he fell or was pushed from a fourth floor dormitory room window during a torture session. Denied medical care, he became a cripple for life. Eventually he was reunited with his family. Deng and his wife gave him loving care as they attempted to heal the wounds of the Cultural Revolution among their exiled family. Each day, Deng walked the compound of his simple home, thinking and keeping himself fit. He walked almost four miles daily. Deng still believed that he had a future. It was a belief that never wavered.[21]

Mao could not tolerate the idea that someone might someday become his successor. Those he promoted to a position of potential succession feared that accepting such a sensitive post would result in their downfall. This usually proved correct, as Mao would build up one successor after another only to turn on them to assure their political demise or death. The emperor's paranoia by now had taken over completely and China was strangling in the grip of a deranged political genius. He had brilliantly risen to the top of the world's largest nation but he maintained his power through intimidation, terror and never-ending revolution.

When the Cultural Revolution began to attack the PLA, a line was crossed. An article in *Red Flag* targeted the army in the Cultural Revolution's next battle against "Capitalist Roader's."

In some respects this moment parallels the right wing assault on the U.S. Army during the McCarthy period in the United States. Charging that the State Department was full of communists was one thing, but taking on the military was quite another.

Mao then made one of his well-known reversals. Following the dialectic theory, when a movement reaches its most extreme manifestation, it is transformed into its opposite. In the mind of Chairman Mao, the Red Guards had become a threat. With the Party apparatus destroyed, Mao moved to strengthen the one institution that could restore order: The Peoples Liberation Army. Mao sent word that he viewed purging the army as "unstrategic." He also approved a directive forbidding seizures of weapons by student Red Guard radicals, and he authorized the army to use armed force in self-defense.

Before it ran its course, the Cultural Revolution cast suspicion on more than ten million people. More than three million people were detained and hundreds of thousands were tortured or beaten to death. In some areas, alleged traitors were killed and their livers eaten at "banquets of human flesh" as proof of the victor's revolutionary commitment. The fortunate survivors were sent to labor camps. Mao finally moved to quell the extreme excesses of the revolution, but it was not easily defused. Many times troops were sent into provinces that had experienced violence between Red Guard factions. The shutdown of the Cultural Revolution cost another one million lives.

As the revolutionary fervor quieted, more and more military leaders were designated as members of local committees, essentially placing most of the country under military rule. At the next Party Plenum, Mao supplemented the depleted Party membership with military officers. The meeting designated Lin Biao as the successor to Chairman Mao.

Defense Minister Lin Biao began to gaze longingly at the position of ultimate power – the Dragon Throne itself. Rumor and intrigue were rife and factionalism had splintered the leadership badly. Mao, now 76, was still the center of power but he had grown more unpredictable with age and had become completely paranoid. Philip Short, in his epic *Mao: A Life*, has written, "The Cultural Revolution Group, in the late 1960's, was even more a nest of vipers than the Politburo a decade before." [22]

The Ultimate Opiate is Power

Behind the praise for Chairman Mao, a secret struggle for succession began in 1970, when Chen Boda was purged. His disgrace came as a result of his attacks on politburo members who were not fully supportive of a more glorified role for Mao. Mao was immediately suspicious of Chen Boda's motivation and acted swiftly to have his old comrade arrested. But Mao also harbored deep suspicions centered on Lin Biao, Mao's designated successor, who also supported a glorified role for the Chairman.

Defense Minister and Vice Chairman, Lin Biao was a strange and complex figure. A man of slight, almost frail build, with piercing dark eyes, he was a close ally of Jiang Qing and was an enthusiastic supporter of the most extreme elements of the Cultural Revolution. In the 1940's he had become addicted to opium and later to morphine. He had supposedly been cured of his addiction during a stay in the Soviet Union, but he was still known for erratic behavior. He was afraid of wind and light and was absolutely terrified of water – even the sound of running water would give him diarrhea. He refused to drink liquids. His wife assured his liquid intake by dipping steamed buns into water for him. He would not use a toilet, but insisted on using a bedpan while wrapped in a quilt. He was given to periodic depression. Addiction was not uncommon in the communist high command. Many had depended on sleeping pills or opium since the days of the "Long March." Mao himself could sleep only with the aid of sedatives. Morphine and other opium derivatives were used in medical practice at the time and some believe that Mao's detachment from reality may have been rooted in drug addiction.

In the spring of 1971, several of Lin's closest military commanders were informed that they were under suspicion by the

Chairman. By summer, Mao was drawing a direct bead on his Defense Minister by stating, "A certain person is anxious to become state chairman, to split the party and to seize power."

While Lin Biao himself remained somewhat detached, his staff, including his son, who was an air force officer, began to plot against Mao – even planning his assassination. By September, Mao was told of unusual activities at air force headquarters. He reacted by reinforcing his personal security detail and changing his schedule.

On September 13, Lin Biao and his party departed China, defying a nationwide ban on air travel. Zhou Enlai reported the departure to Mao. There were indications that Lin Biao's plane was headed for Mongolia. Reportedly the Chairman commented, "The skies will rain; widows will remarry; these things are unstoppable. Let them go." The next day it was learned that the plane had crashed in Mongolia and all on board were killed. Mao had again targeted a potential rival, and had destroyed him.

The Lin Biao affair took a toll on Mao, however. He was soon confined to bed, suffering a deep depression for more than two months. He was locked in a struggle with the Russians that had erupted into a shooting war on the border, relations with India were deplorable and the plot to kill him was widespread enough to require nearly one hundred of Lin's associates to be arrested in the wake of the plane crash. Mao's credibility also suffered. He had purged many of his closest colleagues and his heir apparent had been branded a traitor. Some bold stroke was urgently needed to break the cycle of failure in China. [23]

Despite the difficulties that Mao faced during those days and the strain of the Lin Biao affair, he had the audacity to initiate a stunning, almost unthinkable breakthrough in diplomatic relations. After several months of back channel discussions with the U. S. and a secret visit by Henry Kissinger, China was on the verge of an act so far removed from the established pattern of events that it would shock the world: President Richard Nixon would officially visit China as the guest of Chairman Mao.

Undeterred by his increasingly frail condition, Mao was
ready for this diplomatic drama and very excited by Nixon's visit. Zhou Enlai met the Presidential party and a hastily planned
first meeting took place, as described by Kissenger:

> *[In] Mao's study... manuscripts lined bookshelves along
> every wall; books covered the table and the floor; it looked
> more the retreat of a scholar than the audience room of
> the all-powerful leader of the world's most populous na-
> tion...Except for the suddenness of the summons, there
> was no ceremony. Mao just stood there... I have met no
> one, with the possible exception of Charles de Gaulle,
> who so distilled raw, concentrated will power. He was
> planted there with a female attendant close by to help
> steady him... He dominated the room – not by the pomp
> that in most states confers a degree of majesty on the
> leaders, but by exuding in almost tangible form the over-
> whelming drive to prevail.* [24]

As an observer of deceptively simple small talk during this
discussion, Kissinger was impressed by Mao's phrases, which
"communicated a meaning while evading a commitment ...
[like] passing shadows on a wall." This was one of Mao's greatest triumphs and soon other western nations would hurry to
Beijing to establish ties. This diplomatic breakthrough was a
victory of real politic over ideology for both Mao and Nixon,
as the revolutionary emperor and the conservative president
focused on the common interests of both countries.

The issue of succession in the aftermath of the Cultural
Revolution and the death of Lin Biao still remained unre-
solved. Mao made a decision to select Wan Hongwen, a thirty
nine year old political leader from Shanghai, as his new man.
He believed that a dark horse would bring little baggage with
him. And, in a move that would have a much more profound
impact on China, Mao rehabilitated Deng Xiaoping. On April
12, 1973, after disgrace and years of exile, Deng walked into the
Great Hall of the People for a banquet for Cambodian Prince
Sihanouk, as if he had been on a short holiday.

Jian Qing, leader of the group that Mao himself had designated as the "Gang of Four," began to make assaults on policy
with Deng Xiaoping as their target. Mao was now eighty and so
frail that he talked openly of his own death. With the death of
Zhou Enlai, in 1976, the final struggle for succession began.

Earthquake!

Zhou Enlai was the consummate survivor and a highly effective government operative. Mao had no personal affection
for him and therefore he was not accorded a ceremonial funeral. But his passing had an astonishing result – more than a
million citizens lined the streets to say their last farewell to the
former Premier of China. While none of the leadership had
noticed, Zhou had captured the hearts of the Chinese people,
perhaps because he was so quietly effective in keeping the ship
of state afloat, despite the madness of each revolutionary wave
that engulfed the nation. More than two million people visited
Tiananmen Square to honor their late Premier with wreaths
at the Monument to the People's Heroes, in direct defiance of
the government's policy. Speeches during these ceremonies
denounced Jiang Qing as the "mad empress" and her allies as
"wolves and jackals." Some even denounced Mao himself.

As the war for succession raged, Mao grew progressively
weaker. Deng dropped from sight, but he did not capitulate to
his tormentors. He knew that Mao's days were numbered, so
he held firm. When Mao stripped much of the power from a
Deng supporter, Jiang Qing moved into action, now so close to
the Dragon Throne that she could almost taste the power that
she might soon acquire as the "Red Empress" and successor to
her husband, Mao Zedong.

On the night of July 28, 1976 one of the greatest earth-
quakes of modern times, registering 7.8 on the Richter scale,
struck the city of Tangshan, near the capital. 242,000 people
died in Tangshan and another quarter of a million perished
in nearby Tianjin and Beijing. Only a few weeks later, a political earthquake struck China. In late summer, Mao weakened

further and in the early hours of September 9, 1976 Chairman Mao died after suffering a massive heart attack. The public did not react with emotion as they had with the passing of the Premier. They were shocked and apprehensive about the future but showed almost no emotion or sense of personal loss. The Politburo immediately turned against Jiang Qing. The deference that her position required when Mao was still alive turned into animosity caused by her years of scheming cruelty and personal viciousness.

Deng was in Canton under the personal protection of his longtime friend, General Ye Jianying. Despite feverish plotting by the "Gang of Four" to gain military backing, General Ye had secured extensive army support during his meetings with key military leaders. His tactic was simple – he asked the question, "Whom do you trust, us or Jiang Qing?" A notice was sent out that the Standing Committee of the Politburo would meet in Zhongnanhai on October 6 at 8 p.m. As each member of the Gang entered the hall they were denounced and arrested by Ye's military allies. Jiang Qing was seized at her villa and taken away in hysterics.

The launching of Mao's Cultural Revolution in the spring of 1966 created a social upheaval unlike any other in history. While Mao was still suffering politically from the catastrophic Great Leap Forward, he believed that by launching a "violent revolutionary storm" he could solidify his power, crush his enemies and reenergize the national fervor. He succeeded, but in the process he terrorized the nation through its children, who assaulted, beat, maimed and murdered their own teachers, elders and parents. The careers of millions of people were destroyed and an entire generation lost their opportunities for education. The death toll was enormous.

Chairman Mao had conjured up a form of mass hysteria that gripped the nation and his mysterious authority kept his subordinates "transfixed like rabbits in front of a cobra," until his death. Then, as if emerging from an evil spell, the survivors of the ordeal blamed the decade- long orgy of madness on the gang of four. Jiang Qing and her closest associates were all sentenced to prison terms after a show trial in 1981. Jiang Qing committed suicide in prison a decade later.

The way was cleared for Deng Xiaoping's comeback and his succession to the position as the leader of all China. Mao had been right about Deng all along. He was a capitalist roader, but he also was in touch with the pulse of the people. They wanted no more of Mao's revolutions. They wanted prosperity. Mao had been a towering figure – a poet, a philosopher and a man of "fiendish cleverness." But he was also a man who caused suffering and death on a massive scale. Perhaps the judgment of an earlier age regarding Emperor Qin Shihuangdi could also apply to Mao:

> *The King of Qin is a bird of prey... there is no benefi-*
> *cence in him, and he has the heart of a tiger or a wolf.*
> *When he is in difficulties, he finds it easy to humble*
> *himself. But when he has achieved his aim, he finds it*
> *just as easy to devour human beings. If he realizes his*
> *ambitions concerning the Empire, all men will be his*
> *slaves.*[25]

In his later years, a swollen, corpulent and debased old man with his broad face and receding hairline became the symbol of China to the world. Usually pictured in a revolutionary-style tunic, his countenance seemed bland and flat, with a wide nose, thin lips and a wart the size of a pea on his chin. Mao the man became Mao the icon, and then he became a Warhol painting and eventually an image that commercialized the communist ideal. He was, and is, one of the most enduring figures of the twentieth century.

Mao's dream of permanent revolution did not survive him. China was changed, perhaps forever by Deng's policy to move down the "capitalist road." Mao will be remembered as a visionary leader of modern China, but he was also one of the twentieth century's greatest tyrants, who committed almost unimaginable crimes. During his rule, more than 30 million mostly innocent people were sent to prisons for "Reeducation through labor." His plans for the transformation of China resulted in the murder of millions more. But his greatest crime was the more than 40 million unnatural deaths that have been called "unintended casualties of famine," and were the direct result of his "Great Leap" policy.

In total, Mao was directly or indirectly responsible for the deaths of approximately 70 million Chinese citizens. Rather than a classic racial or ethnic genocide, this mass killing is precisely what R. J. Rummel had in mind when he created the term Democide or "government inflicted deaths." It is a story of destruction that is almost unparalleled in all of human history. But Mao successfully ended the long history of dynasties that ruled China. He was the last emperor, and for that above all else, he will be remembered as a true revolutionary.

CHAPTER 6
Papa Doc and "Baby Doc": Voudou Regime

"Gratitude is cowardice"

François "Papa Doc" Duvalier

European purveyors of the Atlantic slave trade arrived on the West African coast in the late 15th century to begin the greatest forced migration in history. Terrified Africans, who had been seized by rival tribes, were chained together, sold and herded onto ships bound for the New World. The captives became human cargo on the slaving ships and were forced to leave behind their homeland, their tribes, and their families. The only thing they were able to take with them on the horrifying "middle passage" was their belief in the spirits. They called this belief Voudou, derived from the word for "spirit" in the language of the West African Yoruba people.

As the slave trade developed, many unfortunate Africans landed in the western part of the Caribbean island of Hispaniola – a tropical hell, then known as Saint Dominique. This colonial outpost, founded in 1664, became the richest of all French colonies, producing sugar, coffee, cotton and indigo. The trade with this colony employed more than a thousand ships and fifteen thousand sailors. French planters worked their slaves literally to death rather than feed the older and less productive ones. This required an ever-increasing number of

fresh African slaves to operate their plantations. The slaves of
Saint Dominique were disciplined severely – burned with boiling cane, branded with hot irons, smeared with molasses and
fed to ravenous ants or mutilated by amputation. They were
often beaten with whips, nail-studded paddles or with brine-
soaked bulls' penises. [1]

Enslaved Africans were forced to work from dawn to dusk
in the unrelenting tropical heat. Most went to bed hungry
every night. Slave women rarely bore babies that survived and
few wanted to bring children into a world of such savagery. A
continuing stream of captive people was brought to this colony
of bondage, cruelty and death. During one hundred years of
slavery in this small colony more than one million Africans
perished. It is no wonder that Voudou chants, which could
be heard around island campfires at night, swore vengeance
against slave owners.

Two races inhabited the plantation society of Saint Dominique in the early days – black and white. But a hybrid racial
group soon emerged. The third group was mulatto or mixed-
blooded people, usually conceived from the lust of white slave
owners for their black female slaves. Sometimes white men
kept mulatto mistresses, who bore children even whiter than
the previous generation. Elaborate racial laws were enacted to
restrict the rights of mulattos, who were in a category between
blacks and whites, but separate from both. Amid this culture of
discrimination and distrust a seething racial gumbo was created. By 1791 this Caribbean caldron was ready to boil over. [2]

On the night of August 22, the sound of drums pierced the
dense, tropical night near a coastal plantation in Cap Haitian.
A renegade Jamaican Houngan (priest) named Boukman Dutty
sent a message through the talking drums that a ceremony
of Voudou rites was to occur. At the appointed hour, more
than one hundred slaves assembled to drink warm blood from
freshly sacrificed pigs. They vowed freedom or death. Boukman stood and prayed to conclude the service:

> *The god who created the sun, which gives us light, who*
> *rouses the waves and rules the storm, is hidden in the*

clouds, but still he watches us. He sees what the white man does. The god of the white man inspires him with crime, but our god calls upon us to do good works. Our god, who is good to us, orders us to revenge our wrongs.... Listen to the voice of liberty, which speaks in the hearts of all of us! [3]

The revolution born that night lasted for thirteen bloody years. The bitterness and suffering of generations exploded and runaway slaves burned every plantation in their path. Believing that the spirits of Voudou protected them, slaves rushed armed Europeans screaming, "bullets are as dust." They were fearless because for many death was preferable to bondage. White plantation owners were savagely killed and white women were raped and murdered. Thousands of plantation animals were slaughtered. The sinister forms of torture that the slaves had learned from their white masters were turned on the overseers. Many mulattos joined with the blacks to attack white slave owners.

The leader of the rebellion was Toussaint L'Ouverture, a remarkable former slave, grandson of an African King, expert horse trainer and respected folk veterinarian. Known as Médecin General by rebel forces, he was a devout Catholic, a friend of the Jesuits and reportedly, a Freemason of a high degree. L'Ouverture was freed from slavery at the age of thirty four and rose to become a brigadier general, then Governor of Saint Dominique after leading the first successful slave rebellion since the revolt of the Roman gladiator, Spartacus, in the first century B.C. [4]

Under L'Ouverture's leadership, the slaves of Hispaniola defeated Spain in 1794 and England the following year. The slave revolt defeated Napoleonic France in 1803. The French forces offered L'Ouverture safe conduct to negotiate the terms of a treaty, but betrayed and imprisoned him in France, where he died in April of 1803. On January 1, 1804, the emancipated nation declared itself free, adopting the Arawak Indian name of Haiti, meaning "land of mountains."

Other countries commercially ostracized the newly independent nation of Haiti for more than a century. The idea that black slaves could defeat white European armies was unthinkable and slave-owning nations, including the United States, were determined to bring the breakaway nation to its knees. Haiti's agriculture had been virtually destroyed by the long and bitter war. Tension between blacks and mulattos continued to smolder and ineffective political leadership doomed the new nation to poverty and economic chaos for generations. Through it all, the desperate Haitian people clung to the only hope they knew – the mysterious and powerful Voudou spirits they called loa.

Voudou ceremonies were held around a pole, called a poteau-mitan, to summon the spirits and were accompanied by the beat of drums and the incantations of the Houngan or female priestesses, called Mambos. The ceremonies were profoundly emotional experiences for believers. Dancing in a circular pattern, the tension mounted and the rhythm intensified as worshipers communed with their loas. An animal (usually a pig) was ceremonially sacrificed by slitting its throat and the blood was collected. Ecstatic dancers usually drank the warm frothy blood, which intensified their frenzy. Ample supplies of homemade rum frequently fueled the dancing. Finally, someone may have been "mounted" by a loa, or possessed by the spirit's mysterious power. With eyes rolled back, dancers undulated with the percussive rhythm and might have uttered deep groans or a howled like a dog baying at the moon. As the ceremony ended the possessed dancer frequently collapsed, usually remembering little of the experience of the mounting. [5]

One especially significant loa in the story of Haiti is Baron Samedi, guardian of the graveyard, who has been linked with death and sexuality. This spirit is believed to wear undertaker's clothes and to display an ostentatious black cross. It is believed that the Baron dwells in the tombs of the dead. This dark spirit became a powerful influence during the Duvalier era, as Doctor Duvalier, a skilled practitioner of Haitian Voudou, frequently dressed in the style of Baron Samedi.

Voudou Houngans were the primary healers throughout the countryside of Haiti and they provided services to people who were so poor that many had never seen a medical doctor in their entire lifetime. Houngans frequently combined herbal medicine, folklore and various types of magic to treat or cure ailments. The mystic intersection of healing and spiritual power was destined to become the essence of the Duvalier legend.

Haiti's Contentious Society

The former slaves of Haiti developed a culture that became known as "Africa in the West Indies." Living at the edge of survival and practicing the most primitive form of subsistence agriculture, these impoverished people denuded the hillsides, stripping lush Haitian forests of vegetation in a desperate search for wood to produce charcoal. Their small plots of land were eventually divided among their children, rendering them even less productive for the next generation. Over time what had been some of the most fertile land in the world became desolate, barren earth that yielded only starvation. An exodus from rural poverty created Haitian cities that quickly turned into fetid urban slums. Each day in the tropical heat, the sole imperative was a struggle for survival. Sustained only by a belief in Voudou spirits, this "low world" of African culture was surrounded by whites and mulattoes who both despised and feared the blacks.

Above the slums, in the cooler hills, the culture of the "high world" developed. Here, a small elite class of inbred mulattos became heirs to property and wealth from the landholding class. The mulattos were intensely political people. They were merchants and civil servants, who supported themselves through exploitation of black Haitians or by taxing their labor. The parasitic mulatto government and business leaders favored their friends and families, who enjoyed the benefits of patronage and economic monopoly.

The government itself became a mechanism for extracting funds from the masses and funneling the spoils to the elite. But the denizens of the "high world" needed black labor to cook their food, raise their children and serve as their domestics. There was a constant temptation, especially for a "low world" black man, to "put a little milk in his coffee" – to add prestige to his family and lighter skin to his bloodline through liaisons or marriage with mulatto women.

This racial mélange was the poisonous legacy of the French slave owners – a caste system that designated dozens of racial categories distinguished by skin color, facial features and hair. Mulattos were raised by black servants and frequently were introduced to sex by an African housemaid or prostitute. The mulattos were the progeny of black Haitians and white slave owners, both of whom they hated. [6]

The future dictator of Haiti was the product of a black Haitian family of little means. His father, a man named Duval Duvalier, worked diligently to remain just above the squalor that surrounded him. First a schoolteacher and later a Justice of the Peace, he earned only a pittance, but his position elevated him from the masses and gave him modest respectability in the "low world."

He married a woman who worked in a bakery. We know little about her, except that she too was black and she was emotionally unstable. Not far from the National Palace, in Port-au- Prince, on April 14, 1907, Duval's wife, the former Uritia Abraham, gave birth to a son named François. Soon after his birth, François' mother was confined to an asylum and labeled a madwoman. She was a source of shame to the family. Little François was raised in the shadow of the National Palace where he was a witness to the political turmoil in the country.

He was raised by his aunt but he rarely talked about his upbringing. His mother remained shut away until her death when François was fourteen but his father doted on him. Despite his poor eyesight, François was studious. He attended Lycee Petion, a school of high reputation in Haiti. As a young man, François enthusiastically embraced Pan-Africanism, a consciousness of African social solidarity and black emancipation.

François and his friend, Lorimer Denis, began to write together under the name "Griots," a title used by African magicians and storytellers. Their writings were a call to arms for a black pride movement in Haiti that became known as "noirisme." Their editorials attacked racist Catholic priests, while extolling the virtues of Voudou. These writings developed a large following among the oppressed Haitian masses. [7]

During his medical studies, François met and courted his future wife, a young nurse named Simone Ovide. She was the daughter of a mulatto businessman, Louis Faine and an attractive, but illiterate black domestic. Her mother abandoned her at an early age and she was raised in an orphanage in Petionville, an upper class suburb in the hills above Port-au-Prince. Simone developed a fanatic devotion to Voudou, a bond that she and François would share.[8]

The American Occupation

Haiti struggled to survive for more than a century but France and the United States exerted a great deal of control over the country through financial pressure. In 1905, the U. S. seized control of the finances of Haiti's neighbor, the Dominican Republic. When the Americans became convinced that European powers might use Haitian debt as a pretense for invasion, the U.S. began to consider the occupation of Haiti.

Caco rebels ruled the rural north of Haiti in the summer of 1915. They were bandits but they were also nationalistic and urged defiance of foreign domination. The Caco's, who took their name from the cry of a native bird, also despised the ruling mulatto elite. The rebels gradually gained popular support as they fought against the tyranny of Haitian President Vilbrun Guillaume Sam. The president was chased into the streets by a mob where he was hacked to death and castrated. The savage murder of the president gave the U. S. the opportunity it had had been waiting for. On the next day, July 28, 1915, Rear Admiral William Caperton ordered five companies of U. S. Marines ashore in Haiti.

The primary purpose of the occupation was to reduce the influence of France and to prevent any opportunism by the Kaiser's Germany, but there was also a powerful economic incentive for the United States to occupy Haiti. According to U. S. Marine

Major Smedley Butler, "when the National Assembly met, the Marines stood in the aisles with their bayonets until the man selected by the American Minister was made President." The new American puppet, Philippe Sudre Dartiguenave, signed a treaty with the U. S., which ceded it the right to administer Haiti for the next 20 years.

The Haitian constitution was amended to allow foreign ownership of plantation land and Haitian businesses. Washington replaced the Haitian military with a police force trained by Butler's Marines. Major Butler presided over the death of Haitian democracy by forcing the National Assembly to dissolve itself under the guns of the new police force. Legislators hissed their disapproval but armed force prevailed. A writer for *The Nation* commented during this period, "The present Government of Haiti, which dangles from wires pulled by American fingers, would not endure for twenty-four hours if United States armed forces were withdrawn; and the President, Dartiguenave, would face death or exile."

The American Marines referred to the Haitian's as "coons, niggers and apes." According to one American high commissioner, "Haitian mentality only recognizes force, and appeal to reason and logic is unthinkable." Drunken Americans became a frequent sight in Haiti, as they patronized the many saloons and brothels that sprang up to serve them. Light-skinned Dominican girls, preferred by American Marines, staffed most brothels. America brought military order and Jim Crow laws to Haiti and soon entire neighborhoods and even Catholic masses were segregated, just as in colonial times.

The American administration instituted major road construction projects, to enable access to the regions dominated by the rebellious Cacos. A postal service, a hospital and telephone lines were built. The old forced-labor law, known as the corvee, was reinstated to accomplish construction of these public works. Haitians were roped together like slaves, overworked and underfed. Those who attempted to escape were shot on the spot. These repressive measures added to the sense of unrest, enhancing the appeal of the Cacos, who continued an insurgency from the bush.

Charlemagne Peralte, leader of the Cacos, soon became a
folk hero to the people and, as a consequence, he became a
target of the Marines. Camouflaged with blackened faces, they
infiltrated the Caco chieftain's camp, shot Peralte and paraded
his body on a crucifix for viewing by the dispirited rebel forces.
The murder of Peralte turned him into a martyr to patriotic
Haitians; however, the Americans had prevailed again through
the use of force.[9]

There was an unintended consequence of the American
occupation. The black pride or "noirisme" movement became
an underground phenomenon, along with an increase in the
popularity of Voudou. American administrators tried to crush
the belief in Voudou spirits but failed miserably. The people
were ready for a new leader, someone who could give them
back their pride and their religion – someone who understood
their longing. As a young medical student and aspiring noirisme poet, François Duvalier, captured the emerging spirit of
Pan-Africanism in a poem he wrote during the occupation:

> *The sons of the jungle,*
> *Whose bones during 'the centuries of starry silence'*
> *Have helped to create the pyramids.*
> *And I continued on my way, this time with heavy*
> *heart,*
> *In the night.*
> *I walked on and on and on*
> *Straight ahead.*
> *And the black of my ebony skin was lost*
> *In the shadows of the night.*[10]

As a medical student, François participated in a student
strike against the American occupation. On December 6, 1929,
the Marines bombed the town of Cayes, prompting mobs of
peasants to attack the Marines with stones. In response, the
Marines killed more than two-dozen people and wounded
scores more. The event bonded Haitians in national mourning
and prompted the Hoover administration to begin planning for
withdrawal of the occupation.

A month after François Duvalier received his medical diploma, the occupation ended. Although the relationship between the Haitians and their occupiers had been troubled, in the nineteen years that Haiti was ruled by American administrators there had been many improvements in the Haitian infrastructure. The country had come out of its isolation and the nation had more than one thousand miles of roads, three thousand vehicles and a series of provincial airfields. There were automated telephone exchanges and even radio stations. Great progress in public health was aided by the construction of 147 clinics and 15 hospitals during the occupation. The currency was pegged to the dollar and offered general financial stability. The new army or Garde D' Haiti was greatly improved over the former rag tag military organization. On July 28, 1934 the Americans left Haiti, and a wild national celebration took place.

The Rise to Power

Haiti continued to suffer after the American occupation ended. Cane cutters from Haiti had traditionally served as low-wage workers performing backbreaking labor for many Caribbean nations. In 1937, Cuban dictator Batista abruptly expelled the Haitians from his country. Desperate for work, they surged into cane fields across the border, in the neighboring Dominican Republic. At that time Rafael Trujillo ruled the Dominican Republic with an iron hand and he despised "a weakening of the national blood" due to racial commingling with blacks. On October 2, Trujillo's troops rounded up thousands of Haitians living near the border (aptly named the Massacre River) and murdered nearly all of them. They were beaten, bayoneted and hacked to death with machetes. Some were herded into the sea, where the sharks feasted on them as the surf turned crimson with blood. In just three days, between 20,000 and 30,000 Haitians were murdered.

This genocidal crime became known as the Dominican Vespers and it had a shameful aftermath. Trujillo bought his way out of blame by paying off the Haitian government with

$525,000. The funds never reached the survivors or families
of the victims. The mulatto elite in Haiti quickly grabbed the
money and absolved Trujillo. The British Ambassador was
shocked by "the contempt in which the educated Haytian holds
the peasant, whom he regards as belonging to a race apart, and
with whom he has little real sympathy."

The Dominican Vespers was another grim reminder of the
hopelessness of black Haitians. There was no work at home
and now, very little chance to work outside the country, even at
slave wages. Haitian President Vincent, who had been complicit in the cover-up of Trujillo's crimes, was exiled and Elie Lescot
succeeded him. An anti-populist mulatto, Lescot was a supporter of the Catholic Church and the anti-Voudou campaign it
was waging. But sullen black peasants refused to let go of their
beloved loas. Disgusted with their president, they began to seek
a leader who reflected their racial identity and beliefs.

American Dr. James Dwinelle came to Haiti in 1943 to direct a medical effort to eradicate yaws, a crippling tropical disease that afflicted most of the population. Entering the body
as a spirochete through bare soles of the feet, the disease leads
to deformed limbs and ulcerations on the body. Many victims
lose their noses or lips and yaws appears much like leprosy.
Dr. Dwinelle hired a young, myopic, English-speaking black
doctor to work in a clinic in Gressier, near Port-au-Prince. As
he traveled throughout the countryside, Dr. Duvalier bonded
with the common people. He was black like them and he
shared their faith in Voudou. He soon he became a folk hero.
Although antibiotics defeated yaws, the people believed that
it was the man they called "Papa Doc," who made them well.
His star rose, and when Dumarsais Estime' was swept into the
presidency with the slogan "a black man in power," Duvalier
became Under Secretary of Labor, and later Public Health and
Labor Minister.

Estime' was a noiriste advocate, who raised the minimum
wage and created badly needed jobs. Black Haitians believed
that things were beginning to change, with visible evidence
represented by blacks in positions of power. Estime' harbored
a well-known hatred of mulatto and white domination, but he

had a weakness for mulatto women. He owned a tan Oldsmobile, called "The Tomb of Virgins," in which he seduced many.
Estime's black Haitian ministers were as tempted as their predecessors by easy access to government funds. The tradition of
corruption in Haiti was well established.

When the Estime' government was exposed for financial
irregularities, the mulattoes saw a chance to regain power. A
black Colonel named Paul Maglorie successfully conspired with
mulatto business leaders to overthrow Estime'. Maglorie then
was elected president. Duvalier was incensed at the betrayal of
black Haitians and refused to serve in the new administration.
He returned to his medical work in the countryside.

The collapse of a black-run government was a bitter blow
to Duvalier, and a formative event in his political education.
Based on Maglorie's treachery, he vowed never to trust the
military. Duvalier co-authored *The Problem of Classes Throughout
Haiti's History*, a highly charged political treatise. It was a black
manifesto, destined to become a noiriste classic.

During the next decade Duvalier emerged as a revolutionary philosopher and a political renegade. With a deep faith in
Voudou, his beliefs were politically opportunistic; however, they
did reflect his social values. His black power views were steeped
in Pan-Africanism, and were sealed by a philosophy that was
rooted in the African soil. Duvalier's writings further explain:

> *Voudou is essentially cosmogenic, philosophic and spiri-
> tual. It explains the origin of life by asking nature for
> symbols to show the play of cosmic forces. And doesn't
> science daily evolve towards an ever-clearer conception
> of the universality of that cosmic force? Voudou is phil-
> osophic since it provides concepts of both the material
> being and the soul. And it is spiritual because it pro-
> claims the survival of the soul in sanctifying the spirit
> of the Ancestors.* [11]

Duvalier's published views presented an encompassing
system of belief – a folk religion from Africa, brought to the
new world by slaves and nurtured through bloody sacrifice

that survived all efforts to purge it. Voudou was the force that launched and sustained Haiti's fight for independence. It was the philosophy that gave Haitian's an identity and it was the only belief system that gave meaning to the suffering of the people. Duvalier understood the almost narcotic effect of Voudou on the Haitian masses and he recognized the power it could bring to his political ambitions.

As a political dissident, Duvalier became immersed in his Voudou beliefs, with an intensity that has been described as "pathological." He became a student of power, studying Machiavelli's *The Prince*, and drawing to his side loyalists who were dedicated to his thinking and unified by a common faith in his future. These followers included Luckner Cambronne, who would become a Duvalier bagman and Simone Duvalier's lover. Colonel Marcaisse Prosper, chief of police of Port-au-Prince, was also part of Duvalier's inner circle and provided him with assurances of personal safety. Most important of all was Clement Barbot, who was to become Duvalier's most loyal and dedicated killer.[12]

Duvalier learned to operate by deceit and careful political calculation. His fear of the government prompted him to carry guns at all times, even while making love. Weapons were hidden throughout his home, ready for use at any threatening moment. This practice may have been an early sign of a developing sense of paranoia.

By 1956 the government began to implode and President Magloire became increasingly ineffective. The public declared a strike and stores did not open. Students refused to go to school and workers refused to work. The populace was so poor that they had little to lose, so they withheld the only thing they still possessed – themselves. Without workers the Haitian economy collapsed. Magloire quickly fled to Jamaica.

President Papa Doc

Papa Doc gained the support of Madame Estime', the former First Lady and positioned himself as the heir to the Estime'

legacy. He established an organization known as Faisceau
Feminin, or Feminine Torch, a women's group supporting his
candidacy. Duvalier came across as a man of sincerity, seemingly without artifice or pretensions. He maintained a proper
presidential image and was always impeccably dressed in a black
suit and hat in winter and white suit and hat in summer. His
wife, Simone, personified respectability and was always at his
side while he was campaigning.

In 1957, the campaign for president proceeded under the
shadow of violence and intrigue. There was a riot on May 18
and even greater unrest on May 25. Scores were killed. One
candidate fled into exile and another dropped from the race.
By the September election, only Duvalier and Louis Dejoie
remained. In accordance with a carefully developed plan, Du-
valierists swarmed to the polls as they opened, then spent the
balance of Election Day intimidating opposition voters. Duvalier swept the voting by a margin of 3 to 1, a decided advantage
in the controversy that followed the balloting.

On October 22, 1957, in a formal ceremony at the National
Palace, François "Papa Doc" Duvalier was sworn in as President.
Some Haitians were concerned that the methods used in Duvalier's election created the potential for the abuse of power but
no one had any idea what was to come under Papa Doc. Soon
however, Haiti's new leader began to act on the dark suspicions
that haunted his mind. With Clement Barbot taking a leading
role, Duvalier's team of hooded goons known as Cagoulards
(Leopards) began a savage repression of those Duvalier considered his political enemies.

One January evening in 1958, armed Cagoulards broke into
the home of Journalist Pierre-Edouard Bellande and his wife,
Marcelle Hakime. At home were their eight children and Marcelle's beautiful sister, Yvonne, an outspoken critic of Duvalier.
Yvonne was forced into a car by the hooded intruders and taken
to a remote area where one at a time, the Leopards viciously
raped her. She was then subjected to a brutal beating. The victim's unconscious, naked body was thrown into a ditch. Duvalier was personally present during the attack, wearing a military
uniform and he personally ordered his Cagoulards to "finish

her off." The bullets that riddled her body somehow failed to kill her and later a friend found her and saved her life.

A few days following the attack on Yvonne Hakime, soldiers brought three truckloads of bound and gagged supporters of Duvalier's opposition to a pit in the capital's largest slum. The pit was partially filled with wet cement. The trucks emptied the captives into the cement pool as the victims fought to escape. Some managed to remove their gags and cried out in terror. Men in civilian clothes pushed the victims into the gray slime as they thrashed and fell upon each other. The children among them were the first to die, suffocating under the thick concrete goop. Soon only a few moans could be heard. More concrete was poured into the pit and it was leveled, leaving only a silent gray slab, guarded by soldiers. The macabre tomb was topped with a wooden cross, stuck into the wet concrete, a symbolism that a local priest called "satanic." [13]

When the soldiers left, uncomprehending citizens came from their homes to see the site of the massacre. Many of the victims were never identified, but the message was clear. The community, once a hotbed of anti-Duvalier sentiment, would never be safe from the dictator. The word spread and fear of Duvalier began to dominate the peasant folklore of Haiti. According to these stories, Duvalier's knowledge of Voudou allowed him to commune with the spirits and invite them to live with him in the National Palace, where a special mystic room had been prepared. The spirits, it was said, accepted his invitation and no living being could depose Duvalier, because he was assured lifetime power by the Voudou spirit world. The man the people had revered as "Papa Doc," not only used violence and murder in his repression, but he turned the Voudou spirits into evil demons, who conspired with him to terrorize the people.

Not all of Duvalier's suspicions were unfounded paranoia. Nine months into his presidency, a former Captain in the Haitian military, Alix Pasquet, led a small invasion force determined to overthrow Duvalier. Civilians supported by Cagoulards and soldiers attacked the conspirators. Some of the plotters were beaten or hacked to death and their bodies were

stripped and dragged through the streets. The mutilated corpses became trophies for a vengeful mob of Duvalier supporters.
Only one conspirator escaped, the leader, Alix Pasquet.[14]

Despite its failure this event was a shock to Papa Doc. Duvalier invoked nightly curfews and began filling the jails with
dissidents. He emasculated the army, swiftly firing many in
the officer corps and replacing them with younger men. The
armed forces were unified under presidential direction and
he created a new Presidential Guard for his personal protection. Most important of all, he converted the Cagoulards into
an armed militia, named Volunteers of National Security and
called the Tonton Macoutes.

The literal translation of the Haitian Creole for the words
Tonton Macoute is "uncle knapsack." In folk tales they were
bogeymen, who prowled at night capturing bad children by
putting them into Macoutes, the straw satchels carried by most
peasants. But Papa Doc's Tonton Macoutes were armed and
allowed to kill on a whim. Recruited by the thousands from the
most deprived elements of society, the Macoutes were essentially armed thugs, responsible only to Duvalier. They were not
paid, but were given free license to torture, kill and extort.

Of all the evil creations of Papa Doc, none was more diabolical than the Tonton Macoutes. It has been described as a
"strange amalgam of popular militia, religious sect, mass political organization, secret police, protection racket and terrorist
unit." But it was even more sinister than the usual instruments
of state terror because its very existence excited the darkest and
most terrifying fears of the Haitian people. The Macoutes represented Papa Doc, who was believed to be the earthly incarnation of Baron Samedi, the Voudou spirit who ruled the under-
world of the dead.

Known for ritual savagery, Macoutes frequently left a victim's body in the streets, reeking of death, to perpetuate the
people's sense of dread. The Macoutes sometimes mutilated
their victims and cut off heads as trophies for their master, Papa
Doc. Many victims of the Macoutes simply disappeared into the
darkness, never to be seen again. Haitians are a mystical people, who possess almost nothing in this world but their dreams.

Papa Doc turned those dreams into nightmares of abject fear, not just of death, but of deeper terrors that might follow in the spirit world. Haitians expressed their complete despair under his regime with the saying, "Papa Doc taught us to exist without money, eat without food, to live without life."

The structure of his sinister organization was simple. Thousands of virtually all-black Macoutes had complete power over the people, mulatto merchants and the military. Led by Clement Barbot and other Duvalier fanatics, the Tonton Macoutes were above the law and reported only to the president. Perhaps the best description of their national role was provided by the president himself who said of the Macoutes that they "have but one soul: Duvalier; know but one master: Duvalier; struggle but for one destiny: Duvalier in power." Regional leaders of the Macoutes were a valuable source of intelligence for Duvalier. Their ranks included many Houngans who infused the organization with a powerful Voudou belief. The Fillettes Laleau led by Madame Max Adolphe, was the female organization of Macoutes. Its reputation was even more notorious than the men.[15]

In May of 1959, when Duvalier was 52, he suffered a massive heart attack. Papa Doc had been a diabetic since early adulthood and he required insulin shots daily. He also suffered from degenerative arthritis and from chronic heart disease. His appearance was frail and he weighed only about 150 pounds. Journalist Lyonal Paquin described him as "owlish looking," with a likeness to "a sad frog with a heavy lower lip." He took a large number of pills daily for pain. According to Duvalier's personal physician, Dr. Jaques Forucand, he went into a diabetic coma at the same time the heart attack occurred. The doctor administered insulin, but only the intervention of Clement Barbot saved his life. Barbot, who had no medical training, gave him glucose and then contacted the American Ambassador, Gerard Drew. United States Navy cardiologists from Guántanamo, Cuba rushed to Haiti to save the president. Duvalier never fully recovered and he was never physically well again. But his unstable mental condition worsened and became the most important result of his near-death experience. Medical professionals believe that he had been incorrectly medicated during his comatose state and suffered irreversible neurological damage. His American specialists described lapses into insanity. Clement Barbot told friends "Duvalier is a madman." The common people believed that he had become a zombie.

In April 1961, Duvalier dissolved the Legislature and ordered rigged national elections. He was overwhelmingly elected to a second six-year term, winning by a remarkable vote of 1,320,748 to zero. According to the New York Times, "Latin America has witnessed many fraudulent elections throughout its history, but none has been more outrageous than the one which has just taken place in Haiti."

A month later, dictator Rafael Trujillo was assassinated in the neighboring Dominican Republic. The shock of Trujillo's murder further strengthened Duvalier's resolve to tolerate no dissent whatever and to root out his enemies preemptively. Duvalier turned on the Catholic Church, deporting priests and sending the Macoutes on raids of churches where worshipers were beaten and jailed. Murder, torture and disappearance became commonplace in Haiti and roadblocks manned by Macoutes appeared everywhere. Terrified citizens were extorted for money, sometimes for as little as a dime.

Under the rule of Papa Doc no one was safe. Eventually his closest political henchman, Clement Barbot, who once saved the president's life, was arrested for his comments about Papa Doc's mental state. Barbot was imprisoned and held in a torture center for eighteen months. Following his release he became a religious man, driving to prayer meetings in a new car provided by Papa Doc. Perhaps Duvalier felt obligated to Barbot, since he owed the man his life, but nevertheless Papa Doc kept Barbot under constant surveillance. [16]

President For Life

The war between Duvalier and his military escalated with each perceived threat to Papa Doc's power. Several Haitian colonels planned a coup in early April of 1963 but Papa Doc's spies informed him of the plot. Duvalier summoned the colonels to the presidential palace. Colonel Charles Turnier, the only one to appear, was interrogated, beaten and shot dead. His rotting corpse was left on the parade ground as a warning to other potential plotters.

On the morning of April 26, 1963, gunmen armed with pistols attacked Duvalier's children as they entered a school near the presidential palace. The children, eleven-year-old Jean-Claude and his fourteen-year-old sister, Simone, were not hurt, but their chauffer and three bodyguards were killed. An orgy of killing began that very afternoon. Military officers all were considered suspects in the attack on the presidential family. Every active or retired military officer located by the Tonton Macoutes was murdered.

The actual mastermind of the attack on the children was, in fact, former Duvalier supporter Clement Barbot, but Duvalier would not believe it. He was convinced that ex-Lieutenant Francois Benoit, a crack marksman, was the shooter. Benoit's home was machine-gunned and his parents, infant son, family friends and servants were killed. Even the family dog was not spared. Benoit and his wife were not at home, but the Macoutes raged into the streets, murdering Benoit Armond, a passing pedestrian apparently because his first name was the same as the last name of the accused. The slaying of this family along with the murders of the military personnel prompted the Organization of American States to order an investigation. President Kennedy cut U. S. aid and sent an American warship and a Marine Expeditionary Brigade into Port-au-Prince Harbor. Duvalier imposed a nightly curfew and declared martial law. On May 7, American dependents were evacuated from Haiti, amid speculation that an invasion was imminent.

Papa Doc stalled for time by purchasing tickets to Paris for his family and making preparations to depart Haiti. The president scheduled a press conference for May 15, which suggested an abdication was only days away. Roadblocks were removed and the killings were halted. Anti-American rhetoric on Haitian radio was muted. Duvalier denied all charges of repression

and accused the U. S. of creating unrest in Haiti. Papa Doc's
cunning paid off. The OAS investigated but failed to take action, the U. S. did not invade and the Duvalier family cancelled
plans to flee to Paris.

Duvalier gradually became convinced of the true identity of
the leader of the plot against his children and a manhunt for
Clement Barbot was launched. Barbot and his brother, Harry,
a pediatrician, were gunned down by the Tonton Macoutes in
a sugar cane field after a cane fire set by Duvalier's men drove
them into the open.

During the night of November 22, 1963, although the city
was blacked out, the palace in Port-au-Prince was ablaze in
celebration. Duvalier and his supporters reveled in the news
of the assassination of President Kennedy in Dallas earlier that
day. Papa Doc credited his own use of the blackest of magic,
an Ouanga or Voudou charm to strike down the U. S. President
who had dared to cut off aid to his regime. Duvalier height-
ened his religious retribution against the nation's Catholics.
They now could only attend mass celebrated by Haitian priests,
who were armed agents of the Duvalier administration. Confes-
sional admissions were reported to the authorities and used for
political repression.

The people were cowed into submission through a campaign
of organized terror, torture and murder. But in Duvalier's mind
the fear expressed by Haitians from all walks of life were signs of
love and adulation for him. In his *Memoirs of a Third World Leader*, he wrote that the first support of lifetime leadership for the
president had come from the people themselves. "The fantastic
crowd," he wrote, "raised up for the first time cries of Duvalier,
President for Life, Duvalier President forever."

A nation-wide referendum on June 14 affirmed Duvalier as
"President for Life" by a margin of more than 2.8 million votes,
despite the fact that less than 2 million persons were registered
voters. It was no longer possible to remove the dictator, short
of his death, and many Haitians believed that his relationship
with the spirits protected him from harm.

During the 1960's, Haiti was a tiny country of less than
3.5 million people. Based on estimates made by the Toronto

Star, The Guardian of London and the Los Angeles Times, the
Duvalier administration murdered between 50,000 and 60,000
people, in addition to the tens of thousands more, who just
"disappeared." More than a million Haitians fled Duvalier's terror into exile. More than 80% of the professional class of Haiti
were deported or put to death. Papa Doc stripped the nation of
its most valuable human resources and doomed the country to a
future of poverty and squalor.

Duvalier's life-long hatred of the mulatto class was based on
his noiriste beliefs and the sociology of the island, which relegated blacks to the bottom of the economic ladder. This hatred
exploded in an episode still known as "The Vespers of Jeremie."
A small group of expatriates from the Jeremie region set sail
from Miami in an effort to free Haiti. They landed at the town
of Dame Marie. Of the thirteen invaders, twelve were mulatto
and all were members of Young Haiti, a resistance group based
in the U.S.

During the first skirmishes with Haitian soldiers, a Young
Haitian named Yvan Laracque was killed. "Bring me his
body," demanded an enraged Duvalier. The corpse was flown
to Port-au-Prince, where stinking of decomposition and bloated from the heat, it was placed in a garden chair at a major
downtown intersection and guarded for ten days by Tonton
Macoutes. "We mustn't forget that Castro began with little
forays too," Duvalier said, as he planned a brutal campaign
against the remaining invaders. Most of Duvalier's victims
were not even related to the conspirators but were perceived
to be guilty because they were mulattoes from Jeremie.

The roundups and killings in Jeremie continued for
days. Respected citizens were beaten, humiliated and killed,
their bodies pitched into shallow graves. Many women
were subjected to sexual assault before their deaths. Firing
squads were set up at Numero Deux, a wooded area near
the airport. Each night, with wailing sirens and the crackle
of gunfire heard in the distance, trucks brought the victims
to face the Killers. Nearly the entire Pierre Sansaricq family
was taken to their deaths singing "Nearer My God to Thee."
When they arrived at Numero Deux, one young member of

the Macoutes shouted, "to be a Duvalierst you have to be bloodthirsty," as he drove a knife into the heart of the Sansaricq 2 year-old grandchild, Regine. Lighted cigarettes were pushed into the eyes of her 4 year-old brother when he cried over the death of his sister. As he writhed in pain, he was stabbed to death. His killer said that he "wriggled just like a worm."

Night after night the killing went on and the Macoutes turned over the possessions of the slaughtered mulattoes to the masses. By week's end, all but two of the Young Haitian invaders had been exterminated along with a large number of completely innocent mulattoes. Duvalier, suspicious of the body count, ordered that their severed heads be brought to the palace for his personal inspection. The final two surviving Young Haitians were taken prisoner and executed before a large crowd that was forced to witness the grisly spectacle. These killings were broadcast on television to the nation repeatedly for weeks afterwards.

Duvalier owned the people's hopes and dreams. He also owned their souls, and to prove it the government issued a booklet called *Catechism of a Revolution*, which included the following "prayer":

> *Our Doc, who are in the National Palace, hallowed be Thy name in the present and future generations. Thy will be done at Port-au-Prince and in the provinces. Give us this day our new Haiti and never forgive the trespasses of the anti-patriots who spit every day on our country. Let them succumb to temptation, and under the weight of their venom, deliver them not from any evil.* [17]

Squalor, Greed and Death

Duvalier became the object of a perverse reverential fear by terrified Haitians. This allowed Duvalier and his cronies to increase their theft of public funds. Heavy taxes on state monopolies of autos, sugar, flour, cement and other necessities were imposed. Most of the money was siphoned off by Duvalier for his high living family members. His wife Simone, now derisively called "Mama Doc," dressed in haute couture and traveled extensively. The elite of Duvalier's loyalists helped themselves to riches in all sorts of business ventures that depleted state coffers. Duvalier's personal bagman, Luckner Cambronne, was allowed to extort anyone he chose. He had a relationship with Simone, who secretly shared his bed for many years. The economy slumped so badly that Haiti became one of the few nations on earth to show negative growth in 1965 and 1966. Haiti had the highest infant mortality in the western world along with the lowest literacy, the lowest caloric consumption and a life expectancy of only 40 years.

The squalor of Haiti's slums was almost unimaginable. In the poorest sections of Port-au-Prince one could barely stand the stench of open sewers, where swarming flies were everywhere and naked children with distended bellies roamed the streets seeking food. Adults, weakened from hunger, fell prey to a wide range of illnesses. Many had absolutely nothing to eat on a typical day, except for a few scraps of food they might steal. With unemployment of 70% or higher, they had little hope of earning any money.

During the time of Duvalier the survival instinct in Haiti created its own curious resources. The Creole term "Terre," refers to mud biscuits, still sold today in the street markets of Haiti. These culinary inventions are created by vendors who combine clay dirt, water, a little margarine and a pinch of salt. Sometimes they will crumble a cube of bouillon into the mixture, which they stir, shape into discs the size of a saucer and leave to bake in the Caribbean sun. These mud cakes are sold and eaten as "food."

The world that Duvalier created in Haiti was a tropical horror that rivaled anything found in the earlier slave colony of Saint Dominique. Most of the Macoutes were enthusiastically sadistic and had perfected the use of physical coercion and torture. Some leaders of the Tonton Macoutes had cells for this purpose constructed in their homes. Duvalier was increasingly thrilled by torture and had peepholes drilled into the walls of his palace so he could enjoy watching especially brutal sessions. He ordered the inside walls of the palace painted rust brown to more easily hide the victim's splattered blood.

The center of torture in Haiti was Fort Demarche, a military facility originally built by the Americans during their occupation. Cells were so overcrowded that inmates had to sleep in shifts. Food was disgusting and had little nutritional value. Prisoners were allowed only one-minute showers daily and that sixty seconds would provide all the drinking water they would receive for the entire twenty-four hours. Toilets were rarely changed buckets of slop. In these conditions every prisoner's health quickly declined and most inmates suffered from severe dysentery. There were deaths daily and the corpses were hauled away on the same wagons that delivered food. Bodies were buried in shallow graves, near the prison walls. Each night the rotting corpses were dug up and eaten by bands of roving dogs.

Madame Max Adolphe, as a leader of the Tonton Macoutes, became the ruler of the Fort Demarche death house and took sadistic delight in viewing torture sessions. She especially enjoyed live pornographic displays, in which naked prisoners would have their genitals torn by implements in the hands of her Macoutes thugs, skilled in the art of sexual mutilation. Most victims of these ghastly violations did not even know why they were incarcerated. They had no legal or civil rights and there were no courts to intervene. The Macoutes reported directly to Duvalier, and only he could grant a pardon.

Duvalier's crimes of torture and mass murder were not only political in nature, there was also racial and class motivation for slaughter. As demonstrated by the campaign in Jeremie, many of those targeted for death were members of the upper classes and primarily mulatto. It would be difficult to make a case that the political terror in Haiti was genocide in the strictest sense, since many blacks were also victims. But atrocities committed by the Duvalier regime were a morbid outgrowth of his well-known noiriste philosophy, which was, by its very nature, racial.

Duvalier's regime was denounced by the International Commission of Jurists, which reported, "The rule of law was long ago displaced by a reign of terror and the personal will of its dictator, who has awarded himself the title of Life President of the Republic, and appears to be more concerned with the suppression of real or imaginary attempts against his life than with governing the country." And yet, the clever little doctor arranged a state visit by Ethiopia's Haile Selassie, honors from the state of Israel (which sold him Uzis) on the tenth year of his reign, and a new agreement or concordat with the Roman Catholic Church.

Duvalier's health continued to decline although he was still able to make public appearances to assure the nation that he was in command. The U. S. ambassador told UPI, "President Duvalier's position seems solid to me. The Armed Forces and the people seem absolutely loyal to the Government."

On November 12, 1970 Papa Doc suffered what seemed to be a mild stroke. As his condition worsened and then turned dire, he made one final decision. He wanted to extend the Duvalier legacy and protect the hundreds of followers who might be killed in a blood purge at the end of the regime. The dying president named his slothful eighteen year-old son to succeed him. Because the successor was only eighteen, the voting age was lowered. The constitution was amended to make Jean-Claude President-for-Life. Papa Doc, in a delirious state, told his supporters, "We all know that Caesar Augustus was nineteen when he took Rome's destinies into his hands, and his reign remains 'The Century of Augustus.'"

A national referendum confirmed the son's ascension. Huge posters of father and son together were hung throughout Haiti. The caption read, "I have chosen him." Voters dutifully went to the polls and rendered their verdict on the succession. 2,391,916 voted yes and zero votes were opposed. With the unsavory Luckner Cambronne as regent, the schoolboy-president-in-waiting celebrated his bed-ridden father's sixty-fourth birthday on April 14, 1971. On April 21, Duvalier tried to sit up and with a few unintelligible words, his heart failed and the President-for-Life passed the torch to a new leader.

"Baby Doc" in Power

It was not an easy transition. The country was on the edge of complete starvation, the economy was in shambles and most of the educated class had fled Haiti for exile in more friendly countries. The Haitian government continued to steal from the people and the masses were in a state of complete terror of the Tonton Macoutes. The Macoutes numbered in the hundreds of thousands and one person in twenty was now a member. Their power was pervasive. They controlled the people through the ruthless exercise of terror, effectively ruling the nation.

Macoutes used the funeral of Papa Doc to whip up a frenzy of support for the continuation of Duvalierism. The funeral was televised live and lasted for six hours. As the bronze casket moved through the streets of Port-au-Prince in a black Cadillac hearse, a cyclone-like wind seemed to follow the procession. Some spectators cried out, "The evil ones from Trou Foban [caves of the spirits] are following their master." But others believed that his spirit had infused the son. For these followers, the cry was, "After Duvalier, Duvalier." And so it was. [18]

Jean-Claude had never wanted the power of the presidency and had tried to avoid it. He wished only to continue his indolent lifestyle. He was profoundly lazy and his obese body and incurious mind were evidence of his slovenly life. He was nicknamed "basket head," due to his outsized cranium. Jean-Claude's weak character made it easy for his domineering mother, Simone and her greedy lover, Luckner Cambronne to assume powerful roles in his administration.

The new President, Jean-Claude Duvalier, attended ceremonial functions and read prepared remarks, but he was not really engaged in governing. He continued to pursue womanizing, hunting and the high life. He loved fast cars and motorcycles and he ate great quantities of food but he was not a heavy drinker. He engaged in plenty of casual sex, but had never been in love. He had a weakness for beautiful women, but his sex partners were not always female. Jean-Claude was reported to be a somewhat clumsy lover, but he had stamina and could maintain an erection for hours.

He toured the nation in his fast cars, followed by frantic security guards. But he really needed no security. The mild-mannered playboy was a relief to the citizens of Haiti after the diabolical doctor. He was warmly greeted everywhere. The level of violence in Haiti subsided and the tourists (mostly Americans) returned. The sudden turn of events brought a resumption of American aid, and steady increases in U. S. assistance. Despite the appearances of improvement, business as usual continued in Haiti. The Duvalier family persisted in the practice of skimming millions of dollars into their Swiss bank accounts.

Duvalier loyalist Luckner Cambronne was making a fortune in his blood-plasma business. He shipped five tons of plasma each month to American laboratories that were eager for Haitian blood, earning him the nickname, "Vampire of the Caribbean." Because the Haitian people were so poor and so sick, Haitian blood was rich in antibodies, and therefore in great demand. Cambronne also owned a thriving cadaver business. Poorly nourished Haitians were very thin, so their cadavers did not force medical students to slice through layers of fat to reach vital organs in dissection classes. Cambronne paid only three dollars per cadaver in the underground market. When supplies ran short, he stole bodies from funeral homes. There were even reports of the murder of the urban poor to meet the demand of his cadaver business. This rumor was never proven, and may have been prompted by an offhanded Cambronne comment. When told of the poor condition of some of the corpses arriving in the U. S., he said, "All right, I'll start shipping the bodies up alive. Then when they need them, they can just kill them."

There were a few cosmetic governmental reforms, but very little really changed in Haiti. One of the most lucrative practices of the regime and its corrupt ministers was to siphon aid dollars received from the U. S. Lucien Rigaud, a Swiss-trained mulatto businessman with a Swiss wife became entrapped in the foreign aid game. Rigaud had excellent relations with U. S.

commercial interests and succeeded in increasing U. S. foreign
assistance by $9.3 million. The money lined the pockets of
American contractors, Haitian firms and government ministers.
When Rigaud balked at direct graft for the Duvaliers, Air Force
Major Roger Cazeau set him straight. "You don't understand,"
he stated, "You are going to die. The Duvaliers are crooks,
and if you don't bring them something you are contemptible
to them and dispensable." Rigaud stood firm, saying, "Certain
things are out of the question."

In 1975, Rigaud was framed on a charge of murdering his
own handyman of thirty-two years, although the man had actually been shot by police. Despite a confession by the policeman
who committed the murder, Rigaud was arrested. At first he
was held in a filthy cage, so small that he could not stretch out.
Later, his wife was successful in transferring him to the penitentiary. By this time he was dirty and disheveled, but he witnessed
people in far worse condition. Men and women moving in and
out of interrogation rooms exhibited signs of beatings, and
many had broken bones, smashed heads and bleeding flesh.
He soon learned that Jean-Claude was personally supervising
his fate. A presidential order read: "Transfer Rigaud, and put
him in with the common prisoners. And then make garbage
out of him—turn him into a vegetable."

For more than eighteen months Rigaud tried to avoid the
gruesome fate that he witnessed in the prison around him.
Although the commander of the penitentiary received $5,000
a day to feed his 2,000 prisoners, he skimmed off most of the
money and starved the inmates. Rigaud was spared much of
the worst treatment through the bribery of his guards. His wife
brought Amnesty International and the Swiss and American
embassies into the case, but they were unable to obtain her husband's release. Inmates suffered physical decay that was clearly
visible. Death was common and several prisoners died every
day.

In the Duvalier's Haiti, the power to terrorize and kill represented the ultimate political weapons and many more inmates
died as a result of torture than by slow deterioration. The culture of death that had been developed for years by the evil little

doctor continued under the son. The things Lucien Rigaud witnessed in prison in Haiti would stay with him for a lifetime. He was horrified by the fate of the political prisoners, who received the most inhumane treatment. Many had been confined without sunlight for so long their skin appeared to be bleached white. Most were toothless, emaciated and filthy. Almost none of the political prisoners would leave prison alive.

Rigaud witnessed firsthand the hideous prison fate of many children. Every two weeks, a sweep was made of the streets and terrified street urchins – eight, nine and ten year old boys, were arrested. The guards had only one purpose in holding these children, to sell them to inmates who would pay to rape them. The children became diseased from use as sex slaves and were replaced regularly. The system was well established and continued without change under Jean-Claude, despite the happy face he put on the "new Haiti."

Each day Claire-Lise Rigaud visited her husband, enduring the body searches by leering guards as they groped her breasts and genitals "searching for weapons." Her husband bribed his way into the prison hospital where they could meet and avoid her systematic molestation. But soon they learned that Jean-Claude was planning to have him transferred to Fort Demarche for execution.

He and his wife concocted a plan that involved selling his car, and when Claire-Lise brought the car to the hospital, they managed to drug the guards with Valium in soft drinks. Then they boldly escaped. Rigaud reached the Mexican Embassy where he sought and was granted asylum. His wife was less fortunate. She was arrested and beaten so badly that she could not stand. She eventually was able to flee to Switzerland with her children. While Rigaud stayed in Haiti at the Mexican Embassy, he and his wife kept the pressure on Amnesty International and other humanitarian organizations to look into the abuses of the Haitian prison system. Eighteen months later Rigaud escaped from Haiti.

"Baby Doc," as Jean-Claude was now being called, had more pressing concerns than Lucien Rigaud. He was concentrating on creating the appearance of reform in Haiti and to that end he signed the Inter-American Convention on Human Rights. Jean-Claude wanted to prove that he had a plan to improve on two decades of a completely degenerate dictatorship. In a reference to the Bible he stated, "The Gospel of Christ did not destroy the Old Testament. On the contrary, it came to explain it, to complete and realize its promises." Thus, the son was to fulfill Papa Doc's grotesque legacy. He would build on the sins of his father and would even surpass them for avarice, greed, cruelty and corruption.

In 1979, a shocking report appeared a *New York Times Magazine* story entitled: "BABY DOC'S HAITIAN TERROR." The story was an interview with Lucien Rigaud, written by journalist Wendell Rawls, Jr. It described Rigaud's experiences and exposed the absolute evil that Duvalierism had become. Despite the exposé American aid to Haiti continued because there were simply too many U. S. companies that outsourced work to Haiti in order to utilize labor that was paid only $3 per day.[19]

Despite the promises made by the young Duvalier, many Haitians continued to endure severe hunger and malnutrition. During the time of "Baby Doc," a woman in Gonaives unintentionally became a spokesperson for the most desperate of Haiti's poor after a profound family tragedy. Upon the birth of her eighth child, she quietly strangled the baby to death. When she was taken to jail she told the police, in complete sincerity, "I did it so he wouldn't have to live gnawed by pain and hunger, and I did it so that he wouldn't starve the other seven, who already have little enough to eat."

A Regime at War with Itself

Jean-Claude found the love of his life in Michele Bennett, the light skinned daughter of a mulatto coffee exporter. Michele's background was not pristine. Her father, Ernest Bennett had served time in prison for financial misdeeds and was a recognized source of drug transshipments for the criminal cartels. She also had been married to Alix Pasquet, who had attempted a coup against Papa Doc's regime. Michele had two children by

Pasquet while living with him in the United States, where he was hiding from Haitian authorities. She was good looking, high living, with expensive tastes and loose morals. Her reputation for being a sexual adventuress brought her to the attention of Jean-Claude, who took her to his bed after knowing her just long enough for them to enjoy dinner together. [20]

He told his friends that he had "finally met his match", and he soon exhibited scratches all over his body from their frenzied lovemaking. His family was not pleased by his selection of a "mulatto slut" for a bride, who was known to have slept with nearly every well-connected man in Port-au-Prince. Jean-Claude's mother, Simone, arranged for her to be grabbed by Macoutes and taken to the airport, bound for exile, but "Baby Doc" rescued her. Jean-Claude finally stood up to his mother, but Michele was to become an even more domineering woman than Baby Doc's mother.

The wedding in 1980 was listed in Guinness Book of World Records as one of the three costliest on record, at that time, costing an estimated $3 million dollars. Michele wore a lavish white gown by Givenchy and a hairdresser was flown in from Paris for the occasion. The ceremony was held at the aging main cathedral, which had been refurbished for the event, at great expense to the treasury. More than $100,000 was spent on the fireworks display following the wedding.

Michele was willful, cunning and totally amoral. She engaged in a tug-of-war with Simone and the advisors surrounding her husband. As Michele's influence grew, the decline of the second Duvalier regime began. Many government ministers were fired at Michele's urging. Tension at the palace was constant, as Michele ruthlessly separated Jean-Claude from his government ministers, his friends and from his overbearing mother, Simone. A blue and green African parrot was imported by Michele and taught to speak in the barroom slang that she used so often. It was installed outside Simone's bedroom, so that each morning the mother of the president would be greeted by the parrot with "Fuck you. Fuck you."

Ninety-six members of Simone's extended family were eventually exiled from Haiti, most at the urging of the new first lady. They joined the million of Haitians who were by then expatriates. More than a quarter of Haiti's former citizens were living abroad. Most made their exit from Haiti by ship or plane, but the poor did not have those options. The world became aware of the plight of these sad refugees, as the word "boatpeople" became familiar to nations in the Caribbean region. Increasing numbers of starving and destitute Haitians arrived in the Bahamas, the U.S. and elsewhere. During 1980 and 1981, more than 1,200 Haitian's a day arrived in south Florida. They were detained in the Krome Detention Center or transferred to Fort Allen in Puerto Rico, which was almost as horrible as the prisons of Haiti. According to Congresswoman Mary Rose Oakar, it was, "very much like a concentration camp. These poor people are living, caged animals. Their souls are being taken away." Baby Doc's solution to the embarrassing spectacle of the boatpeople was to kill them as they attempted to escape and Macoutes were put on constant lookout for those attempting to flee.

Things became even more unbearable for the people of Haiti with the devastating outbreak of Porcine Swine Fever in the summer of 1981. This disease attacked the one source of financial and dietary security still owned by many of the poor in Haiti – their pigs. Haitian pigs represented a critical element in both the food chain and the economy. The hardy, long-snouted decedents of those brought to the island by European settlers had become very important in the lives of the peasants. Even the poorest people owned a few pigs. They required little care and ate anything and everything, including human excrement. After about two years, they could grow to nearly 100 pounds and could birth piglets. Their meat, served spiced and fried in oil, was a favorite of Haitians, providing the high calorie fat so essential to people near starvation. The pigs also represented a form of savings for the poor. When money was needed for an illness, death or wedding, a pig could be slaughtered and sold.

When the Program for the Eradication of Porcine Swine Fever and Development of Pig Raising (PEPADEP) was begun in 1982, it devastated the Haitian countryside. Four hundred

Americans and French Canadians slaughtered 380,000 pigs and
paid out $9.5 million dollars in compensation. Haitians resist-
ed the program by hiding their pigs in caves and in woodlands
of the countryside. They began to truly hate the president for
his collusion with the outsiders who came to kill their pigs.
Without pigs, the peasants were deprived of desperately needed
food and their only source of savings.

   As the Duvalier dynasty faltered further, a new plan was devised to regain international legitimacy in the form of a visit by
Pope John Paul II. Catholic Church officials would only agree
to a Papal visit if Jean-Claude would restore Rome's power to
name all bishops and the archbishop in Haiti. Jean-Claude
reluctantly agreed, sensing the disrepute that his regime was
held throughout the world. The Pope shrewdly made his dis-
taste for the Duvalier's clear, though unspoken, during his visit
in March of 1983. His speech was in Haiti's Creole language.
The Pope's theme of: "Where are you?" (Kote nou?), suggested
that the Haitian people should make themselves heard. They
welcomed him by the millions and in response to his question,
they roared, "Here we are." He told the people of Haiti that
the world knew all about what was happening in their country,
stating: "Things have got to change here!" Later, during his
visit, John Paul refused Michele's invitation to a lavish state
feast, taking a simple meal with fellow priests. He made only
a brief stop at the palace and departed from Haiti by nightfall,
secure in the knowledge that he had quietly brought a message
of hope and change to the sad little island nation. [21]

   The Pope had aroused the spirit of the Haitian people.
They were no longer willing to remain silent as the elite plundered the country. In late May of 1984, a pregnant woman
was beaten to death in Gonaives and a crowd surged into the
streets. They were hungry, desperate and still enraged that the
government had killed their pigs. The crowd wanted Michele
and her family expelled from Haiti. The incident turned into
a riot that lasted for two days, during which at least 40 people
were killed. A week later more than 25,000 rioted in Cap Haitian, provoked by word that CARE warehouses full of food had
been sold by the government instead of being distributed free

to the poor, as intended. Riots and public disturbances continued for months. With the death toll mounting, the situation in
Haiti seemed untenable.

Political storm clouds first appeared during the fall of 1985,
high in the Mountains of Laboule, at the home of prominent
attorney, Gerard C. Noel. It was here that the first discussion of
real change began between Noel, Haitian Army Chief of Staff,
Lieutenant General Henri Namphy and Army Colonel Williams
Regala. The small band of conspirators formed an alliance
with American officials to plan the end of the Duvalier Dynasty.
They all agreed that Baby Doc could not continue to rule Haiti.
The plotters were assured that the power of the United States
would not be used to prop up the regime. American Ambassador Clinton McManaway Jr. also gave them assurances that
the U. S. would recognize a coalition government following the
overthrow of Duvalier. As the conspirators were preparing their
plan, Michelle's outrageous behavior became the catalyst for a
revolt. She went on a lavish shopping spree in Paris, spending
$85,000 in airfare for her entourage and more than $1.7 million in furs, jewelry and art. When the news media reported on
her excess it brought the people into the streets.

The Haitian public expressed a new feeling of power. Im-
provised barricades were put up on roads. Cars belonging to
regime members were torched. Inflammatory leaflets appeared
saying that the "homosexual" Jean-Claude must go, along with
his "lesbian" wife. Stores were closed by strikes. The Haitian
currency, known as the Gourde, plunged in value. Macoutes
ran wild in the streets shooting innocent civilians, in a show of
bravado that masked their fear of the people. Schools, hospitals, stores and food warehouses were looted. Tourists fled to
the safety of their cruise ships and sailed away. Jean-Claude
wanted to stop the public violence and he ordered the army to
"massacre them," but Namphy's instructions were clear. "Hold
your fire," he told his soldiers, and the army obeyed.

By January 1986, the rolling rebellion had intensified and the
Macoutes had increasingly become targets of the mob. The Duvaliers isolated themselves in the palace, becoming more and more
paranoid and using drugs to remain calm. Without Jean-Claude

even asking, several embassies informed him that they would not offer asylum in their countries. In fact, Michele had put out feelers to the most inhospitable countries she could think of as a way to stiffen Jean-Claude's resolve to stay and fight. But then, in a crippling blow, the U. S. State Department announced the suspension of $26 million in aid money previously promised to Haiti, due to the inability to confirm progress on human rights issues. The Macoutes were in fear of the mobs, support for the regime was almost depleted and now Haiti's rich uncle had cut them off. It was only a matter of time for Baby Doc.

The Duvalier's Final Curse

Haiti's darkest hour came at 4 a.m. on February 1, 1986, the National Assembly declared a state of siege. All radio stations were ordered off the air. When news of Baby Doc's refusal to depart reached the masses, they attacked the Duvalier's vacation home and stripped it of its elegant furnishings, Persian rugs and fine Limoges china. In Petit Goave, homes of the Tonton Macoutes were attacked by mobs who hacked off the legs of one leader of the Macoutes, then dragged the dying victim through the streets as he bled to death. In Leogane, mobs burned cane and banana fields.

Nearby, in the village of Belloc, Macoutes with Uzi's responded by murdering protest marchers, creating a mass of corpses. As word of the massacre spread, families of the victims dragged their dead loved ones away for a secret burial to avoid reprisals against entire families by rampaging Macoutes.[22] The Haitian people devised a new implement of rebellion that was reminiscent of the French revolution's guillotine – it was the "necklace," or gasoline soaked tire put around someone's neck and then set aflame. Mobs began to attack government buildings all over Haiti. Cars and trucks were burned. Schools, charitable institutions and private homes were looted. Many of the Macoutes homes were burned and their owners were driven into the streets, where many were beaten to death, or roasted alive with a "necklace"

At the palace, Jean-Claude was wavering but Michele had no intention of leaving Haiti quietly. "If I have to leave, I want to walk in blood from the palace to the airport," she shouted at the bewildered "Baby Doc" and his advisors. She ordered a Voudou ceremony in the palace on February 5 that was meant to bring a curse of horrible death upon the next person to occupy the presidential suite. Houngan Simon, who performed the ritual, provided some of the macabre details. He arranged to purchase two babies. Under such emergency conditions, the price for sacrificial children was ten times the "normal" $40. These were usually newly born children, whose mothers would be informed that the children had died in the nursery. It was a believable cover story, because most of Haiti's filthy hospital nurseries were infested with rats.

When one of the babies was found to be a girl, Simon refused to use her for the Voudou rite. Only males were acceptable to the spirits, so this Haitian infant female was spared a horrible and violent death. After the two sacrificial male babies were brought to the presidential bedroom, Houngan Simon began the ceremony, with only "Baby Doc" and Michele in attendance. The details of what took place there are not fully known, however incantations were made, prayers were offered and the sacrifice was concluded. The small corpses, reeking of rum, were removed for secret burial. The presidential couple had a comfortable night's rest in Michele's room. The curse was complete.

The next morning, February 6, Jean-Claude called in his advisor Georges Salomon and said, "Minister Salomon, we are finished here. We must leave before Carnival, before more people are killed." At 2 p.m. that afternoon, Salomon contacted both the French and United States embassies. Plans were made for the Duvaliers to be exiled in France.

That evening the ministers were advised of the plans and General Namphy was provided a long list of those to be executed in the wake of Baby Doc's departure. The General was horrified by the list, prepared by Jean-Claude and the Tonton Macoutes. Then he adjusted his glasses, and with a pen he added one name. Looking up he said in Creole, "Men mwen," (I'm here). General Henri Namphy had written his own name. As Jean-Claude stared at him, Namphy said, "Put your own name down here too, Mr. President. You are a wicked man." With this gesture, Jean-Claude's confusion cleared. "It was you who countermanded my orders?" he inquired. Namphy squared his jaw and pronounced, "Yes. You have to leave." Michele, who was in the room, screamed, "Kill him, Jean-Claude! Shoot him! Kill him, you fucking queer." She was hysterical, tears streaming down her face, smearing her makeup. But Jean-Claude did not kill anyone. Colonel Regala drew his pistol and spoke his first words in this drama. "If Henri Namphy has so much as a headache," he said, "the army is in a position to blow the pair of you away."

Michele refused to be silenced. She knew that only steps away, outside the president's office were a group of Macoutes who could come to their rescue. She opened her mouth to scream, but Colonel Prosper Avril reacted quickly, slugging her in the jaw and knocking her unconscious. He quietly placed Jean-Claude in handcuffs. The death order in Namphy's hands would never be carried out. Literally thousands of people throughout Haiti had unknowingly been saved from execution. As the meeting concluded, the Duvaliers were released but kept under armed guard for "security" reasons. [23]

That night, Jean-Claude, Michele and those closest to them held a party while they were under house arrest. Champagne was served at midnight as the Duvaliers remained true to their vain, self-absorbed characters. Just after 2 a.m., the escape plane, a U. S. Air Force C141, arrived at François Duvalier International Airport. When the Duvalier motorcade arrived for departure, Jean-Claude and Michele were exempted from the metal detector, in deference to their rank as president and first lady. Deceitful to the end, both carried loaded pistols. At 3:47 a.m., on February 7, 1986, the big jet rumbled down the runway and, lights blinking, it banked into the pre-dawn darkness over Port-au-Prince.

As the sun rose over the capital, crowds swelled into the streets waving flags and palm leaves, blowing horns, conch shells and banging pots. Joy at the departure of the Duvaliers and the expression of love for Haitian soldiers quickly turned to a mood of revenge on the Tonton Macoutes, who remained the most visible symbol of the regime within reach of the masses. A crowd of people went to Papa Doc's grave, but did not find his body, which had been removed by Macoutes. The mob grabbed a body from a nearby crypt, that of General Gracia Jacque, and threw the decomposed corpse into the streets to be crushed beneath the wheels of passing cars. More Macoutes became victims and were "necklaced." Their charred corpses were put on poles to the cheers of the throng. In the days to follow many more Tonton Macoutes were killed.

In the aftermath of the Duvaliers, the Haitian people were literally starving to death and desperate for a government that would replace repression with compassion. They had been left with a collapsing economy, a depleted treasury, rampant corruption and what has been called a "state of insecurity." The people were greeted nearly every morning with corpses rotting in the streets, evidence of nighttime killings. Following the departure of Baby Doc, the violence actually increased as politicians and the military battled over the remains of three decades of Duvalier tyranny.

Bloody reprisals against the Macoutes and their supporters became commonplace and many citizens joined vigilante groups. The people spoke fearfully of le Fauteuil – the Chair, or the seat of power that transformed political leaders into murderous monsters. They knew their government to be violent and chaotic, infected with rampant, avaricious corruption. The evil hand of Papa Doc had bequeathed to Haiti a succession of repressive rulers and a continuous struggle for power. One minor politician who understood this phenomenon expressed it simply when he said, "Duvalier still rules this land. He will rule it for fifty years."

And what became of the exiled leaders of the Duvalier regime? Michele lives the high life in the south of France, having divorced her slothful husband. Baby Doc is now broke and broken, living a meager existence in France on the charity of friends and family. The violent legacy of the Duvaliers continues in Haiti, where the people have suffered a second American occupation, the restoration of a primitive form of democracy, and a "quiet coup" that forced President Jean-Bertrand Aristide into exile. The International Herald Tribune reported in April 2008 that, "three quarters of the population earns less than $2 a day [less than under the Duvaliers] and one in five children is chronically malnourished." Haiti is now a semi-permanent UN protectorate. Violence and food riots there are as common as hunger and disease. In January of 2010 Haiti suffered a massive earthquake that destroyed Port-au-Prince, killing about 250,000 people and making most people in the capital homeless.

There is a proverb in Haiti, "Deye mon, gen mon – Beyond the mountains, more mountains." The Haitian people, in their own folk wisdom, understand that their suffering is endless.[24] Today, in the cities and countryside of Haiti the downtrodden Haitian people continue to endure poverty, starvation and premature death. Their plight is the final curse of the Duvaliers.

CHAPTER 7
Idi Amin: A Feast of Blood

"I want your heart. I want to eat your children."

Idi Amin Dada

The ancient people of the Nile believed that the river was a gift from the Gods. It provided them with the abundance to sustain a mighty civilization. During flood season, the river yielded a layer of silt that the Egyptians called "black land," which fertilized and energized the soil for planting. Some years brought enormous floods that drowned entire villages, while other years brought drought, famine and hardship. Because the Nile was so vital to the fortunes of Egypt, the Pharaohs eagerly sought greater knowledge about the river's behavior and its source.

The first question asked by Alexander the Great in 331 B.C., when he came to the temple of Jupiter Ammon in Luxor was, "What caused the Nile to rise?" Julius Caesar once said that if he had only one question to ask the gods it would be where the Nile originated. Roman Emperor Nero sent two centurions to follow the Nile to its origin, but they were unable to determine its source.[1]

For thousands of years, knowledge of the river was limited to the map that the Greek geographer, Ptolemy, developed in the second century AD. It showed the river arising from a great lake at the foot of what Ptolemy called the "Mountains of the Moon." In 1622, a Portuguese missionary, Padre Páez, located the fork of the river which split off at Khartoum and in 1770

Scottish explorer, James Bruce, confirmed that Lake Tana, in Ethiopia, was the primary source of this tributary, known as the Blue Nile.[2]

In 1858, British explorers Richard Burton and John Hanning Speke traveled to Africa in search of lakes that were rumored to be the source of the Nile's other fork, the White Nile. Their journey took them to Lake Tanganyika and to the Ruwenzori Mountains. In mid-journey Burton took ill, but Speke continued on, eventually becoming the first European to see Lake Victoria. Although Speke claimed to have discovered the origin of the Nile in 1864, it has recently been confirmed that the White Nile arises from natural springs in the mountains of Rwanda and Burundi. Speke's discovery was not the river's true source.

But Speke discovered something else in the heart of Africa. In 1862, he encountered an isolated civilization that was completely unknown to Europeans. Speke was the first white man to discover the people who lived along the shores of Lake Victoria, in a region known as Burganda. They were the descendents of tribes that had flourished there for more than two thousand years.

More than a million people lived in a highly organized society ruled by a King or Kabaka. Speke marveled at the capital's broad roads and graceful thatched huts surrounding the Kabaka's compound. Speke had discovered the ancestors of the people of modern Uganda, who were living by the lake and along the banks of the Nile that flowed southward, into Ethiopia, Nubia and Egypt. On this plateau, located at the equator amid the "green hills of Africa," was a society of cultivators who relied upon fertile land and abundant rainfall for their livelihood.

The nation of Uganda today includes the Bantu-speaking people of the former kingdoms of Burganda and Banyoro. It also includes the Nilotic-speaking Acholi and Langi people from the north. In the west Nile region live several Ugandan tribes that are considered Sudanic, including the Kakwa, who speak their own distinct dialect. In recent times, the Ugandan government has broadcast news in as many as 24 different languages and dialects.

When Arabic speaking ivory traders arrived in Africa during the 1840's, their Islamic culture and religion conflicted with traditional beliefs. Later, Muslims clashed with Christian missionaries who arrived in 1877and a four-year long civil war ensued. The Christians defeated Islamic forces only to become engaged in a violent struggle between Protestant and Catholic converts in 1892. Violence was not limited to Muslims and Christians. The Kabaka of Burganda practiced a terrifying level of brutality upon his people. In his court men known as Binders stood ready to "bind" and drag away to their death, anyone who displeased the Kabaka. He routinely condemned slaves and members of the court to death for such mundane transgressions as failing to close a door properly. No one was allowed to sit or speak in the presence of the Kabaka, who was a figure of awe and dread.

Eventually, the British established control over the region with the support of Nubian mercenary troops. When the Nubian mercenaries mutinied in 1897, the British sought the assistance of the people of Burganda, who were allies and fellow Christians. As a reward for their support, the Kabaka's people were granted a high degree of autonomy in Uganda, which preserved their status as the dominant tribal group in the newly formed British colonial protectorate.

Asians of Indian and Pakistani decent were brought to Uganda by the British to build the Ugandan Railway, which was completed in 1901. Over time the Asians came to dominate the merchant class and key industries. During the post World War II era, resentment by native tribes against British rule and Asian domination grew in the colony. In 1949, during a political crisis and rioting, the houses of pro-government chiefs were burned by mobs. Gradually the unrest led to consideration of self-rule and a proliferation of political parties.

The special status of the Kabaka became a political problem for the British colonial governor. The British exiled the Kabaka, then a chief called King Freddie. He was sent to London in 1953. When it became apparent that his presence was necessary for peace, he was returned to the colony. As the nation moved towards independence, the issue of the special status of

Burganda continued to simmer. Political leader Milton Obote formed a Protestant faction, known as The Uganda People's Congress (UPC), which initially opposed the Kabaka's special status. Another faction, The Democratic Party, led by Benedicto Kiwanuka was predominately Catholic and also opposed the Kabaka's privileged role in the nascent independent state of Uganda.

An alliance between Obote's UPC and the forces supporting the Kabaka was arranged by British administrators. This marriage of political convenience held together long enough for a government to be formed. Uganda became independent in October 1962. Milton Obote was its first Prime Minister and the Kabaka, King Freddie, was named head of state. Uganda became a sovereign nation and a member of the British Commonwealth. The new nation had a favorable climate, wonderfully fertile soil, a well-organized economy and an efficient civil service. Young Winston Churchill once called Uganda the "Pearl of Africa." It had great potential for success, but it was also rife with tribalism that threatened to undermine the appearance of calm. The first challenge to the new nation, however, did not come from tribal violence, but from a mutiny by its military forces.[3]

The Military in Uganda

During the early colonial period, the British formed a military unit made up of 300 Sudanese soldiers to protect the interests of the British East Africa Company. Following the establishment of a British protectorate in 1893, the colonial authorities organized a force of 600 regular soldiers and 300 reservists, most of whom were Sudanese Nubians. They were trained by a small number of Arabic-speaking British officers. This force subdued most of the tribes in the region and consolidated the British hold on the colony of Uganda. In 1897, the Uganda Rifles, as the force was called, revolted and killed their commander and five other white officers, forcing the British to bring troops from India to suppress the mutiny.

The mutiny spurred the British to change the composi-
tion of the colonial military. The number of Sudanese soldiers
was reduced and significant numbers of other Ugandans were
added. In 1902, British officials consolidated all forces within
East Africa and British Somaliland into the King's African
Rifles. The organization was racially segregated, with separate
battalions for Asian and African soldiers, under the leadership
of white British officers. The King's African Rifles became a
legendary force, fighting in western Kenya between 1902 and
1906 and then against Shaykh Muhammad Abdulla Hassan,
known as the "Mad Mullah" in British Somaliland in 1909. The
Rifles conducted an expedition into southern Sudan (then
called Jubaland) in 1914.[4]

Uganda's civil service was trained and well educated but its
military relied on a poorly paid, uneducated force of soldiers
who were not a part of mainstream society. Although the new
military was more racially and ethnically integrated as a result
of British policy, many of its soldiers were still illiterate Sudanese.

In many respects the British military of Uganda enabled
Idi Amin's rise to power. He was born between 1925 and 1928
in the poor farming village of Koboko, in the northwest corner of Uganda. Idi Amin Oumee was a member of the small
Kakwa tribe, which is Nubian-Sudanic, and he was the third of
eight siblings. Nothing is known of his father and his parents
separated near the time of his birth. His mother was from the
Lugbara tribe, also a Nubian-Sudanic people. Amin was raised
a Muslim, in a nation that was primarily Christian.

His mother became a camp follower of the Kings African
Rifles. It is not surprising that an African boy with no father or
education would have been attracted to the mystique and authority of British military service. Idi Amin was a large, strong
boy, who was highly athletic and eager to please. His introduction to military life began in 1946, at the age of about eighteen,
when the King's African Rifles employed Amin as an assistant
cook.[5]

Idi Amin was promoted to corporal within two years because he met the British officers' criteria for a reliable native

soldier. "Not much gray matter, but a splendid chap to have about," one officer stated. The British officer corps put a high premium on spit and polish and the willingness to obey orders without question. In the closing days of the Second World War, he was assigned to the 4th Uganda Battalion. Idi Amin was a gifted athlete, and had learned the British style of boxing well. In 1951, Amin became the heavyweight-boxing champion of Uganda, a title he held until 1960. [6]

While serving during Kenya's Mau-Mau rebellion, Amin learned highly coercive techniques to gain the cooperation of local tribes. During a subsequent campaign to quell the cattle raiding activities of the Karamajong, nomadic tribes of northeast Uganda, he persuaded each warrior to partially disarm by surrendering all but one of their eight matching spears. His method was direct and brutal – he simply brought the offending tribesman into camp and had the man's penis placed upon the safari table. Then, wielding a panga, "a particularly lethal Ugandan machete," he threatened him with sexual amputation unless his spears and warrior shields were produced.

In 1959, Amin was promoted to warrant officer, with the rank of "effendi," a position created for noncommissioned Africans with leadership potential. A former commander described Amin as "a splendid type and a good (rugby) player, but virtually bone from the neck up and needs things explained in words of one letter." In 1961, he was promoted to lieutenant, one of only two native Ugandans to earn that rank during British rule. Amin possessed a kind of "animal magnetism," and he mastered a "sadistic skill," to "frighten, dominate and command." His regimental records from this period showed that Amin was repeatedly infected and cured of venereal disease. He was said to be fond of bordellos.

Amin attended paratrooper training in Israel, where he developed a unique relationship with the Israelis. Upon his return to Africa, he acted as a conduit for arms and ammunition directed to Israeli-backed rebels fighting in southern Sudan. The Israeli government was attempting to create an additional front against Arab forces during an especially tense time for the young Israeli nation.

In 1962, Amin's conduct caused an inquiry during an operation to suppress cattle stealing along the northeastern border of Uganda near the Turkana region of Kenya. The inquiry followed an incident known as the "Turkana Massacre" and charged that troops under Amin's command had victims "tortured, beaten to death and, in some cases, buried alive." Evidence of these crimes was provided through postmortems on bodies of the Turkana dead that were found in shallow graves. However, the British authorities were reluctant to court-martial a Ugandan officer for "overzealous" methods with independence only a few months away. When independence came, in October of 1962, Prime Minister Milton Obote overlooked the allegations. Amin was again promoted.

In 1964, Prime Minister Obote began to actively support a revolution in neighboring Congo. The Prime Minister wanted to keep the Ugandan government's role secret because it involved meddling in the affairs of a sovereign neighbor. Clandestine radio codes were established allowing Obote to maintain direct contact with Amin in the region. The rebels needed guns and transport equipment but were not able to pay for them in cash. So they paid Amin in gold and ivory, which he sold to purchase arms for the rebels. However, Amin began to skim large sums from the transactions for himself. His new affluence was noticed. When Amin's accounts at Ottoman Bank were publicly exposed, an inquiry was launched that became known as the "Congolese Gold Scandal."

In February 1966, the Prime Minister suspended the constitution and fired several cabinet officials. Opponents of Obote called this act a "revolution." The Prime Minister defused the case against Amin by claiming that the transactions in question caused funds to become "stuck" in Amin's bank account, making them "appear" improper.

Free of constitutional restraints, Obote designated himself president and decided to confront the Kabaka. King Freddie had been a thorn in his side since the uneasy political arrangement with the British had put Obote and the Kabaka into a power sharing coalition. Amin was elevated to Commanding General, clearing the way for him to operate with impunity at

Obote's direction. In late spring of 1966, there was widespread bloodshed resulting in 700 deaths, as Amin's troops hunted down supporters of King Freddie. The Kabaka found himself cornered in his palace compound during the violence. As Amin closed in on King Freddie a torrential storm broke over Kampala, allowing the Kabaka to escape to Burundi and then to Britain. He died in exile three years later.[7]

Although Obote had prevailed, he had destroyed nearly all of his political support, leaving him completely dependent upon the army and General Amin. Henry Kyemba, who wrote the inside story of Amin's regime, *State of Blood,* explains the situation in Uganda during late 1966:

> *In the space of just a few months, Uganda had gone from a peaceful democracy to something very close to a military dictatorship. With the Kabaka gone, and the Baganda [people of Buganda] quelled by force, there was no possibility of a lasting, working parliamentary majority for Obote. Hundreds of prominent citizens were imprisoned without trial (including the former Army Commander, Shaban Opolot).* [8]

Obote's seizure of control of the government was disturbing to many countries beyond the borders of Uganda. He was a dedicated leftist and began planning "a new political culture," based on an authoritarian form of Socialism. His plans to nationalize or confiscate a share of more than eighty U. K.-owned businesses in Uganda came as a shock to London.

A Clandestine Plan

Three Western nations that had significant interests in Uganda at the time were Israel, the U. S. and Great Britain and all three contributed to the demise of the Obote government. The British feared the appropriation of their business assets, the Israeli's were supporting a neighboring revolt on Uganda's Sudanese border and the U. S. was attempting to blunt the

inroads of communism in Africa. A plan for regime change
of the Ugandan government was conceived and skillfully con-
cealed by the covert agencies of these governments for more
than two decades.

The first hints of their secret actions appeared in 1978, with
the publication of *The Last Adventurer*, a book written by a West
German national named Rolf Steiner. At age 17, Steiner joined
the French Foreign Legion and saw combat in Indochina. He
later supervised a commando unit on the Biafran side during
the Nigerian civil war and subsequently became a mercenary in
southern Sudan. During the late 1960's, Steiner was assisting
a rebel group in Sudan called the Anya-Nya. The Israelis had
long been suppliers of arms and financial support to these rebels. Steiner claims that he was merely seeking additional help
for his rebel clients in southern Sudan when he learned that
British mercenaries were using the conflict as a cover for a plan
to assassinate Obote and replace him with Idi Amin.

According to *The Last Adventurer*, a British associate told
Steiner, "the British knew Idi Amin well and he was their first
choice because he was the stupidest and the easiest to manipulate." He was also told, after the fact, that men working with
British intelligence had planned a December 1969 assassination
attempt on Obote's life. Henry Kyemba was an eyewitness to
that failed attack, writing, "The President had had an extraordinarily lucky escape," when a grenade failed to explode. A shot
fired at Obote only missed his brain by a few inches and "entered his jaw." Kyemba was slightly wounded by the same bullet
after it exited Obote's neck. The British presumably orchestrated this attack with Israeli and American concurrence, but this
has never been confirmed.

Amin's reaction to the attempt on Obote's life immediately
made him a suspect. When soldiers arrived at Amin's residence
he fled barefoot over a back fence. He later said that he feared
for his life, suggesting knowledge of the assassination attempt
and his expectation that Obote was dead. Brigadier General
Pierino Okoya accused Amin of involvement in the plot and
of desertion. A few days later Okoya's wife was bathing on the
veranda of their home near Gulu when she was fatally shot

twice in the chest. When Brigadier Okoya opened the door he
was shot dead on his front porch. Amin immediately became
a suspect in the couple's murders and further implicated himself by obstructing the investigation. In June 1970, there was
another attempt on the life of Obote, who became increasingly
suspicious of Amin.

In September of 1970, a dossier was compiled against Amin
containing details of the attempts on Obote's life and the killing of the Brigadier General and Mrs. Okoya. General Amin
was placed under house arrest. Despite the murder investigation, he did not comply with detention, walked away from
his informal restraint and began to appear at civic events in
full uniform. This bold challenge to the authority of Obote
increased tension in the capital. For several months nothing
happened publicly, but there was a great deal of activity in the
shadows.[9]

On two occasions during the latter part of 1970, Amin was
seen in southern Sudan. He was reported to be in constant
contact with the Anya-Nya rebels. This was reported to Obote,
who had shifted his support from the rebels to the Sudanese
regime of Jafaar Numayri. Amin's continued involvement with
rebel forces was one more sign that Amin had his own agenda
and was perhaps in league with foreign governments. In December, Rolf Steiner, the German expatriate mercenary, working closely with the rebels in Sudan, crossed the border and was
"entertained as a guest" by Ugandan troops. But within a few
days he was arrested. Amin Biographer, David Gwyn provides
details:

> *Steiner was taken to Entebbe Airport with a sack over
> his head...was placed on a Sudanese government air-
> craft by a Ugandan police party under the direction of
> Hassan, the head of Uganda's Criminal Investigation
> Department.* [10]

According to Steiner's book, upon his arrival in Khartoum,
the capital of Sudan, he was tortured and interrogated about
his role with the rebels. He remained in the custody of the

Sudanese government. Several years later, Steiner was released from a Sudanese prison, through the efforts of the West German government.

In January 1971, Obote left Uganda to attend the British Commonwealth Conference in Singapore. It was a trip that he would soon regret. Henry Kyemba reports that Obote had arranged for his security apparatus to arrest Amin in his absence. Kyemba has written that the night the Commonwealth Conference concluded, he overheard Obote and his staff attempting to reach Kampala by telephone to learn about the status of Amin's arrest. "There had been no arrest," he writes, "Amin had already struck."

Amin was apparently not acting alone. During an especially heated conference session, Presidents Kaunda of Zambia, Nyerere of Tanzania and Obote of Uganda pressed British Prime Minister Edward Heath about their strong opposition to British military assistance to the white apartheid regime in South Africa. They went so far as to threaten to withdraw from the Commonwealth over the issue. An enraged Heath, perhaps revealing too much, was quoted as saying "I wonder how many of you will be allowed to return to your own countries from this conference.

Indeed, Obote would not return to Uganda, for at that very moment, Amin's troops were moving to seize strategic locations in Kampala. The President's entourage fearfully boarded their homeward flight, not knowing the fate that awaited them. About two hours from Bombay, they learned from a BBC radio report that Obote had been overthrown and the military had taken over the country. The stunned group of stateless officials headed for Nairobi, where Obote was accorded treatment as a deposed head of state. "The next day," Kyemba writes, "we were put on board a new East African Airways DC-9. It was to have made its inaugural flight to Entebbe that day. Instead, we left unceremoniously for Dar-es-Salaam."[11]

Neither Obote nor Western intelligence services had ever truly controlled Amin. While intending to use his "brute force" tactics to achieve their own ends, they consistently underestimated his primitive cunning and his unwillingness to become a puppet for anyone. Within a week of the coup the British press embraced Amin. The Daily Telegraph printed, "Good Luck, General Amin." The Daily Express praised the General's take-over, stating glowingly, "Military men are trained to act." The fawning acceptance of a military takeover was a reflection of British relief at the end of Obote's regime.

The British recognized the new Ugandan government before the week was out. This was quickly followed by recognition from Israel and the United States. *New African Magazine* reported that, "Amin…denationalised several of the British companies taken over under Obote and in July 1971 came to London where he had lunch with the Queen and meetings with Heath's cabinet." Amin was treated as a hero in Uganda. He released most of Obote's detainees, including General Shaban Opolot, once his commander, who was granted full back pay for the five years he had spent in prison. Amin also released most of the imprisoned supporters of the Kabaka and arranged for the return of the Kabaka's body for reburial in Uganda. Amin cleverly claimed that it was he who had allowed the Kabaka to escape during the siege of 1966.

Although Idi Amin was a physically huge man and cut a commanding profile in his military uniform, he remained, in many ways, a child in a man's body. He presented himself as a leader, but he understood nothing of national governance. He was illiterate and suffered from psychic wounds that were clearly visible. He longed for legitimacy but he harbored grievances that would divide the nation by race, ethnicity and religion. In a world he did not understand he suspected conspiracies by the elites, whom he could not trust. Amin would rule through the devices he knew best – violence and bestial brutality. His incompetence, delusion and uncontrollable rage would unleash a primitive form of terror upon Uganda.

The Bloodbath

Following the takeover, Amin stated, "I am not an ambitious man, personally. I am just a soldier with a concern for

my country and its people." Outwardly, he seemed committed
to good government for Uganda. His appointees were well
qualified and balanced between Christians and Muslims. A
few isolated incidents of violence within Uganda were generally dismissed as the predictable aftermath of a military coup.
Major Emmaneul Ogwal, a pro-Obote officer, was hunted down
through the streets of the capital and killed during a shoot out.
He had sought refuge in the home of an unsuspecting doctor,
who was later seized and taken to the Malire military barracks
where he was "crushed to death with a tank." Maybe the African proverb is true, which says, "You can never see what is in
the darkness of a gun barrel."

Amin's seemingly "random announcements," to the media
frequently became the statements of official policy. Amin's
ministers began to listen carefully to broadcasts of his words
so they could follow his instructions. People found this habit
amusing and the media portrayed Amin as jovial, charming
and well meaning. Within days of the coup those suspected
of being enemies of Amin (generally officers from Acholi and
Langi tribes, closely identified with Obote) were singled out for
retribution. A number of senior officers were beaten to death,
including Brigadier Suleiman Hussein, the Army Chief of Staff.
According to Henry Kyemba, "It was rumored that his head was
later taken to Amin, who kept it in a refrigerator overnight."

The former Minister of Public Service and Cabinet Affairs in
Obote's government was arrested in March and confined to Ma-
kindye prison. He reported the death of thirty-six army officers
and one enlisted man, who were shot, beaten and slashed to
death. The former minister was forced to clean up the remains
and reported that, "the floor was a quarter of an inch deep in
blood....Along with the blood, there were pieces of skull and
teeth, brain tissue and empty shell cases." Thirty-two Langi and
Acholi officers were blown up with explosives at the Malire barracks. Beyond the military killings, atrocities were taking place
on a wider scale. In May 1971, Amin gave his troops authorization to shoot anyone on sight that was suspected of having committed, or who might be planning to commit, a crime. He also
issued a decree that allowed detention without trial.

The military killings escalated and the targets of these murders were usually members of the Acholi and Langi tribes. It was beginning to look like a planned extermination based on tribal ancestry. Amin's Nubians, who seemed to enjoy killing Ugandans, committed many of these crimes. There were ritual murders committed every Friday night at a bridge over the Karuma Falls, where the victims' were thrown into the Nile. The crocodiles did not consume all of the bodies and the slow current failed to carry away much of the remains, which were left "bumping and rotting against the banks amid the papyrus." Decomposing bodies endangered the health and very lives of many Ugandans who relied on the river for bathing and drinking. Soon Nile perch were no longer safe to eat, because most had consumed rotting human flesh.

Additional massacres of Acholi and Langi soldiers were reported in early July. Two Americans, journalist Nicholas Stroh and university lecturer Robert Siedle attempted to investigate these murders, but they too were killed. An inquiry by the American embassy prompted a cover-up of the crime. The Americans' bodies were exhumed, placed into sacks and then disposed of in the river. Their car, burned and hidden in a mountain location, was discovered during the inquiry. Amin dismissed the accusations of murder and cover-up as the work of a "prejudiced mind."

There were no written instructions from Amin regarding these or other murders because he never learned to write. But certain phrases used by Amin were code for the action he demanded. "Give him the VIP treatment," meant death after torture. Amin frequently spoke the word "kalasi," a Nubian word meaning "death." Few Ugandans spoke this dialect so they did not understand Amin's death orders. Nubians soldiers were not bound by any code of honor and they killed without mercy. By mid-1971, promotions of Amin's favorites "put sergeants and sergeant majors in charge of battalions." Most of the new men were untrained and illiterate.

Amin blamed Kondos (violent robbers), saboteurs, Asians, the British, "imperialists," and the Tanzanian government for the mounting military death toll. By the end of Amin's first year in power nearly 6,000 of Uganda's 9,000 soldiers had been murdered, most without ever being charged with a crime or provided a trial in a court of law. Amin expanded the army by flooding the ranks with additional soldiers from trusted sources, who were mostly Muslim. The greatest number came from his own Kakwa tribe followed by Nubians and Sudanese. Biographer David Gwyn tells of an officer, later killed, who supervised a small military barracks during 1971. His statement about the prevailing mentality is chilling:

> *It was not good and it got worse. They were savages from the Muslim Kakwa. Every day, and sometimes twice or three times a day, they would come and ask for more prisoners to play with. I knew what this meant: soldiers of other tribes were held in the cells because they might be dangerous. They would take them out a few at a time and torture and kill them. This was now their amusement. It was for them like television for children.*[12]

As the slaughter raged on within the military, the terror of Amin's policies began to affect the civilian population. The practice of "government by radio announcement" was no longer amusing. Many men heard about their own demise on the radio and some learned that they had been named a "saboteur." David Gwyn explains the significance of these broadcasts:

> *The attacks were personal, against individuals; the result was often death or "disappearance." There was little advantage in being forewarned, because there was nothing to be done during the period of warning. If a man was named, he was certainly watched. You could not call on him without involving yourself. It was dark every night at 7 p.m. If you moved around you might run into troops. So men sat alone and waited to be killed.*[13]

Amin's systematic killing of his perceived enemies was a policy that evolved into genocide, because the criterion for death was primarily tribal. But there were many random murders.

Amin did not liberate Uganda. He instead unleashed a culture of violence and chaos by his soldiers that has been described as "wanton decentralized brutality." An officer might see a car on the streets of Kampala that appealed to him. It could be seized in broad daylight, and the owner shot, so the officer could enjoy a new Jaguar convertible. A soldier might murder a man behind a dance hall at night, simply to take his woman. It was unpredictable and terrifying because no one was safe from the military anarchy that ran rampant in the streets and roadways of Uganda. Casual murder was a common occurrence by soldiers who had been given life and death power without restraint or responsibility. Ali A. Mazrui, wrote in the Afterward of *Idi Amin: Death Light of Africa,* "On balance, many more people must have died, or been mutilated, in Uganda as a result of decentralized violence than in response to purposeful brutality by the regime."

In September of 1971, Michael Kagwa, President of Uganda's Industrial Court, became the first high-ranking civilian official to die by order of the new regime. Kagwa committed no crime and he was not a tribal enemy. In fact, he did nothing to provoke Amin or his newly appointed assassins in the Bureau of State Research. But Amin was sexually attracted to Kagwa's girlfriend, Helen Ogwang. Amin's men snatched Kagwa at the Kampala International Hotel swimming pool. He was shot and his body was stuffed into his new Mercedes, which was then torched. No investigation was conducted. A terrified Helen Ogwang arranged a transfer to the Ugandan embassy in Paris, where she defected.

Amin's purges stripped the nation of many of its finest civil servants, and business was hampered by the confused state of governmental operations, budgeting and management. Amin knew nothing about finances and tens of millions of dollars were spent on unproductive projects, mostly for military infrastructure. According to Henry Kyemba, Amin's "financial irresponsibility and total ignorance of economic realities also has a personal dimension. He does not differentiate between personal and governmental expenditure."

A Family Man

Amin married five wives, all of whom were quite beautiful. He had about 30 mistresses and an estimated 34 children, although there is no definitive record of his progeny. His first wife, Malyamu was the daughter of a teacher and the sister of the former Foreign Minister. She was "a statuesque six-footer in her early twenties," when they became a couple, while he was serving in the King's African Rifles. By the time they married in 1966 she had several children by Amin. Before the union to Malyamu was formalized, he had chosen a second wife, Kay Adroa, a student at Makerere University and a beauty queen. Her skin was deep ebony and she is described as "a dignified, quiet and self-possessed girl." Within a year of this marriage he acquired a third bride, Nora, a Langi from an area that strongly supported Obote. This was a marriage of political convenience, although she bore him several offspring. By the time of the coup, he had fathered about fifteen children by his three wives.[14] Amin continued to engage in countless extramarital relationships, described in *State of Blood*:

> *He regards his sexual energy as a sign of his power and authority. He never tries to hide his lust. His eyes lock onto any beautiful woman. His reputation for sexual performance is so startling that women often deliberately make themselves available and his love affairs have included women of all colors and from many nations, from schoolgirls to mature women, from street girls to university lecturers.*[15]

As evidenced by the murder of Michael Kagwa, one of the darker aspects of Amin's amorous activities was his propensity to casually kill in order to achieve a sexual conquest. The prominent Judge he ordered killed for the opportunity to seduce his girlfriend was not the only murder for sex he had committed. One of his mistresses was Sauda Amin, a woman he did not marry, but who nonetheless used his name and bore him several children. She became his paramour after her lover was murdered. A secretary at the Ministry of Culture sexually attracted Amin in 1971 and soon thereafter her husband was murdered. When Amin became interested in the wife of a hotel manager, the man in his way was killed and Amin thoughtfully helped to expedite the payment of the insurance benefit to the widow. Amin's interest in a senior female police officer resulted in her husband's arrest, and then his murder.

Once women were drawn into Amin's harem as a wife, mistress or girlfriend, they ran great risks to themselves or their companions if they ever were seen with other men. Amin's spies were ever vigilant, especially in government ministries and abroad at Ugandan embassies. Amin was sexually hyperactive and never stopped seeking new sexual partners or additional wives. Shortly after the coup, he was became transfixed by a dancer from Buganda who was the star of the *Heartbeat of Africa* Troup. Her name was Medina and, she was "quite simply, stunning…slim-hipped, with well-formed breasts, and was a ferociously agile dancer. She was in a class by herself," writes Henry Kyemba. His marriage to Medina, Amin's fourth, was announced in 1972. [16]

A Black Man's Nation

A national census taken in 1969 counted about 74,000 Asians in Uganda, a tiny minority in a nation of 9.5 million. In December of 1971, Amin accused the Asian minority of "economic sabotage." He charged that the Asians "milked the cow, but never fed it." At the time the Asian population of Uganda controlled nearly 80% of the nation's "floating capital," due to their prominence as merchants. Amin's verbal attacks increased the pace of the already brisk capital flight from Uganda. On August 4, 1972, Amin announced that he dreamed that God had ordered him to deport all Asians from the country. They were given 90 days to leave.

The Asian population was a convenient scapegoat for Amin's failure on the economic issues facing Uganda. They were generally unpopular with Africans and were easily singled out for persecution. Some have called them "the Jews of East Africa." Amin allowed them to take only three hundred dollars per person out of the country. The Asians were forced to leave behind their homes, thriving businesses and huge land holdings. A vital cog in the economic wheel of Uganda simply vanished from a country that could ill afford to lose the ingenuity, skill and work ethic represented by its Asian citizens.[17]

The deportation was accompanied by many cases of abuse and injustice. Many Asians were arrested as the deportation deadline neared and many were forced to pay bribes to secure their freedom. Biographer David Gwyn told one of the saddest tales of cruelty about a relatively humble family of Asians, who were victimized 48 hours before the deportation deadline:

> *Troops broke into their apartment and looted it. In the scuffle, the family's three-month-old baby was killed. The parents were hospitalized for two days. When they left the hospital they tried to find the body of their baby for burial. They were told that the body would be returned – on payment of $1,000.[18]*

Amin's racist policy led to an even greater economic disaster. The business assets of the Asian families were given to Amin's loyalists, especially the Nubians, whose families arrived like vultures in Kampala to await the distribution of the confiscated wealth. But the people who received the assets were untrained, uneducated and had no business experience. They simply stripped all the valuable items from homes, factories and shops, sold the assets and closed the businesses. Soon Uganda was experiencing shortages of milk, salt, sugar, bread, cheese, automobiles, concrete and many other items required for daily life. Millions of dollars in invested capital that had sustained Uganda for decades was squandered and the plunder reached massive proportions.

Amin's policy towards the Asians was partly motivated by an underlying sexual issue. Many Asian men "took African mistresses or used African prostitutes," while the reverse did not seem to happen. As a result, the Africans felt disrespected

and tension between the races was exacerbated. A year after
the expulsions Amin expressed these feelings, when he told
the British newspapers, "We felt they were very unhappy bed-
fellows with us, so we sent them over to you in the hope that
they would be happier here. Before long they will marry white
women. Before long you just won't be able to tell who is Asian
and who is white."

While the nation was being torn apart internally by the ethnic cleansing against the Asians and genocide against Amin's
tribal enemies, tensions with neighboring African nations were
growing. Amin had always harbored hostility towards Julius
Nyerere, the President of Tanzania, for providing sanctuary to
the exiled Milton Obote following the coup. He feared that
Tanzania might attempt to reestablish Obote in Uganda. To
preclude this possibility, he attempted to obtain jet aircraft
from Britain to "bomb Dar es Salaam," the Tanzanian capital.
Neither the British nor the Israelis would provide the aircraft
he sought. It appeared that Amin's patrons did not trust him
with high-performance aircraft that could be used to expand
his killing spree into neighboring African nations. Amin flew
into a rage at the Israelis, who he believed were his last hope
for obtaining the planes.

In early 1972, Amin visited Libyan leader Colonel Muam-
mar Gaddafi, seeking financial and military support. High
on Amin's agenda were the airplanes that would allow him to
attack his Tanzanian neighbor and neutralize the perceived
threat represented by the collusion of Obote and Nyerere.
During his visit to the desert kingdom, Amin apparently re-
discovered his Islamic roots. A joint Ugandan/Libyan communiqué was broadcast upon his return to Kampala and the
nation was shocked to hear Amin's vituperative denunciation
of Israel. Israeli advisors were absolutely blindsided. Amin
refused to meet with the Israeli ambassador and continued to
broadcast hate-filled attacks on Zionism and the Jewish state.
Amin accused Israel of stealing Arab land during the 1967
war and he stated that Israel should be wiped from the face
of the earth. He then ordered the Israeli advisors to leave
the country.

The Invasion

In the midst of Uganda's economic and ethnic chaos, on September 17, 1972, forces loyal to former President Obote invaded Uganda from Tanzania. They planned to engage two of Uganda's border garrisons, while a mutiny was simultaneously launched at the barracks near Kampala. The episode was a farce with little chance of success, since the one thousand invaders were not properly trained or equipped. The invasion was halted near the border with the assistance of Libyan air support. About 3,000 troops sent by Gaddafi drove the invaders back or slaughtered them. Amin took the opportunity to claim that the invasion was intended to stop his Asian expulsion policy.

Amin also used the invasion to justify a massive wave of killings that followed. The highest profile victim was Benedicto Kiwanuka, the Chief Justice of the Ugandan High Court. Kiwanuka made the mistake of releasing a British citizen who had been arrested by Amin's men. Seized directly from his courtroom, the judge was forced to remove his shoes and then he was taken away. Empty shoes became a symbol of state terror. The judge was never seen again. The killing of Judge Kiwanuka marked a shift in the regime's genocidal priorities. The judge was a prominent Catholic and from this time forward Amin instituted a state policy of murdering Catholics.

Shortly thereafter, Father Kiggundu, Editor of the Catholic newspaper, *Munno,* disappeared and was murdered. His killing followed the typical pattern – he was snatched by security men, shot at close range, then his body was burned beyond recognition in his own vehicle. Father Kiggundu's shoes were found at the spot of his abduction. In October 1972, the radio prematurely announced the disappearance of the Vice Chancellor of Makerere University, Frank Kalimuzo. The educator refused to flee and he waited for Amin's thugs, telling friends who frantically called that he had "done nothing wrong." The Chancellor's body was never found.

Tens of thousands of ordinary citizens also went missing. A new industry known as "body finding," was spawned. Families were willing to pay to recover their loved one's remains for a proper burial. Teams of "body finders" worked with Amin's death squads, an arrangement that was profitable for both the body finders and the killers. Fees based upon the rank or prominence of the victim ranged up to 30,000 shillings ($4,000). A ghoulish spin off of the practice was bogus finders who took the money of bereaved families and then disappeared. By 1974, the death toll in Uganda had risen to nearly 100,000.

Amin's racism became more pronounced than ever. He publicly praised the massacre of Jewish athletes at the hands of the "Black September" terrorists at the Munich Olympics in 1972. He sent a diabolically insensitive telegram to Israeli Prime minister Golda Meir, following this tragic event stating, "Germany is the right place, where when Hitler was Prime Minister and Supreme Commander he burnt over six million Jews. This is because Hitler and all the German people know that the Israelis are not people working in the interest of the people of the world."

Amin's erratic behavior occasionally became macabre. Members of Uganda's medical profession have attested to bodies being dumped by Amin's thugs at hospital mortuaries with missing lips, livers, noses, genitals and eyes. These were not random mutilations, but are said to have followed a barbaric but "well-defined pattern." In fact, the killers were acting on Amin's specific instructions. Amin's intention was to violate the bodies of those he had killed in a ritualistic way. In 1974, a Foreign Service officer named Godfrey Kiggala was shot, his eyes were gouged out and then his body was partially skinned. Two other victims, Minister of Works, Shabani Nkutu, murdered in 1973 and Minister of Foreign Affairs, Lt. Colonel Michael Ondoga, killed in 1974, were both cut open to allow tampering with internal organs, according to medical reports.[19]

Rumors of cannibalistic practices have long been attributed to Amin personally. However, the African custom of "blood rituals" puts his behavior in context. Minister Kyemba, writing in *State of Blood,* reported several occasions when Amin insisted on being left alone with the body of one of his victims. He goes on to explain:

> *Hardly any Ugandan doubts that Amin has, quite lit-*
> *erally, a taste for blood...Like many other societies, the*
> *Kakwa, Amin's tribe, are known to have practiced blood*
> *rituals on slain enemies. These involve cutting a piece*
> *of flesh from the body to subdue the dead man's spirit or*
> *tasting the victims' blood to render the spirit harmless –*
> *a spirit, it is believed, will not revenge itself on a body*
> *that has become, in effect, its own.[20]*

Although the practice of blood rituals helps to explain why charges of cannibalism have persisted regarding Amin, it does not account for all of the allegations. There are eyewitness reports about Amin's "taste for blood" and Kyemba states, "on several occasions he has boasted to me and others that he has eaten human flesh." He quotes Amin's acceptance of cannibalism in time of war: "In warfare, if you do not have food and your fellow soldier is wounded, you may as well kill him and eat him to survive." On another occasion, Amin stated, "I have eaten human meat. It is very salty, even more salty than leopard meat."

Amin's Islamic faith has been associated with a cult of Nubians who were descendants of former slave soldiers from southern Sudan at the time of the Mahdi's Islamic uprising in the late 1880's. Men who were members of the cult were identified by a marking of three vertical lines on the face, known as "One–Elevens." The marks can clearly be seen in photos of Amin. His unique link with this warrior cult explains why they were employed as killers in his regime. His killing apparatus was, "all staffed by southern Sudanese, Kakwas and Nubians; they all respond to Amin's direct orders; and their activities overlap to comprise a powerful, merciless machine of terror that reaches into every corner of Uganda and seizes victims from even the highest level of Ugandan society, at will and with impunity."

The primary apparatus of terror utilized by Amin was the State Research Bureau. Originally bodyguards, they were also used for special killing missions. Later, Amin established the Public Safety Unit specifically to serve as death squads. These units grew quite large, eventually totaling about 18,000 members.

Although some terror unit members were in the military they generally wore plain clothes, usually "flamboyant flowered shirts," and dark glasses. They had wide latitude to pursue their intended victims, who could be anywhere in the country and at any level of society. It was common for victims to be snatched off of the street or from their workplace. Most of the victims were never seen alive again. In many cases their shoes were left behind as a warning to the public. This death symbolism was highly effective in maintaining abject fear of Amin and his terror organizations.[21]

Bad Blood in the Family

Following his fourth marriage Amin had little time for his first three wives. He was occupied by compulsive womanizing and the passionate relationship with his newest wife, Medina. All three less-favored wives lived in isolation in his Presidential Lodges and had taken lovers. On March 25, 1974 they threw a party for their lovers, in open defiance of the dictator. Amin's security men called to inform him of the party. Amin was enraged by his wives' insolence and he became abusive and threatening on the phone. The women, who had been drinking, told him to keep Medina and to "go to hell." The very next day, Amin divorced all three wives, in the Muslim tradition by stating, "I divorce thee," three times. The divorces were announced over Kampala radio. Amin claimed that Malyamu and Nora were "involved in business," which was true, since both had been given textile shops by Amin that had been looted from the Asian expulsions, the prior year. He claimed that Kay was a cousin and was too closely related to be a wife.

On April 11, Malyamu was arrested for smuggling a bolt of fabric into Kenya. She was detained for two weeks, then fined and released. The following March, she was injured in an auto accident, after Amin's thugs rammed her vehicle. Amin visited during her long hospitalization to humiliate and berate her. She left the country for medical treatment and never returned. In August 1974, Kay was arrested for possession of a pistol and ammunition, both of which had been given to her by Amin.

After Amin arrived at the jail to verbally abuse her, she was cautioned and released. A few days later she disappeared. The next day Kay's physician, Dr. Mbalu-Mukasa and his wife and five children were all suspiciously hospitalized with overdoses of sleeping pills. There was almost no doubt that Kay's disappearance and her doctor's family tragedy were somehow linked.

Shortly thereafter, a woman's dismembered body was brought to a Kampala mortuary. Health Minister Henry Kyemba, suspecting the worst, reported by telephone to Amin. Kyemba was ordered to personally identify the body and to report his findings immediately. What he described is grotesque:

> *The sight that confronted me was the most horrible I have ever seen; it is one that still haunts me. The body was indeed that of Kay Amin, but it had been dismembered. The legs and arms had been cut off. Lying on the shelf was the torso, face up, with the head intact... The dissection had been neatly done; no bones were broken; the ligaments in the joints were carefully cut; there had been no tearing. The job had been done by an expert with the correct surgical instruments. Too appalled even to speak, I took a step back in shock and simply nodded to the attendants to slide the shelf shut.*[22]

When Kyemba phoned Amin to inform him of the details, the General expressed no surprise and told Henry to go home. Later, Amin instructed that Kay's limbs were to be sewn back onto the body. The next day he brought their three children to see her remains, which were covered only by a sheet. According to Kyemba, "His behavior was quite appalling...he reviled his former wife, and used her body to humiliate them. 'Your mother was a bad woman,' he shouted at the children, 'See what has happened to her!'" Amin did not attend her funeral.

Kyemba believes that Kay's death was due to loss of blood during an attempted surgical abortion and that her lover, Dr. Mbalu-Mukasa, dismembered her remains in preparation for the disposal of the body. Others believe that Amin was directly involved in her death and mutilation, pointing out that the doctor's expertise

could have been utilized to establish a plausible story as a cover
for Amin's role. Since the doctor died without recovering consciousness the true story of Kay's death will never be known. Her
children remained with Amin and have told their schoolmates
that, "their daddy killed their mummy." The most fortunate of
the three wives was Nora, who never had an intense relationship
with Amin. Amin's relationship with Medina continued to be passionate and sometimes extremely violent, when his rage could not
be controlled. He beat her brutally many times and once fractured the base of his wrist while punching her in the head. There
was an occasion when he beat and kicked her so severely that she
miscarried.

Amin later married Sarah, wife number five and a go-go
dancer with a jazz band. When he met Sarah she was pregnant and Amin strangely claimed paternity of the child that
he knew was not his. Amin forbid her to see the child's real
father. The young man then vanished, almost certainly killed
by Amin's men. Amin married Sarah in August of 1975. She
bitterly disappointed Amin, when she failed to conceive again.
Perhaps she was traumatized by the murder of the father of
her only child. According to Henry Kyemba, "She has told her
doctors that she dreams of his murder, and is so thoroughly
frightened of Amin, that she can never enjoy sexual relations
with him."

Despite the mounting death around him and the tragedies
of his personal life, Amin continued to mug for the cameras
and posture for the international press. Many African countries boycotted the OAU meeting held in Kampala in August
1975. Attendees were greeted at Entebbe Airport by bare
breasted dancers and native drummers. Amin arrived at the
reception of ministers, with his 280-pound bulk carried aloft in
a sedan chair by a group of spindly and thoroughly humiliated
white Kampala businessmen. Another white flunkey carried a
parasol. It was a reverse racist image of "white man's burden,"
which could be seen in many old photos from the Victorian era.
The image of this event was carried in newspapers throughout
the world. During the summit meeting, Amin played a few
songs on the accordion to entertain his guests and proudly

showed off his personal zoo, which included a crocodile, an ostrich, a leopard and a chimpanzee.

The Ugandan dictator used the word Dada in his formal title. Dada, literally meant grandfather, but Amin intended it as something like "Big Daddy," both as a spoof and a measure of his authority. His titles were as contrived as his image and included His Excellency Field Marshal Idi Amin Dada, VC, DSO, MC, Conqueror of the British Empire, and King of Scotland. The King of Scotland title was based on his love of bagpipe music and kilts, which he wore on special occasions. According to biographer David Gwyn, "Amin was like an addict – hooked on two drugs, blood and publicity."

By late 1975 the press was beginning to understand the full dimensions of the genocide underway in Uganda. Behind the public image of the jovial Amin, the slaughter continued. It is estimated that more than 150,000 persons had died or disappeared, by the end of 1975. Many of Uganda's best educated and most productive citizens had left the country. The poor slipped across unmarked sections of the borders into friendly African countries, while many of the higher-ranking ministers went into exile in the West. The brain drain in Uganda added to the hardship, in an economy that was failing badly. The inflation that was fueled by Amin's fiscal mismanagement and his eager use of the currency printing press was running above 400% annually.

The base of Amin's political support was noticeably shrinking. The Ugandan military was fractured by four years of blood purges and the civil service was shattered. The economy was in shambles and the forces of terror unleashed upon the nation kept the population so afraid that normal life was impossible. Amin himself was now more isolated than ever and the circle of his most extreme loyalists who could execute his erratic and unpredictable orders was shrinking. Biographer David Gwyn tells us that these men "became more dangerous and ruthless as their numbers decreased." Despite the misery, death and deprivation that Amin's rule had brought to Uganda, his image in the West was that of an amiable buffoon. Then in 1976, a startling event occurred that put Idi Amin on the front page of every newspaper in the world.

The Raid on Entebbe

On June 27, 1976, Air France flight 139 departed from Ben Gurion Airport, Israel, bound for Paris via Athens with 246 passengers aboard. During the stopover in Athens, the plane was hijacked and forced to divert to central Africa. The hijackers were members of Dr. Wadia Hadad's Popular Front for the Liberation of Palestine (PFLP), a wing of the Palestine Liberation Organization (PLO) and two former members of the German Bader Meinhof gang.

The flight landed in Kampala on June 28 and the hostages were taken to the old terminal building at Entebbe Airport. The hijackers transmitted a list of demands to the Israeli government via Paris. The primary demand was for the release of 53 convicted terrorists held in Israel, France, Germany, Switzerland and Kenya. The hijackers threatened to blow up the airplane and its passengers at 2 p.m. on July 1st if their demands were not met. The non-Jews were told they could leave but the captain and crew refused to abandon their Jewish and Israeli passengers. Another Air France aircraft arrived to fly the 101 released hostages to Paris. The Air France crew, the Israelis and non-Israeli Jews, a total of 105 men, women and children remained at Entebbe.

An Israeli team established communications with Idi Amin and the hijackers agreed to extend the deadline to Sunday, July 4 at 2:00 p.m. The delayed deadline allowed the Israeli's to assemble a commando team to execute a rescue plan. The team assembled the equipment for the mission, including five C-130 Hercules aircraft, a 200 man assault force, two Boeing 707's for medical and communications teams (which would not land at Entebbe), and a Mercedes limo and Land Rovers, which were to be used to fool the Ugandan guards. The assault team was assigned to the command of Lieutenant Colonel Jonathan Netanyahu. Israeli Defense Force (IDF) pilots practiced landing without runway lights, late into the evening of July 2.

On Friday night, July 2, the IDF discovered an error in their plan. A white Mercedes limousine had been delivered, but Amin's was black. The IDF sprayed the white vehicle black. By late that evening the commando team completed a series of drills to simulate an assault on the Entebbe Airport. All was ready by 1:00 a.m. on Saturday, July 3. Operation Thunderball, as it had been designated, was given final approval. At 1:30 in the afternoon, the team was airborne, heading south to Ophir on the Sinai Peninsula. Each of the five planes took a different path in order to assure operational secrecy.

After refueling, the C-130's resumed their flights deeper into Africa, followed by the Boeing planes. The ministers in Israel took a final unanimous vote – the operation would proceed to Entebbe Airport. Struggling through a storm in Ethiopia, the pilots knew that despite the difficulty in flying, the storm would make radar detection impossible. Over Lake Victoria, they flew directly through massive cloud cover, with conditions so threatening that the cockpit windows flashed blue from discharges of static electricity.

As the Israeli flights leveled out on their landing path, the Israelis could see that the landing lights of the Entebbe Airport were still on. The commando team boarded their vehicles. The first aircraft landed at 11:01 p.m., with the engines of the vehicles on board running and the ramps already down, allowing them to roll the cars onto the tarmac at the moment the aircraft came to a stop. As the caravan of cars approached the old terminal, Ugandan sentries ordered them to stop and began firing when they did not obey. The sentries were shot down by pistol fire from the Mercedes limousine. Those in the terminal now realized that they were under assault. Some of the hijackers were shot. One was killed while throwing a grenade towards the commandos, who were able to evade the blast. Using a bullhorn, the commando's shouted in English and Hebrew, "This is the IDF, stay down." The team's commander, Netanyahu, lay on the tarmac fatally wounded after being shot by a sniper on the roof. The assault of the old terminal had taken three minutes.

Additional aircraft landed, according to plan. Just as the control tower was secured, the final aircraft landed, ready to take aboard the hostages. All heads of hostage families were asked to confirm that everyone was accounted for. It took

seven minutes to board all hostages. The bodies of hijackers
were left behind and the assault team brought out the Israeli
dead and wounded. Commandos made a final check of the old
terminal building and signaled the aircraft to takeoff. At 11:52
p.m., the first aircraft took off headed for Nairobi, just 51 minutes after the first plane had landed.

At 12:40 a.m., the final members of the Thunderball team
departed Entebbe and thirty minutes later, they joined the
others in Nairobi for refueling. On Sunday, July 4, 1976, as the
United States celebrated its Bicentennial, the first Hercules
flew low over the city of Eilat as the IDF aircraft finally reached
Israeli territory. The pilots were astonished to see people in the
streets below waving and clapping. By mid-morning the former
hostages reached Ben Gurion International Airport, where they
had departed on a routine flight only a few days before.

It was later learned that the Ugandans had fired upon the
limousine caravan as it approached the old terminal at Entebbe, because they knew that Amin had recently purchased
a white Mercedes limo, as a replacement for the older black
model. This one operational detail may have caused the loss of
the Israeli commander. The mission was renamed by the IDF as
Operation Jonathan as a tribute to their fallen leader.[23]

One hostage, 75-year-old Dora Bloch was at Mulago Hospital in Kampala at the time of the rescue. She had been admitted on Friday night after choking on a piece of meat and had
reported difficulty breathing. Although she had recovered by
Saturday, Health Minister Henry Kyemba arranged for her to
remain in the hospital for one more night. He thought she
would be more comfortable there than on the cold floor of the
old airport terminal. His consideration would doom her to the
mercy of a vengeful Idi Amin.

In the morning Kyemba looked in on Mrs. Bloch and later
approved a visit by Peter Chandley, an official from the British
High Commission. Chandley left the hospital to obtain some
European food at Dora Bloch's request. After he departed,
four armed State Research men arrived at Mulago Hospital.
Two of the men, later identified as Major Farouk Minawa, head
of the State Research Bureau and Captain Nasur Ondoga,

Amin's chief of protocol, proceeded to Mrs. Bloch's room and forcibly dragged her into the hall and down the stairs. She screamed all the way to the front door of the hospital and then was forced into a car and taken away.

Forty-five minutes later Amin called Kyemba to discuss those injured in the raid and the funerals for those killed. Then he said, "Oh, by the way, that woman in the hospital, don't worry about her – she has been killed." Kyemba felt disgust at Amin's actions and terrible guilt for having kept her at the hospital. Kyemba's act of kindness had prevented Dora Bloch from being among those rescued.

Amin ordered Kyemba to lie to international officials and tell them that Mrs. Block was returned to the airport before the rescue. Kyemba did as he was told. "I felt sickened by my actions," he wrote. Dora Bloch's murder became public knowledge when her body was dumped by the side of the road to Jinja, outside of the capital, near the village of Lugazi. An abortive attempt had been made to burn her body but she was easily identifiable. A well-known Ugandan reporter took photos of her corpse. He was soon picked up near his office at *the Voice of Uganda* newspaper. His body was found later "riddled with bullets and lacerated with knife wounds."

Amin ordered the murder of more than 200 airport staff members and senior government officials in retribution for the Entebbe raid. He began to expel foreigners and launched a new wave of killings throughout Uganda. But the raid on Entebbe marked a turning point for his regime. Amin was no longer seen as a powerful leader, despite his tyrannical rule of Uganda. The press no longer laughed at his jokes. Because of the IDF rescue mission, Amin had been publicly humiliated in the eyes of the entire world. The events at Entebbe strengthened the resolve of Ugandans to resist the Amin dictatorship. Throughout Africa, Amin's enemies were emboldened.

The world did not forget Dora Bloch. The press provided the grisly details of her killing by Amin's henchmen. A few Ugandan government officials knew the location of the unmarked grave where she was buried, but they did not disclose it to the dictator for fear, "of further ghoulish interference by

Amin." Local villagers also knew where Mrs. Bloch had been buried and most believed that the Israelis would return for her remains. The villagers were right. In 1979, Dora Bloch's remains were recovered and forensic evidence proved her identity. Her body was returned to the care of her family in Israel.[24]

The Agony of Uganda

Amin desperately wanted to reassert his authority after the humiliation he had suffered and the beating he was taking in the international press. The method he chose was to attack the Christian churches in Uganda. In response, attendance in Christian churches actually rose. The Christian community directly challenged Amin by turning to their faith in even greater numbers.

The Anglican Archbishop of Uganda, Janai Luwuum took exception to Amin's insults to the Christians of Uganda and demanded a meeting with the dictator. Amin rejected Luwuum's demand several times and the Archbishop was arrested. On February 16, a phony proceeding was held at the Nile Hotel, complete with the display of a huge cache of weapons that were supposedly seized as proof of subversion on the part of the Archbishop and two Cabinet ministers. Following the charade, the three men were taken to the State Research Bureau headquarters, where they were murdered. A fake auto accident was arranged to cover up the killings, but the bodies were sent to the mortuary at Mulago Hospital where they were reported to be, "bullet riddled." A false postmortem report was filed and the bodies were buried by the military, making verification of the crime impossible.

In early 1977, Makerere University students held a party to which they had invited a number of hospital nurses. Later that evening, the bus returning the nurses to the hospital was stopped by a State Research vehicle. The University security officer on the bus and the driver were overpowered by armed security men, who hijacked the bus, taking it to the State Research headquarters in Nakasero. The male passengers were taken into another section of the building. The female nurses were forced to undress and then were paraded around to be viewed by the leering security men. Then they were raped. The State Research men telephoned others to "come help themselves to the nurses." Other terror squads returning from patrols joined what became a nightlong gang rape. Some nurses were returned to the hospital, while others ran away and hid until daylight. The male bus passengers were roughed up and released. No charges were ever filed and no one was held responsible.[25]

During the remainder of 1977, conditions in Uganda continued to deteriorate and the social fabric began to completely unravel. The combination of economic hardship and military dictatorship made life unbearable and the violence was so debilitating that Uganda was rendered completely dysfunctional. Henry Kyemba has called this condition "degenerative paranoia," which leads to, "the disintegration of the national character and the paralysis of the body politic." People with the means to escape fled from Uganda. In April of 1977, Kyemba spirited his family across the border and went into exile in London following a World Health Organization conference in Geneva. He arrived in London on May 17, emotionally spent after more than six years of misrule by Amin, during which his own brother had been murdered by the regime.

Kyemba recognized that his defection came at an opportune time, since the Conference of Commonwealth Nations was scheduled to begin in London on June 7. It would include thirty-five countries, twelve of which were from Africa. Kyemba wrote a two-part exposé, published on June 5 and June 12, in the London Sunday Times. His revelations of the events of Amin's rule in Uganda were received by arriving delegates with shock and horror. As a direct result of his article the delegates adopted this condemnation of Amin:

> *Cognizant of the accumulated evidence of sustained dis-*
> *regard for the sanctity of life and of massive violation of*
> *base human rights in Uganda, it was the overwhelming*
> *view of the Commonwealth leaders that these excesses were*

*so gross as to warrant the world's concern and to evoke
condemnation by the heads of government in strong and
unequivocal terms. Mindful that the people of Uganda
were within the fraternity of Commonwealth fellowship,
heads of government looked to the day when the people of
Uganda would once more fully enjoy their basic human
rights, which now were being so cruelly denied.* [26]

But still the world was not aware that the death toll in Uganda under Amin was now nearing 300,000 victims. Although the British broke off diplomatic relations with Uganda following the Entebbe raid and U. S. President Jimmy Carter publicly denounced Amin, saying, that his rule "disgusted the entire civilized world," both countries continued to covertly support his regime.

The British provided a vital lifeline to Amin through what was known as the "Stansted shuttle," which consisted of several flights a week between Stansted Airport in Essex, England and Entebbe Airport in Kampala. The British government accepted Ugandan tea and coffee for "the necessary supplies for Amin's survival." By way of the shuttle, Amin received luxury goods, which he sold on the black market at enormous profits. These shipments included specialty items, such as Land Rovers (28 in all) that were "bristling with sophisticated electronic equipment for monitoring broadcasts, jamming and other capabilities." This clandestine lifeline was exposed in the Sunday Times in June 1977, but the "Stansted shuttle" continued to operate until the final days of the Amin regime.[27]

In Uganda, Amin was slowly losing his stranglehold on power. Most of his ethical military and civilian employees were either dead or in exile and the government was now consuming itself in internecine violence. As the killing in Uganda increased, it had become very dangerous to remain close to Amin, which his most trusted associate, General Mustafa Adrisi, learned when he was the severely injured in a highly suspicious auto accident. Troops loyal to Adrisi became restive, and in October the formerly reliable Malire Mechanized Regiment along with several other units began to mutiny. Amin dispatched loyal troops to quell the uprising, but many of the mutineers fled across the border into Tanzania.

Like so many dictators, Amin felt invincible. He was surrounded by sycophants who flattered his ego and catered to his whims. There were whispers that he suffered from advanced syphilis, which rendered him deranged. Whatever the cause, he was reliant on the military, arrogant regarding his own capabilities and reckless about committing his forces into battle. Perhaps he believed that other nations would cower before him as his fellow Ugandan's had. But Amin continued to worry about what might happen to him if his Tanzanian neighbors decided to remove him. He accused Tanzania of plotting war against Uganda and ordered his troops across the border into Tanzanian territory. Ugandan forces crossed the Kagera River border on November 1, 1978. Amin claimed an area of about 700 square miles within Tanzania as Ugandan territory and formally annexed what was called the Kagera Salient.

The Ugandan Army occupied the town of Kyaka, Tanzania, where up to 8,000 people were massacred and thousands more were forced to flee from their homes. Nyerere quickly augmented his military forces with Ugandan exiles to defend the integrity of his borders. The small force of Tanzanians halted the Ugandan advance and began to force a Ugandan withdrawal. By December the Ugandans were expelled from Tanzania, but Nyerere's forces did not stop at the border. On January 20, 1979, as many as 10,000 Tanzanian troops crossed the Kagera River and began an advance deep into Uganda.[28]

With Ugandan troops in full retreat and Tanzanian forces closing in on Kampala, Amin called on Colonel Gaddafi for help. Libya provided 3,000 troops and Russian made fighter/bombers. The Libyan reinforcements slowed the Tanzanian advance, but Amin's men continued to flee, looting as they escaped the fighting. Gaddafi then withdrew his forces and his support. Amin, expecting the worst, sent his family to Tripoli. As the Tanzanian forces closed in on his capital, Amin departed, joining his family in Libya. Kampala fell on April 11, 1979 and the Tanzanian troops and Ugandan exiles were welcomed as liberators.[29]

Amin eventually settled in Jeddah, Saudi Arabia. He was provided a villa and a modest stipend in return for the assurance that he would make no public statements and would stay out of politics. This arrangement precluded any further embarrassment to Islam. During the next twenty-four years, Amin rarely communicated with the outside world. There were a few reports from Jeddah indicating that he led a quiet life with several of his women, residing in a modest home. It was reported that he had been seen driving a Range Rover and a powder blue Cadillac for shopping trips and visits to the airport where he often received gift packages shipped to him from relatives in Uganda.

One of his wives, Sarah, went into exile with Amin, but he later divorced her and she was reported to have moved to Germany, where she was penniless. On occasion, Amin telephoned former underlings, among them Robert Astles, a former English operative who headed Amin's secret police and was known as "the white rat of Uganda." According to Astles, the former dictator was convinced that he was being spied upon.

In late July of 2003, Amin's wife Medina reported that he was on life support and in intensive care at the King Faisal Hospital in Jeddah, where he had been receiving treatment for high blood pressure since being admitted on July 18. On August 16, 2003, he died of multiple organ failure and was buried in Jeddah's Ruwais cemetery just hours following his death. There were many scathing obituaries of Amin in newspapers throughout the world, but perhaps the most insightful appeared in *The Sydney Morning Herald* on August 18, 2003:

> *Amin's tragedy, like that of so many Africans, was to have admired a civilization whose external trappings he strongly desired, but of whose internal workings he had no idea, while at the same time he was partly enclosed in the mental world of a primitive tribalist.* [30]

It is difficult to explain Idi Amin's cruel tyranny in Uganda. Because he was illiterate and resentful of his lowly position in society, perhaps his behavior can be attributed to his need for revenge against tribes who were prominent, ethnic groups who were prosperous or religious people who did not share his Muslim faith. He did not comprehend the ways of civilized society and relied upon brute force, in a display of chaotic violence that almost resembled a tantrum against the forces he could not understand or control. Amin represented a return to the law of the jungle, where the strong victimize the weak and all creatures are either predator or prey.

Idi Amin had no ideals and he never strived to provide anything of social or economic value to the Ugandan people. The simple facts are that Amin's purpose was power and his method was murder. Robert Kayanja, a prominent Ugandan churchman, said of Amin, "He raped the whole country of morality, of integrity. He implemented a trend of corruption in a people who were not corrupt. He raised a generation of people who wanted to steal rather than to work for personal gain." Uganda after Amin remained a troubled society. Milton Obote, who preceded Amin and also succeeded him, said that Idi Amin was, "the greatest brute an African mother has ever brought to life." However, Obote's second administration was not much better and nearly equaled the 300,000 death toll of the eight years of Amin.

A former military leader, Yoweri Museveni, seized power in 1986 and conducted a relatively productive administration, but it was plagued by a vicious insurgent group, known as The Lord's Resistance Army that has become synonymous with abduction, rape, mutilation and murder. The LRA steals children for use as fighters and sex slaves. During the past several years it has been responsible for the abduction of at least 20,000 children and the displacement of more than one million people in northern Uganda and southern Sudan. LRA violence continues today.

Idi Amin was one of Africa's first post-colonial warlords and his example of corruption and disregard for human rights has paved the way for a new breed of brutal African strongmen. Men like the LRA's Joseph Kony and Liberia's Charles Taylor have utilized mercenary armies that specialize in the wholesale slaughter of innocent civilians. Following in the footsteps of Amin, this generation of ruthless tyrants may doom the African continent to many decades of death and despair.

CHAPTER 8
Pol Pot: Cultivator of Killing Fields

"To keep you is no benefit, to destroy you is no loss."

Pol Pot

The highest of all mountain ranges, Himalaya, was named with a Sanskrit word meaning, "abode of snows." It is the source of the great rivers of Asia – the Ganges, Indus, and Brahmaputra flowing southwest and the Yangtze, Yellow, Salween and Mekong, flowing to the southeast. Just as the snows of the Himalayas melt to form southward rushing rivers, human migration followed the watercourses to populate the continent. Along these great waterways, entire tribes of people migrated into temperate regions and river valleys.

The ethnic groups moving south included the Mons, Shans, Karens, Chins, Kachins, Burmans and a group closely related to the Mons – the Khmer people. The Mons followed the Salween River into the hills of what is today Myanmar and Thailand, while the Khmers followed the Mekong River into the fertile region around the river's delta in about 2000 B.C. The Khmer established a kingdom called Kambuja, named for the wise hermit Kambu and the celestial nymph Mera, according to mythology. They became vassals of the kingdom of Funan, which was dominant in Southeast Asia during the Fourth Century. The

Khmers adopted the Sanskrit language, Hinduism and other aspects of Indian culture.

The Khmers rose to power and extended their realm, conquering Funan in the seventh century A. D. In 706 A.D., the Khmer kingdom split in two, forming upper and lower Chenla states, which spanned the entire region of what is to-day Cambodia, the Mekong delta of Vietnam and portions of eastern Thailand. An ambitious Chenla king once expressed the desire to have the head of the Sailendra ruler of Java on a dish. Hearing this story from an Arab traveler, the Sailendra king invaded lower Chenla in 790 A.D. and killed the talk-ative Khmer monarch. He then sent the embalmed, decapi-tated head of the Khmer king to the ruler of upper Chenla. Although it was meant to intimidate the surviving Chenla ruler, this bloody event galvanized the Khmers. The power-ful Khmer leader, Jayavarman II, consolidated the kingdom and expelled the Sailendras. This marked beginning of the Khmer empire.[1]

The source of Khmer wealth was agricultural abundance created by an innovative water management system. Under the supervision of King Jayavarman II, the Khmers turned the Angkor plain into the most productive rice-growing region in all of Indochina. A unique feature of the terrain is the Tonlé Sap (Great Lake), which is connected to the Mekong by the Tonlé Sap River. From May to October, when snowmelt from the Himalayas and monsoon rains cause the Mekong to swell, the flow of its tributary, the Tonlé Sap River is reversed, caus-ing the Great Lake to grow dramatically.

Through the construction of enormous reservoirs, known as Barays, monsoon rainwater and overflow from the rivers was collected and utilized on a year-round basis. Using the natural slope of the land, the Khmers controlled several billion cubic feet of water, which supplied more than 12.5 million acres of intensive rice production. Their ingenious hydraulic sys-tem and a series of canals, dams and dikes facilitated three to four rice harvests per year, producing a vast surplus and great wealth for the kingdom. Like the Egyptians of the Nile River Valley, the Khmers used waterways linking their agriculture to transport building materials for the construction of temples, palaces and monasteries.

Carved into the edifices of Khmer temples and statuary is the history of a grand civilization, providing a detailed record of the succession of kings who expanded the empire and continued to build temples for more than five centuries. The splendors of the Khmers comprise the largest religious monument in the world, which stands as a tribute to Khmer creativity and devotion to spiritual enlightenment. Jayavarman VII became a devotee of the Buddha and artistry from this religious tradition stands alongside the great Hindu epics such as the Ramayana and the Mahabharata in the bas-reliefs of the temples of Angkor. Spiritual enlightenment and Buddhist compassion prevailed over former Hindu beliefs, although Hinduism did not disappear.

The magnificent bronze and stone sculptures and the remarkable bas-reliefs seen on the walls of the great temples of Angkor tell of a civilization devoted to beauty and religious principles. Essential characteristics of Khmer sculpture include elegant facial details and a radiant luminosity, suggesting a spiritual power from within. Although the gods were beyond earthly form, these remarkable works are anthropomorphic manifestations of the divine.

Gradually, the treasury of the Khmers became strained by the cost of building 100 hospitals, 101 rest houses for pilgrims and 20,000 shrines. More than 30,000 monks and priests were supported by the Khmer state. Additional thousands of artisans and laborers were required to maintain the temples and to fill them with statuary. A further drain on the resources of the empire was the constant warfare between the Khmers and neighboring states, especially the Thai and Vietnamese, who repeatedly encroached on Khmer territories.

Following a Thai invasion in 1430, the kingdom of Kambuja, began a long decline. The reservoirs and canals fell into disrepair, becoming malarial swamps and forcing the court to move away from the plain of Angkor. Although the jungle overtook the great edifices of Angkor, they were never forgotten or completely abandoned by the Khmer people. [2]

Years of Subjugation

Between 1450 and 1860 the Khmer people and their fallen
empire became vassals of neighboring states. For short periods
there was a revival of the kingdom and some temporary military
success, including a period when the Cambodian court briefly
reoccupied Angkor, but in general the civilization suffered decline and evanescence. In 1857, France invaded Vietnam and
took political and military control of most of Indochina. Cambodia was made a French protectorate in 1863 and four years
later it was integrated into the Union Indochinoise, the vast
French colonial empire of Southeast Asia. [3]

The period between the World Wars was the golden age
of French imperialism in Indochina, with the rubber industry
dominating the economy of the region. The global depression
of the 1930's brought economic hardship to the plantation
economy and fostered a "dictatorship of police and civil servants." However, the preservation of Angkor for the French was
a "labor of love that transcended economic interests or imperial power politics." The dedicated efforts of a number of French
archaeological experts resulted in the perfection of many new
restoration techniques.[4]

It was within this colonial world that Saloth Loth raised his
family on the banks of the River Sen, in a village known as Prek
Sbauv. Loth owned a rice paddy of 50 acres, considerably more
than most villagers, and he resided in one of the largest homes
in the village. Loth's sister, Cheng, held a post in the royal
household and her daughter, Meak, became a royal concubine
to the heir apparent of the Cambodian throne. Loth's oldest
daughter also became a royal concubine.

Loth raised a family of six children. The youngest two
were Sar, born in 1925 and Nhep, born in 1927. The two
brothers were especially close and enjoyed playing together
and swimming in the river. The family lived in a traditional
elevated Cambodian home near the riverbank. Rivers are
essential to life in the countryside, as the rainy season makes
roads impassable. Phillip Short explains the essence of village
existence:

Cambodian life has an earthy, elemental quality. Nature teams and fructifies. The sun beats like an iron hammer, the jungle steams, the land pulsates with the heat and colour of the tropics... Girls flower into women as soon as they enter their teens, and fade when they reach twenty.[5]

Loth's family was of Chinese extraction and he had a pale complexion, which is highly prized in Cambodia. Sar means pale, so the next youngest in the family carried a name that described an attractive feature of the entire clan. His father, Loth, is remembered as a disciplinarian, who was strict but even-tempered, rarely showing humor or anger. His son, Sar, who would one day become the notorious Pol Pot, had a similar, almost enigmatic demeanor.

Sar has related to intimate associates some of his earliest memories of the spirits that were part of village life in Cambodia. They are stories of a sometimes-gruesome netherworld, where spirits feed on human intestines and fetuses are ripped from mother's bellies. The fetuses are known as kun krak or "smoke-children," and are believed to offer powerful protection from the forces of evil. Life in the Cambodian countryside has always included a hint of menace and unpredictability.

At the age of nine, Sar like other boys in the family, attended school in Phnom Penh, at Wat Botum Vaddei, where he was taught the Buddhist Eightfold Path along with reading and writing of the Khmer language. A year later he changed schools, continuing his studies in the French language, under Vietnamese and French priests, where he learned about Christianity, along with history and culture from a European perspective.

Cambodians traditionally have suffered from a sense of national inferiority to the Vietnamese, who ruled before French colonialism, and who formed the core of the civil service under the French protectorate. But Sar was reminded of Khmer greatness during visits to the royal palace to see his sister and his aunt. There he witnessed the power of a semi-divine ruler, which was reminiscent of the Khmer's grand civilization. These were times that he remembered with great fondness.

Although Sar was still considered a child at 15 and young
enough to visit the women's quarters, he was old enough to
attract female attention in his school uniform. Young women
gathered around him, teasing and fondling him. On some occasions they would masturbate him to climax. This seemingly
peculiar behavior is not untypical in harems, where sequestered
women seek whatever sexual stimulation they can find. [6]

As World War II loomed over the horizon, Sar completed
his studies at the College Preah Sihanouk at Kampon Cham,
located on the Mekong River, some fifty miles north of Phnom
Penh. He was not an impressive student, but his classmates
considered him an "amusing companion," who was pleasant to
be with.

The French Vichy government ruled Cambodia and its
weakness was evident to the Cambodians as it fell under the
domination of both Germany and its Asian ally, Japan. In
March of 1945, facing military defeat, the Japanese decided to
take more authoritarian control in the region. The Japanese
army seized power and arrested French officials and civilians.

For the first time, Cambodians saw Asians in control of
white colonialists. During this period, Sar and several other
students visited the temples of Angkor Wat. It was a trip that
thrilled and overwhelmed the students as they reflected on
the glories of their Khmer past. By the time the French resumed control at the end of the war, the Cambodian view of the
French had changed. The occupation by the Japanese had seriously damaged French legitimacy and the arrest of the Cambodian prime minister only increased the hostility engendered by
the return of French colonialism.

Cambodian passions spilled over into violence in April
1946. Followers of the arrested prime minister joined Khmer
freedom fighters, known as the Khmer Issarak, in an attack on
the Grand Hotel in Siem Reap, home of many French military
officers in Cambodia. After six hours of fighting, the Khmers
were driven off, leaving seven French officers dead. The rebels
used the ruins of Angkor Wat as a stronghold for a week, and
then fled into the Dangrek Mountains near the Thai Border.

An armed struggle broke out in neighboring Vietnam against the resumption of French authority. The Vietnamese revolutionary forces, known as the Viet Minh, were affiliated with Ho Chi Minh's Indochinese Communist Party (ICP). But due to ban on war coverage, students like Sar knew little of the war next door in the summer of 1948.

Sar continued his education at the prestigious Lycee Siso-wath School, in Phnom Penh but failed to gain admission to the upper division classes and he subsequently enrolled in a technical school. It was, however, a blessing in disguise for Sar. He won a coveted scholarship through the technical school to study in France.

Sar was remembered for a winning smile. His was the famous Khmer smile – "that indefinable half-smile that floats across the stone lips of the Gods at Angkor." But it was, in Sar's case, also a mask hiding his real ambitions and innermost thoughts. Although he was only a student, he was beginning to develop a taste for revolution.

Student Revolutionaries

Sar and his student companions arrived in Paris on October 1, 1949, the very day that Mao Zedong proclaimed the establishment of the Peoples Republic of China, in Beijing. Although Sar's Parisian friends considered him a "bon vivant," some noticed that he was a bit of a loner and seemed burdened by a deep inner sadness. They assumed his melancholy to be longing for the girlfriend he had left behind. She was Soeung Son Maly, a young woman who was beautiful, serious and from an excellent family. Sar was an improved student in Paris and he passed his exams at the end of the first year. He made many close friends among the small Cambodian community of students including Keng Vannsak, who was older and who became a mentor to Sar.

The young Cambodian students began to see themselves as patriots, with a firm determination to end French colonialism. But they were not yet communists. By the spring of 1951, the Cambodian students in Paris accepted the communists as friends and allies because the communists "opposed colonialism." By the fall of that year, however, the Khmer students veered more sharply to the left and a few students were invited to join the Cercle Marxiste, a secret organization with distinctly communist views. Saloth Sar became a member of the Cercle Marxiste the following winter, but Sar remained in the background, stating many years later, "I did not wish to show myself."

Within a few months Sar joined the French Communist Party. As he delved more deeply into communist ideas, he was especially influenced by Stalin's book written in 1938, after the launch of the Great Terror. Entitled, the *History of the Communist Party of the USSR*, this book has been called a "crucial formative influence" on the young student. In this work, Stalin emphasized "the Party grows ever stronger by cleansing itself of opportunist elements," suggesting that the response to opposition should be "pitiless repression."

Ieng Sary emerged as a leader of the Cambodian student group and Sary and Sar devoted all of their waking energy to preparation for the class struggle that they were certain would soon come. In studying Mao Zedong, the students found Stalin's intolerance of dissent reinforced. Mao had written, "Whoever wants to oppose the Communist Party must be prepared to be ground into dust." The young Cambodians became part of what then seemed to be an inexorable tide of world communism. They were not theoreticians and had little interest in the more arcane aspects of Marxist theory. In their view, they had learned how to throw the French out of Cambodia.

Perhaps an equal influence on Sar's thinking, as the works of communist leaders was a book entitled, *The Great Revolution*, by Russian anarchist, Petr Kropotkin. It emphasized the importance of an alliance of intellectuals and peasants against the monarchy in the French Revolution. Although later, Sar would say that he "did not understand all of it," he sensed that aspects of such an alliance could be applied in a peasant-dominated society like Cambodia. Sar and his fellow students developed a fascination with Robespierre – the radical of the French revolution who disdained compromise. But Kropotkin believed that the French revolution had failed to go far enough and he wrote, "Once a revolution has broken out, it must develop to its furthest limits." These were powerful images to the young Sar, and would influence the profound absolutism that became the hallmark of the Khmer Rouge movement.

In Cambodia, a new level of anti-French activism was developing. The King, Norodom Sihanouk, wanted Cambodian independence under the leadership of the Monarchy. While this plan was self-serving, it also reflected his observation that colonial democracy had failed miserably in Cambodia due to corruption, incompetence and greed. The students in Paris took a direct role in Cambodian politics for the first time, with a special issue of their magazine featuring a statement that the students considered the king to be a traitor. It was written by Keng Vannsak and stated in part: "The French oppress the whole country, the King trades on his Crown, the Palace and its parasites suck the people's blood..."

Saloth Sar's initial writings were clearly influenced by his mentor. He wrote that the monarchy was "as foul as a putrefying sore" and that "the King's words are good but his heart remains evil." The students reflected increasingly strident views and agreed that they should adopt uniquely Khmer concepts and not imported, Western ideas. Paradoxically, Sar's views of the French Revolution and Marxism were not Asian ideas, but Western political theories. Only the emphasis on the Khmer civilization's lost greatness was authentically Cambodian.

Sar volunteered to return to Cambodia to "carry out a reconnaissance" on the students behalf. Some said that he took the opportunity to visit his girlfriend, but others felt that, with his royal household contacts, he was the best choice for the mission. He departed for Indochina in December of 1952 and his ship docked in Saigon on January 13, 1953, the day that troops surrounded the parliament building in Phnom Penh. The King had announced a suspension of civil liberties and rule by decree. King Sihanouk stated, "any individual or any political party that opposes my policies will be declared a traitor to the nation..." [7]

The Rebel Apprentice

After spending three years in Paris, Sar found his nation suffering from a low-grade insurgent war. While it was not on the scale of the war in Vietnam, it was enough to cause hardship for the people. Sar recalled, "The Cambodian countryside was being pauperized. Having lived in Europe, seeing these things hurt my heart." Colonial troops, in their attempt to isolate the rebel Khmer forces and to deny them provisions, destroyed rice supplies and burned entire villages, causing many casualties and deaths. One veteran Cambodian government soldier recalled tests of strength that made macabre use of the surviving infants of murdered villagers. The babies were grasped by the legs and literally pulled apart.

Khmer rebels also committed grisly atrocities, including the torture and murder of anyone thought to be a government spy. In some cases, bodies of alleged spies were cut open while they were still alive, their livers torn out, then fried and eaten by the accusers. This practice was thought to allow the killer to gain the strength of the victim for himself. Rebel leaders frequently engaged in gruesome forms of sorcery, for example carrying mummified fetuses or "smoke children" as amulets for protection while in battle, a traditional practice among Cambodian fighters.

Sar remained in Cambodia, but provided a written overview of the situation to his fellow students. He reported that the Khmer Viet Minh were the most effective Cambodian resistance group because they were the most disciplined and enjoyed the support of their Vietnamese allies. The students decided to actively support the Khmer Viet Minh, while simultaneously working to free the Khmer rebel group from its subservience to the Vietnamese.

Eventually the French government began to seriously consider Sihanouk's demands for independence as the most practical means to preserve their influence in Cambodia. After months of deliberation in Paris, military powers were transferred to the Cambodians on October 17. On November 9, 1953, Cambodia became officially independent. The nation was politically free of its colonial masters; however it was still economically dependent on the French.

While parades and celebrations were held in Phnom Penh, Sar and a companion made their way into the liberated zone of Cambodia, only three miles from the Vietnamese border. They could not accept modified colonialism and were dedicated to promote true revolution. Upon arrival in the rebel Khmer Viet Minh camp, they were given a uniform of shirt and trousers, dyed black from makloeu berries, car tire sandals and a red and white checked krama or scarf that became the trademark of the Khmer rebel movement. Sar recalled that as newcomers they were not trusted and that the Vietnamese made all decisions. According to Sar, "We Khmers were just puppets."

Sar's original objective of freedom from colonial rule had been achieved, but this was no longer enough. He now wanted to impose a comprehensive social and political system of his own creation on the people. His revolutionary scheme was part Marxism, part French revolution and part personal ambition. Behind his enigmatic smile, he was a developing a plan to impose something more draconian than anyone could imagine. While living with the Khmer Viet Minh, he learned their techniques of subduing the people through methods that combined indoctrination and terror. These practices complimented the lessons from his student days that Sar would not forget and they were fully compatible with a revolution taken to "its furthest limits."

As Sar began his rise through the ranks of the rebel organization, Cambodia was engaged in a triangular struggle between the King, the French and the rebels, who themselves were not completely unified. King Sihanouk was determined to win over the insurgents, to form a unified Cambodian political structure. But the French were just as determined to keep him from forming an alliance with the Viet Minh, with whom they were fighting in Vietnam. The King seemed to make political headway when two rebel groups pledged allegiance to him, but without support of the French military, the Cambodian army was steadily losing ground to the Khmer Viet Minh.[8]

On May 7, 1954, the French garrison in Vietnam was defeated at Dien Bien Phu. The battle lasted for 209 days, and during the final 54 days the French were under constant attack by Viet Minh forces. It was more than just a military defeat. It became a symbolic triumph of indigenous Asians over people from the developed world. It was a shock to all the Western powers, but especially to the U. S., which by 1954 was underwriting about 80% of the French costs in Indochina.

A formal cease-fire between the French and the Viet Minh was negotiated at Geneva. The Viet Minh believed that they had been double-crossed by the Chinese, who insisted that the insurgents accept a partition of Vietnam rather than complete control of the country. Although a military truce was established, there was no solid political settlement and this lack of resolution eventually led to the second war in Vietnam.[9]

Under the terms of the peace accords, the Viet Minh were forced to return to Vietnam. However, before leaving their weapons were carefully greased with beef fat and buried in the forest, for the future time when the war could be resumed. In October of 1954 about 1,900 Khmer rebels went to Vietnam with their Viet Minh allies. Sar made his way to Phnom Penh to shift from armed revolution to a political struggle.

In the election campaign of 1955, Sihanouk shocked the nation by abdicating his throne, which Keng Vannsak later acknowledged to be "a stroke of genius." Free to pursue his political goals and willing to use political strong-arm tactics, Sihanouk and his party swept the elections. Cambodia became a single party state under the rule of a prime minister and former king who was charming, clever, ruthless and autocratic. After the abdication, Sihanouk's father became King.

The politics of Cambodia became increasingly opaque. The King was a figurehead and the French continued to control the country economically, but the political tide was shifting in favor of the communists. Now the prime minister, Sihanouk held power precariously. Intelligence sources have claimed that Sihanouk privately had agreed to allow a limited number of Viet Minh cadres to operate in the border regions of Cambodia to support their communist allies in the war in South Vietnam. In return, Sihanouk received communist assurances of non-intervention in Cambodian political affairs.

Living a Double Life

Saloth Sar's home in the capital was simple, furnished with only a sleeping mat on a wooden floor. But Sar had another side that wanted the good life and a government job. This was the side of his personality that wanted to marry Soeung Son Maly, a society girl who he had begun to court again since his return from Paris. This was the Sar who drove around Phnom Penh in a black Citroen sedan and was an aspiring political leader. Soeung Son Maly hoped the Democratic Party would win a great victory and that when Sar was an important official, they would marry. Sar may have hoped for this as well. But when the Democrats were crushed, his girlfriend ended their relationship and according to intimate friends, Sar became a bitter man.

He returned to his revolutionary ways with grim determination. Then, somewhat surprisingly, he married a dedicated activist, "on the rebound," according to his mentor, Keng Vannsak. Khieu Ponnary was thirty-six, five years older than Sar, and was emotionally very fragile. She has been described as "a very traditional Khmer woman," who was extremely modest and never wore makeup. Sar took a job as a teacher of French literature at a private school. However, he continued to lead a double life that involved intrigue and prevarication. This well dressed and well-liked teacher attended clandestine meetings with groups that were essentially cells of revolution.

Sihanouk was engaged in a delicate balancing act between the great powers, while at the same time trying to stabilize his government and fend off an incipient revolution. The Cambodian leader was politically sophisticated enough to see the dilemma which faced his nation and the undeveloped world during the post-war period. Sihanouk wrote the following observation:

> *The Western conception of Democracy seems to me the only one that is worthwhile from the viewpoint of the*

human condition, of human rights and freedoms. Its superiority resides in the fact that it places man at the summit, while Communism reduces him to the state of a slave to an all-powerful State.... But the great weakness of Western Democracy is its failure to deliver social justice... In most countries where they build up military forces as a rampart against totalitarian, freedom-hating communism, our American friends close their eyes to the violations of Democracy perpetrated by the governments concerned – violations which lead to a system no less totalitarian than the one they are fighting against and without the latter's advantages... The West must try to understand that... its aid will never cure the Red fever if it is used to prop up regimes, which lack the support of their own people.[10]

In 1960, Sihanouk's father, King Suramarit, died. The son then used his political wiles to amend the constitution, making him Head of State for life. The same year, a group of leading rebels formed the Kampuchean Labor Party, run by a four-man group that included Saloth Sar. In 1962, one of the Committee members, Tou Samouth, was arrested, taken to the home of the Defense Minister, Lon Nol, tortured and then murdered. This inflamed the Khmer rebels and put Sar essentially in control of the new revolutionary party.

Sihanouk began to call the communists "Rouges" or reds, as distinguished from the Khmer Roses, or pink progressives of the Democratic party. Sar's Khmer revolutionaries were not yet a force and had no clearly defined organization. The rebels did not see their struggle as between good and evil, but instead they had a distinctly Khmer view. To them it was a struggle between srok and brai, "village and forest." They saw the conflict between the people in cities and towns and people of the countryside and jungles.

In much the way Mao had concentrated his efforts among the peasants, the Khmers would now turn to the wild parts of Cambodia to expand their movement. Sar departed Phnom Penh on the night of April 13, 1962, and although he did not know it, he would not return for more than a decade. He was bound for jungle camps run by Vietnamese communists, where along with comrades, Ieng Sary and Son Sen, he would build a revolution.

Sar and his fellow Khmer rebels soon arrived at a base run by the National Liberation Front (NLF) in the dense jungle, on the Vietnamese side of the border, where there was little food and almost no sunlight. The Vietnam War was raging around them and they lived like hunted animals. The serious lack of food led them to eat elephant, wild dog, monkey and almost anything that provided the protein needed to survive. They endured physical and mental isolation. Because they seldom saw the sun, Ieng Sary remembered that their complexions took on "a jaundiced, sickly look." By 1964, Sar had gained permission for the Khmers to have their own camp, known as Office 100. Although it was separate, all operations were under strict Vietnamese control.

In the dark, impenetrable jungle of South Vietnam, Sar and his comrades began to develop plans for the new, communist Cambodia. He has written: "We applied ourselves to [define a direction] and then to put it into practice without knowing whether it was right or wrong." Sar used Marxist principles loosely but the model was Maoist communism. However, he and his comrades developed a distinctly Khmer, and almost mystical system for Cambodia. Their philosophy was utterly ruthless, but it was cloaked in a native mythology that made it mysteriously appealing to the Khmer people.

By this time, the Communists in the South, now called the Viet Cong, were fighting against a Vietnamese government force that was increasingly directed by American advisors. The advisory teams had increased in size and the rules of engagement were changing. Incursions into Cambodian territory in pursuit of the Viet Cong were occurring more frequently, many times with American participation.

During the Spring of 1965, Sar made his way north on the Ho Chi Minh Trail, across Laos, all the way to Hanoi. After a trek of two and a half months he met with Ho Chi Minh himself. During this visit, Sar learned of a Vietnamese plan to incorporate Cambodia into an Indochinese Federation that would be a single integrated territory. He was appalled, and vowed to never again trust the Vietnamese. But he hid his anger behind the typical Saloth Sar smile.

Sar flew from Hanoi to Beijing and he stayed for a month. He never met with Chairman Mao, but his host was Deng Xiaoping, General Secretary of the Chinese Communist Party. In Beijing, Sar found that the Chinese attitude towards his movement was far more positive than the response he had received in Hanoi. Chinese leaders approved his revolutionary plans and offered support for his cause. Upon his return, Sar told his Khmer comrades, "If we want to keep our distance from Vietnam, we will have to rely on China."

Life in the jungles was harsh and unforgiving. Sar contracted malaria, from which he would suffer for the rest of his life. But from their dark tropical hideout came the framework of a new, utopian society. The vision developed by Sar and his colleagues was not humanistic in any way, and was tinged with racial and class hatred. The new society was to be radical in the extreme and would rely on coercion to achieve its goals.

The Revolution Begins

The Cambodian government assembly elected in September of 1966 took a turn to the right, and Sihanouk did not object when they chose the tough-minded Lon Nol, as their prime minister. This advanced the cause of the Khmer rebels, because increased repression sent many ordinary Cambodians rallying to their banner. The practice of taking the heads of communists became widespread and foreigners witnessed trucks filled with severed heads on their way to the capital from outlying towns. The rebels were under a full assault. Their bases in the jungle were bombed and their supporter's villages were burned by government troops. In the fall of 1966 the rebels privately took a new official name, the Communist Party of Kampuchea (CPK), and in December, they adopted the principle of "armed violence." [11]

The disappearance of two members of the assembly gave Sihanouk a reason to force the resignation of Lon Nol, who he believed was encouraging the communists with his hard-line tactics. But there was little let up in the repression. In 1967, Sar was nearly ready to begin his revolution and his plan was revealed in this letter to the Chinese Central Committee:

> *We have reached an important turning point. We have mastered how to undertake the revolution in our country... Our past experiences, notably in using political violence and, in part, armed violence, from the end of 1966 to the middle of 1967 have convinced us that organizationally and ideologically our people are ready... to launch a true peoples war. We are now exerting leadership [to that end] in the country as a whole.*[12]

Sar's brave words had greatly overstated his case. The rebels were subsisting on small amounts of rice and occasionally turtles and lizards, caught with their bare hands. When raids by government soldiers cut off supplies, they survived on roots and tubers. Their weapons were mostly old muskets and Enfield rifles pilfered from government stocks.

Despite the odds against them, the CPK began the revolution at dawn on January 18, 1968, with an attack on an army post at Bay Damran in western Cambodia. The raid was a limited success, costing two rebel lives, but securing badly needed arms. Other attacks followed in which they succeeded in seizing rifles, ammunition and even some machine guns. Following the rebel attack, Lon Nol returned to the government at Sihanouk's request and his scorched earth tactics resumed.

The rebel's jungle base was relocated due to government assaults and it finally settled at a location called K-5, in the mountain area known as the "Nagas tail," where Cambodia, Vietnam and Laos meet. Sar had his own camp, with a separate staff and guards. Gradually, the power of the revolution was becoming concentrated into his hands alone. Sar, who had not yet taken his revolutionary name of "Pol Pot," became enamored of the remarkable qualities of his Montagnard bodyguards. These simple hill people personified the ideal of the "noble savage" and represented the most pure form of Sar's revolutionary objectives. They knew nothing about the decadence of town or city life and they were in Ieng Sary's words, "men who would give their lives for you without a thought." But where would the Khmer Rouge find more such men to fill their ranks?

In the spring of 1969, U. S. President Richard Nixon inadvertently provided the answer to this question with the secret B-52 bombing of Vietnamese sanctuaries in Cambodia. In operation "Rolling Thunder," thousands of sorties were flown over eastern Cambodia under the code name, "Menu." Ben Kiernan, in *The Pol Pot Regime*, underscores the importance of this action:

> *Although it was indigenous, Pol Pot's revolution would not have won power without U. S. economic and military destabilization of Cambodia, which peaked in 1969-73 with the carpet-bombing of Cambodia's countryside by American B-52's. This was probably the most important single factor in Pol Pot's rise.[13]*

The total devastation of the countryside and the massacre of rural Cambodian peasants proved to be the catalyst that Khmer Rouge recruiters needed. The people were caught between government search and destroy missions and American death from the sky. They turned to the rebels as their only refuge. An American advisor to Sihanouk, Charles Meyer, called the U. S. Air Force policy "systematic pillage" of "peaceful and captivating villages, which are disappearing one after another under bombs or napalm." The UPI stated, "refugees swarming into the capital from target areas report dozens of villages... have been destroyed and as much as half their population killed or maimed in the current bombing raids." One eyewitness, named Chhit Do, gave the following testimony:

> *The ordinary people...sometimes literally shit in their pants when the big bombs and shells came... Their minds just froze up and they would wander around mute for three or four days. Terrified and half-crazy, the people*

*were ready to believe what they were told...That was
what made it so easy for the Khmer Rouge to win the
people over.* [14]

The Khmer Rouge began to grow quickly, their ranks swelling from 6,000 in mid-1968 to more than 30,000 only one year
later. With large supplies of arms from the Vietnamese they
were finally becoming a true fighting force and the intensity
of the fighting increased. The war reached new heights of
savagery. Two National Assembly members who arrived in the
village of Kompong Cham to mediate between Khmer Rouge
and the government were attacked and killed by villagers who
supported the Khmer Rouge. Their livers were removed and
fried, then cut up and handed out to the crowd.

The government began gunning down entire villages believed to support the rebels. The Mekong River was frequently
littered with bloated bodies. More than 3,000 Vietnamese
males were arrested near Phnom Penh and shot. The women
survivors of this carnage were raped by government troops.
The brutality of the government policies began to cause wholesale defections to the Khmer Rouge. The tide of public opinion was turning.

Ethnic purity became an important issue to the revolutionaries and cruelty was increasingly directed towards Vietnamese,
Chinese and Cham minorities within Khmer Rouge controlled
areas. Cham women were forced to cut their traditional long
hair and their sarong was banned. They were forced into collectivization and labeled "internal enemies." Chinese-Cam-
bodians were treated similarly. Vietnamese fared even worse.
Muslim Chams refused to eat pork as ordered. Arrests were
made and a number of Chams were killed. They were, perhaps,
the first victims of the Khmer Rouge genocide.

In January 1970, Sihanouk left Cambodia for an international grand tour. Lon Nol had been undergoing medical
treatment in France and Prince Sirik Matak became acting
prime minister. When Lon Nol returned, Matak forced him at
gunpoint to officially oust Sihanouk. Matak then returned to
his royal duties and Lon Nol resumed is role as prime Minister.

Sihanouk was no longer part of the Cambodian government, but he retained his instinct for political survival. When he arrived in Beijing, Zhou Enlai urged him to make a plea for Cambodians to revolt against the new right-wing regime, which he did by radio. The Chinese and North Vietnamese brokered a deal between Sihanouk and the Khmer Rouge. Pro-Sihanouk rioting broke out in Cambodia and Lon Nol's half brother, Lon Nil, was killed, butchered and his liver was cooked and eaten by the mob. Also coming to Sihanouk's side were the communist forces of China, North Vietnam and Laos. On March 18, Sihanouk announced the National United Front of Kampuchea, known by its French acronym, FUNK.

The U.S. countered the new communist unity and North Vietnamese involvement in Cambodia with what it called a "limited incursion," of up to 30,000 American troops and 40,000 South Vietnamese soldiers. The Lon Nol Government was not informed of Nixon's decision to cross the border. The military thrust killed many Viet Cong and North Vietnamese hiding in Cambodia and resulted in the destruction of vast amounts of weapons and ammunition. The incursion, however, drove the rebels and their North Vietnamese allies deeper into Cambodia and it effectively erased the border.

Sar and his wife made their way down the Ho Chi Minh trail to their jungle camp. In June, his wife's behavior became more erratic than usual. Chinese officials in Beijing remembered her as being paranoid about the Vietnamese. "It wasn't possible even to mention the word 'Vietnam' in her presence," one recalled. Over time, she began to exhibit classic symptoms of what was eventually diagnosed as chronic paranoid schizophrenia. Her psychological fragmentation was perhaps a metaphor for the fate of Cambodia, which was in a state of chaos and would be followed by conditions so perverse and inhuman that it could not be imagined by anyone of sound mind.

In late July of 1970, Sar announced that the Khmer Rouge would leave their mountain hideouts and "go down to the plains." "Today we will change our names," he said. His old nickname of Pouk, which referred to his soft-spoken and conciliatory nature, would be abandoned. "From now on I will call myself Pol," he stated. He gave other rebels revolutionary names. His official new name became Pol Pot, which meant "original Cambodian," or something like "noble savage." He proclaimed that the rebel movement would be guided by a philosophy of "independence-mastery." It meant a return to a more pure, idealized lifestyle, from the time of Angkor to recapture the greatness of the long-ago Khmer civilization.

The life of the rebels was Spartan. Alcohol, gambling and extramarital sex were discouraged. Any resistance to the revolution was dealt with harshly and could result in death for the offender and his family, including children. But the Khmer Rouge cadres were careful to treat villagers with respect. When they picked fruit, they usually left payment at the foot of the tree. Their policy encouraged divestiture of private possessions to share with the poorest among them. This garnered support from landless peasants who prospered through these arrangements. Later, they initiated "lifestyle meetings" for correction of errors in thought or deed and to impose a strict code of revolutionary conduct on their subjects. Gradually, the people gave away their property and their privacy. They traded their individuality and freedom for revolutionary vigilance and perpetual suspicion.

Villagers were coerced into work camps that were dirty, cramped and ill prepared to feed large numbers of people. Some villagers killed their livestock rather than give their property away. On May 20, 1973 Pol Pot announced that cooperatives would collectivize everything. A merciless policy was instituted that punished almost every transgression with cruelty, death or forcible conscription to supply manpower for the war. Along with the ethnic minorities, Cambodians who had returned from living in Vietnam were persecuted and denounced as having "Khmer bodies and Vietnamese minds." Most were executed. Intellectuals or those with educations were identified and killed. Militarily, the Khmer Rouge advanced on all fronts and victory was in sight for Pol Pot.

The Khmer Rouge surrounded and cut off Phnom Penh as desperate city dwellers scrambled to exit the capital. The price of rice skyrocketed and the poor began to starve. On April 1,

Lon Nol flew to exile in Hawaii. On April 12, the U.S. Ambassador, John Gunther Dean was evacuated by helicopter to ships waiting off the Cambodian coast. After killing 500,000 Cambodians and spending nine billion dollars (the equivalent to ten years national income for Cambodia), the American presence in Cambodia came to an end.

Life in the capital became eerie and surreal. But the expat crowd continued to enjoy excellent French food and wine in pursuit of the life that the Khmer Rouge had long denounced. It is reported that one April evening, at the Hotel Phnom, a French girl made love in the swimming pool, in both the deep end and the shallow end with two different men, while guests enjoying their poolside drinks cheered her on.[15] The tense city awaited its fate at the hands of the Khmer Rouge. What the people of the cities and villages could not have foreseen was that Cambodia was about to descend into a Kafkaesque nightmare.

The Great Evacuation

At first light on April 17, 1975, armed men dressed in black were seen on the outskirts of the city. The strangers who entered Phnom Penh that morning were completely alien to the people in the capital. Some said they "never smiled" and that they were covered with "jungle grime." Many reported that they barely spoke and were "surrounded by a deathly silence." Soon the people of Phnom Penh realized that these young men were true primitives. They drank from toilet bowls, thinking they were water wells. Some tried to eat toothpaste or to drink motor oil, never having seen tubes or cans. Most were teenagers, some as young as twelve. One observer said, "There was something excessive about their anger," and another speculated, "Something had happened to these people in their years in the forests. They had been transformed."

The same kind of transformation was now planned for every citizen of Cambodia. Orders had come down from the ruling organization, called "Angkar," that the cities were to be evacuated. The apparent purpose was to purge a decadent society and to provide a labor force for the new, agricultural Cambodia. The mysterious and impersonal Angkar masked the real decision makers, who were further obscured by code names: Brother Number One – Pol Pot, Brother Number Two – Noun Chea and only a very few others knew what was to be done and why. "Brother Number One" was shrouded in so much secrecy that Saloth Nhep was shocked to find out that his brother Sar was actually Pol Pot, when the first photograph of the Khmer Rouge leader was displayed on a poster.

While the evacuation of the city was being planned, a massive slaughter of officials and military leaders of the Lon Nol government was carried out. Hundreds and perhaps thousands were shot and buried in common graves on the day Phnom Penh fell. Northern Zone troops began to round up residents to evacuate the city allowing only ten minutes notice. Those who put up any resistance were "liquidated, as enemies of the people."

Books from libraries were burned in the streets, while stragglers were violently ejected from their homes. Eastern Zone troops were more friendly and helpful than the Northern Zone "blackshirts," but none showed any real compassion. Those not able to keep up with the convoy, mostly the old and the sick, were shot. The roads were littered with bodies and the remnant possessions of the city's residents. Many personal items were at first taken along, but later discarded, as it became clear that the greatest treasure was life itself. Refrigerators, suitcases, furniture and all sorts of household goods littered the roads leading out of Phnom Penh.

An eyewitness reported: "We moved very slowly in the heat of the day. Some people were carrying their possessions on their backs or on bicycles... Those with cars were the lucky ones...Children cried out that they were being squashed in the crowd. Everywhere people were losing their relatives." Hospital patients were being wheeled in hospital beds. "I shall never forget," said one evacuee, "a cripple who had neither hands nor feet writhing along the ground like a severed worm, or a weeping father carrying his ten-year-old daughter wrapped in a sheet tied round his neck like a sling..." The pitiful caravan

stretched for miles and was duplicated on every road leading
from the city. Shots fired into the air kept the crowds moving.
Separated from their friends and family, some refugees lost
their composure and many became confused. A large number
quietly wept as they marched. Within a few days all towns and
cities in Cambodia would share the same fate.

After several days on the road, larger-scale killings began.
At first the victims were usually men suspected of having been
government soldiers or employees. Later, the wives and children of the executed men were also killed. People were given
little food and thousands died along the route from exposure
or starvation. The most authoritative estimates are that 20,000
people died during the evacuation of Phnom Penh.[16] Sydney
Schanberg, the *New York Times* reporter whose experiences in
Cambodia were detailed in the film, *The Killing Fields*, wrote of
that time:

> *The Khmer Rouge imposed a revolution more radical and
> brutal than any other in modern history.... Attachment
> to home village and love of Buddha, Cambodian veri-
> ties, were replaced by psychological reorientation, mass
> relocation, and rigid collectivization. Families were sep-
> arated, with husbands, wives, and children all working
> on separate agricultural and construction projects. They
> were often many miles apart and did not see each other
> for seasons at a time. Sometimes children were sepa-
> rated completely from their parents, never to meet again.
> Work crews were often sex-segregated. Those already
> married needed special permission, infrequently given,
> to meet and sleep together. Weddings were arranged by
> the Khmer Rouge, en masse; the pairings would simply
> be called out at a commune assembly. Waves of suicides
> were the result of these forced marriages.[17]*

In the killing fields of Cambodia, if you failed to work hard
enough you would be denied food and when you became too
weak to work, you would be killed. People in the fields were
told that they were not even worth a bullet. Those murdered

were frequently struck by a club on the back of the neck. The victims' bodies were pushed into large mud pits with some dead and others still barely alive.

Khmer Rouge cadres repeated a phrase originated by the leaders, "To keep you is no benefit, to destroy you is no loss." This expression conveyed the complete disregard that Pol Pot and his accomplices had for the people of his country. They were not treated as human beings, not even as well as farm animals. The working conditions were dreadful – twelve to sixteen hours of labor, starvation diets and brutal interrogation sessions. Spies reported to the leadership any deviation from strict rules, which forbade foraging for extra food. Many people became sick and died from disease, as there was little or no medical treatment or medicine. Those who had educations, civil servants, teachers, engineers or doctors, those thought to be clever, or those who merely wore glasses were sent away for "reprogramming," which usually meant they were killed.

People were classified into two primary groups – "Base People," also known as "Full Rights Members" and "New People," who were called "Candidates." The Base People were very poor peasants from the countryside who had lived under Khmer Rouge control for some time. They were given better conditions, more food and were allowed to join the army or to apply for Party membership. The "New People" were mostly city dwellers, rounded up at the end of the war. They were given almost no privileges and less food. These people were under constant suspicion of being spies.

Administration of the work camps was inefficient and capricious treatment was the norm. The lives of Cambodians frequently depended on random events or the whim of their guards. Within a few months some people were relocated to areas where poor rice yields suggested a need for more workers. But more mouths to feed with meager rations led to greater starvation, especially among the "New People."

Pol Pot declared that 1975 would henceforth become year zero, and time would start anew for the Cambodian people. He reinvented the calendar, allowing only a single rest day in ten and he abolished money entirely. There were no wages, no

markets and no financial system. All feeding was done com-
munally and "free" time was filled with mandatory meetings,
indoctrination and interrogations. Pol Pot's collectivization
went beyond even the Chinese Cultural Revolution, which
controlled thought and political discourse but did not destroy
family life or rout people from their homes. One victim, said,
"We never knew when we would ever see the light of happiness
and dignity. The revolution of Pol Pot's Khmer Rouge was the
darkest black."

As in times past, the Cambodian people had no modern
tools or equipment, no fertilizer or technology. Two hundred
small tractors donated by China were allowed to rust because
Pol Pot called them useless "iron buffalos." To employ them
would be contrary to the principles that he sought to instill.
Pol Pot, the social philosopher, was determined to overcome
what he saw as indolence on the part of his people. His solution was violent coercion to force maximum output.[18] Everything was under the control of Angkar, which Pol's former mentor, Keng Vannsak later called:

> An immense apparatus of repression and terror as an
> amalgam of Party Government and State, not in the
> usual sense of these institutions but with particular
> stress on its mysterious, terrible and pitiless character.
> It was, in a way, political-metaphysical power, anony-
> mous, omnipresent, omniscient, occult, sowing death
> and terror in its name.[19]

Angkar was pleased by the progress that they observed
throughout their administration, as a secret document observes: "Compared with the revolutions in China, Korea, and
Vietnam we are thirty years ahead of them. In some places we
gather the peoples force to be active in production day and
night, regardless of rain or wind. So the people new and old,
work hard with no hesitation." In January of 1976, The Communist Party of Kampuchea, or (CPK) was intent on destroying
all ethnicities that were considered potential enemies of the
state. In the words of scholar Ben Kiernan:

By 1975, the CPK Center had effectively Khmerized the administration of the areas with significant minority populations: the Eastern, Western and Northeast Zones of Cambodia. It had destroyed the autonomous Cham, Thai and northeastern tribal minority organizations and administrations in those zones. But as with the defeat, evacuation and Khmerization of Phnom Penh, the purges created many new enemies. And the CPK itself contained a substantial body of dissident opinion.[20]

The Khmer Rouge eliminated religion and it sought to repress a belief in anything beyond the earthly hell that Cambodia had become. Monks were arrested or put to work in the "killing fields." Buddhist temples were converted into prisons and storehouses, while magnificent temple statuary was vandalized and destroyed.

As relocations proceeded, the highways were filled with refugees, being herded under gun barrels. The deportees were stooped creatures, hollow eyed, emaciated, sick and dying. They had suffered the most hideous insults and traumas. One woman was forced to cook her husband's liver, which was removed while he was still living. All of the victims had horror stories, but they could share them with no one. Criticism was punishable by death. Under the Khmer Rouge, Cambodia had become a mysterious and coercive state that forced the people into an apocalyptic world of starvation, misery and death.

A French woman, Laurence Picq, who was married to a Cambodian man and initially a supporter of the cause, is the only westerner known to have survived the rule of the Khmer Rouge. She found that old friends were almost unrecognizable after several months under the nightmare regime of Pol Pot. "Their behavior was studied, measured ...When they spoke it was in the same official formulae that we had heard from countless other cadres... Every action, every word, was placed in a defined political and ideological context."

People were facing a daily test of their physical stamina and emotional stability. Those who could not meet the rigors of the new revolutionary system were doomed. A man named Long

Visalo, who had returned to Cambodia from Budapest, compared it to crossing a river: "There will always be people who
don't make it, who can't get over the fall into the water. You
can't leave those people behind, so eventually you kill them."

The health of Cambodian citizens deteriorated terribly.
Diseases that had been eradicated for many decades like yaws
and dropsy reappeared. Workers in the fields wrapped cloths
between their legs as protection against miniature leaches that
could enter the body through the penis, anus or the vagina,
causing horrible pain. Malaria was widespread and sometimes
as many as 40% of the workers were stricken with fevers.

Food was a constant preoccupation and hunger gnawed
at people every minute. One witness reported that, "people
who stole food out of hunger were taken away by the police,
and starved to death in jail." In the village of Pursat, there
were reports of cannibalism and at least a third of the people
sent to that area were dead within a year of their deportation.
The standard food ration was one tin can of rice (about two
hundred fifty grams) per day. This was barely enough to keep
a person alive and although private foraging was forbidden,
it occurred frequently. Some died when they ate poisonous
plants in a desperate attempt to stave off hunger. Most women
stopped menstruating due to malnutrition.

The Senior Party officials had access to plenty of food and
many of the high command showed weight gain during these
years of famine. It was a form of political hypocrisy seen in
many collectivist tyrannies. Laurence Picq reported: "These
people lived a life apart, in a style beyond anything one could
imagine in a country so puritan and poor. Dinners, excursions,
parties, liquor – and first choice on whatever plunder was going. Like conquerors they were, they never went without." One
eyewitness reported that at one Party headquarters, "there was
always a basket of fresh fruit on the table." Sihanouk himself
remembered the Central Committee commissariat offering
"Japanese biscuits, Australian butter, French-style baguettes,
ducks' eggs... and succulent Khmer crabs, together with locally-
grown tropical fruits, oranges from Pursat, durians from Kom-
pot, rambutans and pineapples." [21]

The Higher Search for Enemies

Over time, food production from the countryside failed to meet expectations. Even when coerced, slaves are less efficient than free workers and most of the slaves in Cambodia were unfamiliar with rural life, since the majority came from cities. Many were unable to effectively perform the physical work in the blazing Southeast Asian heat.

By the end of 1976, even the Party leadership was forced to admit that there were food shortages in more than 75% of the communes. A witch-hunt began to find someone to blame. Although a few acts of sabotage were suspected, the paranoia of the leadership drove the frenzied search for culprits that gripped Kampuchea. A security prison and torture center was established at an abandoned school called Tuol Sleng on the outskirts of Phnom Penh. Known as S-21, it would become a place of almost unimaginable horror. The torture center was the responsibility of Defense Minister Son Sen, who named a former schoolteacher known as Duch to run the facility.

Torture sessions, not surprisingly, produced elaborate confessions of plots involving treason, spying for the CIA, and planning assassinations of the leadership. The leaders did not believe these confessions made under torture, but they provided "evidence" for further purges, most of which were already planned. Security was tightened and Khmer Rouge leaders began to be arrested and taken to S-21. False confessions suggested plots to kill Pol Pot. Later, Ieng Sary confirmed that these conspiracies never really existed, but that cases had been brought against moderates. According to *Pol Pot, Anatomy of a Nightmare*: "In simple language, moderates were traitors."

Increasing numbers of leaders within the Khmer Rouge were fed to the torture machine at Tuol Sleng. Koy Thuon, a member of the Central Committee, was sent to the chamber, as was Toch Phoeun, Minister of Public Works and the Information Minister, Hu Nim. All were accused of being spies for the CIA. By the fall of 1997, five Central Committee members, four division commanders and many lower level Party officials had been tortured and killed. Even Westerners were caught

up in the net, including a British yachtsman who was arrested
by the coast guard, several Americans, a few Australians and
some New Zealanders. All signed confessions and died at Tuol
Sleng.

As the secret police, or Santebal, arrested members of the
Central Committee and the military command, they created a
blowback reaction within the regime. Perhaps the most dramatic example occurred in the fall of 1978, during the seizure
of a group of high ministers who were accused of treachery.
One of the ministers named Cheng An, understanding the
hopelessness of his situation, attempted to warn the people.
As the handcuffed minister was driven to his execution, he
screamed out the window to the workers in a metal factory, "I
am Cheng An! Rebel, everyone! Don't follow Pol Pot, he's a
traitor. He is a murderer!"

Tortures at Tuol Sleng included electric shock, force-
feeding of excrement, pulling out fingernails, suffocation with
plastic bags and immersion to simulate drowning – known as
"water boarding." One guard recalled the use of prisoners to
replenish blood supplies. "They used a pump... they went on
until there was no blood left in them and they could scarcely
breathe. You could just hear this wheezing sound, and see the
whites of their eyes rolling as if they'd had a fit. When they
were through, the corpses were thrown into a pit."

The purges went even deeper into Khmer society, beyond
merely leaders who were suspected as traitors or just moderates.
The Khmer Rouge leadership believed that tendencies towards
treason extended to children. In the words of Ben Kiernan in
Pol Pot Regime:

> *Among the seventeen ethnic Khmer "poor peasants" who
> arrived in Tuol Sleng from the 3rd Division were two
> nine-year-old boys, two ten-year-old girls, and five oth-
> ers, all under 16. Accused by the Santebal of association
> with a dissident tendency, all seventeen, the Santabal
> noted, were arrested because their parents or husbands
> had been. "Kill them all," Duch wrote on 30 May, ap-
> pending his signature.[22]*

A small notebook was found near Tuol Sleng in 1979, entitled "Human Experiments." Like the Nazis, Khmer Rouge prison keepers had devised a series of disgusting acts to be performed on living victims. The notebook details an experiment using a 17 year-old girl, with her throat cut and stomach slashed, who was put in water to see if she would float. Similar details were recorded for a large woman stabbed in the throat, with her stomach "slashed and removed" and "a young girl, still alive, hands tied, placed in water…" There could be no useful medical information gathered from these rituals; only a grisly thrill for the torturers as their victims suffered the agonies of death. The killing in the prison system run by the Santebal rose in direct proportion of the paranoia of Angkar. Eventually, the number of victims of torture and murder at Tuol Sleng rose to nearly 20,000.

The regional jails in the countryside operated without any supervision at all. Here diabolical practices were employed that could only have been fashioned by primitives who believed in a dark form of witchcraft. Survivor Haing Ngor, who became known for his role in the film, *The Killing Fields*, gave an eyewitness account of his arrest, when he was caught foraging for food:

> We stopped at a collection of buildings I had never seen before, at a clearing back in the woods… Some wrinkled black objects hung from the eaves of the roof, but I was too far away to see what they were…In the afternoon the guards brought [in] a new prisoner, a pregnant woman. As they walked past I heard her saying that her husband wasn't a [former Lon Nol] soldier…Later [an] interrogator walked down the row of trees, holding a sharp knife… He spoke to the pregnant woman and she answered. [Then] he cut the clothes off her body, slit her stomach and took the baby out. I turned away but there was no escaping the sound of her agony, the screams that slowly subsided into whispers and after far too long lapsed into the merciful silence of death. The killer walked calmly past me holding the fetus by the

neck... He tied a string around [it], and hung it from
the eaves with the others, which were dried and black
and shrunken.[23]

War With Vietnam

While Khmer Rouge leadership attempted to maintain a
cordial relationship in public with their more powerful neighbor, Vietnam, border skirmishes escalated and there was increasingly open hostility between Khmer Rouge forces and the
Vietnamese military. Long smoldering hatreds erupted, when
on April 30, 1977 Cambodian forces crossed the border into
Vietnam, and conducted a slaughter in Vietnamese villages.
The official Vietnamese record states: "Most barbarous crimes
were committed. Women were raped, then disemboweled,
[and] children cut in two. Pagodas and schools were burnt
down." Vietnam gradually increased military pressure on the
Khmer Rouge and engaged in open hostilities in border areas.

On September 24, 1977 Khmer Rouge forces went into Tay
Ninh province of Vietnam, leaving a wake of atrocities and
death behind them. A journalist who visited the area reported,
"in house after house, bloated, rotting bodies of men, women
and children... Some were beheaded, some had their bellies ripped open, some were missing limbs, others eyes." The
Vietnamese reported nearly one thousand persons killed or
severely wounded.

In December of 1977, 50,000 Vietnamese troops made an
incursion into Cambodia, and the Khmer Rouge became outraged and bellicose. What followed was major struggle between
communist governments – Vietnam backed solidly by the Soviet
Union and Cambodia supported reluctantly by China. A military build-up along the Vietnamese border became a symbol of
Chinese determination to hold the Vietnamese in check.

Sensing a military showdown, Pol Pot took steps to ease the
suffering in Kampuchea. But, some Khmer Rouge leaders were
unable to countenance more permissive measures. Perhaps to
protect himself from a backlash, Pol Pot reversed himself and

authorized a program to seek absolute purification from Vietnamese influence.

Defections from the ranks of the Khmer Rouge had been rising and now reached an all time high. Pol Pot went on a murderous rampage and purged or murdered many military leaders who were essential to the defense of Cambodia. Two leaders, who were given important appointments at the November Party Congress, were the next day arrested and thrown into Tuol Sleng. Pol Pot's suspicion was a cancer that continued to spread and almost anyone within the Khmer Rouge was subject to charges of treason.[24]

On Christmas Day, 1978, a massive Vietnamese invasion force of 60,000 men advanced into Cambodia on a front that extended nearly the entire length of the border. Towns and villages fell quickly and by January 1, the main assault force was on the highway to Phnom Penh. The Khmer Rouge leadership fled for the Thai border, and by January 5 capital defenses were near collapse. There had been no defense plan and no evacuation of wounded. The leadership simply ran for their lives.

At S-21, interrogators killed the remaining inmates, but had no time destroy archives and 6,000 photos that documented their sickening crimes. The Khmer leaders flew to Beijing, where Deng Xiaoping chastised them for excesses and "deviations from Marxism-Leninism." But the Chinese knew that the Khmer Rouge could be kept viable with strategic support from important friends. Pol Pot was alive and the Chinese were confident that the Khmer Rouge would continue its bloody reign of terror. [25]

A New Beginning

China arranged for a massive infusion of supplies and arms to be shipped to the Khmer Rouge with the cooperation of the Thai military government. Thailand maintained relations with Kampuchea, solidly positioning their government with the Chinese and the Americans, who wanted to keep the Khmer Rouge on life-support to thwart the Vietnamese. On February 17, the

Chinese invaded northern Vietnam with 85,000 troops, hoping
to put enough pressure on them to force a withdrawal from
Cambodia. Within a few months the Vietnamese troops did
break off their attacks and some of the Vietnamese forces returned home after looting Cambodia, and stripping it of almost
anything of value they could carry back across the border.

Pol Pot established a headquarters, known as Office 131, on
the western side of Mount Thom, just inside the Cambodian
border from Thailand. Minefields and pits with punji sticks
(a diabolical jungle booby trap) protected the compound and
Thai Special Forces controlled access to the area. In the same
region, Democratic Kampuchea established a government office that was visited by Henry Kamm of *The New York Times*, in
early 1980. He found attractive guest bungalows with, "Chinese
tea and flowers and packs of American cigarettes" and "Vases
of bamboo…were filled with fresh flowers… The plates of fruit
brought from Bangkok were renewed each day. The best Thai
beer, Jonnie Walker Black Label Scotch, American soft drinks
and Thai bottled water were served." Thanks to the Chinese,
the Americans and the Thai's, the Khmer Rouge leaders were
back in business.

Pol Pot initiated a charm offensive to cultivate support
among Western governments that involved proclamations of
respect for human rights and new attire – jungle green for the
troops and white shirts and dark trousers for the administrators.
The young people who worked at Pol Pot's compound were
selected on the basis of ability and some secondary education
was required. One of the new employees observed that these
requirements "would have got us killed before." In October
1980 orders were given to stop all executions and Iang Sary told
Khmer Rouge cadres that there had been "a new beginning."

The Chinese wanted a solid Cambodian political front
against the Vietnamese. In August of 1981, Pol Pot was flown
to Beijing to meet with Deng Xioping, who pressured him to
bring former king Sihanouk back into the fold. Within two
weeks, a joint statement was issued announcing a coalition government to oppose the Vietnamese aggression, which included
Sihanouk.

In December, they made an even more stunning announcement – the Communist Party of Kampuchea was disbanding. This marked the first time in history that a Communist Party had terminated itself and it caused great shock among those still faithful to the cause. The renunciation of communism removed the glue that held together the revolution, but Pol Pot wanted a chance to win back the support of the people. Somehow, despite all the horrors of his regime, Pol Pot assumed that shedding aspects of his sinister past could achieve this goal. He also wanted the support of capitalist countries. In marketing terms, the leadership had "rebranded" itself into kinder and gentler, non-communist Khmer Rouge.

On June 22, 1982, the Coalition Government of Democratic Kampuchea was announced in Kuala Lumpur, with Sihanouk as Head of State. Behind the scenes, China and the U. S. had found a semi-legitimate way to continue the war against the Vietnamese. President Carter's National Security advisor admitted that he encouraged the Chinese to support Pol Pot, saying, " Pol Pot was an abomination. We could never support him, but China could." At the UN, the United States delegation walked out when the Khmer Rouge delegate stood to make a speech, while at the same time, the U. S., team was working behind the scenes to preserve the Khmer Rouge seat in the General Assembly.

While the war between the new-look Khmer Rouge and the Vietnamese continued, Pol Pot was given a full medical checkup in Bangkok and was diagnosed with Hodgkin's disease that would require prolonged treatment. Pol Pot was nearly sixty years old. The approach of old age and the diagnosis of cancer gave him a reason to reflect on his life. But events were closing in on him. A renewed offensive by the Vietnamese forced a relocation of his headquarters. Pol Pot then departed for Beijing to begin a yearlong treatment for his cancer.

By the time Pol Pot returned to Cambodia, in the summer of 1988, the country was being run by Hun Sen, a former Khmer Rouge military commander, who had been appointed by the Vietnamese. Only 34, he had lost an eye during the battle for Phnom Penh in April of 1975 and had defected to

Vietnam during the height of the purges. He was a cunning
leader, and extremely ruthless. In September 1989, the Vietnamese finally completed their pullout from Cambodia.

The Agreement on a Comprehensive Political Settlement
of the Cambodian Conflict was signed in Paris on October
23, 1991. The UN launched a major peacekeeping effort and
Sihanouk returned to Phnom Penh in triumph. Streets lined
by a cheering throng of Cambodians greeted him. With popular support and a deal with Hun Sen accomplished, Sihanouk
turned on the Khmer Rouge. He told a news conference that
he wanted the Khmer Rouge leadership put on trial for their
crimes.

The Final Days

But both sides violated the U N sanctioned agreements.
In January 1993, Sihanouk became completely fed up with the
despotic Cambodian leaders and the weakness of the United
Nations mission. He left Cambodia and took up residence in
Beijing. Pol Pot assumed that he could return to the use of
violence to meet his objectives, but by now history had passed
him by. He and the Khmer Rouge had become irrelevant,
controlling only a tiny strip of land along the Thai border and
less than 5% of Cambodia's population. After some military
skirmishes between Khmer Rouge and government forces, the
parliament declared the Khmer Rouge, "outside the law."

Government military pressure drove Pol Pot further into
the Dangrek Mountains, where he had a cliffside home with
a magnificent view. It was furnished in French colonial style,
had a shaded terrace and orchids growing from coconut shells
that hung from trees. He continued to give political seminars
at a nearby meeting hall. But his movement was dying and so
was his body. He suffered from a dysfunctional aortic valve
and required frequent oxygen. Most of his time was spent with
his second wife and daughter Sitha. The stories he told were
mostly from the past and he enjoyed having someone read him

the David Chandler book, *Brother Number One*, about his life and exploits. He spent hours listening to traditional Khmer music.

The Khmer Rouge had now become merely a gang of bandits. They attacked a train in September of 1994 and took three young backpackers hostage. The young adventurers were a British citizen, a Frenchman and an Australian. The Cambodian government was unwilling to make an offer for them that Pol Pot considered adequate, so he ordered them killed, in keeping with his old adage, "To keep you is no benefit, to destroy you is no loss." The Khmer Rouge cult of death was still operating, even if it was on a diminished scale. About forty peasants were bludgeoned to death for their refusal to submit to the will of Pol Pot. Soon thereafter, Khmer Rouge forces massacred 52 people, including women and children at a small market near Battambang.

By early 1996, Khmer Rouge commanders had begun talks with the government about defecting. By August, it was arranged that several, including Ieng Sary would join the government's side and receive amnesty. Even Pol Pot could see that the end was near. He told his few remaining aids, "We are like a fish in a trap." But Pol Pot ordered some of his remaining leadership, including long-time loyalist, Son Sen murdered. The condemned were killed with their wives and one grandchild. In all, 13 people died in this final execution.

The remaining Khmer Rouge commanders finally decided to act against Pol Pot's tyranny. When alerted to the threat, Pol Pot, his wife and his eleven-year old daughter and twenty bodyguards departed in a chaotic flight along mountain paths, not really knowing where to go. They were observed by Thai spotter aircraft, and detained by Thai troops at the border. Pol Pot was taken back into Cambodia, where his own people placed him under house arrest.

The illusion of Cambodia as a fledgling democracy under U. N. auspices died completely on July 5,1997 Hun Sen seized full control in a military coup.[26] In late July, Pol Pot and three remaining commanders faced a local village council. Nat

Thayer, an American journalist, attended that meeting and filmed the proceedings. He described a surreal scene:

> *[He sat] in a simple wooden chair, grasping a long bamboo cane and a rattan fan...an anguished old man, frail eyes struggling to focus on no one, watching his life's vision crumble in utter, final defeat...Pol Pot seemed often close to tears, [while] the three [detained] commanders, in contrast...had menacing, almost arrogant expressions, staring coldly and directly in the eyes of...the speakers and members of the crowd. They showed no fear...The crowds, though robotic, appeared to be both entertained and awestruck by the event, [but many of] those who had overthrown Pol Pot [were] deferential...[They] spoke in almost gentle, respectful terms about their deposed leader... [When he left], some people bowed...as if to royalty.[27]*

A tribunal sentenced Pol Pot to life in prison. His three loyal commanders were executed. In a final interview with Thayer, the journalist found Pol Pot "chillingly unrepentant." His final public words were spoken to a Cambodian journalist Samkhom Pin, who recorded his statement: "I am in extremely bad health," he said, "the blood does not reach my brain. It hurts every day."

On April 15, 1998, Pol Pot, listening to the Cambodian service of Voice of America, learned that there was a plan to turn him over to international authorities for trial. By that time, government forces were within artillery range of his location. Pol Pot told his wife that he felt faint and he lay down to rest. By 10 p.m. he was dead of heart failure. Pol Pot's body was preserved long enough for journalists to witness his funeral. Thai forensic specialists confirmed his identity, and then he was cremated on a pile of trash and old car tires. Pol Pot's former military commander, Ta Mock, who had turned against him at the end, told a reporter:

> *Pol Pot has died like a ripe papaya. No one killed him, no one poisoned him... He has no power, he has no*

rights, he is no more than cow shit. Cow shit is more
important than him. We can use it for fertilizer.[28]

During the 1930's and 1940's French archeologists, historians
and academics became enamored with the greatness of Angkor,
including Andre Malraux, who wrote a novel, entitled *La Voie
Royale (The Royal Way)* that contributed to a metaphysical vision of
that lost civilization. During his time in Paris, Pol Pot must have
been influenced by such romanticism, and he once stated, "If
our people can make Angkor, they can make anything." It may
have been this almost mystical view of Khmer greatness that was
the root of Pol Pot's diabolical political movement. He dreamed
of a renaissance of the Khmer past. His apparent fear of the
extinction of the Khmer culture unleashed a murderous impulse
against those he suspected of opposing his dream.

Pol Pot's personality was characterized by a paranoid insecurity that led to the most extreme form of communism ever
known. He passed down through the chain of command an
ideology of hate to his soldiers, many of whom were only twelve
or thirteen years old. They implemented his policies with
childlike enthusiasm and adolescent cruelty. Some have suggested that to best understand the governmental administration in Kampuchea would not be to study Marxism, but to read
The Lord of the Flies. With different leaders, the revolution could
have easily resulted in a wholly different political system, without widespread savagery or mass murder.

Biographer Philip Short has attempted to explain some
of the excesses of the regime through concepts derived from
Theravada Buddhist traditions, but Buddhism was totally abolished by the Khmer Rouge and its teachings banned. New York
Times reporter and eyewitness to the seizure of Phnom Penh,
Sydney Shanberg tells us, "Of the sixty thousand Buddhist
monks only three thousand were found alive after the Khmer
Rouge reign; the rest had either been massacred or succumbed
to hard labor, disease, or torture."

Shanberg further explains, "Religion however was only
a starting point. Simply put, the Khmer Rouge marked for
potential extinction all Cambodians they deemed not "borisot"

(pure)…" Pol Pot and his cohorts were obsessive purists, seeking racial, ideological and social perfection, based on an illusory medieval model. There was no restraint on the atrocities they were willing to commit because of their belief in revolution taken to its "furthest limits." Consequently, inhumanity was taken to its "furthest limits," resulting in a holocaust of epic proportions. Much of the killing, but not all, was based on ethnic and racial differences, making the Cambodian killing a case of genocide.

There is no precise count of the number of killings in Cambodia during the Khmer Rouge revolution, since many of the victims were buried in mass graves. What is clear, however, is that about one in five or twenty percent of Cambodians were killed by the Pol Pot regime, or about 1.7 million people out of a total population of about 8 million people. This makes the Cambodian genocide, on a percentage basis greater than Hitler's "final solution; greater than Stalin's "Great Terror" and even larger than Mao's "secret famine" of the Great Leap Forward. None of these horrors approached 20% of the population. [29]

Four Khmer Rouge leaders now face trial: the highest ranking member of the regime, Nuon Chea, 82, known as Brother Number 2, Khieu Samphan, 76, head of state in the Khmer Rouge government, Kaing Khek Ieu (better known as Duch), the leader of the S-21 torture center, and Ieng Sary, former minister of foreign affairs, who was originally given amnesty by the Hun Sen government, but was arrested along with his wife, Ieng Thirith in late 2007. The long delayed trial of the first defendant, Kaing Khek Ieu, began on March 30, 2009. The defendant acknowledged his crimes and asked for forgiveness. He was sentenced to a mere 19 years in prison. The political obstruction that has prevailed for a decade regarding the tribunal leaves little hope for justice, resolution or healing. [30]

After all the horrors the Cambodian people endured during Pol Pot's regime and the politically inspired postponement of justice, there is now a small ray of hope for Cambodia. Ironically, that hope rests upon the shining glory that was the inspiration for the Khmer Rouge revolution – the grandeur of the Khmer civilization. The world of commercial tourism has discovered these wonders and has embraced them with much of the same intensity as past generations did the pyramids and temples of Egypt.

Affluent travelers now flock to Siem Reap and Phnom Penh to see dazzling Khmer architecture and its stunning statuary. Tourists are pumping literally billions of dollars into the Cambodian economy. While corruption may siphon off much of this income, some is destined for the people of Cambodia, in the form of education, jobs and new opportunities. Perhaps, in the end, the greatness of the early Khmers will bring a better life for the Cambodian people.

CHAPTER 9
Saddam Hussein: The Politics of Terrorism

"The hand of the revolution can reach out to its enemies wherever they are found."

Saddam Hussein

Roaming hunter-gatherers began settling Mesopotamia as early as 5000 BC. In this "fertile crescent," where the Tigris and Euphrates rivers spill into the Persian Gulf, the Ubaidian people drained the marshes and irrigated wheat and barley fields beginning in about 3900 BC. They were followed by the Sumerians, who built the first cities and created an ancient alphabet of picture words called cuneiforms. Despite the achievements of early Mesopotamia, the region had no natural defensive barriers, and the "cradle of civilization," became a cauldron of conflict, falling prey to successive invaders.

The Babylonians followed the Sumerians. Their king, Hammurabi, gave the world its first codified laws. In 605 B. C. Nebuchadnezzar became king of an empire that by then extended from the Persian Gulf to the Mediterranean Sea. The Persian armies of Cyrus the Great conquered the Babylonians in 539 B. C. Then, Alexander the Great fought his decisive battle with the Persians on Mesopotamia's northern plains at Gaugamela, in 331 B. C. Persian influence persisted, but in 637 A. D., Arab armies, newly converted to Islam, won an important battle against the Persians at Qudisiyah on the lower Euphrates.[1]

Leadership succession of the new Islamic religion was in dispute following the death of Muhammad in 632 A.D. Many believed that the position of Viceroy of God, or Caliph, should be awarded to a direct descendent of the Prophet, but a majority of believers favored the Prophet's close friend, Abu Bakr. Bakr became Caliph, leaving Muhammad's cousin and son-in-law, Ali ibn Abu Talib, out of power. Abu Bakr was followed as Caliph by Uthman and upon his murder Ali finally became the fourth Caliph, restoring succession by bloodline. Ali's position of leadership was contested, however, and he was murdered at his newly completed mosque on the Euphrates at Kufah, in 661. The majority of Muslims favored the King of Syria as the next Caliph, but supporters of the murdered Ali, who became known as Shiat Ali or partisans of Ali, prevailed on Ali's son, Hussein, to succeed his father. The two sides in the battle for succession met near Karbala on October 10, 680. During the battle Hussein was killed and decapitated.

The battle at Karbala has assumed enormous importance within the world of Islam because it caused a permanent schism among Muslims and created a martyr in the minds of the supporters of Ali's bloodline, who became known as the Shiites. Karbala would become their holy city and the annual mourning of Hussein's death continues, even today, in the spectacular ceremony of Ashura. During this pilgrimage, faithful Shiites march while flagellating themselves with whips and swords.

The followers of Mu'awiyah, ruler of Syria, and his successors became known as Sunnis, which means the Way of the Prophet. The Sunnis prevailed as the dominant sect of Islam and were identified with the upper class. The Syrian King became Caliph, both spiritual ruler and head of the Islamic empire. Shiites meanwhile continued to venerate the Imams, or descendents of the Prophet through the 12th Imam, Mohammed al-Mahdi or the "Guided One." This Imam was the last of Ali's bloodline and he disappeared in the 9th century. Shiites believe that al-Mahdi, the next successor has been mystically "hidden" and that the 13th Imam will emerge sometime in the future, when justice will finally prevail. The Shiites lost the struggle for succession and became the oppressed class of the Islamic world. [2]

The Abbasids, a dynasty that claimed kinship with the Prophet Muhammad, established a Caliphate in Mesopotamia in 750 A. D. Their capital was moved upstream to Baghdad and the full flower of an imperial empire returned to the region. The publication of the *Thousand and One Nights* and other Arabic classics earned Baghdad a place among the cultural capitals of the world. Despite its greatness, the Abbasid Empire was dealt a mortal blow when Mongols from Asia besieged Baghdad in 1258. In 1401, Baghdad was sacked by Timur, ruler of Samarkand and after 1623 Mesopotamia became a sleepy backwater of the Ottoman Turkish Empire.

For the next four hundred years, control of the "cradle of civilization" was the object of a continuing conflict between the Safavid Empire of Persia and the Ottoman Turks. Fearing the spread of Shia Islam to their own heartland in Anatolia, the Sunni Ottomans attempted to maintain the region as a buffer between themselves and the Shiite-dominated Persian Empire. World War I was a turning point for the Ottoman Turks, who were allied with the Germans.

The Paris Peace Conference of 1919 placed most of the region under a British mandate, with Syria falling under control of the French. A Jihad (Holy War) jointly supported by Sunni and Shiite religious leaders was fomented to gain liberation from British colonial rule. The revolt was suppressed in 1921, when the British designated Faisal I, a member of a powerful Hashemite family from Mecca, to rule the newly named Kingdom of Iraq.

Before his death, Faisal I wrote a confidential memorandum that revealed his prescient understanding of the fundamental problem facing Iraq:

> *There is still – and I say this with a heart full of sorrow – no Iraqi people, but unimaginable masses of human beings devoid of any patriotic ideas, imbued with religious traditions and absurdities, connected by no common tie,*

giving ear to evil, prone to anarchy, and perpetually ready to rise against any government whatsoever.[3]

Faisal's observation could have been written today, since the same lack of national cohesion eludes the country, even now. In 1927, oil was discovered in Kirkuk, dramatically altering the nation's economic potential. Consequently, in the aftermath of colonialism this oil-rich nation presented grand possibilities for a ruthless opportunist. But Saddam Hussein, the strong man who eventually seized control of Iraq, would need a repressive political organization and the emergence of Arab nationalism to pave his way to power.

The Rise of the Ba'th Party

Michel 'Aflaq, a young man with a "Christian, Greek Orthodox background," and Salah al-Din al-Bitar, a Sunni Muslim from a deeply religious family, were both born in the al-Maydan quarter of Damascus. Although the two young intellectuals were reared in a common community, they did not actually meet until 1925 in Paris, where they formed an Arab Students Union. Following the defeat of France by the Germans in 1940, the two men created the political organization that later became the Ba'th Party (Ba'th is an Arabic word meaning resurrection or renaissance). Their philosophy set them apart from other nationalist organizations because they were committed to pan-Arabism or the unification of Arab peoples. Iraqi Ba'thists embraced the intense, ascetic 'Aflaq as their "spiritual father." [4]

'Aflaq' believed deeply in a sense of Arab identity and he conceptualized Arab nationalism as a transcendent, almost religious experience. In its first programmatic statement issued in 1943, the Ba'th Party stated that, "We represent the Arab Spirit against materialist Communism." The Party denounced Western ideas, stating, "We represent living Arab history against dead reaction and artificial progressivism." The philosophy of Arab unity sounded inspirational but the new party had another characteristic. 'Aflaq observed that the Arab Nation had a "sickness" that could be cured by an "Idea," but this would require a "Leader" for its eventual implementation:

> *The Leader, in times of weakness of the "Idea" and its constriction, is not one to appeal to a majority or to a consensus, but to translate numbers into the "Idea"; he is not the ingatherer, but the unifier. In other words he is the master of the singular "Idea" from which he separates and casts aside all those who contradict it.* [5]

Ba'thism resembles other totalitarian schemes of the twentieth century in the belief that violence and cruelty are required in the pursuit of an overarching goal. In the case of Ba'thism, it is the "Spirit" or "Idea" of pan-Arabism. The pure "morality" of the movement gives license to violence. On this point 'Aflaq is precise – he specifies that Party members must "engender fierce hatred until death towards those persons who represent a contrary idea." He states, "The antagonistic idea does not exist by itself; it is embodied in persons who must perish, so that it too must perish." 'Aflaq even describes the attitude of Ba'thists during the application of violence:

> *When we are cruel to others, we know that our cruelty is in order to bring them back to their true selves, of which they are ignorant. Their potential will, which has not been clarified yet, is with us, even when their swords are drawn against us.* [6]

In the same way that Hitler's Nazis and Stalin's Bolsheviks were the sole arbiters of policy and belief, the "spiritual father" of the Iraqi Ba'th Party had defined the principles that identified him with the brutally authoritarian regimes of his age.

A rising tide of Arab nationalism and bitter hatred of British occupation resulted in an unsuccessful Wathbah (uprising) against British rule in 1948. The Iraqi powder keg exploded again on July 14, 1958, when King Hussein of Jordan requested Iraqi assistance against an anti-Western revolt in Lebanon. Officers of the

Iraqi 19th Brigade mobilized, but instead of reinforcing Jordan,
they marched into Baghdad and proclaimed a new republic to the
cheers of huge crowds. The leadership of the monarchy and the
Iraqi royal family were killed. The old rivalries of Sunni, Shiite
and Kurd reemerged to plunge the nation into political chaos for
more than three years. Iraq's military leader, Brigadier Abd al Ka-
rim Qasim precariously attempted to balance pan-Arabism against
communism, while at the same time trying to subdue an armed
resistance by the Kurds.

The Life and Politics of Saddam Hussein

When the warlord Timur of Samarkand swept over Mesopotamia, his troops built a pyramid from the skulls of their
victims. The location of this grisly monument was near the
provincial town of Tikrit, on the Tigris River, about one hundred miles north of the capital. This is the place where the
legendary Saladin was born in 1138 and the region where
Saddam Hussein was raised. Saddam was born in the small
village of Ouija, near Tikrit, on April 28, 1937. His birthplace
was a typical mud-brick village where tribal life has changed
little over the years. His father was Hussein al-Majid, a peasant
farmer, who died or disappeared before Saddam's birth. His
mother, Subha al-Tulfah, was a traditional woman who wore the
dark robe of tribal custom. She attempted suicide following
the loss of her husband and she tried without success to abort
her pregnancy.

Little is known about Saddam's childhood beyond the propaganda espoused in his official biography. He was raised and
greatly influenced by his maternal uncle, Khair Allah Talfah, a
former military officer and Nazi sympathizer. When Saddam
was three years old, his uncle was imprisoned following a failed
coup. After his uncle's arrest the boy was returned to his family. Saddam was rejected by his mother and possibly beaten by
his stepfather. His dysfunctional and chaotic childhood taught
Saddam that loyalties to the tribe and the clan were as imperative as the distrust of outsiders. A photo taken when Saddam

was a boy shows his stepfather, Ibrahim al-Hassan, wearing a white headdress and a traditional robe, while carrying a double-barreled shotgun. Predictably, Saddam was prone to violence from an early age and has bragged that he threatened his headmaster with death when he was expelled from school.

When his uncle was released from prison in 1948, Saddam ran away from home to live with him in Tikrit. Saddam later followed his uncle to Baghdad. While attending high school he became involved in Arab nationalist politics and at the age of 20 he joined the Ba'th Party. When the monarchy was overthrown in 1958, a swirling power struggle brought about violent clashes between communist and nationalist partisans.

Saddam was recruited by his uncle to assassinate a prominent communist leader in Tikrit, which he accomplished with a single gunshot to the man's head. He served six months in prison but was released for lack of evidence. Saddam was recruited to commit a second assassination, this time by his cousin and mentor, General Ahmad Hassan al-Bakr, who targeted his rival, Brigadier General Qasim. The plot failed, but a wounded Saddam escaped arrest and fled to Egypt. There he completed his education. Saddam was in Egypt in 1961 when the British declared Kuwait, a former province of Mesopotamia, to be independent. The majority of Iraqis opposed the declaration of independence for the Kuwaitis and never accepted its sovereignty.

The Ba'th Party took power in Iraq following a coup in 1963, in which General Qasim was assassinated. American policy opposed Qasim because he had nationalized part of the Iraq Petroleum Company, an international consortium with rights to produce Iraqi oil. The Americans were pleased with the overthrow of Qasim and according to the CIA Station Chief in the Middle East, "we regarded it as a great victory."

The new Ba'th regime collapsed and Saddam was jailed for his participation in a massacre of those who opposed the Ba'thists. But Michel 'Aflaq put Saddam in charge of the Party security apparatus, known as "Jihaz Haneen" or the "Instrument of Yearning." The theoretician, 'Aflaq and the operative, Saddam, were now joined together through the Party's instrument of terror. In

1968, a second Ba'thist coup was successful. 'Aflaq promoted Saddam Hussein to the Regional Command, the highest-ranking organization of the Iraqi branch of the Arab Ba'th Party. Saddam achieved his initial step up the ladder of power by direct order of the "spiritual father" of the Party for his work in its first secret police organization.

In 1969, Saddam appointed Nadhim Kzar chief of Internal State Security, one of only a few Shiites to gain real power within the Ba'th Party. Kzar proved disloyal to Saddam when he attempted a takeover of the regime in 1973. Kzar was executed along with thirty-five others on orders from the Revolutionary Command Council (RCC), which was the new supreme authority in Iraq. In a speech that followed the execution of the dissidents, Saddam provided his own context for the internal struggle facing the Ba'th Party:

> *Throughout all its stages, the Revolution will remain capable of performing its role courageously and precisely without hesitation or panic, once it takes action to crush the pockets of the counter-revolution. All that we hear and read about, including those crimes which have taken place recently, are new devices to confront the Revolution and exhaust it psychologically. These are not sadistic crimes as some imagine; they are crimes committed by traitorous agents. Those who have sold themselves to the foreigner will not escape punishment.* [7]

Saddam formally launched the politics of terrorism when he reorganized the secret police apparatus. He invented a new definition for treason that was more abstract and indefinable than ever before. Henceforth, treason could be in people's thoughts as well as in their deeds. Kanan Makyia observes, "Once treason was ensconced in this fashion, police work logically became the substitute for all politics." Saddam transformed the old Amn, or State Internal Security Department into the Mukhabarat or Party Intelligence Network, which became a "distinctly political body, not merely a professional organ of the state charged with safeguarding national security."

He also established the Estikhbarat, or Military Intelligence, which facilitated control of Iraqi nationals abroad. Saddam consolidated power by purging his enemies, reestablishing his authority and legitimizing the use of terror in politics.

During the 1970's the Ba'th Party solidified its control of Iraq by continuing the persecution of its enemies, including communists and Kurds. Hundreds of communists were tortured and killed. Saddam's family ties to the leadership of Iraq were strengthened by the presence of his uncle and guardian, Khair Allah Talfah, who was a member of the RCC. A further unifying element was Saddam's marriage to Talfah's daughter, Sajida. The marriage had been arranged when Saddam was 5 years old and Sajida was 7.

In 1979, following the fall of the Shah of Iran, Saddam cunningly arranged the transfer of presidential power to himself by the RCC at the expense of his cousin, General Ahmad Hassan al-Bakr. Al-Bakr was forced to resign and was arrested. He remained in custody until his death in 1982. At the age of 42, Saddam became President of the Republic, Chairman of the Revolutionary Command Council (RCC), and Secretary-General of the Ba'th Party, Prime Minister and Commander-in-Chief of the Armed Forces. He also granted himself the military rank of Field Marshal.

Saddam's personal power was underscored by means of a savage and dramatic performance that is legendary in Iraq. During the week of July 18, 1979, he summoned all members of the RCC along with high Ba'th Party officials to Baghdad for a series of important meetings. The meetings were carefully staged and videotaped for the purpose of spreading terror throughout the Party and the nation. Saddam announced to Party members that there were "conspirators" in their midst. One man, who had already been tortured, confessed his guilt. He then began to name others who he accused of treason.

Those who protested the charges were screamed down by Saddam, who shouted "Itla!" "Itla!" – "Get Out!" "Get Out!" Slowly and ominously, the names of sixty traitors were read. They were then removed from the hall by security men. Saddam came to the podium to tearfully repeat the names of the traitors. Those in the hall also began to cry, emotionally spent by the experience and absolutely terrified. He called on everyone still present to join the firing squads of the traitors. They shouted their approval and rose to their feet clapping, their tears mixed with hysterical laughter. The Party and the nation then understood that Saddam was the absolute leader of Iraq and that no one would ever be safe again. [8]

War With Iran

Saddam sought to take advantage of Iran's weakened military after the fall of the Shah. On September 22, 1980, the Iraqi air force bombed air bases inside Iran and began what became an eight-year war. Within two years about 50,000 Iraqi soldiers had been killed and a similar number captured. Fear began to mount among the Arab Gulf States that Iraq might actually lose the war to the hated Iranian Shiites. Sunni Arab regimes generously bankrolled Saddam's war costs. The United States, still reeling from the Iranian hostage crisis, provided important strategic intelligence, including satellite photography. Despite this support, the Iranians pushed the Iraqi forces back across the border in 1982. Iraq withdrew all of its forces and sought a peace agreement to end the fighting. The enraged Iranian leadership was determined to overthrow Saddam as punishment for the invasion so the war continued.

A sectarian struggle within Iraq complicated the conflict because many Shiites in southern Iraq were openly sympathetic to Iran's Shiite leadership. When Saddam visited the town of Dujail on July 8, 1982, a group of Daiwa Party Shiite militants shot at his motorcade. In an action reminiscent of Nazi retribution, Saddam responded with collective punishment. More than 140 men and boys of fighting age were taken into custody and never seen again. About 1,500 men, women and children from the town were seized. After more than a year in prison most were exiled to a camp in the desert. Their homes were bulldozed and their orchards demolished. The Shiites would not forget Saddam's savagery. [9]

During the war Iranian forces had taken heavy casualties from Saddam's use of mustard gas and nerve agents including tabun and sarin. Iran too, used chemical weapons during the war. Each side had committed carnage on a huge scale and by the end of 1987, both nations were completely exhausted. In August of 1988, the United Nations brokered a cease-fire that finally ended the conflict.

With characteristic bravado, Saddam proclaimed Iraq the victor in the war. He named the war Qadisiyyaat Saddam, evoking the great battle fought between Arabs and Persians on the plains of Qadisiyyah, in southern Iraq in 637 A. D. The claim of victory was arrogantly overstated. But Saddam had built a true regional military power, with an army of fifty-five divisions, a tank force of four thousand and rockets that could reach both Tehran and Tel Aviv.

The so-called Victory Arch was a vulgar display of Saddam's egotism – a massive sculpture of his own hands holding two crossed swords. Any claim of achievements related to the war with Iran could not obscure the terrible price paid by Iraq. Casualties were estimated to be at least 200,000 Iraqi dead, 400,000 wounded and perhaps 70,000 taken as prisoners. The Iraqi debt was nearly $80 billion owed to the Gulf States and the industrialized world, plus loss of oil revenue due to wartime supply disruptions.[10]

By the end of the Iran-Iraq war, Saddam Hussein had transformed his nation into a land of fear, repression and terror. Saddam implemented the most frightening aspects of the Ba'thist belief system, completely robbing the people of their sense of self. He replaced it with a sense of mortal dread of his all-pervasive security state. The people were so filled with fear that they would believe anything Saddam told them to believe. His power over the people was reinforced by a culture of cruelty that elevated hideous tortures into monstrous theatrical art forms. The eyes of children were gouged out to force confessions from their parents, enemies were murdered and dismembered, their body parts left on the doorstep of the widow. Poison gas was used to exterminate entire towns. Saddam created a "Third-World style of barbarism," that eventually spawned a tribal and religious genocide within Iraq.

According to a 2006 interview by Newsweek with Susannah Sirkin, Deputy Director of Physicians for Human Rights, a systematic horror was perpetrated in northern Iraq beginning in 1988. Tens of thousands of Kurdish refugees fled into southern Turkey claiming that their villages had been subjected to chemical weapons attacks. Physicians for Human Rights sent a team to investigate but they were denied access to the area. Saddam's government categorically denied the use of unconventional weapons. But the evidence was unmistakable. Ms. Sirkin described the findings based on eyewitness interviews:

> *They had been some distance from the bomb they described as being dropped from the air. Those who were closer to the bomb died. The refugees described the bodies they saw as they ran away. They said the people who died turned black and blood-tinged fluid seeped from their noses and mouths. Their skin turned thick and leathery. They also described how small animals died within minutes around them. The people we'd interviewed had somehow survived, but the symptoms they described confirmed to us the use of mustard gas: eye irritation, skin blistering, throat burning, dizziness, pain from breathing, shortness of breath.*[11]

Physicians for Human Rights provided testimony to the Congress of the United States about the suspected use of mustard gas but no action was taken regarding these atrocities because, at the time, Saddam was a U. S. ally in the war against Iran and was receiving American military and intelligence support. It would not be until 1992, when Human Rights Watch gained access to northern Iraq that the full dimensions of Saddam's war against the Kurds would be recognized. The organization's Middle East Watch Kurdistan Project conducted a series of forensic examinations at mass gravesites during 1992 and assembled a dossier of captured Iraqi intelligence archives, including signed government decrees ordering mass executions. While the world was unaware, genocide had been committed across northern Iraq.

The Extermination of Rural Kurds

The Kurdish people have lived in the mountains of central Asia for at least four thousand years and yet they have never been able to establish a national homeland. Iraqi Kurds are a fiercely independent people, who have consistently challenged the authority of the national government. Oil discovered on Kurdish ancestral land and appropriated by Iraq added to their grievances against Baghdad. When the Iraq Petroleum Company was nationalized in 1972, the Kurds made a formal claim to the Kirkuk oilfields. Saddam viewed this claim as a virtual declaration of war against his authority. In an aggressive response to the Kurdish claim, Saddam reconfigured the old province of Kirkuk and began a program of "Arabazation." Iraqi Arabs from the south were offered jobs and assistance to move north to the cities of the Kurdish homeland. In the late 1970's, a program of mass relocations forced hundreds of thousands of Kurdish people to move to resettlement camps.

During the early1980's, as Iraqi troops were shifted to the frontline of the war with Iran, Kurdish fighters known as Peshmerga gained strength and recruits. One Kurdish faction, the Kurdish Democratic Party (KDP), began limited operations as scouts and guides for the Iranians, leading to an Iranian victory at the strategic border town of Haj Omran. Saddam was furious about what he considered treason and he began a series of savage reprisals. According to Human Rights Watch, "Between five and eight thousand Barzani [KDP] men from Qushtapa and other camps were loaded into large buses and driven off toward the south. They have never been seen again..."

During 1987, Saddam moved to exterminate the rural Kurds, in a siege that some consider the final phase of the Iran-Iraq war. This gruesome program was actually a series of campaigns, known as al-Anfal. The Arabic word, al-Anfal means "spoils of war." The term comes from the eighth chapter or sura of the

Qur' an, which tells the followers of Muhammad to pillage the lands of nonbelievers. Although Kurds have long been Sunni Muslims, Saddam developed a religious justification for what was to become a grotesque policy of ethnic genocide. Saddam selected his cousin, Ali Hassan al-Majid, a man known for his brutality, to direct the campaign to eliminate the Kurds. He was called "Chemical Ali," because the battle plan he devised utilized unconventional weapons to "solve the Kurdish problem and slaughter the saboteurs." Chemical Ali ordered the use of aircraft to drop poison gas on both PUK and KDP villages. Loyalty to the government was not considered. This scheme of ethnic annihilation was based on Kurdish identity alone.

There were only a few Peshmerga fighters present on the afternoon of April 16, 1988, in the Jafati Valley when the village of Balisan was attacked. As the people returned to the village from their fields, they heard an aircraft approach, causing them to run to their homes and air raid shelters. They next heard several muffled explosions, with less blast noise than from typical high-explosive charges. On this cloudy spring afternoon, Saddam Hussein's regime became the first government in history to attack its own people with poison chemicals. This action was a gross violation of the Geneva conventions and all standards of civil conduct.

Official government videotape recorded the attack. Looming columns of white and gray smoke drifting in the cool evening breeze can be seen on the tapes. The scents reported by some witnesses were quite pleasant at first, like flowers or apples. Others, however, recalled the unpleasant odor of insecticide. Then the world darkened and many people became blind. A large number vomited and some people's faces turned black. Many experienced painful swelling in their limbs and a yellow watery discharge ran from their eyes and nose. A second attack followed an hour later.

Those who did not die immediately staggered into hospitals seeking treatment. Many victims' eyes were so dry that they seemed to be glued shut. Soon a huge number of bodies were delivered for burial. The entire operation was shrouded in secrecy and morgue workers were given orders, under penalty of death, not to disclose the names of the dead to anyone. Doctors were not allowed to touch or examine the bodies. Intelligence Service guards handled the burial details, amid strict security, utilizing bulldozers as the numbers grew larger. The bodies of victims were not even washed or prepared for burial in accordance with Islamic tradition. Nor were they turned to face Mecca, as is the Islamic custom. According to one security officer, "Dogs have no relation to Islam." [12]

The al-Anfal continued through 1987 and 1988. A series of eight campaigns were conducted. Each was precisely planned and executed by the Iraqi military. The victims, largely civilian Kurds, were exterminated village-by-village. The use of gas was almost always followed by an assault, destruction of the village and finally, removal of the surviving people. The men and boys were usually taken to remote desert locations to be machine-gunned to death and then buried by bulldozers in mass graves. Survivors have described the details of firing squads that murdered Kurdish males (and sometimes females) by the thousands.

An incident that is representative of this policy is the mass execution of an estimated 2,000 women and children that took place in 1988 between Tikrit and Kirkuk. This slaughter was witnessed by a twelve-year-old boy named Taymour Abdullah Ahmad from Kulajo. His father was taken away and the child never saw him again. Soldiers with Kalashnikov rifles took him with his mother and sisters in a convoy of vehicles to a remote desert location, where the entire group was cut down by firing squads. The boy was wounded and left for dead among the piles of corpses. Somehow, he managed to escape. Through the mercy of a kind Bedouin, who took him in, and a friendly Arab family, who cared for him for two years, he was eventually reunited with his uncle in the village of Kalar. His story was related for the first time in October 1990, following the failed Kurdish uprising.[13]

Perhaps the most infamous unconventional weapons attack of the al-Anfal campaign was the horror of Halabja. Kurdish PUK fighters captured the village of Halabja on March 15, 1988, accompanied by members of the Iranian Revolutionary Guard.

Eyewitness testimony was collected by Physicians for Human Rights. British filmmaker Gwynne Roberts was in Halabja and filmed the attack. There were numerous media witnesses to the attack, including Guy Dinmore of the Financial Times, who was about eight kilometers outside Halabja with a military helicopter when the Iraqi MIG −23 fighter bombers flew in. "It was not as big as a nuclear mushroom cloud, but several smaller ones: thick smoke," he said. The scenes he encountered upon arrival in the town shocked him, though he had seen gas attacks before, during the Iran-Iraq war:

> *It was life frozen. Life had stopped, like watching a film and suddenly it hangs on one frame. It was a new kind of death to me. You went into a room, a kitchen and you saw the body of a woman holding a knife where she had been cutting a carrot. The aftermath was worse. Victims were still being brought in. Some villagers came to our chopper. They had 15 or 16 beautiful children, begging us to take them to hospital. So all the press sat there and we were each handed a child to carry. As we took off, fluid came out of my little girl's mouth and she died in my arms.*[14]

An estimated 5,000 people died in Halabja. Many survivors have suffered long-term medical complications. Christine Gosden, a medical geneticist from Liverpool University, conducted the only study on the Kurdish victims and confirms that mustard gas, sarin, tabun and VX were all used in Halabja. This was clearly an act of genocide. Human Rights organizations have been unanimous in their condemnation of this as a "crime against humanity." Although Halabja was larger in scope than other attacks and better documented by witnesses and the media, it was similar to the other attacks of al-Anfal, which continued until September 1988. By the end of the extermination program more than 3,500 Kurdish villages, or 90% of them, no longer existed. The areas surrounding the villages were littered with land mines to prevent resettlement. Subsequent investigations by Human Rights Watch estimated the Kurdish civilian deaths numbered about 100,000. The Kurds say that the total was closer to 182,000. "Chemical Ali" was outraged when, after his arrest, he was told of the estimate. He exclaimed, "It could not have been more than 100,000."

Saddam next turned his attention to Kuwait, a former province of Iraq and the oil riches of that tiny kingdom. With his expanded military power (obtained with loans from Kuwait), it appeared to be an easy target after the grueling eight-year struggle with Iran. In July of 1989, Republican Guard units were deployed near the Kuwait border. The U. S. ambassador may have misspoken when she told Saddam on July 25, that the United States had no opinion on "your border disagreement with Kuwait." Saddam interpreted this as an expression of indifference to Iraqi military action.

The Invasion of Kuwait

Since most Iraqis had never accepted the British-imposed arrangement for Kuwait's independence, Saddam believed that his claim on that country would be viewed as legitimate. Border skirmishes between the countries were frequent and Iraq had accused the Kuwaitis of using slant drilling into to Iraqi territory to steal 2.5 million barrels of oil from its Rumaila oil field. Saddam also believed that overproduction of oil by Kuwait had driven down world oil prices, hurting his government financially. "The oil quota violators have stabbed Iraq with a poison dagger," stated Iraqi Foreign Minister Tariq Aziz, emphatically expressing the Iraqi position.

Despite the bellicose rhetoric, most Gulf States did not seriously believe that Saddam would dare to invade and occupy his Kuwaiti neighbor. Even the Iraqi leadership expected that Saddam would make a limited incursion into Kuwait only to seize the disputed oil field, which was virtually on the Kuwait-Iraq border. Shortly after midnight on August 2, 1990, about 150,000 Iraqi troops surged into Kuwait, overwhelming the 20,000 man Kuwaiti military force. By daybreak Saddam's troops had seized control of Kuwait City. His troops originally

posed as liberators to appeal to those in Kuwait who opposed
the Kuwaiti monarchy, but this cynical ploy failed to gain any
significant Kuwaiti support. The UN Security Council and the
Arab League immediately condemned the invasion and within
the week the UN Security Council imposed a strict embargo
on trade with Iraq. Saddam responded by formally annexing
Kuwait.

More than half of all Kuwaitis fled the country during the
occupation but many of those who remained attempted to form
a resistance. This futile effort cost many Kuwaiti's their lives.
Disdainful Iraqi soldiers assaulted the prosperous little kingdom of Kuwait with brutal police-state tactics. Anyone with an
anti-Iraqi slogan on his home was executed, without a trial or
a hearing. Shoot-to-kill orders were issued for members of the
resistance and for even minor violations of an Iraqi-imposed
curfew. The Iraqi invaders committed indiscriminate murder and torture. Human rights organizations reported cases
in which ears were cut off, tongues were torn out, eyes were
gouged out and men were castrated. More than 1,000 rapes of
Kuwaiti and expatriate women were reported. Many more went
silently unreported.

The international community quickly recognized the threat
posed by the hostile seizure of a country that produced 10% of
the world's oil supply. An even greater threat was discovered
by U. S. intelligence reports, which confirmed that Iraqi forces
were poised to strike at Saudi Arabia, the world's most important energy provider. Within a week of the invasion a massive
coalition of international military forces began to gather in the
Saudi Kingdom.

Saddam was given a deadline of January 15, 1991 to withdraw from Kuwait. He defied this final demand and coalition
forces began a massive air assault on January 17. On February
24 the coalition launched a land offensive. Using rapid armor
assault tactics, they surrounded Kuwait, trapping Iraqi forces in
northern Kuwait and in southern Iraq. Within two days of the
beginning of the ground war Iraq began a complete withdrawal
from Kuwait. The withdrawing troops set fire to many oil wells
as they retreated, creating massive environmental damage and

engulfing Kuwait in greasy black petroleum soot that fouled
the air and made the battlefield look like the first phase of
Armageddon. The looting, destruction and killing by withdrawing Iraqi troops was horrific. Failing to hold the wealth and
resources of Kuwait, the Iraqis seemed determined to destroy
them.[15]

The retreating Iraqis were slowed by the massive amount of
loot that they attempted to carry away. The Second Armored
Division of the U. S. Marines, known as "Hounds of Hell," conducted a pursuit of the Iraqis that resembled a hunt more than
it did a war. One U. S. officer called it a "turkey shoot." Kanan
Makyia describes the macabre nightmare of retreat through
Mutla' Ridge in *Cruelty and Silence.*

> *...A ramshackle panic-stricken convoy of stolen cars,
> buses, vans and armored vehicles was turned into
> a ghoulish traffic jam of scrap metal and roasted oc-
> cupants, filling all four lanes of a sixty-mile stretch of
> highway from Jahra to the Iraqi border...Nine men in a
> flat sided supply truck were killed and flash-burned so
> swiftly that they remained naked –skinned and black-
> ened wrecks in the vulnerable position of the moment of
> first impact.[16]*

On February 28, one hundred hours after the start of the
land war, a cease-fire was ordered and Iraqi officers accepted
its terms. Saddam's forces had sustained between 20,000 and
35,000 casualties. The coalition reported the loss of 240 and
776 wounded. Iraq was "economically devastated, militarily
defeated, and politically isolated." But Saddam's elite military
forces had managed to escape, almost unscathed. The terms of
the cease-fire allowed the Iraqi military the use of helicopters,
which would become an important factor in assuring Saddam's
political survival.

The United Nations imposed and maintained an economic
embargo on Iraq after the war. In 1995, the UN amended the
sanctions to allow Iraq to sell limited amounts of oil so the nation could afford food and medicine. One might have thought

that Saddam Hussein was completely spent as a force in Iraq
and on the world stage. But he proved to be surprisingly resil-
ient and fiendishly clever. Out of the ashes of defeat, he rebuilt
his power base and maintained control of Iraq for more than a
decade after the Kuwait war.

The Uprisings

At about the time the formal cease-fire was ordered, at 5:00
a.m. on February 28, 1991, a column of fleeing Iraqi tanks that
had escaped Kuwait neared the downtown square in the southern Iraqi city of Basra. They parked before a huge portrait of
Saddam Hussein and next door to the Ba'th Party headquarters. Without any warning, the commander of the lead vehicle
stood on his tank and addressed the portrait, "What has befall-
en us of defeat, shame, and humiliation, Saddam, is the result
of your follies, your miscalculations, and your irresponsible actions." The tank commander aimed at the portrait and blasted
it with several shots from the tank cannon, to the delight of a
throng of cheering Shiites. A wild rampage ensued. The governor's residence was burned and security offices were looted.
The rioters seized the center of the city and within hours a general rebellion was underway in all of southern Iraq.

In the holy Shiite city of Najaf a full-scale battle erupted
between Saddam's security forces and a mob of mostly young
Shiite men who attacked them with swords, clubs and pistols.
The fighting was intense and resulted in about thirty killed on
both sides. When it was over, the rebels controlled Shiism's
holiest shrine. Then they turned on police headquarters. After
a night of furious fighting the rebels swarmed into the police
building, killing anyone who opposed them and releasing only
those who surrendered without a fight. Outside the city, army
soldiers fled from what had become an increasingly brazen and
bloodthirsty rebellion.

The Kurds in the north began an uprising of their own, killing thousands of Ba'this and known Kurdish collaborators with
Saddam's regime. On March 6, Baghdad ordered Iraqi troops

to "suppress popular demonstrations" and to seal off the roads. But Saddam's security men were overwhelmed by the demonstrators. Many small towns were liberated and by March 20, with the seizure of Kirkuk, the entire north was under Kurdish control for the first time in history. In almost every town children were burning portraits of Saddam. The sense of spontaneous liberation was infectious and a wave of celebration and joy swept the rebellious provinces. Despite the attempts of both Kurdish and Shiite leaders to control excess violence, the mobs wanted more blood.

In the northern town of Raniyah, an enraged band of rebels dragged local police and Ba'th Party officials to the roof of a building and one by one pushed them to their deaths. Below an angry crowd of Kurds attacked the broken bodies on the ground, shredding them with knives. In Sulaimaniya, a two-day battle at Central Security Headquarters resulted in the death of four hundred security men. Another three hundred were taken prisoner, then slaughtered, when the rebels discovered "torture chambers equipped with metal hooks, piano wire, and other devices, smeared with blood." In the south, mobs killed government employees of all types, then looted and torched government offices. Units of the Badr Brigade, Iraqi forces trained in Iran, swept into southern Iraq to proclaim the "Shiite Islamic Republic in Basra." The lawless rampage continued, with seemingly no end in sight until the forces of Saddam Hussein began a counterattack.

A Republican Guard ground assault supported by helicopter gunships was unleashed in southern Iraq against the city of Najaf on the morning of Wednesday, March 9, 1991. Government soldiers forced their way into the city, using women and children as human shields. Loudspeakers mounted on helicopters announced safe evacuation routes for civilians, which then became streets of violent death as fleeing refugees were strafed by helicopters with heavy machine guns. In Basra and Asmara, Shiites were weighted down with concrete blocks and thrown into rivers.

Homes were ransacked and looted. Women were raped and then forbidden to wear their veils, as a symbol of their dishonor.

Children who refused to turn in their parents were doused with
gasoline and burned alive, forcing many parents to surrender
to spare their children this horrible fate. During the first ten
days of the counterattack in Najaf more than 4,000 people were
killed. Shiite shrines were desecrated and treasuries of holy
sites were looted. American warplanes flew high overhead,
observing the slaughter and photographing it, but the pilots of
these over-flights were under orders not to intervene to prevent
Saddam's terrible revenge.

Government savagery in the north followed a similar pattern. Republican Guards used ground troops and tanks, supported by helicopter gunships to crush the Kurdish uprising.
Despite the encouragement by U. S. President George H. W.
Bush, the United States did not intervene to help rebel Iraqis.
On April 2, Saddam's forces took the northern city of Sulaimaniya, the last stronghold of the Kurds. In the aftermath of
the counterattack, more than two million terrified Kurdish
civilians fled into the mountains, fearing a repeat of the poison
gas attacks. The coalition had reversed Saddam's seizure of
Kuwait, but it was a "triumph without victory." [17] In the wake of
Saddam's deadly revenge, the Kurds and Shiites were left with
nothing but tears and shattered lives.

During the 1990's, covert plans were developed by the
United States to overthrow Saddam. The CIA recruited two significant Iraqi operatives. Ahmad Chalabi had been a convicted
embezzler, who was responsible for the collapse of Petra Bank
in Jordan. Iyad Alawi was a former Ba'thist assassin for Saddam,
who had fallen out of favor with the tyrant. Chalabi and Alawi
would eventually head the Iraqi National Congress and the
Iraqi National Accord, respectively.

These two competing and antagonistic entities worked for
Iraqi freedom from a comfortable and gilded exile in Europe.
The U. S. Government provided $40 million to these groups
during the first year of their existence. As the administration
of George H. W. Bush came to an end, this covert legacy was
handed to the new administration. In the words of *Out of the
Ashes, The Resurrection of Saddam Hussein*:

However halfheartedly, Washington was now inescap-
ably involved in the political affairs of one of the most
complex, divided and violent societies anywhere. [18]

The CIA created a large and growing pressure group, aided by its own propaganda arm and a steady flow of funds, courtesy of the American taxpayer. While the pressure group itself did not bring down Saddam, it slowly and imperceptibly worked to influence American public opinion to increasingly accept war to remove him from power.

Saddam Hussein and WMD

As early as 1982, Saddam Hussein had begun to lavish his oil wealth on a project to develop nuclear weapons. The use of both chemical and biological agents during the war with Iran and the al-Anfal campaigns was proof that he had a ready supply of other unconventional weapons, including gas and nerve agents. The UN Security Council passed Resolution 687, which created a Special Commission, UNSCOM, to supervise on-site inspection of Iraq's biological, chemical and missile capabilities, as well as "nuclear weapons or nuclear-weapons-usable material." The sanctions were to remain in force until all weapons of mass destruction were in compliance with the requirements of Resolution 687.

On July 7, 1991, Saddam secretly decided to destroy many of his hidden weapons, in order to save key components that could be reassembled after the inspections had ended. The elimination of weapons was carried out about a month later in a riverbed near Tikrit. But the inspection teams learned of this destruction and demanded a detailed description of what had been destroyed.

Following a CIA tip, the inspectors discovered what was considered the "mother lode" of documents on September 24. When the copied documents were examined thoroughly, they proved conclusively that Saddam had been developing nuclear weapons for delivery on missiles. According to *Out of the Ashes, The Resurrection of Saddam Hussein*:

> *A pattern had been established that was to endure for the next seven years: Iraqi denials, followed by partial disclosure, followed by further investigations by the UN inspectors, leading to further Iraqi admissions.* [19]

As the inspection game continued during the 1990's, so did the economic deterioration of Iraq. The UN sanctions began to change the face of the entire nation. Catholic Relief reported that people in Baghdad were selling personal possessions to buy food. Incomes were falling precipitously, while inflation was raging at annual rates in excess of 600%. A UN official reported that, "Iraq has, for some time to come, been relegated to a preindustrial age." The specter of famine stalked the country. By May of 1996, the World Health Organization reported "the vast majority of the country's population has been on a semi-starvation diet for years." The UN Food and Agriculture Organization estimated that 576,000 Iraqi children had died of starvation, due to the deprivation caused by the continuing sanctions. But Saddam, his family and his high command did not suffer. They evaded many sanctions and maintained a lifestyle that rivaled the splendors of the Babylonian Empire.

The Royal Family of Iraq

Saddam had a tattoo of three dark blue dots in a row on his right hand, near the wrist. This symbol reflected his pride in his humble past and his tribal affiliation. He believed that he possessed extraordinary qualities that elevated him within his nation, but also to a position of leadership for the entire of the Arab world. He was a tribalist and believed that his power came from the kinship of his people. As he rose through the ranks of the Ba'th Party as an assassin and a security official, he utilized charm and brutality easily and interchangeably. Like many despotic rulers, Saddam Hussein has been described as a "malignant narcissist," who covered deep insecurities with the projection of a grandiose self-image. He also suffered from a pathology common in many tyrannical personalities that leads them to express aggression in cruel and sadistic ways against anyone who fails to submit to their will.

Saddam feared the existence of plots in the shadows that might cost him power, or even his life. For that reason he rarely slept in the same location twice in succession and his schedule was erratic and unpredictable. In the Middle East where water is precious, Saddam surrounded himself with water themes in each of his palaces. They all had pools and most included other prominent water features – fountains, indoor streams and elaborate man-made waterfalls. The water chemistry at each palace was always carefully monitored to detect poison that might attack him though bodily orifices while he swam every morning as therapy for a slipped disk in his lower back. About twenty of his favorite palaces were always fully staffed. Three complete meals each day were prepared in case he might arrive on short notice. His staff insured that food preparation was always secure and when dining at a restaurant, the food was inspected and tested to prevent any possibility of poisoning.

In the midst of the Iran-Iraq war, during the late 1980's, Saddam's confidant and food taster, Kamel Hannah Jajo, introduced him to a beautiful ophthalmologist named Samira al-Shahbander. Samira secretly became Saddam's second wife and the mother of his new son. The Iraqi dictator enjoyed many mistresses but until Samira, none had threatened the position his first wife, Sajida. She and members of her clan were livid when they learned of the relationship and the son Saddam had fathered with the new woman. Seeking revenge, Sajida enlisted the aid of her oldest son, the cruelly erratic Uday.

One October night in 1988, Jajo threw a large party on an island in the Tigris called Umm al-Khanazir (Mother of Pigs). Uday, who was not invited to the party, wanted to provoke a confrontation with Jajo, but he did not wish to be seen as the instigator. Near midnight Jajo began firing a submachine gun into the air in a typical Iraqi celebratory gesture. From his neighboring villa, a very drunk Uday ordered the firing to cease. Jajo sent back a message to Uday that he would obey "only the president's orders." Uday then crashed Jajo's party and attacked the host with a battery-powered electric knife, which he used to slice Jajo's throat. While his victim was writhing in agony on the floor, Uday shot him twice with a pistol. He then fled, leaving behind horrified party guests.

Saddam arrived soon after the killing, to accompany Jajo to the hospital in an ambulance but his friend was already quite dead. Saddam was extremely angry about the murder. Uday was sent to Switzerland to spend some time with his Uncle Barzan. The Iraqi defense minister, who was also Sajida's brother, made the mistake of taking her side in this deadly family feud. He died in a suspicious helicopter accident the following year. Uday was eventually forgiven and reinstated into the good graces of his father but he had been exposed as a dangerous psychotic.

Saddam's second son by Sajida was named Qusay. Like his deranged brother, Qusay had accompanied his father to witness torture and killings as a child. He grew up to be much like Saddam, disciplined and serious. He even dressed like his father, wore a similar mustache and smoked the same cigars, Cohiba Esplendidos. As a commander of the Republican Guard, he was responsible for crushing the uprising of Shiites in southern Iraq at the end of the Gulf War. By all accounts, he behaved exactly as his father would have, personally shooting Shiite prisoners in the head while screaming "Bad people! Dirty People!" He was the architect of a number of Shiite exterminations and he killed enthusiastically. Qusay was considered the second most powerful man in Iraq. But no one could challenge his older brother as the most dangerous man in the country.[20]

People generally avoided Uday, especially men with attractive daughters, who were terrified of Uday's penchant for rape. A report in Time Magazine provided a number of eyewitness accounts of Uday's bizarre sexual exploits:

> *Uday demonstrated an insatiable sexual appetite. Five nights a week, some two dozen girls, all of them referred to him by his friends, were taken to the posh Baghdad Boat*

Club on the bank of the Tigris to meet Uday, close associates of his confirm. After drinks, music and dancing, the young women would be lined up like beauty queens for Uday's approval, and all but one or two would be dismissed. Those who stayed would join Uday in his bedroom at the club and leave with a gift of 250,000 dinars ($125), gold jewelry or sheer lingerie. "He never slept with a girl more than three times," says a former butler. "He was very picky." Uday took two days a week off from girls. He called it "fasting," his close associates say.[21]

Uday frequently abducted women or girls for sex, some as young as eleven. More than once, he killed a man in order to have access to a woman. Repeated episodes of his perverse cruelty had earned him many enemies. A four-man hit squad followed his gold Porsche on the evening of December 12, 1996 and riddled the car with volleys of fire from their AK-47 rifles. Uday survived despite 17 bullet wounds, but he became a cripple for life and partially impotent. The incident ultimately resulted in the torture and death of an entire family that was affiliated with a group of resistance fighter's known as "15 Shaaban," named for the date of the Shiite uprising. According to published reports, "Uday's physical ailments seemed to heighten his sadistic tendencies." He once cut off the ear of one of his guards and then applied a welder's torch to the man's face.

Not long after Uday emerged from his long and painful convalescence he attended the races at the plush Jadriyah Equestrian Club. There, he noticed an attractive 14-year-old in a lovely yellow dress, who was with her highly respected and prominent family. Uday instructed his bodyguards to make a proposition on his behalf. The offer was rejected. Later the girl was snatched from the parking lot and physically carried to the back seat of Uday's car. Bodyguards muffled her screams for help. The girl was returned home three days later with a new dress, an expensive watch and a substantial amount of cash.

The girl's frantic parents had her tested for rape. The test was positive. When they learned about the test results, Uday's men threatened the doctors and ordered them not to report the rape. The girl's outraged father complained publicly about his daughter's treatment. Uday then sent a message to the father, telling him that must bring the girl who he had raped and her12-year-old sister to Uday's next party, to be his "girlfriends." If he failed to comply, the entire family would all be "wiped off the face of the earth." The terrified man, realizing that Uday meant it, surrendered both of his daughters for Uday's enjoyment.

About a year later, Uday crashed a wedding at the exclusive Hunting Club in Baghdad. The bride, a beautiful 18-year-old, disappeared suddenly, causing general panic at the event. Uday left the scene with the girl and his bodyguards sealed the building so that no one else could depart. The cries and wails of the women reflected the despair of the entire wedding party. The groom shot himself to death. There are many similar stories, which Time magazine has confirmed through witness interviews, including the story of a young woman who was kidnapped, raped, tortured and murdered. Witnesses saw acid burns on the face and shoulder of the victim's body when it was removed wrapped in a military blanket from one of Uday's palaces.

Uday's personal staff consisted of 68 people, including two trainers for the lions he kept on the grounds of his lavish al-Abit palace. But his brutal and decadent lifestyle could not compensate for the injuries he suffered in the 1996 shooting. He tried every possible healing method – acupuncture, multivitamins, Chinese herbal medicines and even breast milk from a new mother. According to Time, "Uday sucked her nipples for what he believed would be vitamin-rich milk."

Both brothers lived opulently in ornate palaces. Qusay employed a procurement officer who went shopping twice a month to Beirut or Amman and sometimes Paris, where he spent about $100,000 each trip on luxury items for the family. The purchases always included Qusay's favorite liquor, Johnny Walker Blue Label, which he drank in excess. Qusay and his brother Uday frequently had ugly shouting matches. Uday was intensely jealous of Qusay. On a few occasions, Uday showed up Qusay by having one of his younger brother's conquests brought to him so he could also enjoy her. Several of Uday's sexual victims had their buttocks branded with a red-hot horseshoe, which produced a U shaped scar and marked the woman as Uday's personal property.[22]

Iraq's "royal family" was a twisted reflection of Saddam's ego, cruelty and corruption. The spiteful act of revenge by Saddam's first wife that compelled her oldest son to commit murder, the criminality of both sons and the degeneracy of Uday is evidence of malignant dysfunction in the first family. Saddam and his family believed that people were possessions to be dominated, controlled, tortured and even branded as property. The primary weapon Saddam and his sons used to control Iraq was terror. For more than twenty years it worked.

The Defectors

Saddam arranged strategic marriages to politically strengthen his family. His daughters, Raghad and Rina, were married to Hussein Kamel and Saddam Kamel, their al-Majid cousins. This bound Saddam to the family of "Chemical Ali," a connection that paid important dividends in times of trouble. Hussein Kamel played a major role in the savage repression of the Shiites in southern Iraq, following the war against Kuwait. His most important duty was leader of the Republican Guards. He was competent but extremely arrogant. His younger brother, Saddam Kamel, was not as well respected, but both brothers demonstrated the loyalty and brutality that Saddam required. But their positions in the hierarchy of the Iraqi power structure dramatically changed on the evening of August 7, 1995.

On that evening, Lt. General Hussein Kamel led his brother, their wives, children and about fifteen other family members into Jordanian exile in a convoy of Mercedes limousines. Iraqi border officials dared not intercept or delay the high-level motorcade as they crossed the frontier on the highway to Amman. The defection was the result of political infighting that had cost the al-Majid family leader, Ali Hassan, his position in the Defense Ministry. The poison gas campaigns against the Kurds by Ali Hassan should have been proof of his loyalty to Saddam. But, no one, not even Chemical Ali, was safe from Uday's manipulations.

Hussein Kamel and his brother decided to flee Iraq less than two weeks after the fall of "Chemical Ali." They had accumulated several million dollars in cash for use in a possible defection. On the night of the Kamel's escape, Uday had crashed the annual commemoration party of the victory over Iran in 1988, with violence on his mind. He was gunning for Saddam's half brother, Watban Ibrahim, who had spoken ill of him. Uday attacked his uncle with a machine gun, severely wounding him and killing six young gypsy dancers who were entertainers at the festivities. The victims were being driven to the hospital and the morgue just as the defectors reached the al-Amra Hotel in downtown Amman.

Lt. General Kamel's press conference in Amman, on August 13, provoked a dramatic change in Baghdad's position on the inspections by UNSCOM. Foreign Minister Tariq Aziz blamed all previous inspection interference on Kamel and pledged full cooperation with UNSCOM. He also admitted that Iraq had manufactured biological weapons for use with missiles. On the same day that these admissions were made, the Iraqi's provided half a million documents to the inspectors.

The defection of high-level members of Saddam's military organization was a shock to his regime. The Kamel brothers were denounced in the most vituperative terms and compared to biblical traitors, Cain and Judas. The Kamel brother's uncle, Ali Hassan also announced, "His family has unanimously decided to permit, with impunity, the spilling of blood." This was a virtual death sentence for both Kamel brothers.

Life in Amman was difficult for the Kamel brothers and Hussein Kamel faced charges for threatening the life of a prominent Jordanian journalist. Slowly and skillfully as a spider lures his prey into a web, Saddam began to send messages of conciliation to the defectors, at first through Kamel's father and later through the mother of Saddam's daughters, Sajida. The families assured them that they could return without recriminations. "Do you think I could harm the father of my

grandchildren?" asked a seemingly sincere Saddam. Although
it seems preposterously naive, on February 20, 1996, after seven
months in Jordan, the Kamel defectors loaded up their convoy
of Mercedes limos and departed for Iraq.

Periodically on the road to Baghdad, General Kamel would
get out of the car and pace, clearly nervous about their fate at
the hands of his father-in-law. Uday met the motorcade at the
border but he did not arrest the Kamel brothers. He simply
transferred his sisters and the children into his vehicles. A
security officer watching through field glasses on the Jordanian
side of the border saw that they were separated and he softly
said into his phone to the palace in Amman: "Khallas," meaning, "He's finished."

Uday's television station announced that his sisters had
divorced their husbands. The broadcast charged that the
women had been taken to Jordan against their will and had
been, "deceived and misled by two failed traitors." Soon after
the announcement 40 men, led by the revenge seeking "Chemical Ali," surrounded the brothers' house. In keeping with tribal
custom, the brothers were provided with a car full of guns and
ammunition to mount a defense. The battle raged for more
than thirteen hours and two attackers were killed. When the
defectors ran out of ammunition Hussein Kamel was shot dead
and his brother was killed with a rocket-propelled grenade.
Their father, aunt and her children were killed inside the
house. In the words of their uncle, Ali Hassan, "We have cut off
the treacherous branch from our noble family tree." Saddam's
daughters never forgave their father for killing their husbands.
They continued to live in the family home in Tikrit, in complete seclusion.[23]

In Washington, the CIA moved covertly against Saddam.
But the dictator had already infiltrated the exile groups and
he struck before the planned coup was ready. Eventually his
security sweep netted some 800 plotters, many in high positions
within the Iraqi regime. It was a debacle for U. S. intelligence
that ranked alongside the "Bay of Pigs" operation in Cuba.
Two months later, Saddam's forces crushed a covert operation
involving the Iraqi National Congress in northern Iraq. Their

operatives were forced to run for their lives and many were killed.[24]

The Invasion of Iraq

As early as 1991, following the collapse of the Soviet Union and the success of the Gulf War, U. S. President George H. W. Bush spoke of an era of "enduring peace," to establish a more secure world. On March 1991, he stated:

> *We can see a new world coming into view. A world in which there is the real prospect of a new world order... in which the principles of justice and fair play... protect the weak against the strong.* [25]

Some American defense hawks wanted a very different "world order" – one that was created and guaranteed by U. S. military power. These people believed in a grand strategy to capitalize on the American position as the world's mightiest nation, sometimes called a "hyperpower." Their plan was to bend the will of the world, not through leadership, but through violent domination. The Americans who advocated these ideas became known as neo-conservatives, or Vulcans, a term coined by author James Mann, from the Roman God of fire and conflagration.

When the younger George Bush became president in 2000, many of the Vulcans were appointed to important positions in the new administration. A plan for regime change in Iraq was discussed in early administration meetings. The terrorist attacks of September 11, 2001 finally doomed Saddam Hussein by giving the Vulcans the opportunity to put their plans into action. Saddam had no connection to 9-11, but the American desire to remove him gained momentum in the wake of the terrorist attacks on the U. S. The confluence of the Anglo-American thirst for oil, neo-conservative dreams of global domination and an Oedipal psychodrama, through which the new President Bush shattered his father's vision for a "new world order," resulted in the U. S. attack on Iraq. The son would replace his father's multilateral diplomacy with his own style of unilateral militarism.[26]

In the run up to war, the dark specter of Saddam's Weapons of Mass Destruction became the most compelling case for the invasion of Iraq and removal of the dictator. The U. S. and its allies had no doubt that Saddam had at one time possessed dangerous unconventional weapons, but there was uncertainty that these weapons still remained in his arsenal. After considerable debate in the United Nations but no consensus on military action, the United States and about 16 other nations assembled a "coalition of the willing" to proceed with an invasion and occupation of Iraq. The force included a U. S. contingent of 130,000 troops, 1,200 tanks, more than 1,000 aircraft and five aircraft-carrier battle groups. About 45,000 British troops and 2,000 Australian Special Forces supported the United States.

With troops massed at the borders of Iraq and the war plan complete, the U. S. made a last minute decision to gamble on a "decapitation strike," – an attempt to kill Saddam Hussein before the outbreak of hostilities. The strike occurred on March 19, 2003 when bombs were dropped in a location near Baghdad known as Dora Farm. The ground attack began almost immediately. The next day Saddam Hussein made a brief appearance on Iraqi television, looking slightly disheveled. His televised presence proved that the strike to remove him as Head of State had failed.

The U. S. Army's 5th Corps crossed the Iraq-Kuwait border to move north through the desert west of the Euphrates. On March 23, in the Nasiriya area, the U. S. military met its first real resistance from Uday Hussein's Fedayeen militia, who engaged them in a blistering firefight. Despite these hit-and-run attacks, U. S. forces were racing to Baghdad less than a week after the start of the war. On March 31, U. S. forces reached the outskirts of the Iraqi capital.

Hundreds of thousands of defenders of Baghdad were available to Saddam, including regular army forces, Republican Guard units and special intelligence services. But a determined defense of the city was never made. On April 3,

Saddam failed to appear on television for a scheduled speech and Iraqi military commanders began to lose faith in Saddam's leadership. The mass defections that the Americans had hoped for didn't happen, but several of Saddam's military units seemed to disappear from the battlefield. On April 4, U. S. forces began to mass for the final battle of Baghdad, which most observers expected to be long and bloody. But Iraqi military morale was beginning to break and the command and control of Iraqi units was becoming dysfunctional. A possible factor was American payoffs to several of Saddam's military commanders.

There were rumors that Saddam was seeking to escape from Baghdad with a Russian diplomatic convoy. U. S. intelligence thought he was still in the city and Saddam was targeted by Coalition bombings on April 7 and 8. On April 9, Saddam was seen on the streets speaking with the public. He was aware that many in his high command had betrayed him and on April 13, he bade final farewells to his bodyguards. He told them, "My regime is over. I know where I should be going." Saddam went underground and disappeared.[27]

Casualties were surprisingly light on both sides during the warfare phase of the conflict. The US/UK battle deaths totaled about 150, half of which were the result of "friendly fire." Iraqi deaths were estimated at 10,000. Only about 8,000 Iraqis were taken prisoner, confirming that many Iraqi soldiers slipped away from the battlefield. On May 1, 2003 the President of the United States declared victory on the aircraft carrier Abraham Lincoln, stating:

> The battle of Iraq is one victory in a war on terror that began on September 11th, 2001, and still goes on... no terrorist network will gain weapons of mass destruction from the Iraqi regime, because that regime is no more.[28]

In the weeks that followed, despite elections in Iraq and the establishment of the veneer of democratic procedures, it became increasingly apparent that the U. S. and its allies could not completely dominate Iraq. Ba'thists and former Saddamists became the proxies of Damascus and Tehran, working diligently to destabilize the American occupation. They were joined by self appointed al-Qaeda resistance fighters, foreign Jihadi volunteers, Shiite militias, the Badr Brigade, the Mahdi Army and other shadowy bands of Islamic fanatics and criminal gangs. Each of these groups had its own agenda, but they had a common hatred of the American occupation and a willingness to sacrifice many Iraqi lives to achieve their goals.

After an extensive yearlong search, the United States Iraq Survey Group (ISG) was finally forced to admit that Weapons of Mass Destruction could not be found. A major international political reaction resulted. Many could not understand how the intelligence could have been so flawed. In the early spring of 2004, Dr. David Kay, who headed the inspection team of the ISG, and who served in prior UN inspection efforts explained:

> *I'm absolutely convinced that after '95, when two of his son-in-laws, Hussein Kamel being the most important of the two, defected and they decided to get rid of all their weapons stockpile at that point because they thought Hussein Kamel would give them up, did his rationale for continuing to act like he had weapons change and we missed it. For Saddam, and this is the most important thing, really, in understanding Iraqi behavior. For Saddam, the most important thing in the world was survival in the job. For him the weapons program was important for one reason and one reason only. It was the thing than insured, in his view, that the Kurds and the Shia would not rise up again.* [29]

Saddam destroyed his remaining weapons so the defectors could not reveal his stockpiles to the world but all outward appearances remained the same. There was, however, an important internal shift that had taken place in Baghdad. Saddam's objective had changed from preventing discovery of the weapons, to preventing the discovery that he no longer had them. In order to look invincible to his domestic enemies and to his

hated neighbor Iran, he made himself seem menacing to the
world. This strategic posturing ultimately proved his undoing.

Extreme violence soon plagued the American occupation
of Iraq. The primary targets were originally U. S. soldiers and
Iraqis who cooperated with the occupation. For many weeks,
the Americans refused to recognize that the insurgent forces
were exploiting the growing hostility between the Iraqi public
and the U. S. military. American authorities primarily focused
on tracking down former Ba'th Party members and leading figures in Saddam's regime. Saddam tried to remain an influence
in Iraq, despite being underground. On July 8, 2003 in a tape
broadcast by al-Jazeerah, he urged national unity and resistance
to the occupation:

> *Returning to the methods of secret action we started at
> the very beginning is the appropriate method for Iraqis
> to adopt. Based on this and through these methods I ad-
> dress you brothers from inside proud Iraq, to say: Your
> main task now – as Arabs, Kurds, and Turkmen; Shi-
> ites and Sunnis: Muslims and Christians; and under
> all titles and of all religions and denominations—is to
> expel the invaders from our country. [30]*

The effort to maintain an underground insurgency required
Saddam and his sons to meet with their loyalists periodically,
which exposed them to the serious risk of apprehension. For
more than a month, Uday and Qusay had been using a "safe
house" in Mosul at the home of their father's cousin, Marwan
Zaydan. Before dawn on July 20, Saddam's sons, along with
Qusay's fourteen-year-old son Mustafa and one bodyguard were
returning to this location when they were spotted by Kurdish
soldiers. American officials were promptly notified.

On the morning of July 22, U. S. Special Forces knocked
down the front door and entered the home. Three Americans
were wounded by fire from at least one AK-47. The Americans
pulled back and offered the occupants of the house an opportunity to surrender. A very large force surrounded the house
and two OH-58 D Kiowa Warrior helicopters circled above.

The barricaded brothers responded to the surrender demand with automatic weapons fire and grenades thrown from windows. The Americans returned several volleys of withering fire including missile rounds before ground forces made a final rush on the house. A furious firefight ensued and lasted for about three hours. The inhabitants were all killed, including young Mustafa, who was the last to die. The Ba'thist followers of Saddam threatened revenge for the killings.

Although the Americans believed that the demise of Saddam's family would hasten the end of the insurgency, many experts in Arab politics understood that a prolonged struggle was just beginning to take shape. In August, there was an intensification of guerrilla warfare, with Islamist elements taking the lead. Many observers believe that the event that launched the real war for Iraq was the August 7 truck bombing of the Jordanian embassy in Baghdad. This assault was linked to Ansar al-Islam and its leader, a Jordanian named Abu Musab al-Zarqawi, who became the self-appointed head of al-Qaeda in Iraq.

Targeted bombings plunged the capital into a state of perpetual fear and sporadic chaos. On August 19, an Islamist group exploded a sophisticated truck bomb designed to destroy the UN headquarters in Baghdad. The entire building collapsed, killing dozens of people, including the United Nations Chief of Mission. In the face of escalating violence, the Coalition Provisional Authority was forced to withdraw into the heavily fortified "Green Zone," a complex of palaces located in central Baghdad. The American occupation took on a "bunker mentality," further isolating it from the Iraqi people.

Saddam's Last Days

As suicide attacks began to control the flow of events in Iraq, Saddam feared the success of the Islamists was marginalizing his role. Saddam's time had passed and control of the insurgency was now in the hands of a group of extremists. Empowered with a twisted interpretation of the Qur'an, the insurgents claimed to be authorized to kill anyone, even women and

children, in the pursuit of their goals. Saddam's very existence
had become an impediment to the rise of the new militant
leaders, and the $25 million reward offered by the Americans
was looking like an attractive prize for removing him.

Saddam's second wife, Samira al-Shahbander, wanted to
save him from his enemies, who she feared might kill him. So
by telephone from exile she leaked some crucial information
about members of Saddam's inner circle. This information was
relayed to American intelligence. On December 10, Saddam
met two brothers who were confidants. Col. Muhammad Ibrahim al-Omar and Lt. Col. Khalil Ibrahim al-Omar were scheduled to move Saddam to his next safe location but he was taken
prisoner and perhaps drugged by the Ibrahim brothers. He
was placed into a "spider hole," a small shaft leading to an underground chamber. There are indications that they intended
to move him again, but before they could act the Americans
intervened. The information leaked by Saddam's wife enabled
the Americans to capture an informant, who under intense
interrogation, "blurted out Saddam's location."

On December 13, 2003, the Americans launched "Operation
Red Dawn," to locate Saddam. A search of two suspect farmhouses yielded nothing, but the informant insisted that his intelligence was accurate. During a second more intensive search,
beyond the area of the farmhouses, a soldier noticed a crack
in the earth near a mud hut. Brushing the dirt back revealed
a Styrofoam cover to the top of Saddam's hiding place. It was
8:26 p.m. on December 13. It has been reported that Saddam
offered to negotiate but eyewitness accounts indicate that he was
"very much bewildered" and not coherent enough to understand
what was happening. One intelligence officer described him as
"a broken man." The American government hailed Saddam's
capture as "a turning point" in the war in Iraq, but this event,
like so many others, would soon prove a hollow victory.[31]

The highly controversial trial of Saddam began in Baghdad
in October 2005 and lasted for a little over a year. By the time
the trial began the Coalition Provisional Authority had managed to hold elections and to transfer power to a new Iraqi
government. The status of the new government was seriously

challenged by sectarian infighting from the very beginning. The insurgency gradually began to change and Shiite and Sunni violence directed against each other became commonplace. Because the new government was predominately Shiite, the Sunni community was wary and distrustful of their agenda and their conduct of the trial of Saddam. According to the Los Angeles Times:

> Neither Hussein's capture nor his trial slowed the country's descent into civil war. The number of U. S. troops and Iraqis killed continued to accelerate. Hussein himself, long despised and mistrusted by the rest of the Arab world, became a cause célèbre worldwide, as he condemned the trial as a farce and the U. S. backed government of Iraq as a puppet.[32]

On November 5, 2006, Saddam Hussein was convicted of serious crimes following "a contentious, chaotic trial during which three defense lawyers were gunned down and a judge was removed." Saddam was not tried for his most heinous crimes, including the invasion of Kuwait, the extermination of the Kurds and the use of poison gas at Halabja. The Shiites did not care about his crimes against the Kuwaitis or the Kurds. They wanted retribution for the crimes against their people, including the murders in the Shiite village of Dujail that occurred in July, 1982. The outcome of the trial did not bode well for national reconciliation.

After all appeals had been exhausted, the law mandated a 30-day period for the sentence to be carried out. Five days into that period, the Shiite-dominated government of Prime Minister Nuri al-Maliki demanded that U. S. officials turn Hussein over to them for execution. In a "dead-of-night rush to the gallows," key members of the Maliki government were told to assemble at the prime minister's office at 3:30 a.m., on Saturday, December 30, 2006. They were taken by helicopter to a prison in the northern Baghdad suburb of Khadimiya.

The Americans delivered Hussein to the prison and his rendezvous with death. The men who took custody of Hussein from the Americans were from Iraq's Shiite south, identifiable by their accents and darker skin. It is possible that these men were related to victims of Saddam's purges of southern Shiites. As Saddam was taken to the hangman's noose, he was taunted by hooded guards. The execution was not the solemn ceremony of a sovereign nation but the vengeful act of a death squad.

The name of the fiery Shiite cleric, "Moktada, Moktada, Moktada," was chanted as the noose was tightened around Saddam's neck. He replied contemptuously, "Is this what you call manliness?" A voice in the execution chamber issued a curse, "To hell with him." The display of sectarian blood lust and Saddam's surprising courage turned things upside down. In the final moments before execution, his enemies managed to transform Saddam from a criminal into a perverse kind of Sunni martyr. In a dark concrete room, Saddam can be seen in a video of the execution. With a rope around his neck, he appeared "alert and composed" and he looked directly at his tormentors. In his final seconds, he began to repeat a Muslim verse for the dying, "There is no god but God and Muhammad...." Before the verse was finished, the trap door opened beneath his feet and he plunged to his death. "The tyrant has fallen," shouted members of the excited crowd who witnessed the hanging.[33]

An American helicopter flew Saddam's body to a U. S. base outside Tikrit, where his remains were turned over to Sheikh Ali al-Nida, and the leader of Saddam's Albu-Nasir tribe. He was taken by convoy to his birthplace in Ouija and laid to rest in the visitor's center that he had built in the 1990's. The tribe planned to move his body to a final resting place, outside the town, with the remains of his sons, Uday and Qusay.

During 24 years of brutal rule in Iraq, Saddam Hussein further divided an already fractured society. He kept his enemies in a state of perpetual terror of him and his family. His well-known crimes were grotesque and pervasive. He violently suppressed the Shiites, and committed genocide against the Kurds. According to the Documental Center for Human Rights, Saddam murdered more than 600,000 Iraqi civilians during his time in power.

Someday the United States will withdraw its troops. A battle will probably rage on among the national and regional forces that want to dominate Iraq, its vast oil supplies and its great potential wealth. The ultimate outcome is not at all certain. The greatest danger is a wider conflagration that will threaten other governments and the stability of the entire region. It is probable that whatever forces emerge, the new ruling elite will utilize the old ways. British Middle East expert, Dr. Toby Dodge calls this a, "shadow state with its tried and tested use of violence, patronage and favoritism."

Iraq is unique as the only Arab nation with a Shiite majority. It is possible that the removal of Saddam Hussein will usher in a new era for the Shiites. For the first time since Emperor Cyrus the Great in the sixth century B. C., the Persians and their Shiite allies may one day dominate a crescent from Tehran to Beirut. This expansion of Shiite power is certain to be resisted by the Sunni Arab states. The front line of the Iran-Iraq war may then move two hundred miles to the west as the great schism of Islam continues a violent struggle, just as it has for more than thirteen centuries.

CHAPTER 10
Théoneste Bagosora:
Architect of the Apocalypse

"Wage a war that will be long and find many dead."
Colonel Théoneste Bagosora

The African continent is slowly breaking apart along the line of the Great Rift Valley. As the continental plates separate, the Red Sea will one day flood, making East Africa into a huge island. The force that is bringing about this slow geological change, called rifting, draws lava to the earth's surface to form volcanoes. On the western edge of the Great Rift Valley is a chain of volcanoes known as the Virungas, the newest of which still actively smolder as the rifting process continues.

The Virungas reach heights of 14,000 feet and their peaks capture moisture from the passing clouds to produce a magnificent rainforest. Here, in the mist, are the ancestral ranges of the Mountain Gorillas. Abundant rainfall and fertile volcanic soil has created a naturally beautiful landscape of mountains, high plateaus, lush valleys and grasslands. The earth is the color of volcanic sienna, which contrasted against a forest of green hues, is breathtaking. The winding rivers support a vast agricultural bounty, varied flora and plentiful wildlife. Above all are the peaks of legend, the "milles collines." Rwanda is known as the land of a thousand hills. [1]

This Eden-like world of Central Africa naturally attracted people to enjoy its rich bounty. The first to settle here about 4,000 years ago were the Twa, who are related to the pygmies of the Congo basin. These hunter-gatherers were cave dwellers who survived on the plants and animals of the rainforest. About one thousand years after the Twa other settlers migrated from northwest of the Virungas. These Bantu-speaking peoples were agriculturalist tribes, the largest of which were the Hutus. Some five hundred years later, Nilotic-speaking people from the north arrived. They were taller, lighter-skinned and came to dominate the drier savannas north of Lake Kyoga. These were the Tutsis, who raised cattle and exhibited highly developed skills in the art of war. Over time the Hutu and Tutsi acquired the same spoken language, Kinyarwanda, intermarried and began sharing the same religion and culture. Their chiefs, called Mwamis were both Hutu and Tutsi.

Because the people who settled this region had no written language their pre-colonial histories are unreliable and some surviving legends may be outright fiction. However, oral tradition tells us that there was ethnic stratification before European settlement. This trend accelerated during the time of Mwami Kigeri Rwabugiri, a Tutsi who became king in 1860. He expanded his empire and established the Tutsis as leaders and aristocrats, while relegating the Hutu to more servile positions. The Twa continued to be the least populous ethnic group in the region and were distinguished by their small physical size and their distinctive dialect of Kinyarwanda.

When John Hanning Speke published his highly acclaimed, *Journal of the Discovery of the Source of the Nile*, in 1864, he espoused his views of "race science," which stated a hypothesis that the Tutsi were of Ethiopian origin, descended from King David. He compared the darker-skinned tribes to the baboon, while defining Tutsis as a "superior race of men who were as unlike as they could be from the common order of the natives." These observations had no scientific basis but became an accepted part of European mythology as the colonization of Africa began.

In 1885, a conference held in Berlin, established African states without regard to the local tribal kingdoms. Rwanda and Burundi were maintained as separate domains but administered as joint provinces of German East Africa. At the time, no white man had actually set foot in Rwanda, which had become the most densely populated country on the African continent.

The death of King Rwabugiri in 1895 and the German defeat in World War I created what has been described as "dual colonialism." Under this system, the Tutsi elite enjoyed hegemony over the Hutus and served as colonial overseers of the black masses. This stratification prevailed when Belgium was awarded Rwanda by the League of Nations following the war. The established social structure became a pillar of Belgian colonial rule, with Tutsi's given full reign over the Hutu labor force.

In 1931, the Belgians installed a new King, Mutara Rudahigwa, as their puppet. Soon thereafter, identity cards were issued which prevented any claim of change in ethnicity. The population was classified as 85% Hutu, 14% Tutsi and 1% Twa. The Belgian administration essentially established a tribal apartheid, with the Tutsi's serving as overlords on their behalf.

After World War II, Flemish priests began to sympathize with the plight of the Hutus. This encouraged Hutu political activists to demand majority rule. In 1957, a group of Hutu intellectuals produced a "Hutu Manifesto" that declared Tutsis to be foreign invaders, who had denied the natural rights of the majority Hutus of Rwanda. Widespread conflict between the two tribal groups had not yet occurred but was almost inevitable.

On November 1, 1959, a Hutu political activist and subchief named Dominique Mbonyumutwa was badly beaten by Tutsis. Soon Hutus across the nation organized themselves into small groups for a campaign of violence, arson and occasional murder of Tutsis – events that became known as "the wind of destruction." Colonel Guy Logiest, the Belgian military leader sent from the Congo to calm the unrest, saw himself as the champion of democratization. He supported rule by the Hutu majority. In a statement with sweeping implications, he said,

"We have to take sides." In early 1960, he replaced Tutsi chiefs with Hutus, creating a serious social upheaval.

New elections firmly established Hutus in power and Logiest belatedly warned of danger if there was a failure to observe minority rights. After the Rwandan republic was declared in 1961, a UN commission reported that the Rwandan revolution had replaced "one type of oppressive regime with another." The report darkly warned, "Someday we will witness violent reactions on the part of the Tutsis." The Hutu president of the new republic, Gregoire Kayibanda, spoke of Rwanda as "two nations in one state."

The Tutsi/Hutu divide is subtler that it initially seems. They are not separate races and due to centuries of intermarriage, their ethnic differences are blurred. What traditionally divided these groups were tribal origin and class or "caste" distinctions along with some aspects of physical appearance. Nevertheless, a looming sense of rivalry and unrest grew over the next three decades into a malignant but unseen force in Rwandan society.[2]

The Tutsi Diaspora

The shadow of anti-Tutsi violence stalked the Hutu-dominated nation of Rwanda for many years and caused the migration of thousands of Tutsis into neighboring countries. Most Tutsis fled north to Uganda and Tutsi exiles harbored profound resentments of their treatment in Rwanda. Between 1961 and 1967 ten separate military incursions were made into Rwanda by Tutsi militia forces. All were repelled, but following each, Hutu militants slaughtered Rwandan Tutsis in retribution. During the 1960's, more than 300,000 Tutsis fled Rwanda and their Hutu neighbors murdered tens of thousands who could not escape.

In neighboring Burundi, where the tribal makeup was similar to Rwanda's, the ruling Tutsi elite became horrified by Rwandan events, resulting in intensified restrictions on the Hutus in Burundi. In 1972, a failed uprising against Tutsi control of Burundi led to the killing of nearly 100,000 Hutus in that country.

About double that number of Hutus fled Burundi – many to Rwanda, increasing anti-Tutsi feelings among Rwandan Hutus.

The Burundian massacres became a rallying point for a second Rwandan republic, which was established in a "bloodless coup" in July of 1973, when Major General Juvenal Habyarimana seized power. He was a Hutu and the Army's senior officer. Under Habyarimana, all political power was vested in his Hutu-dominated Mouvement Révolutionnaire National pour le Développment (MRND) party. His followers were put into positions of authority all the way down to the commune level – the basic unit of Rwandan administration. Rwanda became a militarized dictatorship whose Hutu majority harbored deep feelings of tribal hatred against Tutsis.

The Army, the Catholic Church and the president's closest associates, known as the Akazu or "Little House," anchored the dictatorship. Gerard Prunier, who has written one of the most important accounts of the Rwandan genocide, has called Habyarimana's MRND, "a truly totalitarian party." The 7,000-man army (Forces Armées Rwandaises, or FAR) and the 1,200-man National Police enforced the Party's will in Rwanda. A fiercely loyal Presidential Guard of about 1,000 troops protected Habyarimana. The Catholic Church was supportive of the Hutu President, although many in the clergy were Tutsi. The Church had supported majority rule even before the Hutu revolution.

The Akazu was an exclusive circle within a larger network of political associates. These were President Habyarimana's most devoted supporters and many were from his home region. "Little House" membership was made up of the wife and relatives of the president, as well as military leaders, like Major Leonard Nkundiye and most important of all, Colonel Théoneste Bagosora. The "Little House" also included groups of business leaders representing parasitic state-sponsored companies. They exercised control of entire sectors of the economy for the private benefit of the elite.

General prosperity boosted the Habyarimana regime for a time. But economic discontent arose when the collapse of the coffee and tea markets plunged Rwanda into debt in the late 1980's. A drought followed that exacerbated the crisis. Cronyism and corruption became more extreme during these hard times, which fomented an organized political opposition to the regime.

In September of 1990, the International Monetary Fund imposed a structural adjustment program on Rwanda, freezing government salaries and devaluing the Rwandan franc. Political opposition soon came from beyond the borders of Rwanda. By 1990 Tutsi exiles in Uganda had formed the Rwandan Patriotic Front (RPF), organizing and training a military force that eventually numbered about 7,000 soldiers. The RPF was financed mostly by international contributions received through Rwandan human rights organizations.

The Roots of Genocide

The Rwandan people harbor a morbid sense of suspicion that borders on paranoia. When people are served drinks in bars or in private homes, the bottle caps are left on and removed only within the view of those who will be drinking. There is a pervasive fear of poison and of people who would use poison or evil spirits to bring harm to others. When death or illness strikes, it is frequently believed to be the result of a virulent potion or a sinister form of sorcery. This distrust combined with deep tribal hatreds to form fertile ground for extreme solutions to Rwanda's social problems.

The tribal divide seemed intractable to many military officers, who believed that eventually the solution would be in their hands. One Officer who held such views was Théoneste Bagosora. He was born in 1941 and grew up in the northwest of the nation, on the banks of Lake Kivu. He has described himself as the son of a "Christian and relatively well-off family." His father was a Hutu teacher. Bagosora's rise to power was facilitated by his military training, which included the Kigali School for Officers, where he graduated with the rank of Second Lieutenant. He held positions as Second Commander of the Higher Military School of Kigali and Commander of Kanombe Military Camp. He would eventually become Cabinet Director to the Minister of Defense in 1992.

Colonel Bagosora enjoyed a prominent position in the Rwandan military, but he was highly competitive with the president and relations between the men were not always warm. Bagosora maintained a low profile while in uniform and was actually retired from military life by early 1993. However, Bagosora was the ranking career professional in the Defense Ministry in the spring of 1994, when Rwanda was forced to endure the most painful period in its history. Military records show that Bagosora was in command of the entire military apparatus and significant elements of its paramilitary forces.

The development of Bagosora's political and social views is not well documented, but it is clear that as he approached the pinnacle of power, he became recognized as a Hutu extremist. He helped to whip up popular sentiment against the Tutsis and served as a leader in the Hutu movement that would eventually sweep Rwanda into the headlines for the darkest of all national acts – mass murder of its own people.

Colonel Bagosora possessed a diploma in Advanced Military Studies from a French Military School and his rise to power occurred when French influence in Rwanda became increasingly important. In the mid-twentieth century, France was the most prominent colonial power in Africa and despite a setback in Algeria, the French played an important role in much of the continent. Since colonial times, the rivalry and competition between the Western powers has frequently been a corrosive influence upon the emerging nations of Africa. France has long feared the creeping Anglo-Saxon influence of the U. S. and Great Britain in the developing world.

By 1990, France had replaced the Belgians as the primary European supporter of the Rwandan government. Africa was a place where the glory of the French empire still thrived in the minds of French politicians. Former French President Mitterrand, who served from 1981 to 1995, has written, "Without Africa, France will have no history in the 21st century." Mitterand's son, who was head of the Africa Office at the French Presidential Palace, forged a bond of friendship with the Habyarimana family and was fully supportive of the regime.

On the afternoon of October 1, 1990 Tutsi forces of the RPF launched an invasion of Rwanda from Uganda, with the stated objective of replacing the Rwandan Hutu regime. This incursion gave President Habyarimana the opening he needed to solidify his political position by rallying Rwandan Hutus against the invaders. His plan was simple: Rwandan Tutsi's would be sacrificed to gain the total support of the nation's Hutu majority.

By October 4, while the invaders were still miles from Kigali, gunfire erupted in the capital and the government spread the word that accomplices of the invading force were attempting a takeover. The government did not limit the enemy to the Tutsi's in their midst. They also lashed out at Hutu opponents of the regime. The fabricated attack on the capital also enabled Habyarimana to gain support from Belgium, Zaire and France. The French immediately dispatched more than 600 soldiers to Rwanda, a force that eventually grew to more than 1,100, according to Human Rights Watch. With the help of highly trained French paratroopers, the Rwandan army repelled the RPF forces back to the Ugandan border. Large-scale shipments of French weapons soon began to flow into Rwanda.[3]

The government arrested more than 13,000 people and a large number of detainees were held for months without charges. Many prisoners were tortured and dozens died. But preparations were being made for a far more ambitious program of reprisals. Most French military officers working in Rwanda clearly understood the danger of a full-scale genocide. A close associate of Rwanda's president, who supervised French military cooperation, actually stated publicly that, "the Tutsi are very few in number, we will liquidate them."

Only ten days after the failed RPF invasion, a foreshadowing of the horror to come was initiated in the village of Kibilira in Gisenyi prefecture. Local officials informed Hutus that their work duty would include fighting their Tutsi neighbors. This village had been peaceful for at least fifteen years, but the Hutu workers did not seem displeased at the prospect of attacking their neighbors. They were seen singing and drumming on their way to the attack. There are no written records of the events that followed but it became a wanton slaughter that lasted for three days. About 350 Tutsi's were killed and more than three thousand fled in fear of their lives. This was not an act of redress or self-defense. The government instigated it as a test, to see how the Hutu majority would perform when assigned a war of extermination against their Tutsi neighbors.

The savage murders in Kibilira were a first step in a social solution envisioned by Bagosora and others who shared Habyarimana's view that the Tutsis should be sacrificed to consolidate the regime's power. The leadership discovered that the Hutus of Kibilira were not reluctant to kill when told that it was their duty – a duty that was encouraged by the prospect of enrichment from the spoils of those murdered. In the early 1990's Rwanda was a nation living in the invisible shadow of an extreme darkness – a virulent hatred that would soon consume the nation.

Members of the Akazu or "Little House," understood that their program to unify Rwanda required a communications network and in 1990, Madame Agathe Habyarimana secretly established a newspaper for this purpose. A paper known as Kanguka or "Wake Up," that had been critical of the government was replaced by Kangura or "Wake It Up." The staff of the original paper was arrested. The new publication was filled with vile slanders directed at Tutsis and it published a list of Hutu Ten Commandments. The eighth commandment was well known and widely quoted. It read, "Hutu's must stop having mercy on the Tutsis." A coordinated program of hate-filled propaganda would reach its peak with the relentless tirades of a government-supported radio station known as Radio Mille Collines (RTLM), which would call on the Hutu people to defend the nation against an invasion of the inyenzi, or "cockroaches."

In December 1990, a group of University faculty members proposed a "self-defense" program for all adult men. Using the theme, "He who wishes for peace prepares for war," the group suggested local training under the command of soldiers. The proposal specified that the members of the self-defense groups should learn to fight with "traditional weapons," because they were more affordable than firearms. This simple plan grew into a comprehensive program for a group named the Intera-hamwe, which means "those who attack together."

Colonel Bagosora was involved in every detail of planning and implementation of the so-called self-defense program. He obtained vehicles and arranged storage locations for weapons. Notebooks belonging to Bagosora identify the city of Kigali and the prefectures of Byumba, Ruhengeri and Gisenyi as the areas where the self-defense program should be launched first. These records show that he specified training techniques and the types of weapons to be used. He also directed that partici-pants should "listen to all radio broadcasts."

As foreign aid poured in to support the Habyarimana re-gime, killers-in-training were armed with weapons received from France, Egypt and apartheid South Africa. When foreign governments questioned reports of sporadic Tutsi killings, these concerns were smoothed over with assurances that these were acts of "self-protection" or "spontaneous anger." Meanwhile, the drumbeat of anti-Tutsi propaganda escalated, even going so far as recruiting famous singers to develop songs to reinforce the message.

Bagosora was never officially a head of state and has not yet been profiled in a biography. He became an almost phantom leader while ruling the defense establishment in Rwanda. His activities remained "under the radar," even as he developed detailed plans for human slaughter. Perhaps his actions were intentionally obscured, because Colonel Bagosora was one of the few who understood the true nature of what was planned. He chaired a military commission that was tasked with develop-ing methods to destroy the enemies of the regime, described as "domestic Tutsis, Hutus discontented with the regime in power, foreigners married to Tutsi women." The final document de-veloped by the commission was widely distributed and became a blueprint for genocide.

In the months that preceded the spring of 1994, Bagosora's planning activities were kept secret and were only later revealed through evidence inadvertently left behind. In a series of pub-lic communiqués, issued under the pseudonym, "Commandant Mike Tango," instructions were provided to a wider audience to

facilitate preparations for the genocide. Human Rights Watch
states that the mystery figure of "Commandant Mike Tango, is
either Col. Théoneste Bagosora, or someone working closely
with him." The secret planning of Colonel Bagosora and the
pronouncements of the mysterious "Commandant," seem eerily
parallel, suggesting that it was actually the phantom leader who
was communicating and preparing hate-crazed Hutus to hunt
down and kill their neighbors.

While Bagosora's killing machine was being built, the international community pressured both sides of the RPF/Rwanda
conflict to come to terms on a cease-fire. Habyarimana was not
inclined to end the war because it was making him and his supporters in the Akazu rich, while it fueled the hatred that radical
Hutu's believed would ultimately result in a "final solution."
Vast sums of money were siphoned from aid programs to line
the pockets of Rwanda's elite.

International diplomats arranged a cease-fire in 1992, but
Habyarimana delayed signing of the accords. After stalling for
more than a year, donor nations used their ultimate weapon,
the cut-off of aid, to force the president to finally seriously consider the Arusha accords to end the fighting in Rwanda.[4] The
diplomats who had negotiated the agreement were very satisfied with the Arusha accords. The agreement established the
rule of law, provided for a transitional government, guaranteed
free elections and provided for the repatriation of refugees. A
UN peacekeeping force was provided to assure compliance with
all provisions of the agreement. The accords that were signed
on August 4, 1993, almost immediately came under attack from
militant Hutus in Rwanda.

While crowds in Kigali celebrated peace, groups of hard-line
Hutus were preparing to take action. By this time Bagosora's
meticulous preparation for the slaughter was in its final stages.
One third of self-defense recruits would be issued firearms,
while others would use traditional weapons, which would include bows and arrows, spears and machetes. From January
1993 through March 1994 approximately 581,000 machetes
were imported into Rwanda. This amounted to one machete
for every third adult Hutu male in the country, according to

Human Rights Watch. These weapons were in addition to local machete production, which was doubled.

Training of the self-defense forces intensified and their offshoot organization, known as the "Zero network" began to appoint death squads. Operations had moved into a new and more active phase and on-the-job-training replaced simulations. Government officials explained the training by claiming that it was preparing the young men to be guards in the national parks and forests. In October of 1993, the training programs began to dispense payments to the militia leaders, while the government was near financial collapse and its treasury was depleted.

The UN peacekeeping force supporting the peace accords was far too small to be of much value. The force commander, General Romeo Dallaire of Canada, had requested 4,500 men but the U. S. only wanted to support 500. On October 5, 1993, the Security Council finally established the UN Assistance Mission in Rwanda (UNAMIR) with a total of 2,548 troops. The final budget was not approved until April 4 of the following year, only two days before the genocide began. UNAMIR did not have adequate reserves of food or medicine and they were short on basic military supplies. Like most UN operations, the force was authorized to use weapons for "self defense only," and it was lightly armed. Dallaire was allowed to use the UN force to prevent crimes against humanity, but he was required to seek approval for any military action directly from UN Headquarters.

In late October of 1993, the assassination of the President of neighboring Burundi set off a wave of killings of both Hutus and Tutsis in that country. The President was a Hutu and had been a popular figure in Rwanda, where he had been a political refugee for a time before his election. This political killing undercut the position of moderates who believed that an integrated nation was possible. With the murder of the Hutu leader of Burundi, hard liners in Rwanda had just the propaganda gift they had most wanted. Radio Mille Collines reported the event with the voice of the well-known announcer, Habimana Kantano, on the evening news:

Burundi first. That's where our eyes are looking now. Even when the dog-eaters are few in number, they discredit the whole family. That proverb was used by the minister of labor, Mr. Nyangoma, meaning that those Tutsi thugs of Burundi have killed Democracy by torturing to death the elected president, Ndadaye. Those dog-eaters have now started mutilating the body. We have learned that the corpse of Ndadaye was secretly buried to hide the mutilations that those beasts have wrought on his body.[5]

False stories of mutilation and castration were run in Rwandan newspapers and even fake photos of a bloated corpse were used to whip up tribal hatred. Following the assassination in Burundi, more than 300,000 fearful Hutu refugees poured across the border into southern Rwanda. A movement known as "Hutu Power" began to hold huge rallies around the nation, in which any subtleties of politics were absent. There was now only one cause: tribal solidarity tinged with extreme hatred for the Tutsis in their midst.

Even one of the Hutu negotiators of the Arusha accords was swept up in the frenzy of hatred, telling one crowd, "The enemy is among us here. We cannot sit down and think that what happened in Burundi will not happen here, since the enemy is among us." Extreme Hutu Power was a threat even to Habyarimana, in the form of vicious criticism of the Accords and his role in signing them. Propaganda by Hutu extremists denounced the president as a dupe of the Tutsi's. The March issue of Kangura, the publication established by the president's wife, ran this chilling banner headline: "HABYARIMANA WILL DIE IN MARCH." The accompanying article explained that he would not be killed by a Tutsi, but by a "Hutu bought by the cockroaches."

The stage was set for the genocide to begin. The Interahamwe were trained and the militias were on standby. The machetes had been sharpened, stored and were ready for distribution. Bagosora, the top authority in the Defense Ministry, had disclosed his agenda months before, when he angrily walked out of a meeting at Arusha. He told Rwanda's future Finance Minister, Marc Rugenera, that he was returning to Kigali, to "prepare for the apocalypse."

Assassination by Missile

By January 1994, almost the entire diplomatic community in Kigali was aware that some kind of terrible violence was becoming more probable with each passing day. It was clear to the diplomats that a plan for house-to-house extermination had been developed with specific names of each individual who would become a victim. The completion of the genocide plan was a major preoccupation of the Defense Ministry under Théoneste Bagosora during this period.

Despite extreme secrecy, word of the government's planning leaked. On January 11, 1994, UNAMIR commander Major General Roméo Dallaire faxed a "Request for Protection for Informant" to his UN superiors. This communication made it clear that UNAMIR had a source deep within the high command of the Habyarimana regime. The informant had been coordinating the activities of 48 plainclothes soldiers and several others in a plot to kill opposition leaders and Belgian peacekeepers during a ceremony at the parliament. The objective of this action was to "provoke a civil war." Dellaire's faxed memo made the following specific points:

- *Since UNAMIR mandate [the informant] has been ordered to register all Tutsi in Kigali. He suspects it is for their extermination. Example he gave is that in twenty minutes his personnel could kill up to a thousand Tutsi's.*
- *Informant states he disagrees with anti-Tutsi extermination. He supports opposition to the RPF but cannot support killing of innocent persons. He also stated that he believes the President does not have full control over elements of his own Party/Faction.*
- *Informant is prepared to provide location of major weapons cache with at least a hundred thirty-five weapons ... He was*

*ready to go to the arms cache tonight if we gave him the follow-
ing guarantee:*

- *He requests that he and his family (his wife and four children)
be placed under our protection.*[6]

Here was factual evidence of the suspicions that most could
feel on the ground in Kigali. Vast shipments of Machetes from
China and the development of an arms bazaar in plain sight
made a mockery of the Arusha Accords provision that Kigali
should be a "weapons free zone." And now a high-ranking
informant had offered to expose stored weapons and a formal
program to exterminate a large number of people – it was the
break that Dallaire had been hoping for. General Dallaire
made it clear that he wanted to grant this informant protection
and wished to proceed with raids on the weapons caches within
36 hours. The fax was marked "Most Immediate." It was signed
off with this phrase in French: "Peux ce que veux. Allons' y"
(Where there's a will there's a way. Let's go").

The response was uncharacteristically swift. On the following day, Iqbal Riza, deputy to Kofi Annan, who was in charge of
UN peacekeeping, sent a response indicating that protection
of the informant was "beyond the mandate entrusted to UN-
MAIR." General Dallaire was instructed to share his information with President Habyarimana and tell him that the activities
of the Interahamwe were a "clear threat to the peace process."
The response further stated: "You should assume that he –
Habyarimana – is not aware of these activities, but insist that
he must immediately look into the situation." General Dallaire
was also directed to share his information with the ambassadors
to Rwanda from the United States, Belgium and France.

Essentially UN Headquarters had dismissed Dellaire's intelligence as an exaggeration. Riza later said: "We get hyperbole
in many reports." However, the failure to act was certainly a
dereliction of duty. Years after the genocide, when the Belgian
Senate conducted a hearing into the savage murders of Belgian
UNAMIR peacekeepers, Kofi Annan, by then UN Secretary
General, refused to allow General Dallaire to testify. He also

refused to provide his own testimony on the memo, citing his "UN immunity."

Théoneste Bagosora left Kigali for a vacation on March 30, but abruptly returned on April 4, according to eyewitness testimony reported by Human Rights Watch. Kigali was extremely tense. Everyone was waiting for something to happen and on the evening of April 6 something did. The president's plane was returning from Dar es Salaam, Tanzania, where he had reluctantly consented to a broadly based transitional government. In essence, his military and civilian leaders, as well as members of the "Little House," were about to be removed from power. Traveling by an aircraft that was a gift from French President Mitterand was Habyarimana accompanied by Cyprien Ntaryamira, the new President of Burundi; General Nsabinmana, chief of staff of the Rwandan army and several other officials.

At 8:23 p.m., as the President's jet began its final approach to the east side of the Kigali Airport runway, it was struck by a ground-to-air missile in the wing area. The damaged aircraft was able to continue on its landing path. It was then struck by a second missile, which brought the plane down. The aircraft actually crashed on the grounds of the Presidential Palace and was witnessed by Habyarimana's daughter. All passengers as well as the French crew were killed.

Eyewitness reports suggest that the missiles were fired from Masaka Hill, a well patrolled residential area near the airport. According to a French report, witnesses saw white men on the hill during that evening. Some observers believe that this report is accurate, since missiles of this type would have to be launched by highly trained technical personnel. This suggests that whoever arranged for the assassination may have used mercenaries as their agents. The Rwandan army later reported the recovery of two SA-16 launchers from the Masaka hill area.[7]

The first group to fall under suspicion for the assassination was the RPF, the sworn enemy of Habyarimana. A BBC analyst, Martin Plaut, provided a statement from a Captain Josue Abdul Ruzibiza who claims to have been part of an RPF plot. The RPF have denied any involvement in the incident.

Next in line for suspicion was Habyarimana's own inner circle of Hutu Power advocates who wished to prevent the installation of a new coalition government. The Rwandan military had control of the airport and the immediate vicinity of the Presidential Palace, supporting the view that only the Rwandan military would have the logistical opportunity for this act. Moderate Hutus were also suspects, based on the theory that killing Habyarimana was their only hope to prevent the planned genocidal violence.

The actual facts will probably never be established, but in the aftermath of the murder of President Habyarimana, a genocidal slaughter began. And the man who assumed command of the entire Rwandan governmental and military apparatus immediately following the assassination was former Colonel Théoneste Bagosora.

Bagosora chaired an emergency meeting, as the senior official from the Ministry of Defense. According to General Dallaire, who was present, Bagosora was also directing military operations through a series of telephone conversations conducted during the meeting. Bagosora had access to, and apparently used, a direct radio link with the Presidential Guard. Within minutes of the assassination, Rwandan soldiers blocked Belgian UNAMIR troops at the airport and the reconnaissance battalion of the Presidential Guard surrounded the home of the Prime Minister. Two hours after the assassination, MRND politicians and their families were evacuated to the security of a military compound and opposition leaders were told to remain in their homes. By midnight, the first government official was killed and by 2 a.m., Interahamwe were patrolling the streets.

The Moderate Hutu Prime Minister, Mme. Uwilingiyimana arranged for UNAMIR peacekeepers to escort her to the radio station for an address to the nation, to assert civilian control of the government. Her escorts never arrived because they had been taken prisoner by the Rwandan military. She was captured the next morning and a National Police captain shot her in the head, blowing off the left half of her face. Her nearly naked body was later found on the terrace of her home with a beer bottle shoved into her vagina. Her husband was also slain.

Most of the UNAMIR soldiers who had been detained were beaten to death by an angry mob. After the arrival of Bagosora at the compound where they were being held, the Rwandan soldiers killed the remaining Belgians. With civilian control eliminated and Belgian UN troops murdered, the way was open for Théoneste Bagosora to begin the plan he had carefully developed for years: the extermination of the Tutsi's in Rwanda [8]

The Genocide Begins

By mid-day on April 7, the Presidential Guard and other elite units had eliminated anyone who could be installed as a legitimate civilian leader of Rwanda. There was no doubt that Théoneste Bagosora was in firm control. On that afternoon, Bagosora issued a press release in the name of the Rwandan military stating that efforts were being taken "to stabilize the situation in the country rapidly." Few in the military were willing to disobey Bagosora's orders and none had the resources to oust him.

On April 8, Bagosora installed a civilian government of all Hutu Power politicians. On April 9, the French government evacuated Madame Habyarimana by plane. During the first days following the assassination approximately 6,000 to 7,000 people were killed, according to Human Rights watch.

More widespread killing would follow, because Bagosora had personally issued orders on the morning of April 7 commanding elite military units to sweep Kigali from one side to another to eliminate Tutsis. Working systematically with lists of those targeted for extermination the troops soon carried out their orders. They went house to house in the search for victims. Terrified Tutsis and moderate Hutus cowered in their homes listening to the sounds of approaching gunfire, as their neighbors were murdered. The RTLM radio announcer urged the killers on:

The population is very vigilant, except in certain sectors... where people are still downcast; otherwise, everywhere else, they have sacked all the houses, the rooms, the kitchens, everywhere! They have even torn out all the doors and windows in all the uninhabited houses; in general they find inyenzi [cockroaches] hidden inside. They have searched everywhere! If they get hungry, they'll all come out before you arrive. That is why you must act very fast. Force them to come out! Find them at whatever the cost.[9]

Soon mass killing was underway throughout the nation. At first, the assailants operated in small bands, killing people wherever they found them – in homes, on the streets and at roadblocks. Terrified people on death lists fled seeking sanctuary. The government promised to protect them if they assembled in selected sites. One Rwandan remarked, "It was like sweeping dry banana leaves into a pile to burn them more easily." When the people arrived at designated churches and stadiums, at first they believed they were safe. But the killers waited until the location was full and until the displaced persons were weakened from lack of food and water. Then they struck – sometimes with guns, other times with clubs and machetes. In a church in Nyange, "people were massacred by a bulldozer that flattened the church and the people inside."

As the killing mounted, more citizens joined in "the work" and at the end of an exhausting day they would go home to feast on food and drink pillaged from their victims. Frequently when those marked for death were more than members of the militia could kill on a single day, the Achilles tendons of their intended victims would be cut so they could not escape. The next day the killers would return to continue "the work."

Members of the Interahamwe militia had been recruited from the lowest elements in Hutu society and they conducted themselves accordingly. At barricades throughout the towns and countryside they were frequently drunk and disorderly, but they exercised life and death power over those who sought to pass. Interahamwe militia patrols sometimes brought people

found hiding in the bush to a roadblock for disposition. Known
Tutsi or RPF supporters were generally killed on the spot. But
in some cases bribes would be taken and the people would be
allowed to pass. Those taking bribes knew that others would
eventually catch them.

Looting became part of the spectacle of slaughter. Bands
of killers ransacked pharmacies to steal drugs. Victims were
frequently transported by bus to locations where a massacre
was planned. Torture was often inflicted on both males and
females before they were killed. One elderly Tutsi woman in
Kibirira had her legs hacked off and was left to bleed to death.
A Hutu man in Cyangugu, who was known as an opponent of
the government, was killed by having each body part severed
while he was alive, beginning with his extremities. Babies were
thrown into latrines to die of suffocation or hunger. Some
victims were forced to kill their children or spouses. A Hutu
councilwoman in Kigali was offering fifty Rwandan francs each
(about thirty cents) for severed Tutsi heads, a practice that became known as "selling cabbages." [10]

Some victims were stripped naked before they were killed,
purely for the purpose of humiliation. Many were not allowed
a decent burial and their clergymen were forced to stay away
from the bodies, which decomposed in the streets. The killers looked at almost every woman as a potential object of rape
or longer-term sexual slavery. Tens of thousands of women
and girls were raped, including a child as young as two. Hutu
men, who considered Tutsi women both beautiful and haughty,
found ways to humiliate these women further during rape sessions. Human Rights Watch has reported cases of breasts being
cut off, vaginas punctured with spears and disfigurement of
body parts that looked particularly "Tutsi."

Many women who were gang raped acquired HIV and some
were impregnated. Tests conducted on 25,000 female Tutsi
survivors of the genocide by the organization, Avega, reported
that "two thirds were found to be HIV-positive." The pain and
humiliation was passed on to the next generation, with tens
of thousands of Rwandan children suffering the loss of their
mothers due to AIDS. [11]

Some who escaped the roadblocks in the cities were pursued into the countryside. But they did not all go to the slaughter like lambs. There are widespread reports of resistance. Tutsis fought, sometimes hand-to-hand, with their assailants in homes and in the bush, at roadblocks and in fields. Frequently they would repulse the initial attack only to be overcome when reinforcements or National Police arrived. Some Tutsis survived, hidden among or under bodies and some fled, hiding successfully for weeks.

There were reports of organized resistance through a tactic known as kwiunga or "merging." This involved lying down in wait until the killers were upon them – then the intended victims would rise up and engage in hand to hand fighting. The attackers were reluctant to shoot at such close quarters fearing that they might kill each other. In Nyakizu, after days of attacks, a strategy of slipping away in small groups at staggered times helped to increase the chances of escape.

The number of resisters at Bisesero was large enough to allow an organized command structure. In this location, on a mountainous ridge in the Kibuye region, Tutsis stood off the militia and the army from April 8 through July 1. One Tutsi survivor explained:

> We fled to the hill because it was high and we could see the attackers coming... It had lots of woods on it and so many hiding places. The attackers would come to kill during the day and at night they would go off to eat and drink.[12]

The attackers at Bisesero divided themselves into two teams – one for daytime assault and another "who went around at night trying to find where people were hiding by smelling or seeing their cooking fires." The government sent reinforcements and insisted that the operation be "finished definitively" by June 20. Of the thousands of Tutsis originally hidden in the wooded hilltop, fewer than 1,500 survived. Some were caught but escaped to return to their sanctuary in Bisesero. One young man did this three times, remarking. "All this was in April, the month that would not end."

Others fled from one place to another and a few fortunate refugees made it to the border. Day after day they played a deadly game of hide and seek with those who planned to kill them. A few of the intended victims were given refuge by protectors, who then sometimes became victims themselves, suffering rape, beatings or murder for their acts of compassion.

Perhaps the best-known case of a protector, who saved many people and survived, is Paul Rusesabagina, the manager of the Hotel des Mille Collines – "Hotel Rwanda" of the movie. This courageous and enterprising man used his wits, bribery with alcohol and his determination to save those who had sought refuge in the hotel, located in the heart of the capital, Kigali. To this hero the horror of what happened "was more than a surprise," he said. " It was a disappointment." Mr. Rusesabagina, a Hutu, along with his Tutsi wife, Tatiana and their children, narrowly escaped death several times. Mr. Rusesabagina was directly responsible for saving the lives of more than 1,200 Tutsis and Hutu moderates.

Although the killings in Rwanda during the spring of 1994 were carried out in a low-tech fashion, mostly with clubs and machetes, the rate of killing was astonishing. Gerard Prunier estimates that "the daily killing rate was at least five times that of the Nazi death camps." A large part of the Hutu population needed to take part, because the killing technique required teamwork and coordination. Videotapes of the killings showed that several (usually three or four) attackers hacked on a single victim. The organizers clearly planned to involve as many as possible in the genocide. Rwandan authorities provided food, drink and sometimes drugs, uniforms and small cash payments to the militias or the civilians who participated in "the work."

Most who did the killing were men, but not always. Women and girls joined the crowds to serve as cheerleaders for the slaughter and some have been accused of betraying their sons or husbands. One nun provided the gasoline used to burn victims alive. Many women and girls were known to have stripped the dead and dying of money, jewelry and clothes.

This brief description cannot begin to capture the full extent of the horror of the Rwandan genocide, during which more than 800,000 people were hacked to death by their neighbors in just 100 days. Only the survivors can provide testimony, for the dead cannot tell their stories. Journalist Fergal Keane, author of *Season of Blood, a Rwandan Journey*, has provided a compelling story of such a survivor, a 13 year-old girl named Valentina. In early April of 1994 she, along with many others sought refuge in a church. This is her story, much of it in her own words:

> *The killing at Nyarubuye began with an attack on Tutsis at the local marketplace. After this Valentina fled to the church with her family. That afternoon the killers arrived, led by Sylvestre Gacumbitsi, the local mayor. Valentina recognized many of her Hutu neighbours among the more than 30 men who surrounded the church. They carried knives and clubs and were supported by soldiers from the Rwandan army.*

> *Among the gang of men was Denis Bagaruka, a 56-year-old grandfather whose own children went to school with Valentina.*

> *She described what happened next: " First they asked people to hand over their money, saying they would spare those who paid. But after taking the money they killed them anyway. Then they started to throw grenades. I saw a man blown up in the air, in pieces, by a grenade. The leader said that we were snakes and that to kill snakes you had to smash their heads.*

> *The killers moved into the terrified crowd of men, women and children, hacking and clubbing as they went. "If they found someone alive they would smash their heads with stones. I saw them take little children and smash their heads together until they were dead. There were children begging for pity but they killed them straight away, "*

she told me. The killings took place over four days. At night the butchers rested, guarding the perimeter so that nobody would escape.

Other infants, crying on the ground beside their murdered parents, were taken and plunged head first into latrines. One of Valentina's classmates, an angel-faced little boy named Placide, told me how he had seen a man decapitated in front of him and then a pregnant woman cut open as the killing reached its frenzied climax.

"There was so much noise," he recalled. "People were begging for mercy and you could hear the militia saying, 'Catch them, catch them, don't let them get away.'"

Valentina and Placide hid among the bodies, pretending to be dead. Valentina had been struck on the head and hands with a machete and was bleeding heavily. Following her child's instinct, she crawled to her mother's body and lay there. During the killing she had seen the militia murder her father and her 16-year-old brother, Frodise.

After several days Valentina crawled to the room where there were fewest bodies. For the next 43 days she lived among the rotting corpses, too weak to stand up and convinced that the world had come to an end.

"I prayed that I would die because I could not see a future life. I did not think that anybody was left alive in the country. I thought everybody had been swept away," she said.

She drank rainwater and rummaged for scraps of food. There was some wild fruit and some grain but she became weaker and weaker as the days progressed. In the weeks that followed, a few other children emerged from hiding places around the church. The stronger ones lit fires and cooked what food they could find, feeding the weaker ones like Valentina.

Then a new hazard appeared: wild dogs that had started to eat the corpses. "The dogs were coming at night and eating dead children in the other rooms. A dog came to where I was and started to eat a body. I picked up a stone and threw it at the dog and drove it away."

There comes a point in the telling of this story where the existing vocabulary of suffering becomes inadequate, where words wither in the face of an unrelenting darkness. As a reporter I found this the most difficult story of my career to tell. As a parent I listened to Valentina's story with a sense of heartbreak. I marveled at her courage but felt deep anger that his should happen to any child. It was difficult to keep those feelings in check when I confronted one of the butchers of Nyarubuye in the office of the local prosecutor.

Bagaruka, the grandfather who witnesses say was an enthusiastic killer, had recently returned from Tanzania. He had spent nearly three years there in the refugee camp at Benaco where he and his family were fed and cared for by the international community. The man who had helped to bring terror to the infants of Nyarubuye was nervous and evasive when I spoke to him.

"You have eight children, how in God's name can you help to kill a child?" I asked him. After a long pause he answered: "You see all those people in the church had children. Many were carrying them on their backs but none survived. Everyone was killed. We couldn't spare the children's lives. Our orders were to kill everyone."

He told me that he himself had been an orphan and a Tutsi man had been his guardian. Bagaruka had seen the man killed at Nyarubuye. "I almost become crazy when I think about that," he said.

Bagaruka has confessed to some of his crimes and has implicated some of his friends and neighbours, hoping to save himself from the firing squad.

Valentina hopes he will never return to the village. She now lives with an aunt and two other orphans. The aunt's husband and three children were killed at Nyarubuye.

The aunt told me that Valentina has a recurring dream. She imagines her mother coming in the middle of the night. They embrace and then Valentina shows her mutilated hand to her mother, saying: "Mother, look what's become of me. Look what has happened to me." And Valentina wakes up crying and sees that her mother has vanished into the darkness. Then she remembers that her mother is dead and gone forever. [13]

The World Watches in Silence

When the genocide began, the Western nations expressed shock and condemned the killing, but they did little to stop the carnage. The French and Belgians sent troops to rescue their own citizens in Rwanda and American civilians were airlifted out, but no attempt was made to save Rwandans who were in danger. On April 11, the Belgian UNAMIR soldiers protecting 2,000 refugees at the Don Bosco School were ordered to the airport in the afternoon. Most of the people they abandoned were killed shortly afterwards. Many of the Belgian soldiers were so ashamed of this action that they shredded their UN blue berets on the tarmac of the Kigali airport. The Belgians departed, leaving the country to the mercy of the Hutu Power extremists.

The UN Security council voted to withdraw most of the remaining UNAMIR troops. The force was reduced from 2,500 to 270. The international press ran superficial stories that suggested the problems in Rwanda were mostly mutual killing and lawless disorder. Nothing could have been further from the truth. It was systematic, premeditated mass murder that had been planned for months, even years in advance. It was genocide. But the U. S. forbade its diplomats to use that word, in order to avoid pressure to do something to stop it. The behavior of the UN was even worse and they were guilty of actually spreading disinformation. Secretary General Boutros Boutros-Ghali said that it was a case of "Hutus killing Tutsis and Tutsis killing Hutus."

On April 21, General Dallaire, who had been stripped of his peacekeeping force by petty UN bureaucrats and fearful Belgian politicians, stated that with five thousand soldiers and a free hand he could put a rapid halt to the killing. But the international community was not listening. The New York Times editorialized on April 23, that "the world has little choice but to stand aside and hope for the best." African nations were horrified by Rwanda's unfolding nightmare and tried in vain to bring back the UN troops, but the major powers, including the United States would have none of it. When several small countries proposed a UNAMIR II mission with 5,500 troops, Washington held this proposal hostage for weeks, and agreed only to a much smaller force of 150 unarmed observers.

The only organization that made any effort to end the genocide was the RPF. It swung into action almost immediately and began a major offensive with the intention of forcing the killers to withdraw from portions of eastern Rwanda. Within a few weeks, the RPF drive southward threatened to overrun Kigali. As they advanced, the full extent of the genocide was broadcast to the world.

The Rwandan Hutu government charged genocide against the advancing RPF forces and the French military began to issue statements about a "two-way genocide." Jacque Baumel, of the French National Assembly, declared that the RPF was "threatening the privileged position of France." Clearly, the

French desperately wanted to save their Rwandan allies. When faced with the invasion of the RPF, the regime of Théoneste Bagosora chose to put greater resources into the killing, in much the same way that Hitler accelerated the holocaust in Eastern Europe as the allies advanced.

The French, who feared loss of influence in Africa, proposed a military expedition to Rwanda under the auspices of the UN. In a masquerade of multilateralism, that included a few Senegalese troops, the French won immediate UN approval on June 22. The UN gave the French permission to use the aggressive force they had denied the peacekeepers. On the very next day, the infamous "Operation Turquoise" rolled into northwestern Rwanda and was greeted by happy bands of Interahamwe killers. Signs proclaimed, "Welcome French Hutus." The "French Hutus" came to the rescue of their genocidal allies and they also provided additional arms to the Rwandan Hutu military to help them fight off the RPF. Meanwhile the international community attempted to impose a cease-fire, which would prevent a further RPF advance. The irony is that military action by the RPF was the only thing that actually stopped some of the killing.

French forces captured much of the western part of Rwanda and within a week stood face to face with the RPF. The "humanitarian" pretense of the French action was then dropped in favor of what they called a "safe zone." Some have asked the question, "safe for whom?" Even the former president of France, Valery Giscard d'Estaing, has accused the French forces of "protecting some of those who had carried out the massacres." The French "safe zone" afforded Hutu Power fanatics a place to continue "the work."

French forces lured desperate Tutsis out of hiding by using the French Flag on their vehicles. When French troops found survivors, they frequently told them to wait for transportation, only to return to transport the corpses. About 14,000 Tutsis were eventually rescued by the French incursion, but French troops were fully cooperative with Rwandan Hutu officials who had participated in the genocide and they openly considered the RPF the enemy. The practical effect of "Operation

Turquoise" was to provide an additional month for the killers
to complete their work, and then to offer a corridor for safe
passage for the murderers to escape, with many of their French-
supplied weapons, into neighboring Zaire.[14]

The Escape of the Genocidaires

Thousands of escaping killers were given the French name
of "Genocidaires." They retreated into "Zone Turquoise"
and continued the killing while spreading stories about RPF
atrocities. Most were untrue, although there have been some
legitimate reports of RPF troops killing civilians. As the killers
retreated they laid waste to the countryside, looting and destroying as they went. Many abandoned their own children by
the roadsides, to facilitate a more hasty escape. They continued
to listen to radio RTLM, and followed instructions provided
by the regime of Théoneste Bagosora. On July 15, the United
States belatedly withdrew diplomatic recognition of the Hutu
government.

Bagosora and his henchmen shifted their base of operations
and the French, although promising to arrest the Hutu leadership, simply provided safe passage to the border for the entire
mob of well over a million people. On July 19, the RPF formed
a coalition government with Rwandan opponents of the former
regime who had managed to survive. Rwanda's Hutu ambassador was then forced from his UN position.

The world community according to the accusations of
RPF General Paul Kagame, "stood around with its hands in its
pockets," but was suddenly swept up into a frenzy of humanitarian concern, as refugees were placed into camps near Goma,
Zaire in late summer. According to the media, the camps made
"great TV." A massive outpouring of aid was sent to support the
refugees. The public knew that genocide had occurred and
assumed that the camp residents were its survivors. They witnessed broadcasts of desperate people dying by the thousands
of cholera and other diseases in deplorable conditions at the

foot of the Nyaragongo volcano, which was belching smoke and ash upon them.

The suffering seen on TV hid a functioning Hutu government in exile. The French provided military vehicles for evacuation and transport of high Hutu government officials. The propaganda broadcasts of radio RTLM continued, and indeed never ceased to broadcast from the "safe zone." These inflammatory broadcasts were designed to terrify the Hutu masses about the RPF advance and to encourage them to flee into Zaire. The mass exodus provided a sea of refugees, allowing the Genocidaires to hide among them.

The Hutu killers also hoped that the refugees could form a new army to expand "Hutu Power." According to Human Rights Watch and Amnesty International, the French continued to provide military training and assistance to the former Rwandan army in the Central African Republic, Zaire and in France itself. And the flow of French arms to the Genocidaires continued for an extended period. By the time of the French withdrawal in August of 1994, not a single killer had been arrested for their genocidal crimes.

The refugee camps became miniature replications of the Hutu Power government. Dedicated NGO's (Non-governmental organizations) were treated as servants and were expected to provide all the essentials of life. When NGO's were not subservient enough, they were threatened by unruly mobs. Tragically, they became unwilling enablers of the Hutu State in exile. One reporter looked up at the volcano and prayed, "God if that thing erupts right now, and buries the killers, I will believe that you are just and I will go to church again every day of my life." Thanks to the weakness of the international community and the continuing support of their French patrons, most of the Genocidaires escaped. But they were not refugees – they were criminal fugitives.[15]

Despite the planned murders of nearly one million people, the public was still confused about what had taken place in Rwanda. The whole world had heard about the killing but they did not see it happen. What they did see were the dead and dying from the cholera epidemic in the camps. So to most of the world the suffering in the camps was merely an extension of the same horror.

The French took advantage of this confusion to spread propaganda that suggested a double genocide. When asked about the genocide, French President Mitterand responded: "The genocide or the genocides?" The plural of the word was rarely used during the slaughter of the Tutsis but in its aftermath, it was applied frequently to include the death of some 50,000 Hutus from cholera.

The camps became a hiding place for the killers who ruled them with an iron fist. Some NGO's realized how they were being used and for that reason, Doctors without Borders shut down its refugee camp program. By 1995, a string of camps for nearly 400,000 refugees spread out all along the Rwandan border. The most famous was the Kibeho camp, where Interahamwe residents threatened those who planned to leave for resettlement. They knew that removal of tens of thousands of refugees would leave them and the other killers exposed. So they prolonged the existence of the camps, particularly Kibeho, which was their headquarters.

Zaire became the home in exile of Théoneste Bagosora where he and his band of Hutu Power fanatics were planning their next murderous campaign. The leadership of the Hutu Power movement had been given special treatment by Zaire's President, Mobutu Sese Seko, a supporter of the Habyarimana regime. He had facilitated illicit arms shipments into Rwanda and provided a staging area for the French as they prepared to implement Operation Turquoise. He now supplied the Hutu Power leadership with military papers allowing Bagosora to travel to the Seychelles to purchase new weapons and other munitions.[16]

It is difficult to imagine that the genocidal war being waged by militant Hutus against their Tutsi neighbors would somehow continue, but it did. The French had pulled out with the closure of "Zone Turquoise" in the fall of 1994, but they had recruited a group of Serbian mercenaries to help their Hutu allies. The French unilaterally resumed financial assistance to Zaire – allowing Mobutu to pass the cash directly to the killers.

A War of Genocide Spreads

In early 1996, the pestilence of genocide, like some kind of hideous plague, crossed the border into Zaire. With thousands of Hutu killers on the loose in Zaire, the Tutsis of that nation became prey. Desperate Tutsi citizens of Zaire sought shelter at the Mokoto monastery on a hillside above the town of the same name, about thirty miles over rugged hills from the UN camps in Goma. The priests took in the Tutsis and listened to their tragic stories about killings in their hometowns of Zaire.

Soon the monastery came under siege from Hutus, threatening nearly a thousand refugees camped around its grounds. On Sunday, May 12, Hutus broke into the church and dragged out many of the refugees and hacked them to death with machetes. When Doctors without Borders reached the monastery with a relief team, they found the road littered with corpses. Some had their hands, feet and genitals cut off. A few of the rotting bodies revealed ghastly slashes in the chest where they had been savagely opened so their hearts could be removed. Now in a new location, the Genocidaires were back in business and "the work" continued.

The attackers had come from the UN camps. Their excellent Kinyarwanda language skills and their well-dressed appearance easily identified them as Rwandan Hutus. They could not be confused with the local Zairians who were hill people and spoke Swahili almost exclusively. It was eventually determined that at least one hundred victims were killed at Mokoto and many others had been wounded or maimed. The Hutu Power killers did not limit their campaign of genocide just to the Tutsi. About thirty thousand members of the Hunde tribe, subsistence farmers of Zaire, were driven from their farms by the wave of violence and became refugees in their own country.

In Rwanda, the RPF had established a new government and began to stabilize the country as best they could. The new

RPF/Rwandan government in Kigali found the existence of camps that harbored Genocidaires intolerable. Support by Mobutu for a continuing campaign of genocide on the Zaire side of the border was completely unacceptable to the new leaders of Rwanda. Despite international protests, the genocide continued and the world again took no action to stop it. France continued its support of the Hutu Power movement and the new RPF/Rwandan government was banned from French-sponsored diplomatic events. Hutu Power's malignant campaign of death seemed destined to be prolonged, perhaps indefinitely as they established a new home in Zaire that they called "Hutuland."

Burundi closed the camps in its territory completely and multitudes of displaced Hutus streamed back into Rwanda. The Rwandan government warily accepted the Hutus, despite the probable role of many in the genocide. Tutsi refugees who reached Rwanda from Zaire became potential recruits to oppose Mobutu and to resolve the growing cancer of Hutuland, as the war in Zaire was rapidly spreading.

The four hundred thousand Tutsis living in the South Kivu region in Zaire were at extreme risk. During the middle of 1996, the Tutsis of South Kivu were ordered to leave their homes by the Mobutu-loyalist deputy governor, an indication that the alliance between Mobutu and Hutu Power had been formalized. The RPF/Rwandan government knew it could wait no longer. Hundreds of well-trained fighters prepared to move into Zaire from Rwanda.

The RPF/Rwandan government closed the camps on their side of the border, but saved the Kibeho camp for last because of the high number of hard-core Hutu fighters hiding among the innocent. A struggle for control between UN forces charged with protecting the camps and the RPF/Rwandan forces left refugees in the middle. Some of those fleeing the violence inadvertently trampled children to death. When faced with unidentified refugees breaking out of the camp, the Rwandans soldiers recklessly opened fire. The scene was one of complete chaos.[17]

The final death toll was between two and four thousand. Most of the victims in this tragedy had been killed in stampedes. The new Rwandan government could not be proud of the action of their troops. But Interahamwe killers hacked and speared many people to death, which prompted the panic that caused the original flight from the camp. Once more, a flood of refugees was created by violence. This time they scattered in various directions. The Tutsi survivors streamed home to Rwanda and most Hutu militants ran for the bush, eager to find sanctuary in Hutuland.

Conditions in Rwanda were grim. The nation was bankrupt, and its productive capabilities were crippled. Its citizens were traumatized. Almost all governmental facilities were in ruins. The coffee and tea harvest was lost for the season and most of the machinery necessary to process the next harvest was inoperable. Rwanda had become the poorest country in Africa, with an average annual per capita income of eighty dollars per year. The nation was filled with refugees. About 750,000 Tutsis had returned. Many Hutus who returned to Rwanda were suspected of complicity in the genocide. Amid suspicion and mistrust, the country faced an uncertain future.

The new government took steps to bring the guilty to justice, and by late 1995 nearly sixty thousand persons had been arrested for participation in the killings. That number rose to more than 125,000 by the end of 1997. A commission was impaneled to sort through the charges. Some who were not charged were released only to become the victims of vigilante justice. The government initiated "gacaca" courts, in which ordinary Rwandans judged their peers, but it became clear that it would be impossible to bring half of the nation to justice. Trial and punishment would have to target the leaders of the genocide. A list of 400 major criminals was drawn up by the new government in Rwanda and was submitted to the United Nations. Paul Kagame and Rwanda's new leaders could do little but plead with the UN for justice.

Under the brutal and corrupt Mobutu regime, Zaire had descended into gangsterism and Mobutu looted the country while the people of Zaire fell into poverty and despair. Harboring the

Hutu Power extremists was the final despicable act of a dying regime. When The Zairian government ordered Tutsis out of South Kivu, the new Rwandan government, acting in concert with Zairian rebels led by Laurent Kabila, launched a bold invasion into their much larger neighbor, Zaire. Although they initially denied outright invasion, Rwandan forces clearly were operating in support of Kabila's rebels to stop the surreptitious genocide that was being committed in Zaire.

Mobotu's undisciplined army fled as the rebels liberated a huge swath of Zaire. The Interahamwe acted in a predictably loathsome way, using almost 750,000 refugees as human shields for their own escape. The innocent victims of war were herded to the Mugunga camp in Zaire, close to the Rwandan border. While the UN debated another humanitarian mission, Rwandan and rebel force circled Mugunga and attempted to separate the Hutu militants from the refugees. Many of the Interahamwe fled deeper into Zaire, while hundreds of thousands of refugees began to walk back to the Rwandan border. The tactic was only a partial success because many of the killers reentered Rwanda hidden among the refugees. But another bloodbath had been averted. About six hundred thousand people eventually made their way back into Rwanda, including Hutus who had been part of the genocide.

Mobutu fled Zaire and died in exile in Morocco. Kabila became president of that country and changed its name to the Democratic Republic of Congo. Paul Kagame became president of Rwanda. Tragically, the Congo still smolders as a multi-sided war there continues unabated. The death count on all sides has become truly grotesque, reaching more than five million people by 2008. More than half of the victims of this continuing conflict are children under five years of age.

U. S. President Bill Clinton made a brief appearance in Rwanda on March 25, 1998, to apologize on behalf of the failures of international community, stating, "It is important that the world know that these killings were not spontaneous or accidental...they were most certainly not the result of ancient tribal struggles...These events grew from a policy aimed at the systematic destruction of a people." It was a small gesture but deeply appreciated by the people of Rwanda, who had endured so much.[18]

Gradually, during the years following the horrors of 1994 in Rwanda, the leadership of the Genocidaires and ministers of the former Hutu government began to slip away into exile. Some of these men sought refuge in countries that gave them protection from justice and of the original 400 leaders named by the new Rwandan government as prime suspects, only a fraction had been arrested and brought to justice. In July 1995, Théoneste Bagosora made his way to Yaounde, Cameroon, where he lived until he was arrested on March 9, 1996. He was transferred to the UN on January 23, 1997 to face trial.

A Tribunal Without Healing

In late 1994, the United Nations Security Council established the International Criminal Tribunal for Rwanda (ICTR), for the purpose of "prosecuting persons responsible for genocide and other serious violations of international humanitarian law committed in the territory of Rwanda..." From the very beginning the court encountered controversy. The new Rwandan government, dominated by Tutsis and the RPF, was highly distrustful of the court's insistence on so called "special investigations," into charges of crimes on both sides. From the Rwandan government's point of view, this would be like prosecuting the Jews for crimes against the Nazis.

Hutus are the primary defendants in the tribunal's proceedings and they view the work of the ICTR as "victor's justice." The tribunal has fallen into what has been described as "extreme tedium," during more than 15 years of proceedings that have been marred by administrative mismanagement, sluggish judicial progress and continual political rancor. The ICTR has more than 800 employees, who draw ample UN salaries, numerous perks and enjoy judicial workloads that are less than rigorous. Defense counsel's are paid $220 per hour and can charge for up to 175 hours each month. Lawyers making as much as $38,000 per month are in no hurry to wrap up their cases. The budget for the tribunal for 2002-2003 was $256.9 million, compared to all foreign aid provided to Rwanda in 2000 of $322 million for the benefit of more than 7 million people. Many observers believe that the tribunal should close its proceedings and distribute the funds to social programs for Rwanda. Some have suggested that ICTR is "just a jobs program for foreigners."

Many Rwandans consider the Tribunal itself to be another crime against their country. When the cost and the time are weighed against the few individuals who have actually been brought to justice, this charge seems justified. In their defense, however, prosecutors have a thin trail of evidence, many reluctant witnesses and a decreasing list of victims still alive to testify. Those who are willing to appear usually require protection because many fear retaliation. Some witnesses, especially women, who were rape victims, have died due to lack of treatment for HIV, before they could appear in court.

There have been a few rewarding episodes during the trials that have taken place. Sometimes, a Genocidaire breaks down with remorse and confesses his crimes, providing a moment of moral clarity to the proceedings. However, this happens infrequently and the primary source of reconciliation has occurred within the 10,000 gacaca's (people's courts) that have been held throughout Rwanda, during which the people themselves have achieved some small measure of healing for their terrible suffering.[19]

Rwanda is a nation that is haunted by both its living and its dead. For those who survived, many of the psychological and physical scars have not healed, even after all this time. No one who lived in Rwanda during the days of death truly escaped the blade. UNICEF reports that 96% of children interviewed in Rwanda witnessed the massacres and 80% lost at least one family member. Nearly a third witnessed a rape or sexual assault. In Rwanda, there are currently more than 300,000 households headed by child survivors of the genocide. These families are struggling to survive and are victimized repeatedly by adults who prey on vulnerable children trying to raise themselves.

General Romeo Dallaire, who was commander of UNAMIR during the genocide, reflected the feelings of many, when he said, "I will never be finished with Rwanda. Those who have experienced it will never be finished." [20]

On June 1, 2007 the five-year trial of Theoneste Bagosora concluded with the former Rwandan Army Colonel maintaining his innocence, in his words, the "victim of ignominious propaganda." On the day his trial ended, he wore a pink shirt and tie – a color that represents solidarity with other convicted Genocidaires. When he appeared in court, Bagosora's broad expressionless face and blank eyes made him seem to be a mere bureaucrat representing the faceless facilitators of genocide. But this impression does not truly reflect his culpability for this monstrous crime. Colonel Bagosora did not merely follow orders to implement the slaughter, he was the mastermind of the genocide itself. His own comment that he was returning to Rwanda from the peace conference to "prepare for the apocalypse," is probably an accurate description of his role. During his seventeen days of testimony in 2005, Bagosora said, "I request people of goodwill to free their minds of intoxication and poison." He was defiant and showed no remorse.

Only thirty-five defendants had completed the trial process through March of 2008. Five had been acquitted, two were deceased, and an additional twenty-eight, including Bagosora were still on trial. Twenty-five were still awaiting trial or transfer. Of the thirty-five persons who had completed the trial process through March of 2008, only seven were serving sentences. [21]

On Thursday, December 18, 2008, The ICTR made the following announcement: "Colonel Bagosora is guilty of genocide and crimes against humanity and war crimes." His crimes, as cited by the court included the murders of the Rwandan prime minister and the head of the constitutional court as well as the 10 Belgian peacekeepers. He was also found responsible for "organized killings by soldiers at numerous sites in Rwanda's capital Kigali and in Gisenyi." Bagosora was sentenced to life in prison.

Former Colonel Anatole Nsengiyumva and Major Aloys Nta-
bakuze were also sentenced to life in prison for genocide. The
ICTR sentenced the late President Habyarimana's brother-in-
law, Protais Zigiranyirazo, a businessman, to 20 years in prison
for genocide and extermination as a crime against humanity.
On the day of the sentencing of these criminals, Chantal Kabas-
inga, president of the Rwanda Genocide Widows Association
expressed her hope for a more full measure of justice, stating, "All of the other Genocidaires still on the run should be
brought to justice as soon as possible." [22]

Despite the "wind of destruction" that descended on Rwanda,
some stories from those dreadful days of April 1994, teach profound lessons. Perhaps the nation can take heart from the courageous acts of a few Rwandan children that occurred during
the height of the genocide at a girl's school in Gisenyi, where
seventeen students were killed. This followed an earlier attack
on another girl's school that resulted in the killing of sixteen
students in Kibuye.

During both attacks, teenage students were confronted by
the Interahamwe, who ordered them to separate into Tutsi and
Hutu, so the "work" could be finished. They refused. And for
this act of courage and humanity they were indiscriminately
beaten and shot to death. Because they would not separate
into the tribal divisions demanded by the killers they died together, martyrs for a socially tolerant Rwanda.

EPILOGUE

"As nightfall does not come all at once, neither does oppression. In both instances, there is twilight. And it is in such twilight that we all must be aware of a change in the air – however slight – lest we become unwitting victims of the darkness."

U. S. Supreme Court Justice William O. Douglas

The heritage of the twentieth century's deadly dictators is a world in which terror, torture, ethnic cleansing and genocide have become common. Remnants of the Rwandan Hutu Genocidaires, who escaped into Zaire (now Democratic Republic of Congo), have continued the killing and slaughtered more than five million people by 2008 – more than in any conflict since World War II. They and other armed groups are also committing acts of ritualized sexual sadism, leaving thousands of women and girls, some as young as three, reproductively impaired for life and forever branded as outcasts in their own society.

The genocidal killing in the Darfur region of western Sudan also continues and although it is well known to the world, not nearly enough is being done by the international community to stop it. The death toll there probably exceeds 250,000 according to U. N. officials. About fifty ongoing conflicts have forced more than 300,000 kidnapped children into sexual slavery or into the horrors of war as child soldiers. According to journalist Sebastian Junger, "the arming of children is among the greatest evils in the modern world." Standards of behavior for all of civilization have been seriously degraded. Tragically, what we see in the new century is that the terrible past still lives in the present.

This nightmarish situation is our legacy from the masterminds of twentieth century genocides. While different from each other in many ways, the criminal despots examined in this book shared many common characteristics. Most were interlopers or outcasts in their own countries and not accepted by the cultured society of the nations they eventually ruled and many suffered personality disorders resulting from perverse events in their childhood.

Stalin was Georgian, not Russian, and he spoke the Russian language with an obvious accent. He was brutalized as a child. Stalin's deformed character surely contributed to his callous disregard for human life. His handwritten instructions to jailers of political prisoners to "beat, beat and beat again," reveals a propensity towards extreme cruelty.

Hitler was not German, but Austrian. His early childhood experiences in a maladjusted and incestuous family shaped his views on sex and race. In the Rise and Fall of the Third Reich, William L. Shirer writes, "There is a great deal of morbid sexuality in Hitler's ravings about the Jews...Mein Kampf is sprinkled with lurid allusions to uncouth Jews seducing innocent Christian girls and thus adulterating their blood."

Kim Jong-il perceived himself an orphan due to the early loss of his mother and the emotional abandonment by his father, who was instead serving as the "Fatherly Leader" of the nation. Kim's role in the death of his younger brother surely contributed to his cold indifference to human suffering. His emotional deformities are evident in North Korea's reprehensible international conduct and its domestic savagery.

Saddam Hussein was rejected as an infant by his mother and probably beaten by a violent stepfather, childhood traumas that undoubtedly established the sadism in his character. His behavior and that of his lawlessly corrupt family are reflections of his own degeneracy.

Idi Amin was fatherless, illiterate and a Muslim in a Christian nation and he spoke a remote dialect not understood by most Ugandans. His psychological alienation was almost certainly at the root of his tribal extermination policies.

Papa Doc Duvalier was born into the lowest social class in Haiti. His mother was afflicted by madness, a stigma that the dictator was never able to resolve. Both were surely causative factors in his monstrous repression of Haiti.

Trujillo had the blood of Haitian slaves in his veins, suggesting that his genocidal slaughter of Haitians was a reaction to his own racial self-loathing.

Clearly, classic symptoms of malignant narcissism were shared by the genocidal dictators of the twentieth century. They were manipulative, antisocial, paranoid and unable to empathize with others. Each of the men profiled in this book seized power through illegitimate means and they all used violence to secure and preserve their positions of absolute authority.

The impact that power itself provokes in human behavior has long been recognized by psychologists. Chemical changes in the brain of individuals who obtain powerful positions in society can distort their thought processes. In cases of extremely powerful individuals, this subconscious mental distortion can become perverse and extremely dangerous. Perhaps this behavioral pattern can best be summed up by Lord Action's famous pronouncement that, "Absolute power corrupts absolutely."

Prelude to Genocide

When totalitarian dictatorships begin to take shape, power concentrates into increasingly fewer hands. During this twilight of human rights, bold acts of resistance by the public may deflect an onrushing cataclysm. Totalitarianism is not inevitable, but it becomes possible because of the passive acceptance by many in society. Opportunistic, contrived crises, such as Stalin's show trials or Hitler's Reichstag fire, can foster a deep sense of public fear, resulting in the voluntary relinquishment of personal freedoms. And, as we have seen, social conditions, such as the economic chaos of Weimar Germany, or the financial shock of falling commodity prices in Rwanda, can lead the public to embrace racial, tribal or class hatred.

The intended victims of genocidal violence are generally viewed as separate, inferior and apart from mainstream society, which makes them seemingly legitimate targets for cruel treatment. A belief in the "otherness" of non-Aryans in Nazi Germany supported the extermination of Jews, Gypsies, homosexuals, Slavs and Russian prisoners. The desire to create a political utopia by returning to the origins of Khmer society caused the elimination of "others" from the Cambodian regime of Pol Pot. Stalin's social suspicions followed this pattern, as the war against the Kulaks gradually came to include such "anti-Soviet elements," as Bulgarians, Armenians, Kurds and Chechens. And during the latter stages of Stalin's tyranny, the killing became increasingly targeted against Jews. Cooperative Dominicans killed even longtime family servants, when the Haitian's became state enemies under Trujillo in 1937. Tribally based genocides in Rwanda and Uganda followed a similar trajectory, as mass killing was used with the intention of creating a homogeneous society.

The first stage in the progression towards genocide is the deprivation of the civil rights of those targeted for repression. Gradually, they are and isolated and dehumanized. The Jews in Hitler's Germany were publicly called vermin and rodents. Those targeted for slave labor or extermination were referred to as "undermenchen" or sub-humans. The Tutsi in Rwanda were described as "cockroaches" in extremist Hutu propaganda broadcasts. In both Russia and North Korea, state enemies were likened to microbes or dangerous diseases. Those persecuted may be publicly marked in some way, perhaps forced to wear symbols or identifying clothing. The intended victims are frequently segregated into ghettos, or forced into camps. Finally, many are murdered.

The final stage of genocide is denial on the part of the killers. Mass murderers generally act to cover up their involvement by removing common graves, burning bodies and destroying evidence. Investigations of the crimes are usually blocked or delayed. When all else fails and the killers are confronted with the consequences of their crimes, they frequently blame the victims.

Many extermination programs, such as those conducted in Nazi Germany, Soviet Russia, North Korea and Rwanda have been committed in a context of war or armed conflict. During World War I, civilians accounted for less than 10% of the war's victims. During World War II, that percentage dramatically increased to more than 50%. During the 1990's and in the early part of the current century, civilian victims of armed conflict have usually represented more than 80% of the victims.

The prevalence of Civil wars, based on ethnic or religious differences, account for much of the rise in civilian deaths. We also see an increasing number of wars of annihilation, where the objective of the war itself is to exterminate an entire people. The world is currently witnessing such a war in the Darfur region of Sudan. [1]

The Use of Torture

As the momentum of power grows, a totalitarian regime feeds on its own mystique. There are strong temptations to exert control over captives through physical cruelty or psychological violation. States that engage in torture usually claim that their objective is to obtain "actionable intelligence," about persons or organizations that the state considers a threat to its security. However, regimes utilizing torture frequently have other sinister purposes. The Inter-American Commission on Human Rights of the Organization of American States has gathered evidence from the bodies of torture victims that indicated the intent to, "inflict a punishment on the person who has engaged in activities considered to be a danger to the government." Based on this evidence, the commission viewed state torture not as a means to gain information, but as a barbaric act of revenge.

It is only a small step from the use of torture as a tool of revenge to the use of this coercive technique for the purpose of mind control. A powerful portrait of state torture for this purpose is demonstrated in George Orwell's classic novel, *Nineteen Eighty-Four*, which focuses on the life of Winston Smith, who works for the Ministry of Truth. Winston is arrested by the Thought Police for deviation from the "general party line." Because he is afraid, Winston confesses to crimes that both he and the Party know he did not commit. It is through torture that the victim learns to accept the authority of Big Brother, who he is told is the protector of the nation. During the process of re-programming, the suspect is asked, "How does one man assert his power over another, Winston?" His response and the subsequent exchange with his captors is illuminating:

> *By making him suffer, he said. Exactly. By making him suffer. Obedience is not enough. Unless he is suffering, how can you be sure that he is obeying your will and not his own. Power is in inflicting pain and humiliation.... But always – do not forget this, Winston – always there will be the intoxication of power, constantly increasing and constantly growing subtler. Always, at every moment, there will be the thrill of victory, the sensation of trampling on an enemy who is helpless.* [2]

Torture is the infliction of physical pain upon the body or psychological suffering upon the mind. It is designed to destroy the victim's privacy, intimacy, sense of trust and eventually his sense of identity. These acts are made more damaging through public humiliation, incessant repetition and the sadistic enjoyment of the victim's suffering. Frequently, after torture, basic bodily functions such as sleep, sustenance and excretion can, in the mind of the victim, become degrading and dehumanizing. The process of torture robs the victim of a sense of self and "can become the equivalent of cognitive death." It has been described as the "ultimate act of perverted intimacy," because the torturer invades the victim's body, dominates his psyche and possesses his mind. To relieve his or her suffering, the victim will agree to just about anything that is demanded by the torturer. For this reason, confessions obtained under torture are inadmissible as evidence in virtually all judicial courts of the world.

One outcome of torture is the well-documented ability of torturers to obtain acceptance of a prepared confession, which is merely a validation of false charges. Stalin was expert at this use of torture, forcing victims to sign false confessions and to implicate others in his state-sponsored witch-hunts. Public humiliation and repetitive denunciation was a characteristic of Mao's use of torture during the Chinese Cultural Revolution. Saddam Hussein's torturers became expert at a wide array of techniques, one of which was the use of an electric drill on the victim's skull, penetrating the brain. This practice continues to be used in revenge killings between Sunni and Shiite factions in Iraq. In 2005, the *UK Sunday Telegraph* disclosed the use of an "electric drill torture." BBC subsequently reported that use of this torture technique "was not an isolated incident."

In contrast, Pol Pot's torture center at Tuol Sleng, appears to have been used as a form of ritual purification. Victims were generally purged from the Party for real or imagined offenses and then nearly all were killed. The goal of the Khmer Rouge was to achieve racial and ideological purity above all else in the utopian society of Pol Pot's twisted imagination.

Sadism appears to be the motivation for much of the torture in Haiti and Papa Doc was perversely gratified by observing torture sessions through a peephole prepared specifically for his use. In Uganda, simple-minded sadists used members of opposition tribes as playthings, in much the way cats play with mice before killing them. Although not centrally planned or supervised, this form of torture was tolerated as the result of a mindless bloodlust unleashed by Idi Amin and his henchmen.

Nazi officials allowed or encouraged torture in many camps operated by the Third Reich. This is true of Dr. Josef Mengele's medical experiments at Auschwitz. Similarly, Professor Carl Clauberg approved testing of injections and x-ray techniques to sterilize

his victims, causing extreme pain and death. These tortures had
no medical value whatsoever. They are classic examples of sadism
that is rooted in deviant sexuality, since the perpetrators enjoyed a
physical intimacy with the victims and were frequently focused on
their reproductive organs.

Even those who attribute noble motives to their acts can
suffer debilitating long-term reactions as a result of inflicting
torture upon others. A French career soldier, now a priest, has
described this process:

> *I have received enough confidences in Algeria and in
> France to know into what injuries, perhaps irreparable,
> torture can lead the human conscience. Many young
> men have 'taken up the game' and have thereby passed
> from mental health and stability into terrifying states of
> decay, from which some will probably never recover.*[3]

Polls taken in 2001 found that 45% of Americans were willing to accept the use of torture if it was "necessary to combat
terrorism." But the British concluded during their long struggle with the Irish Republican Army that torture of IRA prisoners was not only ineffective, it was actually counterproductive.
Upon the disclosure of British torture of captured IRA members, there was a noted increase in sympathy for the IRA cause.
John Conroy author of *Unspeakable Acts, Ordinary People,* wrote
that, "In the year after the torture was exposed, the number of
deaths in [Britain's war with the IRA] rose by 268%."

It is unfortunate that in the twenty first century many seemingly free societies utilize torture as a method of preserving
state security. Their leaders and their people easily fall prey to
the seductive lure of torture due to the same desire for revenge
and domination that appeals to totalitarians. Practices that
violate internationally accepted standards of human rights are
proliferating even faster than weapons of mass destruction.
The fact that one quarter of a billion people were exterminated
during the last century by their own governments rather emphatically makes this point.

Dangers to Democracies

A fine balance exists between chaos and tyranny in many developing societies, which have limited experience with the rule of law. But oppression can endanger even societies where democracy has taken root, especially in the age of terrorism. Two democracies have recently faced this dilemma – Peru during the late twentieth century and the United States, in this century.

While fighting indigenous terrorism during the 1990's, Peru's President Alberto Fujimori addressed the nation's problems rigorously, boosting military efforts against the rebels with intense violence that eventually became lawless. He also launched Auto Golpe ("Self Coup"), a program to secure full control of the government for himself by dissolving Congress, suspending the constitution, purging the supreme court of 13 of its 23 sitting justices and dismissing dozens of other judges. Operating through his shadowy spy chief, Vladimiro Montesinos, the regime bribed public officials and members of the media, looted the treasury for personal gain and authorized death squads to seek out and exterminate suspects of terrorism. Dozens of people were murdered and hundreds of others disappeared.

After a decade of oppression, the regime collapsed in disgrace when its crimes were publicly revealed. Montesinos went into hiding and Fujimori sought asylum in Japan. In 2002, Montesinos was arrested and convicted of illegally controlling Peru's spy agency and was sentenced to nine years and four months in prison. He was subsequently sentenced to an additional thirteen years in prison for other charges. He faces some 70 additional trials.[4]

Chilean authorities arrested Fujimori when he landed in that country en route to Peru to launch a political comeback. On April 7, 2009, a Peruvian court found ex-president Fujimori guilty of mass murder and kidnapping. He was sentenced to twenty-five years in prison. Although Peru defeated the terrorists during the decade of Fujimori's rule, the nation lost its democratic institutions, and the rule of law was destroyed.

Following the terrorist attacks against the United States on
September 11, 2001, the administration of George W. Bush
launched two wars in response to 9-11, including the preemptive
invasion and occupation of Iraq, despite the fact that Iraq had
nothing to do with the attacks on the United States. The Bush
Administration insisted that it had the right to conduct surveillance of U. S. citizens without warrants and maintained that
presidential powers inherent in the Constitution granted this
authority. On February 13, 2006, the American Bar Association
denounced the warrantless domestic surveillance program, accusing the President of exceeding his constitutional powers. On
August 17, 2006, a Federal District Court ruled that these practices violated the First and Fourteenth Amendment to the U. S.
Constitution.

The United States has also secretly engaged in extrajudi-
cial abduction (officially known as "extraordinary rendition").
These actions have been widely criticized by international
human rights organizations as well as the countries in which
these clandestine kidnappings occurred. Extraordinary
rendition has resulted in the transportation of suspects to
other nations, which allow extreme methods of interrogation, a practice that has been called "torture by proxy." The
United States also stands accused of torture in the treatment
of detainees at the Abu Ghraib prison in Iraq, at the U. S. detention facility at Guántanamo, Cuba and at so called, "black
sites," in various countries, which allow torture on a routine
basis. [5]

One of the consequences of terrorism is that free people
become sufficiently frightened that they voluntarily relinquish their values and the protections of the rule of law.
Few Bush administration policies have been vigorously challenged in the political arena. However, judicial vigilance, a
renewed independence by the press and the electoral reaction by the public are reasons to hope that the United States,
with its long tradition of constitutional government, may
avoid the abuses that cost Peru its democracy for more than
a decade.

A Force, Which is Born of Truth

It is almost impossible to imagine the fear that citizens of Russia during the 1920's or Germany during the 1930's must have felt as they witnessed the darkness descending over the people. Some fled their homelands, while others, perhaps not able to believe the worst, remained only to become victims of dictatorship, oppression and war. Many unfortunate targets of state savagery are now among the millions exterminated, after suffering the horror of the death camps or the brutality of the gulag. What could they have done to save themselves in the face of such violence?

Armed resistance has led to hideous reprisals. Examples of such savagery include the extermination of the entire Czech village of Lidice when Czech resistance fighters assassinated Nazi leader Reinhard Heydrich, in the spring of 1942, and the brutal liquidation of 13,000 Jews in the Warsaw Ghetto in Poland, in 1943. In contrast, Denmark's resisters undermined the German occupation through the successful staging of a number of general strikes. In a truly significant achievement, the Danish resistance also rescued all but a few hundred of Denmark's 7,000 Jews from the Holocaust. Military historian Basil Liddell Hart interviewed German generals about their views of nonviolent methods, and he reports:

> *They were experts in violence, and had been trained to deal with opponents who used that method. But other forms of resistance baffle them – and all the more as the methods were subtle and concealed. It was a relief to them when nonviolent forms were mixed with guerrilla action, thus making it easier to combine drastic and suppressive action against both at the same time.* [6]

Non-violent resistance has been used for centuries by ordinary people uniting to reject injustice. Picket lines, hunger strikes, candlelight vigils, petitions, sit-ins, tax refusals, blockades and public demonstrations have a far greater success rate than many realize. National strikes and work stoppages are frequently more threatening to regimes than demonstrations or marches, since these actions can disrupt the economic vitality of a nation.

Non-violent resistance was best described by Mohandas K. Gandhi, the father of Indian Nationalism. Gandhi explained that his concept of Satyagraha, or "firmness in a good cause," is not passive resistance, which is a "weapon of the weak," but "a force, which is born of truth," and therefore a "weapon of the strong." Gandhi has stated, "Even the most powerful cannot rule without the cooperation of the ruled. If enough people withdraw that cooperation, they will shrink the government's legitimacy and raise the costs of enforcing its will." This was the strategy that won Indian independence from Great Britain. Dr. Martin Luther King successfully adopted Gandhi's methods during the 1960's to achieve civil rights in the United States.

There have been many success stories through the use of non-violent action. The 1986 Solidarity movement in Poland used industrial strikes to force the Communist regime to allow a trade union and free elections, which brought Lech Walesa to power and freed Poland from communist tyranny. Between 1985 and 1990, The United Democratic Front in South Africa used boycotts and strikes to force the regime to free Nelson Mandela and abolish the apartheid system. In 1986, after President Ferdinand Marcos stole an election in the Philippines, a million Filipinos demonstrated in the streets and ultimately forced Marcos into exile and established democracy. Chileans organized a "crusade of civic participation" in 1988, to force dictator Augusto Pinochet to step down and the restoration of democracy. In 1989, student demonstrations in Prague and a strike by citizens of Czechoslovakia was called the "Velvet Revolution," and brought about the first free elections in 40 years. In 2003, electoral corruption caused mass demonstrations, forcing the government out of power in Georgia's "Rose Revolution." In 2004, the people of the Ukraine protested the illegal reelection of their Communist leader, when nearly 700,000 people swarmed into Independence Square in Kiev, forcing free elections in the "Orange Revolution."

Today, citizen action is called Strategic Non-violent Conflict. Although it has been remarkably successful, it does not always succeed. The students, who peacefully protested Chinese Communism in Tiananmen Square, failed to win their objectives and provoked a savage retaliatory massacre. The military dictatorship of Myanmar (Burma) keeps Aung San Suu Kyi, the hero of that nation's struggle for freedom, under house arrest. Her dedication to non-violence has not proven successful so far and the killings of peaceful demonstrators and Buddhist monks in that country are examples of dictatorial continuity through the application of force. But power is symbolic. When the legitimacy of an illegitimate regime is publicly challenged, an important pillar upon which the regime bases its control begins to erode. As a leader loses the mantle of authority, the momentum of power shifts to the opposition.

Skeptics of non-violence and those who accept Mao's adage that "political power grows out of the barrel of a gun," do not believe that the regimes of North Korea or Myanmar could ever be overthrown by non-violent "people power." And they point out that the risk of violence, imprisonment, torture or even death is always present when dealing with despotic regimes. However, the objective of strategic non-violence is not to avoid conflict, but to alter the way conflict is conducted. Dictatorial governments are often pressured by non-violent action into acquiescing to demonstrator's demands in order to avoid international condemnation or sanctions. Sometimes the military or the police actually switch sides, which results in "turning repression on its head." [7]

The most essential purpose of mankind is to honor and perpetuate human life and we must all guard against those who would violate the deepest values of the human family. Citizens of any nation who face the prospect of oppressive dictatorship should summon the courage to act before the power of the state is turned against the people. Once a dictatorship becomes a tyranny and begins to kill its enemies, mass murder can threaten all of its citizens. And each act of mass killing may actually hasten the next. As the respect for human life is degraded, more violence may be tolerated, which can lead to the greatest of all crimes against humanity – genocide.

During the 1970's the military government of Argentina was successful in crushing the resistance by defining anyone who opposed the Junta as a terrorist. The military's most potent weapon was kidnapping. We still do not know all the sordid details of this "dirty war," but as many as 30,000 young people were snatched, usually at night but sometimes in broad daylight. In most cases, the kidnap victims were tortured and killed, in a tactic that was successful in terrorizing the population into submission. The victims were known as "*los desaparecidos*"– the disappeared. The mothers of some of the disappeared organized and pleaded with the regime, which ignored them; they petitioned the Church, which remained silent; they went to the Supreme Court, which refused their call for "due process."

Then they decided to gather in the Plaza de Mayo of Buenos Aires on Thursday of each week, wearing distinctive headscarves. The name of a missing child was embroidered on each scarf. It must have taken great courage for these mothers to gather in the Plaza, but they continued their vigil. Soon sympathetic citizens joined them and a few dozen became hundreds and then thousands. The mothers did nothing subversive, "we just sat on benches with our knitting," said one. But the mothers knew that the regime's greatest weapon was silence and they broke through the wall of silence with their weekly pilgrimage to the Plaza.

At first, the Junta did not take the mothers seriously, but when the military finally acted they used the device that they knew best – violence. The leader of the mothers, Azucena de Villaflor and thirteen others were kidnapped. Their disappearance and subsequent murders, however, did not have the effect the Junta expected. "They thought we would be too afraid to go back to the square…it was difficult to go back…but we went back," said Maria del Rosario. Support for the mothers did not diminish, but instead, it grew. The following year, while covering the World Cup in Argentina, the media visited the Plaza de Mayo to see the mothers. While the Argentine team celebrated winning the World Cup, international audiences also read of the story of the mothers of the disappeared, and were outraged. The Junta's prestige was forever tainted.

This painful chapter in South American history demonstrates what Gandhi called a "force, which is born of truth." It took several years to discredit the corrupt Junta that ruled Argentina. Although there has never been a full accounting of "*los desaparecidos*," the nation was freed from the military dictatorship due to the uncommon valor of the mothers. Azucena Villaflor's ashes, along with those of two other mothers, were buried at the foot of the May Pyramid in the Plaza, as a reminder of the price of freedom. The mothers proved that through acts of quiet courage, a morally powerful force can overcome tyranny.

The day of the dictator has not yet passed and the threat of tyranny can still arise through circumstances that cannot be foreseen. But vigilance can illuminate the darkness of an emerging dictatorship. When alerted to oppression, the public can act boldly to reject it. More than a quarter of a billion voiceless victims from a century of genocide beseech us to resist authoritarianism before it becomes cruel subjugation. Unless we are the protectors of our own rights, we risk losing the light of freedom's flame.

NOTES

Prologue

1. Tuchman, *The Proud Tower*, 64
2. Glover, *Humanity*, 16-17
3. Power, "Never Again"
4. Rummel, "20th Century Democide"

Chapter 1. Stalin: Swordbearer of Terror

1. Tucker, *Stalin in Power, The Revolution from Above*, 1928-1942, 13-24
2. Khruscheva, Nina L. "Why Russia Still Loves Stalin"
3. Montefiore, *Stalin, The Court of the Red Tsar*, 25-37
4. Tucker, *Stalin in Power, The Revolution from Above*, 1928-1942, 76-77
5. Montefiore, *Stalin, The Court of the Red Tsar*, 71-81
6. Tucker, *Stalin in Power, The Revolution from Above*, 1928-1942, 7
7. Montefiore, *Stalin, The Court of the Red Tsar*, 82-92
8. Ibid, 5-22
9. Ibid, 106-114
10. Muggeridge, "Dispatch to the Morning Post"
11. Montefiore, *Stalin, The Court of the Red Tsar*, 132-143
12. Tucker, *Stalin in Power, The Revolution from Above*, 1928-1942, 276-296
13. Ibid, 301
14. Ibid, 303-316
15. Montefiore, *Stalin, The Court of the Red Tsar*, 184-193

16. Ibid, 198-209
17. Ibid, 210-218
18. Ibid, 228-229
19. Tucker, *Stalin in Power, The Revolution from Above*, 1928-1942, 441-478
20. Ibid, 441
21. Solzhenitsyn, *The Gulag Archipelago*, Introduction, xxi,xxii
22. Montefiore, *Stalin, The Court of the Red Tsar*, 280-286
23. Tucker, *Stalin in Power, The Revolution from Above*, 1928-1942, 612
24. Montefiore, Stalin, *The Court of the Red Tsar*, 373-377
25. Ibid, 372-393
26. Ibid, 502-511
27. Ibid, 573-591
28. Ibid, 636-650
29. Times Online: "Russia turns its back on the man who denounced Stalin"
30. The New York Times, "Yukos founder Khodorkovsky attacked in Prison"

Chapter 2. Raphael Trujillo: Sexualized Tyranny

1. Brading, *The First America*, 9-58
2. The Conquistadors – Spanish Conquest. 1
3. Frazier, "Columbus, The Original American Hero" The Second Voyage
4. Brading, *The First America*, 58-78
5. James Ford Bell Library, The Manifest, 1
6. U. S. Library of Congress. "Dominican Republic: A Country Study"
7. Crassweller, Trujillo: *The Life and Times of a Caribbean Dictator* 7-22
8. Hicks, Blood in the Streets, 7-27
9. Crassweller, Trujillo: *The Life and Times of a Caribbean Dictator*. 25-37
10. Hicks, Blood in the Streets, 28-30

11. Crassweller, Trujillo: *The Life and Times of a Caribbean Dictator*, 39-73
12. Ibid, 73-80
13. Ibid, 80
14. Ibid, 107
15. Ibid, 109-139
16. Ibid, 140-142
17. Derby, Lauren H. "The Dictator's Seduction" 218-219
18. Crassweller, Trujillo: *The Life and Times of a Caribbean Dictator*, 134
19. Ibid, 149-154
20. Hicks, *Blood in the Streets*, 107
21. Ibid, 165-200 and 213
22. Diederich, Trujillo: *The Death of the Dictator*, 14
23. Ornes, Trujillo: *Little Caesar of the Caribbean*, 231
24. Ibid, 100
25. Derby, Lauren H. "The Dictator's Seduction" 214
26. Crassweller, Trujillo: *The Life and Times of a Caribbean Dictator*, 290
27. Diederich, Trujillo: *The Death of the Dictator*, 5-19
28. Crassweller, Trujillo: *The Life and Times of a Caribbean Dictator*, 409-420
29. Ibid, 403
30. Diederich, Trujillo: *The Death of the Dictator*, 73-260
31. The Mirabal Influence, 1-3

Chapter 3. Adolph Hitler: Mythology and Madness

1. The Holocaust Project. "A brief History of Anti-Semitism."
2. Moss, "Richard Wagner: Zenith of German Romanticism".
3. U. S. Library of Congress. "History of Germany. "
4. Rosenbaum, *Explaining Hitler*, 11
5. Hitler, *Mein Kampf.* Volume One: A Reckoning, Section II
6. Ibid, Section II
7. Shirer, *The Rise and Fall of the Third Reich*, 29-62
8. Friedrich, *Before the Deluge, 127*

9. Rosenbaum, *Explaining Hitler*, 20-21
10. Ibid, 21-22
11. Ibid, 134
12. Shirer, *The Rise and Fall of the Third Reich*, 213
13. Ibid, 226-248
14. Ibid, 322-356
15. Langer, Walter C. "A Psychological Profile of Adolph Hitler"
16. Ibid, (selected excerpts)
17. Operation Barbarossa, www.spartacus.shoolnt.co.uk
18. Shirer, *The Rise and Fall of the Third Reich*, 937
19. The Nizkor Project, Josef Hell, "Aufzeichnung
20. Rosenbaum, *Explaining Hitler*, 385
21. McFee, "Are the Jews Central to the Holocaust?" www.holocaust-history.org/
22. Bachrach, *Tell Them We Remember*, selected excerpts
23. Lengyl, Olga, *Five Chimneys*, selected excerpts
24. Shirer, *The Rise and Fall of the Third Reich*, 793-1045
25. Ibid, 1086
26. Ibid, 1091
27. MI 5 Documents, "60 Years On-Hitler's Last Days"
28. Shirer, *The Rise and Fall of the Third Reich*, 1126
29. MI 5 Documents, "60 Years On-Hitler's Last Days"
30. Rummel, R. J., "Democide: Nazi Genocide and Mass Murder," Table 1.1

Chapter 4. Kim Il-sung and Kim Jong-Il: Despotic Dynasty

1. Cumings, *Korea's Place in the Sun: A Modern History*, Chapter 1
2. Martin, *Under the Loving Care of the Fatherly Leader*, 11-60
3. Becker, *Rogue Regime*, 50
4. Martin, *Under the Loving Care of the Fatherly Leader*, 59
5. Becker, *Rogue Regime*, 53
6. American Military History, Korean War, Chapter 25
7. Becker, *Rogue Regime*, 54
8. Martin, *Under the Loving Care of the Fatherly Leader*, 89

9. Ibid, 190
10. Ibid, 200
11. Becker, *Rogue Regime*, 77
12. Ibid, 71
13. Martin, *Under the Loving Care of the Fatherly Leader*, 289
14. Becker, *Rogue Regime*, 89
15. U. S. Committee for Human Rights, "The Hidden Gulag"
16. Becker, *Rogue Regime*, 85
17. Diamond, "Korea: Inside the Gulag"
18. Becker, *Rogue Regime*, 93-100
19. Barnett, "Revealed: the gas chamber horror of North Korea's gulag."
20. Ibid
21. Human Rights Watch, "North Koreans in the Peoples Republic of China," Chapter. III.
22. Diamond, "Korea: Inside the Gulag."
23. Becker, *Rogue Regime*, 124-145
24. Ibid, 112
25. Amnesty International, "Starved of Rights," Section 1
26. Becker, *Rogue Regime*, 125
27. Nicol, "Famine-struck North Koreans 'eating children'
28. Scobell, "Kim Jong il and North Korea: The Leader and the System", 14
29. Ibid, Forward, vi

Chapter 5. Mao Zedong: Revolutionary Emperor

1. Barmé, "Walled Heart of China's Kremlin", 1-2
2. Salisbury, *The New Emperors*, 6
3. Short, *Mao: A Life*, 58
4. Ibid, 171
5. Ibid, 188
6. Ibid, 203
7. Ibid, 222
8. Ibid, 11
9. Ibid, 356

10. Ibid, 369-407
11. Ibid, 419
12. Salisbury, *The New Emperors*, 70-79
13. Short, *Mao: A Life*, 436-476
14. Ibid, 488
15. Ibid, 499
16. Li, Zhisui, *The Private Life of Chairman Mao*, 138
17. Becker, Jasper. *Hungry Ghosts: Mao's Secret Famine*, 273-274
18. Li, Zhisui, *The Private Life of Chairman Mao*, 331
19. Ibid, 356-364
20. Salisbury, *The New Emperors*, 209
21. Short, *Mao: A Life*, 528-581
22. Ibid, 588
23. Ibid, 593-600
24. Ibid, 604
25. Ibid, 630

Chapter 6. Papa Doc and Baby Doc: Voudou Regime

1. Abbott, Haiti: *An insider's history of the rise and fall of the Duvaliers*, 11
2. Danner, "To Haiti, With Love and Squalor".
3. Abbott, Haiti: *An insider's history of the rise and fall of the Duvaliers*, 14.
4. Bell, *Toussaint L'Ouverture: a biography*. 57-83
5. Mystica, Voudun page.
6. Danner, Aperture, "Postcards from History",6
7. Abbott, *Haiti: An insider's history of the rise and fall of the Duvaliers*, 5-52
8. Rohter, "Simone Duvalier, Haiti's Mama Doc"
9. Abbott, *Haiti: An insider's history of the rise and fall of the Duvaliers*, 38-42.
10. Ibid, 44
11. Ibid,54
12. Danner, "Beyond the Mountains – Part II".

13. Abbott, *Haiti: An insider's history of the rise and fall of the Duvaliers,80-81.*
14. Ibid, 82-89
15. Ibid, 88
16. Ibid 110-111
17. Ibid, 133
18. Ibid,161-163
19. Danner, "Beyond the Mountains" – Part I
20. Abbott, *Haiti: An insider's history of the rise and fall of the Duvaliers ,208-210*
21. Ibid, 261-266
22. Ibid, 267-294
23. Ibid, 311-314
24. Danner, "Beyond the Mountains" – Part I

Chapter 7. Idi Amin: A Feast of Blood

1. The River Nile, University of Texas
2. Mystery of the Nile
3. The History of Uganda
4. Uganda, Military History
5. Keatly, Obituary of Idi Amin
6. Killer File, Idi Amin
7. Gwyn, *Idi Amin: Death Light of Africa, 30-43*
8. Kyemba, Henry, *State of Blood,* 27
9. Hutton, and Bloch, "The Making of Idi Amin"
10. Gwyn, *Idi Amin: Death Light of Africa,* 52
11. Kyemba, Henry, *State of Blood, 33-38*
12. Gwyn, *Idi Amin: Death Light of Africa, 11*
13. Ibid, 71
14. Kyemba, Henry, *State of Blood, 38-59*
15. Ibid, 163
16. Ibid, 145-165
17. Gwyn, *Idi Amin: Death Light of Africa,* 111-124
18. Ibid, 124
19. Kyemba, Henry, *State of Blood,* 108-144

20. Ibid, 109
21. Ibid, 108-127
22. Ibid, 154
23. Israel Defense Force, Entebbe Diary, 1-11
24. Kyemba, Henry, *State of Blood,*166-178
25. Ibid, 123-124
26. Ibid, 237
27. Hutton, and Bloch, "The Making of Idi Amin"
28. Tanzania-Uganda War
29. Time, "Big Daddy's Last Stand?"
30. Idi Amin Killer File, 6

Chapter 8. Pol Pot: Cultivator of Killing Fields

1. SarDesai, D. R. *Southeast Asia, Past and Present,* 10-32
2. Albanese, Marilia. *Angkor: Splendors of the Khmer Civilization,* 11-133
3. SarDesai, D. R. *Southeast Asia, Past and Present,* 128-129
4. Tully, John. *France on the Mekong* 12, 217, 292
5. Short, *Pol Pot: Anatomy of a Nightmare,* 17
6. Ibid, 25-27
7. Ibid, 28-84
8. Ibid, 85-105
9. Bloomer, "An Analysis of the French Defeat at Dien Bien Phu"
10. Short, *Pol Pot: Anatomy of a Nightmare,* 130
11. Ibid, 106-152
12. Ibid, 170
13. Kiernan, *The Pol Pot Regime,* 16
14. Ibid, 23
15. Short, *Pol Pot: Anatomy of a Nightmare,* 153-265
16. Kiernan, *The Pol Pot Regime,* 33-47
17. Genocide Watch. "A Quest for Justice"
18. Short, *Pol Pot: Anatomy of a Nightmare,* 286-295
19. Ibid, 296
20. Kiernan, *The Pol Pot Regime,* 86
21. Short, *Pol Pot: Anatomy of a Nightmare,* 314-353

22. Kiernan, *The Pol Pot Regime,* 394
23. Short, *Pol Pot: Anatomy of a Nightmare,* 370-371
24. Kiernan, *The Pol Pot Regime,* 411-439
25. Ibid, 448-450
26. Short, *Pol Pot: Anatomy of a Nightmare,* 402-440
27. Ibid, 441-442
28. Ibid, 442
29. Sharp, Bruce. "Counting Hell," Cambodia.
30. Brady, Brendan. "Khmer Rouge trial includes a grisly list."

Chapter 9: Saddam Hussein: The Politics of Terrorism

1. U. S. Library of Congress. "Iraq: A Country Study"
2. Time Magazine, "Why They Hate Each Other"
3. Cockburn & Cockburn, *Out of the Ashes,* 66
4. Makiya, *Republic of Fear,* 183-204
5. Ibid, 196
6. Ibid, 206
7. Ibid, 8
8. Bowden, "Tales of the Tyrant,"
9. History 1900's, "The Crimes of Saddam Hussein", http://history1900.about.com
10. Cockburn & Cockburn, *Out of the Ashes,*82
11. Barrett, "Building the Case Against Saddam Hussein"
12. Human Rights Watch, "Genocide in Iraq," Introduction
13. Ibid, Chapter 9
14. Dinmore, "Halabja Poison Gas Attack"
15. Persian Gulf War, Encarta
16. Makiya, *Cruelty and Silence,* 35
17. Ibid, 57-105
18. Cockburn & Cockburn, *Out of the Ashes,* 57
19. Ibid, 107
20. Ibid, 141-163
21. Bennett and Weisskopf, "The Sum of Two Evils"
22. Ibid
23. Cockburn & Cockburn, *Out of the Ashes,* 191-210

24. Ibid, 211-250
25. Mann, *Incoherent Empire*, 1
26. Lobe and Flynn, "The Rise and Decline of the Neocon-servatives,"
27. Bodansky, *The Secret History of the Iraq War*, 164-241
28. Ibid, 274
29. Harvard University, Dr. David Kay: "Iraq WMD: Lessons Learned and Unlearned," 7-8
30. Bodansky, *The Secret History of the Iraq War*, 367
31. Ibid, 469-475
32. Daragahi and Lamb, "Violence Marked his Rise, Rule and Fall"
33. Burns and Santora, "Rush to Hang Hussein Was Questioned"

Chapter 10: Théoneste Bagosora: Architect of Apocalypse

1. The Story of the Virungas
2. Gourevitch, We *wish to inform you..*, 49-62
3. Ibid, 82-84
4. Human Rights Watch, April 1994: "The month that would not end." Introduction
5. Ibid, 'The month that would not end "Choosing War
6. Gourevitch, *We wish to inform you..*, 103-104
7. Human Rights Watch, April 1994: "The month that would not end."
8. Ibid, April 1994: "Choosing War." Bagosora in command.
9. Ibid, April 1994: "The month that would not end." Thorough elimination.
10. Gourevitch, *We wish to inform you..*, 115-141
11. Gendercide Watch, Case Study: Genocide in Rwanda, 1994.
12. Human Rights Watch, April 1994: "The month that would not end." Strategies for Survival.
13. Frontline: "The Rwandan Girl Who Refused to Die"

14. Gourevitch, *We wish to inform you..*, 150-158
15. Ibid, 158-168
16. Keane, *Season of Blood.* 182-191
17. Gourevitch, *We wish to inform you..*,270-290
18. Ibid, 350-351
19. Cobban, "Healing Rwanda"
20. Schow, "Ikuba – Remember"
21. UN International Criminal Tribunal for Rwanda, ICTR Detainee Status
22. Reuters: "Rwanda's Kingpin Sentenced to Life for Genocide"

Epilogue

1. Mann, The Dark Side of Democracy, 2
2. Orwell, *Nineteen Eighty-Four,* 208-211, 219-220
3. Vaknin, "The Psychology of Torture"
4. Human Rights Watch, "Probable Cause Evidence Implicating Fujimori"
5. Gelman, & Becker, "Pushing the Envelope on Presidential Power –Cheney"
6. Sharp, "Politics of Nonviolent Action"
7. Crist, Hentges & Serwer, "Strategic Nonviolent Conflict"

SELECTED BIBLIOGRAPHY

A Newsletter to the Associates of the James Ford Bell Library, "The Manifest," March 1992, University of Minnesota, http://muweb.millersville.edu/~columbus/data/new/MANIFST1.NEW

Abbott, Elizabeth. Haiti: *An insider's history of the rise and fall of the Duvaliers.* New York: Touchstone Books, 1988

Albanese, Marilia. *Angkor: Splendors of the Khmer Civilization.* Bangkok, Asia Books, 2002

Ackerman, Peter & Duvall, Jack, "People Power Primed," Harvard International Review, Summer, 2005 http//hir.harvard.edu

American Military History, *The Korean War,* Chapter 25, www.army.mil/cmh/books/amh/AMH-25.htm

Amnesty International, "Starved of Rights: Human Rights and the Food Crisis in the DPRK," January 2004. http//web.amnesty.org

Bachrach, Susan, *Tell Them We Remember,* New York, Little, Brown and Co., 1994, Excerpt: History of the Holocaust: An Overview, www.ushmm.org

Barmé, Geremie R. "Walled Heart of China's Kremlin": Time. Asia online, 1949

Barnett, Antony, "Revealed: the gas chamber horror of North Korea's gulag." The Guardian, Sunday, February 1, 2004. www.guardian.co.uk

Barrett, Jennifer, "Building the Case Against Saddam Hussein," Newsweek, August 31, 2006

Beah, Ishmael, A Long Way Gone: Memoirs of a Boy Soldier, New York: Sarah Crichton Books/Farrar. Straus and Giroux, 2007

Becker, Jasper. *Hungry Ghosts: Mao's Secret Famine.* New York: Free Press, 1996

Becker, Jasper. *Rogue Regime*, New York, Oxford University Press, 2003

Bell, Madison Smart, *Toussaint Louverture: A Biography*, New York, Pantheon Books, 2007

Bennett, Brian & Weisskopf, Michael, "The Sum of Two Evils," Time, Sunday May 2, 2003. http://time.com

Bloomer, Major Harry D. USA/CSC. "An Analysis of the French Defeat at Dien Bien Phu" www.globalsecurity.org

Bodansky, Yossef, *The Secret History of the Iraq War*, New York, Harper Collins, 2004

Bowden, "Tales of the Tyrant," Atlantic, May 2002

Brading, D. A. *The First America*, Cambridge: Cambridge University Press, 1991

Brady, Brendan, "Khmer Rouge trial includes a grisly list," Los Angeles Times, March 31, 2008

Burns, John F. and Santora, Marc, "Rush to Hang Hussein Was Questioned", New York Times, January 1, 2007 www.nytimes.com

Casson, Lionel. *Ancient Egypt,* New York, Time Life Books,1965

Chandler, David. "Pol Pot" Time Asia 8/23/99 wwwtime.com/ time/Asia/magazine

Chirot, Daniel. *Modern Tyrants: The Power and Prevalence of Evil in our Age*, New York: The Free Press, 1994

Cobban, Helena, "Healing Rwanda," Boston Review, Dec. 2003/Jan. 2004, http://bostonreview.net.

Cockburn, Andrew and Patrick, *Out of the Ashes: The Resurrection of Saddam Hussein*, New York: Harper Collins, 1999

Corbett, Bob & Chatland, Jan. "Descriptions of Various Loa of Voodoo", Webster University, Spring 1990, www.webster.edu

Crassweller, Robert D., *Trujillo: The Life and Times of a Caribbean Dictator,* New York: The Macmillan Company, 1966

Crist, John, T., Hentges, Harriet & Serwer, Daniel, "Strategic Nonviolent Conflict," US Institute of Peace, www.usip.org

Cumings, Bruce, *Korea's Place in the Sun: A Modern History*, New York, W.W. Norton & Company,1998

Danner, Mark. "Beyond the Mountains – Part I", The New Yorker, November 27, 1989 www.markdanner.com

Danner, Mark. "Beyond the Mountains – Part II", The New Yorker, December 4, 1989 www.markdanner.com

Danner, Mark. "Postcards from History." Aperture, Spring 1992. www.markdanner.com

Danner, Mark. "To Haiti, With Love and Squalor." The New York Times Book Review, August 11, 1991

Daragahi, Borzou and Lamb, David, "Violence Marked his Rise, Rule and Fall," Los Angeles Times, Saturday, December 30, 2006

Davies, Roy, "The Rise and Fall of Alberto Fujimori," www.ex.ac.uk/~RDavies/inca/fujimori.html

Dinmore, Guy, Financial Times. "Halabja Poison Gas Attack" www.reference.com

Derby, Lauren H. "The Dictator's Seduction: "Gender and State Spectacle during the Trujillo Regime" Latin American Popular Culture, SR Books, Wilmington Delaware, 2000

De Madariaga, Isabel, *Ivan the Terrible, First Tsar of Russia*, New Haven, & London: Yale University Press, 2005

Diamond, Larry, "Korea: Inside the Gulag," Hoover Digest, 1998, No. 4, Hoover Institution, Stanford University, www.hoover.org

Diederich, Bernard, *Trujillo: The Death of the Dictator*, Princeton: Marcus Wiener Publishers 1990

European Voyages of Exploration: "Christopher Columbus", www.ucalgary.ca

Exploring the Environment of the Mountain Gorillas, Wheeling Jesuit University "The Story of the Virungas," www.cotf.edu, 1997

Factbook on Global Sexual Exploitation. Cambodia. www.uri.edu/artsci/wms/hughes/cambodia.htm

Frazier, Wade. "Columbus, The Original American Hero", wwwahealedplanet.net

Friedrich, Otto. *Before the Deluge*, New York, Harper Perennial Books, 1972

Frontline: "The Rwandan Girl Who Refused to Die," www.pbs.
org.
Gelman, Barton & Becker, Jo, "Pushing the Envelope on Presidential Power –Cheney" Washington Post, June 25, 2007,
http//blog.washingtonpost.com
Gendercide Watch, "Case Study: Genocide in Rwanda, 1994."
www.gendercide.org
Genocide Watch. "A Quest for Justice", www.genocidewatch.
org/cambodia
Glover, Jonathan. *Humanity: A Moral History of the Twentieth Cen-
tury*, New Haven: Yale University Press, 1999
Gourevitch, Phillip. *We wish to inform you that tomorrow we will be
killed with our families*, New York: Farrar, Straus and Giroux,
1998
Gwyn, David, *Idi Amin: Death Light of Africa*: Boston, Little,
Brown and Co., 1977
Harvard University, Institute of Politics, Remarks of Dr. David
Kay: "Iraq WMD: Lessons Learned and And Unlearned,
March 22, 2004, www.iop.harvard.edu/pdfs/transcripts/
kay_03
Hero's and Killers of the 20th Century, "Idi Amin Killer File,"
www.moreorless.au.com/killers/amin.html
Hicks, Albert C., *Blood in the Streets*, New York: Creative Age
Press, 1946
History 1900's, "The Crimes of Saddam Hussein", http://his-
tory1900.about.com
Hitler, Adolf. *Mein Kampf.* Hurst & Blackett, Ltd. London 1939
http://gutenberg.net.au/ebooks02
Human Rights Watch, "Genocide in Iraq," www.hrw.org/re-
ports, 1993
Human Rights Watch, "Leave None to Tell the Story," www.hrw.
org/reports, 1999
Human Rights Watch, "North Koreans in the Peoples Republic
of China." Chapter III, www.hrw.org/reports
Human Rights Watch, "Probable Cause Evidence Implicating
Fujimori", www.hrw.org/reports, 2005

Hutton, Pat and Bloch, Jonathan, "The Making of Idi Amin," New African, February 2001, www.hartford-hwp.com/archives

Israel Defense Forces, Official Web Site, "Entebbe Diary," www1. idf.il/DOVER/site/

Keane, Fergal. *Season of Blood.* London, Penguin Books, 1995

Keatly, Patrick, "Obituary of Idi Amin," Guardian, Monday August 18, 2003, www.guardian.co.uk

Khruscheva, Nina L. "Why Russia Still Loves Stalin", Washington Post, Sunday February 12, 2006

Killer File, Idi Amin, www.moreorless.au.com/killers/amin.html

Kiernan, Ben. *The Pol Pot Regime.* Chaing Mai: Silkworm Books 1997

Kyemba, Henry, *State of Blood,* London: Corgi Books, 1977

James Ford Bell Library, The Manifest, www.muweb.millersville. edu

Langer, Walter C. *"A Psychological Profile of Adolph Hitler",* Office of Strategic Services, Washington, D.C. http://www.ess.uwe. ac.uk/documents/osstitle.htm

Lengyl, Olga, *Five Chimneys: A Woman's True Story of Auschwitz,* Chicago: Academy Chicago Publishers, 1995

LeVine, Steve, *Putin's Labyrinth: Spies, Murder and the Dark Heart of the New Russia,* New York: Random House, 2008

Li, Dr. Zhisui. *The Private Life of Chairman Mao.* New York: Random House, 1994

Lobe, Jim and Flynn, Michael, "The Rise and Decline of the Neoconservatives," Asia Times, November 22, 2006

Mann, Michael, *The Dark Side of Democracy: Explaining Ethnic Cleansing.*Cambridge University Press, 2005, Excerpt, www. cambridge.org

Makiya, Kanan, *Republic of Fear, The Politics of Modern Iraq,* Berkeley, University of California Press, 1989.

Makiya, Kanan, *Cruelty and Silence,* New York, W.W. Norton & Co., 1993

Mann, Michael, *Incoherent Empire,* New York: Verso Books, 2003

Mann, Michael, *The Dark Side of Democracy: Explaining Ethnic Cleansing*, Excerpt, New York: Cambridge University Press, 2004, www.cambridge.org

Martin, Bradley K., *Under the Loving Care of the Fatherly Leader: North Korea and the Kim Dynasty*, New York: Thomas Dunne Books, 2004

McFee, Gordon, "Are the Jews Central to the Holocaust," www. holocaust-history.org

MI 5 Documents, "60 Years On- Hitler's Last Days", www. Mi5. gov.uk

MicroHistory, "The Sumerians," http://www.fsmitha.com

Mitchell, Stephen, *Gilgamesh: A New English Version*, New York: Simon & Schuster, 2004

Montefiore, Simon. *Stalin, The Court of the Red Tsar*, New York: Alfred A. Knopf, 2004

Montefiore, Simon. *Young Stalin*, New York: Alfred A. Knopf, 2007

Moss, Charles K. "*Richard* Wagner: Zenith of German Romanticism ". www.carolinaclassical.com

Muggeridge, Malcom, Dispatch to the Morning Post, June 7, 1933. www.artukrane.com/famineart/muggeridge3. htm

Mystica, Online Resource on Religions and Sects, Voudun Page, www.the mystica.com

Mystery of the Nile, www.nilefilm.com_history.htm

Nicol, Mark, "Famine-stuck North Koreans 'eating children'", Telegraph, UK, July 6, 2004, www.telegraph.co.uk

Operation Barbarossa, www.spartacus.shoolnt.co.uk

Ornes, German E., *Trujillo: Little Caesar of the Caribbean*, Edinburgh: Thomas Nelson & Sons, 1958

Orwell, George, *Nineteen Eighty-Four*, New York, New American Library, 1981

PBS, Behind the Lens: "Filmmaker Interview: Ellen Perry." www.pbs.og/pov/pov2006

Page, Jeremy. Times Online: "Russia turns its back on the man who denounced Stalin", February 25, 2006. www.timesonline.co.uk

Persian Gulf War, http//: encarta.msn.com/encyclopedia

Polgreen, Lydia. "Rwanda's Shadow, From Darfur to Congo."
    New York Times, July 23, 2006 www.nytimes.com
Power, Samantha. "Never Again: The World's Most Unfulfilled
    Promise", Atlantic Magazine, September 2001
Powell, Bill and Zagorin, Adam. "The Tony Soprano of North
    Korea." Time, July 12, 2007. www.time.com
Prunier, Gerard. *The Rwanda Crisis,* New York: Columbia Uni-
    versity Press, 1995
Rangwala, Glen "Allegations about the responsibility for the
    Halabja Massacre," http//middleeastreference.org.uk/Hal-
    abja/html
Reuters: The New York Times, "Yukos Founder Khodorkovsky
    attacked in Prison". April 15, 2006 www.nytimes.com
Reuters: Rwanda's Kingpin Sentenced to Life for Genocide,
    December 18, 2008
Richardson, Rosamond, *Stalin's Shadow,* New York: St. Martin's
    Press, 1993
Rock, Michael. "Haitian Vodou: "Serving the Spirits." Witches
    Voice www.witchvox.com
Rodman, Seldon & Carole Cleaver. *Spirits of the Night: The Vou-
    dun Gods of Haiti,* Dallas
The Free Press, 1994
Rohter, Larry. "Simone Duvalier, Haiti's Mama Doc", New York
    Times, December 31, 1997.
Romero, Simon, "Court Approves Extradition of Fujimori,"
    New York Times, September 21, 2007
Rosenbaum, Ron. *Explaining Hitler,* New York, Harper Peren-
    nial Books, 1999
Rummel, R. J. "20th Century Democide," www.hawaii.edu/
    powerkills/20TH.HTM
Salisbury, Harrison E. *The New Emperors.* New York: Avon
    Books, 1992
SarDesai, D. R. *Southeast Asia, Past and Present.* Chiang Mai:
    Silkworm Books, 1997
Schow, Lila, "Ikuba – Remember," http://goodusgov.org
Scobell, Andrew. "Kim Jong il and North Korea: The Leader
    and the System." Strategic Studies Institute, March 2006,
    www.Strategic StudiesInstitute.army.mil/

Sharp, Bruce. Counting Hell, Cambodia. www.mekong.net/cambodia/index.htm

Sharp, Gene. "Power and Struggle," section 1 of Politics of Non-violent Action, www.fragmentsweb.org.

Shirer, William L. *The Rise and Fall of the Third Reich*, New York: Simon and Schuster, 1960

Short, Philip. *Pol Pot: Anatomy of a Nightmare*. New York: Henry Holt & Company, 2004

Short, Phillip. *Mao: A Life*. New York: Henry Holt & Company, 1999

Solzhenitsyn, Aleksandr, I. *The Gulag Archipelago*. New York: Harper & Row, Perennial Classics, 2002

Tanzania-Uganda War, 1978-1979, www.onwar.com

Time Magazine, "Big Daddy's Last Stand?" Monday April 9, 1979 www.time.com

Time Magazine, "Why They Hate Each Other: Behind the Sunni-Shiite Divide," Feb. 22, 2007

The Conquistadors – Spanish Conquest. Discover Haiti: Haiti History, www.discoverhaiti.com

The Holocaust Project. "A brief History of Anti-Semitism." www.humanitas-international.org

The History of Uganda, www.mongabay.com/reference/country_studies/uganda/all.html

The Mirabal Influence, "In the time of the Butterflies – Sister's Influence" http://gbs.gllenbrook.k12.il.us

The New York Times, "Yukos founder Khodorkovsky attacked in Prison"

The Nizkor Project, Josef Hell, "Aufzeichnung," 1922, ZS 640, p. 5, Institute fuer Zeitgeschichte www.nizkor.org/hweb

The River Nile, University of Texas, www.utdallas.edu/geosciences/remsens/Nile/index.html

The Story of the Virungas, www.cotf.edu

The Torture Papers, review posted on line Cambridge University Press, wwwcambridge.org

Trial Watch, profile of Théoneste Bagosora, 2006, www.trial-ch.org/trial watch

Tucker, Robert C. *Stalin in Power, The Revolution from Above, 1928-1941,* New York: W.W. Norton & Company, 1990.

Tuchman, Barbara W. *The Proud Tower: A Portrait of the World before the War 1890-1914.* New York: Ballantine Books, 1962.

Tully, John. *France on the Mekong: A History of the Protectorate in Cambodia 1863-1953:* Lanham Md.: University Press of America, 2002

Uganda, Military History, The Library of Congress Country Studies, www.photius.com/countries/uganda

U. S. Committee for Human Rights in North Korea. "The Hidden Gulag: Exposing North Korean Prison Camps, Prisoner Testimonies and Satellite Photographs" www.hrnk.org/hiddengulag

U. S. Library of Congress. "Dominican Republic: A Country Study", http://countrystudies.us/

U.S. Library of Congress. "History of Germany" http://home.carolina.rr.com/wormold/germany

U. S. Library of Congress. "Iraq: A Country Study," http//countrystudies.us/

UN International Criminal Tribunal for Rwanda, 2006,http://65.18.216.88/ENGLISH/factsheets/detainee.htm

Vaknin, Sam, "The Psychology of Torture," http://narcissistic-abuse.com/torturepsychology.html

Vladimiro Montesinos Torres, www.desaparecidos.org/peru/tort/montesinos/eng/html

Williams, Joseph J. *Voodoos and Obeahs: Phases of West India Witchcraft,* New York: Dial Press, 1932

World Food Prize. "Malnutrition In Cambodia", www.worldfoodprize.org

ABOUT THE AUTHOR

Terry Stafford has an extensive background in politics and a deep commitment to human rights. His interest in anti-democratic regimes began with a college class in propaganda and the practices of Joseph Goebbels, Hitler's Propaganda Minister. This led to the author's investigation of ways in which societies lose their most cherished freedoms. Deadly Dictators is the result of that research.

CPSIA information can be obtained at www.ICGtesting.com
Printed in the USA
LVOW042305250412

279152LV00018B/70/P